Living in a Nuclear World

The Fukushima disaster invites us to look back and probe how nuclear technology has shaped the world we live in, and how we have come to live with it. Since the first nuclear detonation (Trinity test) and the bombings of Hiroshima and Nagasaki, all in 1945, nuclear technology has profoundly affected world history and geopolitics, as well as our daily life and natural world. It has always been an instrument for national security, a marker of national sovereignty, a site of technological innovation and a promise of energy abundance. It has also introduced permanent pollution and the age of the Anthropocene. This volume presents a new perspective on nuclear history and politics by focusing on four interconnected themes—violence and survival; control and containment; normalizing through denial and presumptions; memories and futures—and exploring their relationships and consequences. It proposes an original reflection on nuclear technology from a long-term, comparative and transnational perspective. It brings together contributions from researchers from different disciplines (anthropology, history, STS) and countries (US, France, Japan) on a variety of local, national and transnational subjects. Finally, this book offers an important and valuable insight into other global and Anthropocene challenges such as climate change.

Bernadette Bensaude-Vincent is a historian and philosopher of science and technology, and Professor (Emeritus) at Université Paris 1 Panthéon-Sorbonne.

Soraya Boudia is a science and technology studies scholar, Professor of sociology at University of Paris.

Kyoko Sato is a sociologist and science and technology studies scholar, and Associate Director of the Program in Science, Technology, and Society at Stanford University.

History and Philosophy of Technoscience
Series Editor: Alfred Nordmann

From Models to Simulations
Franck Varenne

The Reform of the International System of Units (SI)
Edited by Nadine de Courtenay, Olivier Darrigol, and Oliver Schlaudt

The Past, Present and Future of Integrated History of Philosophy of Science
Edited by Emily Herring, Konstantin S. Kiprijanov, Kevin Jones and Laura M. Sellers

Nanotechnology and Its Governance
Arie Rip

Perspectives on Classification in Synthetic Sciences
Unnatural Kinds
Edited by Julia Bursten

Reflections on the Practice of Physics
James Clerk Maxwell's Methodological Odyssey in Electromagnetism
Giora Hon and Bernard Goldstein

Philosophy of Interdisciplinarity
Studies in Science, Society and Sustainability
Jan Cornelius Schmidt

Material Hermeneutics
Reversing the Linguistic Turn
Don Ihde

Post-Truth Imaginations
New Starting Points for Critique of Politics and Technoscience
Edited by Kjetil Rommetveit

Living in a Nuclear World
From Fukushima to Hiroshima
Edited by Bernadette Bensaude-Vincent, Soraya Boudia, and Kyoko Sato

Living in a Nuclear World
From Fukushima to Hiroshima

Edited by
Bernadette Bensaude-Vincent,
Soraya Boudia, and Kyoko Sato

LONDON AND NEW YORK

First published 2022
by Routledge
2 Park Square, Milton Park, Abingdon, Oxon OX14 4RN

and by Routledge
605 Third Avenue, New York, NY 10158

Routledge is an imprint of the Taylor & Francis Group, an informa business

© 2022 selection and editorial matter, Bernadette Bensaude-Vincent, Soraya Boudia and Kyoko Sato; individual chapters, the contributors

The right of Bernadette Bensaude-Vincent, Soraya Boudia and Kyoko Sato to be identified as the authors of the editorial material, and of the authors for their individual chapters, has been asserted in accordance with sections 77 and 78 of the Copyright, Designs and Patents Act 1988.

All rights reserved. No part of this book may be reprinted or reproduced or utilised in any form or by any electronic, mechanical, or other means, now known or hereafter invented, including photocopying and recording, or in any information storage or retrieval system, without permission in writing from the publishers.

Trademark notice: Product or corporate names may be trademarks or registered trademarks, and are used only for identification and explanation without intent to infringe.

British Library Cataloguing-in-Publication Data
A catalogue record for this book is available from the British Library

Library of Congress Cataloging-in-Publication Data
A catalog record has been requested for this book

ISBN: 978-1-032-13063-7 (hbk)
ISBN: 978-1-032-13066-8 (pbk)
ISBN: 978-1-003-22747-2 (ebk)

DOI: 10.4324/9781003227472

Typeset in Sabon
by MPS Limited, Dehradun

Contents

List of figures	viii
Acknowledgments	x
Introduction: shaping the nuclear order	1
BERNADETTE BENSAUDE-VINCENT, SORAYA BOUDIA AND KYOKO SATO	

SECTION I
Violence and order — 21

1 What the bomb has done: victim relief, knowledge
and politics — 23
KYOKO SATO

2 Optics of exposure — 45
JOSEPH MASCO

3 Constructing world order: mobilising tropes of
gender, pathology and race to frame US non-
proliferation policy — 66
JOHN KRIGE

4 The Nuclear Charter: international law, military
technology, and the making of strategic trusteeship,
1942–1947 — 85
M. X. MITCHELL

vi *Contents*

SECTION II
Pacifying through control and containment   109

5 Sharing the "safe" atom?: the International Atomic
Energy Agency and nuclear regulation through
standardisation   111
ANGELA N. H. CREAGER AND MARIA RENTETZI

6 From military surveillance to citizen counter-
expertise: radioactivity monitoring in a nuclear
world   132
NESTOR HERRAN

7 Making the accident hypothetical: how can one deal
with the potential nuclear disaster?   148
MAËL GOUMRI

8 Governing the nuclear waste problem: nature and
technology   166
TANIA NAVARRO RODRÍGUEZ

SECTION III
Normalising through denial and trivialisation   183

9 Trivialising life in long-term contaminated
areas: the nuclear political laboratory   185
SORAYA BOUDIA

10 Continuing nuclear tests and ending fish
inspections: politics, science and the Lucky
Dragon Incident in 1954   203
HIROKO TAKAHASHI

11 The dystopic Pieta: Chernobyl survivors and neo-
liberalism's lasting judgments   222
KATE BROWN

12 Unfolding time at Fukushima   242
HARRY BERNAS

Contents vii

SECTION IV
Timescaping through memory and future visions 259

13 Framing a nuclear order of time 261
   BERNADETTE BENSAUDE-VINCENT

14 Nuclear dreams and capitalist visions: the peaceful
   atom in Hiroshima 279
   RAN ZWIGENBERG

15 Slow disaster and the challenge of nuclear memory 299
   SCOTT GABRIEL KNOWLES

   Contributors 319
   Index 323

Figures

2.1 Stills from high altitude US nuclear detonation   47
2.2 Stills from restored nuclear test film from Operation Dominic   49
2.3 Still and motion picture cameras used during early nuclear testing at the Bikini Atoll   52
2.4 Film credits for EG&G and Lookout Mountain Laboratory   53
2.5 Animation of air force nuclear attack and flash-blindness from *Nuclear Effects During SAC Delivery Missions*   57
2.6 Dosimeter film badges exhibit at the Atomic Testing Museum   58
2.7 Nuclear detonation photographed at millisecond speed   62
4.1 Original Caption: "Natives of Marshall Islands at time of invasion by American forces. They were happy to see the invading Americans and to come down to the shore in their 'Sunday clothes' to shower Marines, who made a bloodless landing, with gifts"   86
4.2 Marshallese scout Michael Madison meets with Islanders during US invasion   93
4.3 Islanders escape from Jaluit Atoll   94
5.1 Original caption: "Modern methods of prospecting for uranium are being applied in a number of countries and the International Atomic Energy Agency (IAEA) in Vienna (Austria) is helping its Member States by technical advice and missions. It is also encouraging research on cheaper methods to recover uranium from low-grade ores and as a by-product from other mineral production. The 1969 technical assistance program will give help in the development of nuclear raw materials to Chile, Ethiopia, Greece, Guatemala, Mexico, Peru and Tunisia. In Tunisia samples are

Figures ix

examined in a laboratory." IAEA/No. 1984. IAEA Archives/E0045-003. 1969 — 115

10.1 Documents on Alison and Shigemitsu Meeting on December 27, 1954, Japanese Foreign Ministry. This document was declassified by request of the author on October 4, 2018 — 212

15.1 Weldon Spring Site Remedial Action Project Disposal Cell, Weldon Spring, Missouri — 300

15.2 Hiroshima Lantern Festival and the "A-Bomb Dome" on August 6, 2015 — 307

15.3 Three Mile Island. cherry tree grove behind former visitor center—a gift of friendship from Japanese nuclear power operators — 309

15.4 Historical plaque across from Three Mile Island — 310

Acknowledgments

This collaborative research project started with the help of a Conference Transfer Grant from the France-Stanford Center for Interdisciplinary Studies in 2017, and was pursued thanks to a 3-year grant from Partner University Fund (2017–2020) of the FACE Foundation. We greatly appreciate the generous funding from both organizations, as well as the support of their professional and capable staff members, especially Isabelle Collignon, Program Manager at the France-Stanford Center; Sandrine Palud-Guérin, Estelle Beche, and Anissa Rejeb, Program Officers at the Partner University Fund. We also want to thank our colleagues Laurence Raineau at Université Paris 1 Panthéor-Sorbonne and John Willinsky at Stanford University for their support in setting up this research program in our respective universities. Many thanks to the Paris Institute for Advanced Studies for hosting our 2018 workshop in a wonderful historical building and to the administrative and financial staff of University of Paris and Stanford University for their help and support in the organization of events along the project.

We are very grateful to the colleagues and graduate students who contributed to our research through their participation in the conferences that we organized along the way at Stanford and Institut d'études avancées in Paris: Laura Barbier, Barton Bernstein, Martin Denoun, Pierre de Jouvancourt, Jean-Pierre Dupuy, Christine Fassert, Quentin Hardy, François Hartog, Gabrielle Hecht, Toshihiro Higuchi, Barbara Rose Johnston, Alfred Nordmann, Sophie Poirot-Delpech, Mathias Roger, Scott Sagan, Anna Weichselbraun and Lisa Yoneyama. We also benefited greatly from our workshops at Fukushima University and Maison franco-japonaise in Tokyo, and would like to thank participants, including Christine Fassert, Nobuyo Goto, Yasuo Goto, Reiko Hasegawa, Toshio Hatsuzawa, Aleksei Konoplev, Yasuo Sato, Rémi Scoccimarro, Hyoe Takata, Seiichiro Takemine, Toshihiro Wada and Masakatsu Yamazaki.

This manuscript only took shape thanks to the precious editorial work of several people. We want to thank in particular Juliette Rogers for her

Acknowledgments xi

translations from French to English and her editing work, as well as Letta Page for her copyediting of the manuscript.

Lastly, we owe many thanks to the editorial team at Routledge, especially Senior Editor Max Novick and Series Editor Alfred Nordmann for their support and guidance.

Introduction: shaping the nuclear order

Bernadette Bensaude-Vincent, Soraya Boudia, and Kyoko Sato

In March 2020, the Olympic flame traveled from Greece to Japan, destined for the Tokyo Games. For Japanese authorities, the grand start of the Torch Relay symbolised their ability to rebuild following an earthquake, a tsunami and a nuclear accident. Some 20 km from the defunct Fukushima Daiichi nuclear power station, the flame, having made it to Japan, would have begun its journey to Tokyo from J-Village, a luxurious national soccer training center funded by Tokyo Electric Power Co. (TEPCO) and restored with Kuwait's donation. Fukushima Governor Masao Uchibori enthused, "We are happy to send out a message, at home and abroad, that any difficulty can be overcome."[1] Yet, at that time, COVID-19 was reaching pandemic proportions, most of the world was locked down, and several economic sectors were slowing, adding to the region's ongoing problems. According to official figures, 41,000 residents near Fukushima were still displaced nine years after the accident—a number many consider an undercount.

Due to the global pandemic, the "Reconstruction Games," as the Japanese government had dubbed this Olympiad, were postponed until 2021. They coincided with the ten-year anniversary of the Fukushima nuclear disaster, which brought the shock and horror reverberating around the world in 2011. The disaster profoundly changed the lives of tens of thousands of Japanese, turning a vast swath of land with communities, farms and natural areas into a semi-wasteland. As we watched that meltdown take place in a nuclear plant run by a prominent corporation in an advanced industrial nation, we were caught off-guard by the scope of the damage, the uncertainty over residents' health and the future of nuclear technology itself.

One mantra: never again

Today, the Fukushima disaster has become ordinary. It no longer captures the public's attention. Still, its repercussions continue in the everyday struggles of the ongoing evacuation, the uncertainty about the effects of radiation and the lawsuits over accountability and compensation. After the

DOI: 10.4324/9781003227472-101

2   *Bernadette Bensaude-Vincent et al.*

2011 disaster, experts were mobilised, risk standards and stress tests were updated and the next wave of nuclear critics voiced their concerns. Yet Fukushima gradually became a thing of the past, a memory. It has been trivialised like the major nuclear disasters that came before—the long list of global nuclear "events" inaugurated by the bombings of Hiroshima and Nagasaki. These events have become so commonplace that their *eventness* is questionable. Their lingering effects are not.

Multiple generations of humans have lived in a nuclearised world. We came close to a full-blown nuclear war during the Cuban missiles crisis. We[2] have witnessed radioactive contamination from catastrophes like Three Mile Island and Chernobyl. Every accident and fallout incident raises similar questions, such as, *What can we learn from this? How can we ensure it never happens again?* Yet our daily lives are barely shaken by these past and recent events. We feel so at home in this world of risk that few really noticed when scientists nudged the needle of the "Doomsday Clock" up to two minutes before midnight in 2018. Invented by atomic scientists in 1947 to indicate the threat of global annihilation, this portentous clock had been fluctuating within 5–12 minutes before midnight for the last few decades. The jump to a two-minute warning should have been a shocking headline worldwide, but it was not.

About 30 nations including Japan rely on nuclear energy, with dozens of new reactors under construction in the Global South and North. How has such a destructive technology assumed such a central place in our societies over the past 75 years? How is it that, despite major disasters and hollow assertions that they won't happen again, nuclear technology has been so widely adopted and accommodated? How did it become mundane?

This volume is driven by the ambition to better comprehend how nuclear technology has forged this world—and how we have come to live within it. This particular technology offers a case study for understanding how adaptation to disasters and the forgetting of crises can be manufactured. In exploring these questions, the volume's essays build on the contributions of numerous academic works, particularly those that pay attention to technoscience, or the idea that science and technology are more than just tools for fulfilling human needs and desires. In fact, science and technology are *constitutive* of our world. Human artifacts, loaded with economic, social and political values, have lives of their own. They are even constitutive of us as humans, shaping our senses, desires and actions.

Nuclear technology is a world-making technology *par excellence*. Since the bombings of Hiroshima and Nagasaki in 1945, this branch of scientific innovation has profoundly changed history, geopolitics, the natural world and everyday human life. The emerging nuclear sector has been hailed as an instrument of national security, a hotbed of technological innovation, and a guarantor of abundant energy (Hecht, 1998;

Introduction: shaping the nuclear order 3

Jasanoff and Kim, 2013). It has also threatened human health, poisoned water and food supplies, and degraded our environment. Radioactive contamination from atmospheric atomic tests was the first planet-wide environmental issue recognised in the 1950s (Higuchi, 2020). In the current Anthropocene debate, radioactive traces are even taken as the quintessential indicators of humanity's impact on Earth (Masco, 2010).

This volume uses Fukushima as a prism through which we tease out the multifaceted ways in which nuclear technology produced our world. To understand the 2011 disaster, we look back to Hiroshima and reexamine the "balance" of good and evil implicit in this dual-use technology. The analyses presented here are based on newly available historical materials and declassified documents, as well as on field research, Anthropocene studies and a cross-cutting examination of recent international scholarship.[3] They move between past and current events, global and local scales, and various geographical areas, with a particular focus on the United States, France and Japan.

The objective of this volume is not to develop fine-grained historical accounts—it would require several books to do that project justice—but rather to provide an interdisciplinary perspective on the construction of the nuclear order. In this respect, this volume partially overlaps with that of Michael D. Gordin and G. John Ikenberry (2020). Instead of focusing on Hiroshima, however, the works included here highlight the violence of nuclear technology, examine the constitutive roles of nuclear expertise along with institutional and material infrastructure and explore the evolving "nuclear order."

Nuclear order refers to the dimensions of the nuclear domain that constitute and mediate our experience of the world. This use of the term is more encompassing than how it is commonly used in fields like international relations to indicate a global order and the means for preventing warfare through strategic approaches such as deterrence and non-proliferation (Scheinman, 1987; Walker, 2000; Ritchie, 2019). Those analyses tend to focus on nation-states and international organisations instead of survivor bodies, representation, expertise and worldviews. In contrast, the authors in this volume embrace the material and institutional infrastructures of nuclear technology, the cultural categories that structure our experience of space and time, and the symbolic and physical traces that pattern our visions of the world and the future. They approach the nuclear order from multiple perspectives, ranging from discussions of its tangible effects on our lives to abstract changes in culture, knowledge and techno-politics. The authors in this book see the nuclear order both as a product of history and as a constitutive element of the future world.

This book is broken into four sections which represent four entangled dynamics that address two seemingly simple questions: *How has nuclear technology shaped the world we live in? How have we come to live with this technology?* The process of seeking answers sheds light on how we

4 *Bernadette Bensaude-Vincent et al.*

have learned to live with world-objects, to borrow Michel Serres's term, which maintain a global reach but remain ungovernable and indomitable no matter how much technical work and political regulation is devoted to controlling them (Serres, 2006).

The chapters in the first section, "Managing violence: categories and demarcation," look at how the dangers of nuclear technology have been downplayed within the nuclear order that emerged after the atomic bombings of Japan. The next section, "Pacifying atoms: control and containment," examines how "peaceful" uses of atomic energy have been promoted and regulatory infrastructures established to erase and contain the violence of nuclear technology. The contributions in "Normalising risks: denial and trivialisation" scrutinise the work of institutions and global networks of experts to build life *with* the dangers of nuclear power and radiation. And finally, "Timescaping: memory and future visions" looks both backward and forward, examining how nuclear disasters affect our visions of the past and the future.

Managing violence: categories and demarcation

Why is there such disregard for the evidence of nuclear technology's destructive potential? On the morning of August 6, 1945, people in Hiroshima experienced an extraordinarily powerful blast. The heat melted metal. A highly radioactive "black rain" poured down. An estimated 70,000–140,000 in Hiroshima and 40,000–80,000 in Nagasaki died within months.[4] Tens of thousands more suffered radiation and burns. The United States justified these bombings as necessary to end World War II, deftly evading responsibility for the humanitarian consequences of introducing a weapon of such deadly capability and unpredictable aftermath. The Cold War arms race that followed would be marked by the well-founded fear that the deployment of nuclear weapons could destroy humanity.

The chapters in the first section of this volume explore how a new order emerged out of these early displays of nuclear violence. A key mechanism for establishing this order was the imposition of a clear-cut demarcation between *bombs* and *energy*. Nuclear bombs were presented as destructive, while nuclear energy was promoted for its ability to improve modern life. The former were to be feared and restricted. The latter heralded a bright future. Thus, the reputation for violence was reserved for nuclear munitions, and the risk associated with other applications of nuclear technology was glossed over. Violence became exclusively associated with weapons and war.

Crucial for this decoupling of violence and nuclear technology on the whole was the persistent official downplaying of the slow afflictions caused by radiation. The US Occupation that followed the bombings in Japan characterised the bombs' destructive capacity as instant: a

Introduction: shaping the nuclear order 5

relatively brief, hot blast. By censoring and controlling the details of *lingering* damage, the Allies purposefully concealed the long-term harm they already had reason to expect among Japanese survivors.

We know today that radiation from bombs, tests and accidents causes various diseases and disabilities as well as fear about social stigma and future health. Downplaying this intrinsic violence has been necessary for expanding nuclear energy programs. Although nuclear weapons continued to proliferate and inspire fear about human extinction, civilian programs, starting with the US Atoms for Peace campaign in 1953, flourished without causing similar alarm. But as disasters like Three Mile Island, Chernobyl and Fukushima reveal, nuclear violence is not bound to formal hostilities. The potential for devastation is embedded within the reactor, in its capacity for producing massive amounts of invisible radiation. The process is not constrained by the intended outcome.

Much of our understanding of the health effects of ionising radiation owes to the *hibakusha*, the survivors of the 1945 bombings. Kyoko Sato's chapter shows how international and national standards that rely significantly on such knowledge have been used to distinguish who is—and is not—worthy of medical and financial support as officially certified *hibakusha*. Survivors and their supporters have challenged the Japanese government's classificatory approaches by providing testimonials about their bodies and experiences and counter-expertise that problematises the authoritative knowledge's limitations. Although this has helped to expand *hibakusha* status gradually, numerous exclusions of aging survivors have added symbolic violence to their physical, psychological and social struggles. Sato argues that the negotiations over *hibakusha* status served as an arena in which the consequences of the bomb and radiation exposure were defined and redefined. These deliberations involved much wrangling over thresholds between high and supposedly safe doses based mostly on each survivor's proximity to ground zero, while devaluing each survivor's lived, bodily experience and evolving knowledge on multiple pathways of radiation exposure and their effects.

Politics around categories and demarcation have shadowed the handling of many instances of risk and damage. Because ionising radiation is invisible, nuclear technology has required practices for delineating the spatial boundaries between contaminated and habitable zones. The booming field of nuclear geography focuses on the human and social aspects of designing, mapping and enforcing exclusion zones in everyday life as well as in disaster areas (Davies, 2013; Alexis-Martin and Davies, 2017). These zoning and compensation practices usually result from tangled compromises involving standardised measurements and negotiations between authorities and citizens.

In contrast to the slow creep of radiation, the violence of nuclear tests is spectacular and swift. On July 16, 1945, scientists viewing the Trinity test at the Alamogordo Range in New Mexico were flooded with feelings

6 *Bernadette Bensaude-Vincent et al.*

of awe and beauty (as well as the fear of a looming Doomsday) that words could not describe. Only witnesses, it seemed, could realise the "nuclear sublime" (Wilson, 1994) in this striking demonstration of force that became so instrumental in shaping a new vision of the world. Following this first live viewing of an atomic blast, film and photographic representations served to reinforce the inescapable impression of violence in the nuclear sublime as the province of weapons alone.

In the 1950s, Kodak and a few other contractors recorded nuclear tests in the Pacific, capturing them visually with cutting-edge imaging technology and registering the effects of radiation using film badges affixed to their workers' uniforms. Joseph Masco's chapter examines the techno-politics of these recordings and dosimeter badges, showing how menacing images of explosions were linked to a slow violence on bodies as well as to the contamination of the global environment. While the curated representations of atomic mushroom clouds became deeply engraved in the popular imaginary, records of radiation exposure, duly recorded and dully considered within safety thresholds, quietly allowed those tests to continue. Masco argues that technical innovations designed to record these nuclear tests have not only influenced our use of images and our understanding of nuclear dangers, but have also created an archive of US nuclear nationalism. These detailed records of both extreme and slow violence may hold immense implications for nuclear accountability.

The selective set of unclassified images that were displayed in museums, films and on TV became iconic of the nuclear era. Together with the pro- and anti-nuclear propaganda of the Cold War, propaganda and government-controlled images helped to frame nuclear issues as matters of survival at a time when the United States and the Soviet Union were frantically building up their nuclear capacities, developing rocket technologies and engaging in espionage. Following Sputnik in 1957, the American series of Apollo space missions captured images of Earth as a "Blue Marble," indirectly molding a global view and contributing to the study of environmental changes on a planetary scale. Inspiring both wonder and trepidation, these images facilitated what Sheila Jasanoff (2015) calls "sociotechnical imaginaries," or the visions of social orders and desirable futures that could be achieved through technoscientific advances.

Boundaries are prominent in nuclear imaginaries—not only geographic boundaries but the boundaries between military and civilian applications, between worthy and unworthy uses of nuclear technology. In the hazy rhetoric of fear and security, destructive pursuits come from "bad guys" while "good guys"—identified as Western, White and male—work with non-destructive atoms. Only the "other" needs policing, screening and improvement.

John Krige's chapter describes this rhetorical effort via boundary work, in which tropes of gender, race, and pathology were mobilised to create a "nuclear apartheid" that denied "others" access to nuclear

Introduction: shaping the nuclear order   7

weapons. In other words, dual-use was established according to externalised malice (Rabinow and Bennet, 2012: 123) against internalised good intentions to support the illusion that "we" are entitled to split atoms. From the dawn of the nuclear age, Krige argues, US leaders have framed nuclear weapons as an existential issue and American leadership as key to controlling proliferation and maintaining a stable world order. Colonialist and imperialist worldviews are so deeply embedded as to be virtually indistinguishable from the entire endeavor (Churchill and LaDuke, 1992; Hecht, 2012).

Neo-colonialist visions were manifested in the ways the United States unflinchingly changed the legal status of Micronesia and created a flexible nuclear network for weapons testing in the Marshall Islands. The territorial grab would spare the US homeland the risks of nuclear testing while dooming to harm the indigenous islanders and unanticipated others (including the Lucky Dragon No. 5's Japanese fishing crew, operating in the area of the Bravo tests). Describing the emergence of this unique arrangement from the perspectives of both the islanders and the US authorities, Mary X. Mitchell's chapter exemplifies the complex entanglements of nuclear technology and imperialism that reinforced the post-war, neo-colonial world order of White and non-White countries.

The externalisation of malice initiated during the height of atmospheric nuclear bomb testing in the 1950s still fuels fears of "Islamic bombs," "rogue states" and "nuclear orientalism" (Gusterson, 1999). To cope with the violence of detonation and radiation, a tentative nuclear order has been established according to demarcation strategies between good and bad, safe and dangerous, contaminated and habitable. Despite the emphasis on what is good and safe, radioactive fallout from bombs, tests and reactors has lasting and possibly immeasurable effects on humans and their environments.

Pacifying atoms: control and containment

The violence inherent in splitting atoms had to be domesticated to secure the technology's acceptance. It took considerable work to pacify global concerns about the access to nuclear arms and build a convincing system for preventing their use. The attention to atomic bombs generated by the Cold War arms race proved foundational for instituting containment and deterrence efforts. Shortly after the detonation of the first nuclear bombs, a world peace movement took on this global threat (Wittner, 1993; 1997), with scientists and intellectuals calling for the creation of international nuclear governance.

A complementary logic of pacification was at work in the promotion of nuclear applications in medicine and energy. Shoring up the boundary between military and civilian atoms, this strategy used intense publicity efforts to create a positive image of civilian nuclear applications. Scholars

8 *Bernadette Bensaude-Vincent et al.*

have described the huge investments made in promoting non-military nuclear technology on the political stage and in the public arena, beginning with speeches on the greatness of a nation (Hecht, 1998) and followed by the Atoms for Peace campaign in the 1950s (Krige, 2006). During the 1970s oil crisis, nuclear reactors promised abundant energy. Today, amid concerns about climate change, nuclear energy has been rebranded as a green technology that does not emit planet-warming gases.[5]

Scientific expertise has played a key role in producing the pacified atom. The Manhattan Project, for instance, resulted in an unprecedented concentration and coordination of expertise and investment to master a complex and uncertain technology for producing bombs, reactors, and radioisotopes (Hughes, 2002; Oreskes and Krige, 2014). Cold War efforts to discern the terrestrial, atmospheric and oceanographic conditions in which nuclear bombs could be used, along with the race to understand the effects of radiation, contributed to the creation or profound transformation of entire scientific fields such as environmental sciences and climate research (Doel, 2003; Turchetti and Roberts, 2014). Nuclear knowledge has also served as a tool for foreign policy, notably in the late 1940s and into the 1950s, when the United States shared knowledge and isotopes to help improve relationships with other nations, foster European integration and entice nations to the American side of Cold War geopolitics (Creager, 2015; Krige, 2016).

In this second section of the volume, path-breaking scholars scrutinise how pacification efforts were embedded in the distribution of knowledge about nuclear technology, the creation of infrastructures and instruments for radiation and risk measurement and the global standards proposed and adopted during the postwar years. It emphasises how this advancement of knowledge and control paradoxically *also* produced ignorance and blind spots. Based on fear initially, the postwar nuclear order was rebuilt on "rational foundations" by scientists, engineers and experts who framed a regime of global surveillance, oversight and regulation that legitimised nuclear activities in the public eye. Certain of these scientists rose to prominence within global networks while serving national interests and mediating between nuclear institutions and political authorities regarding the dangers of fallout.

One key actor in this work, as Angela N.H. Creager and Maria Rentetzi's chapter shows, was the International Atomic Energy Agency (IAEA). Founded in 1957 with the stated aim of promoting the "peaceful" uses of nuclear technologies while preventing the diversion of these resources to military uses, the agency has twin divergent goals. That the IAEA simultaneously promotes and seeks to control these technologies has never been reconciled or even officially acknowledged. By promoting, advocating and monitoring the development of atomic energy in its member states, the IAEA embodies a new regulatory presence that decisively directs the dissemination of technologies, materials, laboratory

Introduction: shaping the nuclear order   9

designs and safety practices (though it once lacked the explicit authority to enforce its recommendations). Yet, although the promotion of civilian nuclear technologies resembles other postwar programs for economic development in the Global South, the dual uses of atomic energy necessitate a different regime of geopolitical control.

Networks for monitoring radioisotopes and radioactive contamination are another mechanism in building the image of mastery over nuclear technologies. Nestor Herran's chapter considers the role of these networks in the emergence of the nuclear order and the specific regimes of global surveillance. He shows how the development of radiation monitoring was initially motivated by military concerns—specifically, whether the enemy had developed its own atomic weapons. Later, this activity coalesced with 1950s-era concerns about tracking radioactive fallout because of controversy over the health risks of nuclear tests. The expansion of nuclear power stations in the 1960s was accompanied by early efforts at international coordination on monitoring radiation. The Chernobyl accident accelerated these efforts and saw the emergence of citizens' counter-expertise platforms that shaped new forms of communication within the state-controlled apparatuses (Topçu, 2013).

As we contend with 75 years of nuclear waste and fallout, containment is a crucial part of civilising nuclear development. The IAEA and other experts funded by nuclear advocates invest heavily in the production of concepts and doctrines concerning risks and how they should be managed (Boudia, 2014). In this vast market, serious accidents akin to the explosion of a bomb are a central theme.

Thus, in his chapter, Maël Goumri demonstrates how, when faced with a body of studies, nuclear engineers and other experts can go from denial of the reality that an accident could occur to patiently developing the concept of "hypothetical accidents" to make major risks conceivable yet manageable. Using cases from the United States and France from the 1950s to the 1980s, Goumri shows how these experts framed severe accidents as improbable and "theoretical," relegating the possibilities of accidents to a "residual" domain instead of tackling them head-on or learning from actual experiments. Goumri argues that these strategies depended on technical and social work that embedded them within the material and institutional infrastructures of nuclear governance.

Containment strategies are central to Tania Navarro's chapter on the transnational governance of nuclear waste. Documenting past and present decisions regarding radioactive waste management, Navarro reveals how French experts and decision-makers saw a partnership between nature and technology as a way to solve disposal problems. She argues that the conceptual shift from waste *disposal* to waste *storage,* and the correlated change in action from dilution to containment, which took place globally, came directly out of the scientific and social concern that increased right alongside the increasing volume of radioactive waste.

10 *Bernadette Bensaude-Vincent et al.*

Surveillance of installations, regulation of risk and the monitoring of radiation are indispensable companions in the nuclearised world. Nuclear physicist Alvin R. Weinberg observed that the "military priesthood" set up to control the proliferation of atomic weapons had to be extended to other uses of radioactive materials (Weinberg, 1972). The "Faustian bargain" between nuclear professionals and society offered cheap and clean energy, but required that society ensure the longevity of expert institutions and buy into a defanged acknowledgement of risk.

Normalising risk: denial and trivialisation

The quest to control and contain radioactivity, reactor products and waste is fundamental to nuclear technology. However, accidents and the production of counter-expertise undermine this "containment doctrine." After 75 years, the cumulative damage caused by nuclear technology is considerable. The chapters in the third section consider how nuclear institutions and their advocates (including national governments) have worked to minimise these nuclear hazards and their aftermaths, developing new ways of governing the consequences of living amid toxic ruins.

There are several mechanisms of secrecy that intentionally render nuclear activities and their effects invisible. From the beginning of the nuclear age, practices of secrecy were constructed around the technical details of weapons and reactors (Galison, 2010; Wellerstein, 2021) as well as the effects of radiation at Hiroshima and Nagasaki—details that were not fully disclosed for decades (Lindee, 1994). Far from exceptions, these patterns of retention and dissimulation of information are distinctive features of the nuclear milieu.

Hiroko Takahashi's chapter focuses on an episode that took place in 1954, when politics and diplomacy dictated the terms of scientific debate over the effects of radiation and thereby terminated diagnostic testing and the collection of empirical data. After a Japanese fishing boat was exposed to fallout from a US thermonuclear test in the Marshall Islands, the Japanese government responded to public fear and anti-nuclear mobilisation by initiating a short-lived program to inspect tuna catches for radiation. Those fish sufficiently contaminated were destroyed. Takahashi argues that the so-called full settlement that resulted from this case was crucial for the United States and its continued nuclear testing program. The agreement was bolstered by Japanese and American scientists who downplayed the health consequences of radiation during a Tokyo conference.

The multiple logics and methods that contribute to dissimulation and invisibilisation have been articulated by historians. Censorship and press codes restricted early discussions of the bomb (Braw, 1991; Takahashi, 2012), but for decades, scholars have interviewed the inhabitants of Bikini Atoll and the Marshall Islands (Johnston and Barker, 2008; Takemine, 2015), veterans of atomic tests, African uranium miners (Hecht, 2012),

Introduction: shaping the nuclear order 11

and nuclear plant workers (Jobin, 2017) to backfill crucial data. Practices of disqualification and denial have, in turn, been maintained through psychological and physical violence, as illustrated in communities around Chernobyl (Kuchinskaya, 2014; Brown, 2019). Tactics include refuting the suffering of victims, denigrating opponents, and sometimes engaging in threats, surveillance, imprisonment or death sentences (perhaps its own sort of nuclear waste containment and disposal—simply applied to the human evidence of ongoing risk).

Kate Brown's chapter brings us to Chernobyl, where the politics of medical knowledge and the legacy of the Cold War are borne out among parents who failed to mobilise and bring foreign attention to their children's illnesses. Because of the influx of Western medical experts following the accident, Brown reasons, Soviet medicine's focus on environmental causes of disease gave way to individualist approaches that attributed cancer and other maladies to behaviors, psychological states or genetic coding. The "experts" working for UN and national nuclear agencies built these Western assumptions into their reviews and presentations, dismissing the effects of fallout and even blaming Soviet citizens for their "addiction" to state welfare.

Denials of nuclear danger take many forms and different degrees of sophistication depending on the political context in which they are issued. In his chapter, Harry Bernas argues that the 2011 Fukushima disaster resulted from a long social, economic and political process. That is, it was a "normal accident," according to Charles Perrow (1984), rather than an "unforeseeable" event caused by natural disaster, as Japanese authorities claimed. Bernas shows how power utilities, ministries and safety overseers largely ignored or denied the possibility of major accidents despite considerable knowledge that a major earthquake and tsunami along the Fukushima coastline were, seismologically speaking, overdue. It seems the drive to accrue profits and power, as well as bureaucratic inertia, allowed authorities to underestimate risks, tolerating or even encouraging uncertainty and criminal malpractice in the approval and siting of nuclear facilities along Japan's fault-ridden coastlines.

The mechanisms for minimising hazards and their consequences often fall under what Gabrielle Hecht calls nuclear exceptionalism (2012). Hecht uses several studies to show that exceptionalism consists of singularising each case, justifying it according to local and contextual circumstances, and mobilising cultural explanations for local outcomes that are often tainted by stereotypes. In the exceptionalist view, the Chernobyl accident could be dismissed as the consequence of using an old Soviet-era reactor, inferior to those at work in Europe, while Fukushima can be dismissed as an outcome of extraordinary circumstances—of an earthquake, a tidal wave and a cascade of technical failures exacerbated by a culture of obedience in which people did not feel empowered to improvise and take initiative to counteract a new and unusual threat.

12 *Bernadette Bensaude-Vincent et al.*

The flip side of exceptionalism is the simultaneous normalisation and trivialisation explored throughout this volume. Making nuclear technology non-problematic despite its many uncertainties requires political maintenance work, a whole host of techno-political initiatives that make nuclear institutions resistant to challenge and criticism. By constantly re-adjusting their technologies within shifting economic and political contexts, nuclear actors labor to convince the world that nuclear technology is indispensable. The maintenance work that keeps nuclear industries running occurs through different mechanisms, including the production of knowledge and technical innovation, the implementation of safety and security, the presentation of public expertise, the construction of categories and the development of governance technologies.

Soraya Boudia's chapter takes a historical perspective on global nuclear governance, which has long been a political proving ground for designing and testing ways of managing hazards. Nuclear governance, this chapter argues, is characterised by a succession of three intermingled paradigms—containment, risk assessment and adaptation—forged and promoted through transnational expertise and regulatory institutions such as the IAEA, International Commission on Radiation Protection (ICRP) and United Nations Scientific Committee on the Effects of Atomic Radiation (UNSCEAR). Focusing on the adaptation paradigm, Boudia shows how Chernobyl and Fukushima prompted a series of social experiments endorsing the continuation of daily life in "sustainably contaminated" areas, as well as how these political devices are being applied in other areas.

A vast array of instruments and practices have gone into the repertoire of initiatives developed by nuclear institutions to overcome crises and criticisms during the past 75 years. The approaches and tools used to characterise, delimit and manage risks have accumulated their own intrinsic contradictions and tensions, becoming a source for new risks and undermining the legitimacy of institutional models without hampering the ability to pursue nuclear development despite the exorbitant economic and environmental costs.

Timescaping: memory and future visions

The violence of nuclear technology and the efforts to tame it have deeply affected humans' experience of space. The fear of destruction has led institutions such as the IAEA to create a global system of surveillance that collapses national borders and allows scientists and politicians to transcend the confines of earth. The iconic image of the Blue Marble afforded humans their first view of Earth from the outside—a view from nowhere (Grevsmühl, 2014) that turned our relationship to the planet inside-out. It facilitated "the withdrawal from terrestrial proximity" that

Introduction: shaping the nuclear order 13

Hannah Arendt describes as "earth alienation" and which is considered the hallmark of modern science (Arendt, 1958: 264–265).[6]

If the nuclear age reshaped our experience of space through a dual process of globalisation and abstraction, has it also affected our experience of time? Jeremy Rifkin observed, "Time is our window onto the world. With time we create order and shape the kind of world we live in" (Rifkin, 1987: 7). The questions addressed in the fourth section of this volume are inspired by the notion of the order of time and its relationship to the nuclear order of the postwar age.

A number of European historians have tried to characterise the categories that frame ways of dealing with the past, present, and future. Because we take time for granted, we are usually unaware of these categories and their performativity. Observing the changes in the experience of time prompted by modernity's promise of emancipation and progress, Reinhart Kosseleck introduced the concept of the "horizon of expectation" (2004). François Hartog (2015) coined the phrase "regime of historicity" to describe the connecting of past, present, and future in a way that is specific to a given period. The modern future-oriented regime of historicity has such a coercive power that it constitutes an "order of time."

> No one doubts that an order of time exists—or rather, that orders of time exist which vary with time and place. These orders are, in any event, so imperious and apparently so self-evident that we bow to them without even realizing it, without meaning to or wanting to, and whether we are aware of it or not. All resistance is in vain. For a society's relations to time hardly seem open to discussion or negotiation. The term "order" implies at once succession and command: the times (in the plural) dictate or defy, time avenges wrongs, it restores order following a disruption, or sees justice done.
> (Hartog, 2015: 1)

Of particular interest for this book, however, is Barbara Adam's concept of a timescape. The timescape view emphasises the coexistence of multiple forms of time within a temporal regime. Adam attends closely to the entanglement of physical and cultural temporalities that generate multidimensional and complex timescapes, asserting that humans cannot embrace time without simultaneously encompassing space and matter—that is, without embodying it in a specific and unique context (Adam, 2010: 1).

Science fiction in literature and film strongly links technology with visions of the future, a relationship explored by decades of science and technology studies. In particular, "desirable futures" are central to Jasanoff's "sociotechnical imaginaries," defined as "collectively held, institutionally stabilised and publicly performed visions of desirable

14 Bernadette Bensaude-Vincent et al.

futures, animated by shared understandings of forms of social life and social order attainable through, and supportive of, advances in science and technology" (2015: 4). The role of media such as radio and television in disseminating far-ranging visions of scientists, engineers and science policymakers is also well established (Nieto-Galàn, 2016). But so far, visions of the future have been the only expression of the technological footprint on the cultural frameworks of time.

This section's chapters broaden this scope in two respects. First, they demonstrate the intimate ties between visions of a nuclear future and visions of the past and the present, without separating questions raised by the nuclear order of time from questions about space. They next discuss questions such as the extent to which Hiroshima and Nagasaki reconfigured the modern regime of historicity, with its promises of a better future. In order to tackle such issues without reifying the nuclear order (Hughes, 2002), this section focuses on the particular cases of the world's three leading nuclear countries: the United States, France and Japan.

Because nuclear technology was first used in a global war, it could be considered simply another form of mass bombing that targets cities and kills civilians. The conventional practice of airborne attacks did not raise moral issues in 1945, and no serious objections were prompted by the shift from German to Japanese targets that was the impetus for launching the Manhattan Project (Bernstein, 1995). Does this mean that the first atomic bombs were perceived as just local operations meant to impact a global conflict, or did they generate a deep, unsettling fear of the future?

In the aftermath of Hiroshima and Nagasaki, it is obvious that nuclear technology reconfigured our sense of place and the world around us. The bombings were epoch-making events. The actors and witnesses who commented on Hiroshima and Nagasaki were quick to realise that these local bombings would reconfigure the future. They talked about the "dawn of a new era" that became known as the "nuclear age," thus conveying the image of a global transformation.

The authors in this book emphasise the striking contrast between the locality of the bombings and their global impact. Hiroshima and Nagasaki raised awareness that the human species had the power to destroy itself, to bring biblical warnings of apocalypse to fruition. In her chapter, though, Bernadette Bensaude-Vincent argues that the emergence of catastrophic visions by no means eroded the promise of a better tomorrow. Nuclear technology nurtured both catastrophic and optimistic visions of what was to come. A strikingly ambivalent order of time emerged to allow the promise of a "bright future" atop the ruins of atomic bombings.

Ran Zwigenberg (2014) has described the unabated desire for Hiroshima to be born anew, a dream the city's mayor articulated on the first anniversary of the 1945 bombing. In his chapter here, Zwingenberg tackles the critical issue of understanding why Japan, a victim of atomic bombing, came to embrace nuclear power. Atoms for Peace played a

Introduction: shaping the nuclear order 15

crucial role in combining a culture of memory with plans for modernisation. Many in Hiroshima and the anti-nuclear weapons movement who supported nuclear power were motivated by a strong desire for modern life and its comforts. Japan embraced nuclear power enthusiastically in the decades following the bombing while transforming Hiroshima into a symbolic sanctuary dedicated to world peace.

Scott Gabriel Knowles closes the volume with a look at the cultural practices of memorialising nuclear catastrophes in a broader perspective. Memorial practices often center on "events," but nuclear disasters, as you will read in every chapter of this book, span multiple timescales. To emphasise the difficulties in memorialising these tragedies, Knowles introduces the notion of a "slow disaster" in which risks and fears are known long before and long after any single "event." Museums, filmmakers, artists and citizens in Japan and across the world have worked to bring dignity to victims and survivors of Fukushima and knowledge to the public. They do so in a fog of uncertainty, a fog that clouds the fate of many displaced people and raises questions about the future of life on earth.

What now? Open questions for further research

Is it possible to predict the end of the nuclear age? Nuclear technology has profoundly shaped our societies, influenced political and economic trajectories and colonised swaths of our lives. With the exception of radionuclides used in medicine, nuclear technologies have been controversial since the dawn of the "atomic age." Arms protesters have never weakened their stances, regularly assembling in Hiroshima and playing strategic roles in non-proliferation negotiations around the world. At the same time, rising environmental movements have also tempered their opposition to civilian nuclear power since the 1990s when zero-carbon energy policies started to favor nuclear power plants over more traditional mining and refining efforts. It is an uneasy moral balance when the slow disaster of nuclear fallout and the slow disaster of climate change compete in public discourse.

Nuclear technology is, in fact, aging, and its future is open to debate. The first generation of nuclear reactors is being decommissioned, while a new generation of EPR reactors comes online and other "advanced" reactors are being designed. Even in countries that have opted out of nuclear activities and claim to be "atom-free," reactor decommissioning will take decades and there will still be a demand for radionuclides for therapeutic and research purposes. Moreover, nuclear waste has a lifetime far exceeding that of political regimes.

Nuclear technologies are here—not forever, but for a duration that exceeds our power of anticipation. The world cannot be denuclearised by political decisions alone, so it seems that *there is no end of the nuclear age* in sight. Future generations must coexist with material artifacts and

16 *Bernadette Bensaude-Vincent et al.*

contamination from this technology. The question, then, is how to adjust social and political timeframes around the inexorable lifetimes of radioactive materials. The easy solutions of storing waste aboveground or burying it underground are made complex because of the toxicity of radioactive matter. Isolating the technosphere from the biosphere is utopian thinking, since many organisms can flourish in extreme milieus and new life forms will undoubtedly make harmonious arrangements with manmade radionuclides, as is already visible in the thriving wildlife populations surrounding Chernobyl. Separation is not an option, and so adaptation becomes the only possibility.

Again, our nuclearised timescape defies the naïve hope of a foreseeable end to the nuclear age, save a Doomsday scenario. The abolition of nuclear weapons is a globally divisive issue. On the one hand, the historic Treaty on the Prohibition of Nuclear Weapons was passed by the UN in July 2017, with 122 countries voting in favor, and entered into effect in January 2021. ICAN, the International Campaign to Abolish Nuclear Weapons, received the 2017 Nobel Peace Prize for its work in helping to secure the treaty. The organisation has been working closely with survivors of Hiroshima and Nagasaki. On the other hand, not a single nuclear-weapons state supports the treaty. Not even Japan, the only country to have endured atomic bombings, supports it.[7] Furthermore, the treaty bans only the military use of nuclear weapons and does not address civilian nuclear technology.

This limited, variegated success is a call to consider the place of nuclear technologies in the global environmental crisis and to probe the connections between the nuclear order and the Anthropocene. After much debate, a working group of geologists in charge of classifying geological periods settled on nuclear technology as the best marker for the beginning of the Anthropocene; the plutonium released by nuclear tests in the mid-twentieth century fulfills the three criteria for marking a new period: it is man made, operates on a planetary scale, and lasts long enough to be relevant on the geological timescale.

We are living in an age marked by nuclear technologies so powerful that they affect Earth systemically. Not only a nuclear apocalypse threatens our lives and our safety but also the slow disaster of the technology's ongoing, mundane uses. The disturbing possibilities of a world shaped by the nuclear alert us to the emerging character of the adaptive Anthropocene—the complex relationships between planetary warming, global health issues, ecological crises, and the nuclear order.

Notes

1 M. Ishigami, Japan's Post-Disaster Reconstruction Symbol Re-Opens with Kuwait's Help, *Arab Times*, April 21, 2019, p. 3. Available at: http://www.arabtimesonline.com/wp-content/uploads/pdf/2019/apr/21/03.pdf [Accessed June 9, 2021].

Introduction: shaping the nuclear order 17

2 "We" refers to humans in general rather than people whose lives have been severely disturbed, affected, or broken by the impacts of nuclear explosions or radiation. It does not mean the abstract Anthropos, the generic notion used in the term "Anthropocene." A lesson learned from Fukushima is that "we" members of the human species are bound to Earth, dependent on the drift of continents, the occasional earthquake, storms, tsunamis, winds, land, and fish.
3 These perspectives benefit from two workshops that brought together historians, anthropologists, STS scholars, and philosophers to discuss key moments in the nuclear world.
4 Wellerstein, A. (2020). Counting the Dead at Hiroshima and Nagasaki. Bulletin of the Atomic Scientists, August 4. Available at: https://thebulletin. org/2020/08/counting-the-dead-at-hiroshima-and-nagasaki/ [Accessed July 4, 2021].
5 For instance, American business magnate and philanthropist Bill Gates has been an active supporter of increasing nuclear power production to cut emission. Clifford, C. (2021). Bill Gates: Stop Shutting Down Nuclear Reactors and Build New Nuclear Power Plants to Fight Climate Change. CNBC, June 11. Available at: https://www.cnbc.com/2021/06/11/bill-gates-bullish-on-using-nuclear-power-to-fight-climate-change.html. [Accessed July 4, 2021]. Conca, J. (2021). Wyoming to Lead the Coal-to-Nuclear Transition, With New Reactor Planned by Bill Gates-Backed TerraPower. *Forbes*, June 5. Available at: https://www.forbes.com/sites/jamesconca/ 2021/06/05/wyoming-to-lead-the-coal-to-nuclear-transition/?sh= 7090a8e56de1 [Accessed July 4, 2021].
6 This ambition to overcome our earth-bound condition seems to be the opposite of the movement, prompted by the Anthropocene, from the "infinite universe to the closed world." The planetary view of the world from the outside gives way to a view from the inside. To emphasise this radical change, Bruno Latour contrasts the condition of "Modern Humans" with that of "earthlings," humans belonging to the small fringe of the planet between the atmosphere and the soil (Latour, 2018).
7 As of June 2021, 54 states have ratified the treaty.

References

Adam, B. (2010). History of the Future: Paradoxes and Challenges. *Rethinking History*, 14(3), pp. 361–378.

Alexis-Martin, B., and Davies, T. (2017). Towards Nuclear Geography: Zones, Bodies and Communities. *Geography Compass*, 11(9). DOI: https://doi.org/1 0.1111/gec3.12325

Arendt, H. (1958). *The Human Condition*. 2nd edition. Chicago: University of Chicago Press.

Bernstein, B. (1995). The Atomic Bombings Reconsidered. *Foreign Affairs*, 74(1), pp. 135–152.

Boudia, S. (2014). Managing Scientific and Political Uncertainty: Risk Assessment in an Historical Perspective. In: S. Boudia and N. Jas, eds., *Powerless Science? The Making of the Toxic World in the Twentieth Century*. New York: Berghahn Books, pp. 95–112.

Braw, M. (1991). *The Atomic Bomb Suppressed: American Censorship in Occupied Japan*. Armonk, NY: M. E. Sharp.

18   Bernadette Bensaude-Vincent et al.

Brown, K. (2019). *Manual for Survival: A Chernobyl Guide to the Future.* New York: Norton.

Churchill, W., and LaDuke, W. (1992). Native North America: The Political Economy or Radioactive Colonization. In: Jaimes, A., ed., *The State of Native America: Genocide, Colonization and Resistance.* Boston: South End Press, pp. 241–266.

Creager, A. (2015). *Life Atomic: A History of Radioisotopes in Science and Medicine.* Chicago: University of Chicago Press.

Davies, T. (2013). A Visual Geography of Chernobyl: Double Exposure. *International Labor and Working-Class History,* 8, pp. 116–139.

Doel, R. (2003). Constituting the Postwar Earth Sciences: The Military's Influence on the Environmental Sciences in the USA after 1945. *Social Studies of Science,* 33(5), pp. 635–666.

Galison, P. (2010). Secrecy in Three Acts. *Social Research,* 77, pp. 941–974.

Gordin, M., and Ikenberry, G. (2020). *The Age of Hiroshima.* Princeton, NJ: Princeton University Press.

Grevsmühl, S. (2014). *La terre vue d'en haut. L'invention de l'environnement global.* Paris: Seuil.

Gusterson, H. (1999). Nuclear Weapons and the Other in the Western Imagination. *Cultural Anthropology,* 14(1), pp. 111–143.

Hartog, F. (2015). *Regimes of Historicity: Presentism and Experiences of Time.* New York: Columbia University Press.

Hecht, G. (1998). *The Radiance of France: Nuclear Power and National Identity after World War II.* Cambridge, MA: MIT Press.

Hecht, G. (2012). *Being Nuclear: Africans and the Global Uranium Trade.* Cambridge, MA: MIT Press.

Higuchi, T. (2020). *Political Fallout: Nuclear Weapons Testing and the Making of a Global Environmental Crisis.* Stanford, CA: Stanford University Press.

Hughes, J. (2002). *The Manhattan Project: Big Science and the Atom Bomb.* New York: Columbia University Press.

Jasanoff, S. (2015). Future Imperfect: Science, Technology, and the Imaginations of Modernity. In: S. Jasanoff and S. Kim, eds., *Dreamscapes of Modernity: Sociotechnical Imaginaries and the Fabrication of Power.* Chicago: University of Chicago Press.

Jobin, P. (2017). "Nuclear Gypsies" in Fukushima before and after 3/11. In: L. MacDowell, ed., *Nuclear Portraits: People, Communities and the Environment.* Toronto: University of Toronto Press, pp. 274–311.

Johnston, B., and Barker, H. (2008). *Consequential Damages of Nuclear War: The Rongelap Report.* Walnut Creek, CA: Left Coast Press.

Kosseleck, R. (2004). *Futures Past.* New York: Columbia University Press.

Krige, J. (2006). *American Hegemony and the Postwar Reconstruction of Science in Europe.* Cambridge, MA: MIT Press.

Krige, J. (2016). *Sharing Knowledge, Sharing Europe: US Technological Collaboration and Nonproliferation.* Cambridge, MA: MIT Press.

Kuchinskaya, O. (2014). *The Politics of Invisibility: Public Knowledge about Radiation Health Effects after Chernobyl.* Cambridge, MA: MIT Press.

Latour, B. (2018). *Down to the Earth: Politics of the New Climatic Regime.* Cambridge, UK; Polity Press.

Lindee, S. (1994). *Suffering Made Real: American Science and the Survivors at Hiroshima*. Chicago: University of Chicago Press.

Masco, J. (2010). Bad Weather: On Planetary Crisis. *Social Studies of Science*, 40(1), pp. 7–40.

Nieto-Galàn, A. (2016). *Science in the Public Sphere*. London: Routledge.

Oreskes, N., and Krige J. (eds.) (2014). *Science and Technology in the Global Cold War*. Cambridge, MA: MIT Press.

Perrow, C. (1984). *Normal Accidents: Living with High-Risk Technologies*. New York: Basic Books.

Rabinow, P., and Bennet, G. (2012). *Designing Human Practices: An Experiment with Synthetic Biology*. Chicago: University of Chicago Press.

Ritchie, N. (2019). A Hegemonic Nuclear Order: Understanding the Ban Treaty and the Power Politics of Nuclear Weapons. *Contemporary Security Policy*, 40(4), pp. 409–434.

Scheinman, L. (1987). *The International Atomic Energy Agency and World Nuclear Order*. Washington, DC: Resources for the Future.

Serres, M. (2006). Revisiting the Natural Contract. *CTheory*. Available at: https://journals.uvic.ca/index.php/ctheory/article/view/14482/5325/ [Accessed June 21, 2020].

Takahashi, H. (2012). *Fuuin sareta Hiroshima, Nagasaki—Bei kakujikken to minkan bouei keikaku*. [Classified Hiroshima and Nagasaki: US Nuclear Test and Civil Defense Program.] 2nd edition. Tokyo: Gaifusha

Takemine, S. (2015). *Masharu shoto: Owari naki kaku higai o ikiru*. Tokyo: Shinsensha.

Topçu, S. (2013). *La France nucléaire. L'art de gouverner une technologie contestée*. Paris: Seuil.

Turchetti, S., and Roberts R., eds. (2014). *The Surveillance Imperative: Geosciences during the Cold War and Beyond*. Basingstoke, UK: Palgrave MacMillan.

Walker, W. (2000). Nuclear Order and Disorder. *International Affairs*, 76(4), pp. 703–724.

Wellerstein, A. (2021). *Restricted Data: The History of Nuclear Secrecy in the United States*. Chicago: University of Chicago Press.

Wilson, R. (1994). Techno-Euphoria and the Discourse of the American Sublime. In: D. Pease, ed., *National Identities and Postnational Narratives*. Durham, NC: Duke University Press, pp. 205–229.

Wittner, L. (1993). *The Struggle against the Bomb, Volume 1. One World or None: A History of the World Nuclear Disarmament Movement through 1953*. Stanford, CA: Stanford University Press.

Wittner, L. (1997). *The Struggle against the Bomb, Volume 2. Resisting the Bomb: A History of the World Nuclear Disarmament Movement, 1954–1970*. Stanford, CA: Stanford University Press.

Zwigenberg, R. (2014). *Hiroshima: The Origins of Global Memory Culture*. Cambridge, UK: Cambridge University Press.

Section I
Violence and order

1 What the bomb has done: victim relief, knowledge and politics[1]

Kyoko Sato

On November 24, 2019, in his historic speech in Nagasaki, Pope Francis condemned the unspeakable horror of nuclear weapons and called for their abolition. Later that day, he traveled to Hiroshima and met with *hibakusha*, survivors of the atomic bomb, at the city's Peace Memorial Park.

Just three days earlier, amid growing anticipation of the papal visit, Japan's Supreme Court had rejected a lawsuit filed by 161 survivors of the atomic bombing of Nagasaki who sought official recognition as *hibakusha*. The plaintiffs were all within 12 km of the hypocenter at the time of the bombing, yet outside the area officially designated as "affected"—an oval-shaped zone that stretches 12 km north to south but only 7 km east to west. In 2002, the Japanese government had started classifying these survivors as "*hibaku taikensha*," people who "experienced exposure to the bomb," as opposed to *hibakusha*, those who were exposed to the bomb. Unlike officially certified *hibakusha*, who are eligible for free medical care for a wide range of physical and mental illnesses wherever they live, *hibaku taikensha* can receive free care only in Nagasaki Prefecture and, importantly, only for certain psychological conditions such as post-traumatic stress disorder (PTSD) and their accompanying complications. This is due to the official stance that people in this category were not exposed to radiation in a manner consequential to physical health, but the "experience" may have caused PTSD and other mental disorders. The November 2019 ruling marked the second time the top court denied *hibaku taikensha* claims that, just like those with the *hibakusha* status, their health conditions—physical or mental—and medical needs stem from exposure to the bomb's radiation. The first had been a ruling against 387 plaintiffs in December 2017. According to Nagasaki City's latest records, 4,919 survivors belonged to the category of *hibaku taikensha* as of March 2018.[2]

Today, having just marked the 76th anniversary of the atomic bombings of Japan, the survivor population is shrinking. Yet who among them qualifies for what kinds of recognition, public services and financial resources is still an unresolved, contested matter. The globally acknowledged

DOI: 10.4324/9781003227472-1

24   *Kyoko Sato*

Japanese word *hibakusha* (被爆者) directly translates as "those exposed to explosion," though during the postwar period it came to refer specifically to survivors of the atomic bombings of Hiroshima and Nagasaki. This lay definition may be simple enough, but who legally qualifies for the *hibakusha* status and associated medical support and allowances is a complex and unsettled question that has shaped and been shaped by our evolving understandings of the bomb's consequences and meanings. On one hand, A-bomb survivors' bodies and accounts have played a crucial role in the production of myriad technical knowledges relevant to nuclear technology, such as the bomb's destructive capacity and radiation's health and genetic effects. These knowledges have served as a significant basis for various national and international standards and protocols for radiation safety and protection. On the other hand, such knowledge and standards have also been used to draw boundaries among the affected, between "legitimate" and presumably "illegitimate" survivor claims to aid eligibility and recognition. Against this backdrop, survivor groups and their supporters have continuously challenged and helped expand the criteria for *hibakusha* and the kinds of supports available to them through political mobilisation and legal challenges, which then contributed new knowledge on radiation damages.

This politics of survivor classification is an important arena of nuclear history in which divergent views of the bomb's consequences, their temporal and spatial scopes, and the locus of accountability have clashed, been articulated, changed and been reaffirmed. The rationale for providing official and ongoing survivor relief has primarily hinged on the delayed health effects of radiation exposure, deemed unique harms of the atomic bomb.

The official framework, which explicitly refers to dominant scientific knowledge and international standards as its logical basis, has, however, been challenged by survivors and experts in several significant ways. First, they contend, the official designation regards radiation's damaging effects as spatially and temporally contained in ways that are not scientifically plausible. In order to gain the *hibakusha* status, to be considered a person affected by radiation, one had to be within the designated area at the time of detonation or enter it within a certain period of time. Despite various known ways radiation can affect a human body, from direct exposure to the blast to delayed exposure to residual radiation and fallout to internal exposure from the ingestion of contaminated materials, the government frameworks conceptualise the bomb's harm mechanistically, in terms of distance from the hypocenter at the time of explosion, with some consideration of physical barriers that may have mitigated the bomb's effect on any given person. Second, radiation's numerous health effects are not wholly known, even 76 years later, yet the Japanese government has recognised only a limited set of diseases and conditions (such as cancer) as legitimate and relevant effects in survivor designation. Other health effects, including very common symptoms such as severe chronic fatigue (the so-called *bura bura* disease[3]) are excluded, even though some researchers have since traced these to radiation exposure. And third, the survivors' movement has consistently and iteratively shown that the bomb's harmful consequences go well beyond radiation's effects. Specifically, although the trauma of experiencing the bomb and witnessing its aftermath is increasingly recognised as a valid claim in recent years, survivors attest to a much wider range of psychological difficulties than officially recognised, including the loss of family members and friends, survivor's guilt, fear and uncertainty about the lingering and still unfolding effects of radiation exposure, and social stigma and discrimination. Many had their physical health damaged from not only radiation but also heat and blast. Some live with irreparable scars. Some lost breadwinners and guardians. Many endured social isolation and intolerance.

Another area of contention is whether *hibakusha* relief is state compensation or social security. Survivors' organisations have long called for the government to provide aid as formal state compensation for its war responsibilities, rather than mere social security. They thus demand the *hibakusha* relief be extended to those killed by the bomb (as a benefit to be paid to their family members). Framing the question of aid as one of state compensation, activists suggest, is an important symbolic step if Japan hopes to live up to its commitments to preventing future bomb victims by abolishing nuclear weapons and facilitating world peace. Still, the government has narrowly defined *hibakusha* relief as social security for those who have suffered unique damage due to spatially and temporally bounded radiation exposure from the bomb.

Notably, whereas the Japanese government has tried to make the bomb's damages legible through the standards and boundaries of bureaucratic "high modernism" (Scott, 1999), presuming their knowability and manageability, survivors have been forced to live with the far messier—and often invisible—"slow violence" (Nixon, 2013) of the unfolding after-effects of the bombing. In addition to diverse physical and psychological pains, they have long endured persistent fear around their tenuous health and the uncertainty that surrounds the health of their offspring. The tension between these conflicting positionalities on how to address the bomb's violence reveals the paradoxical process: Diverse bodies and survivor accounts have been abstracted and incorporated into the formal knowledge, standards and policies that so significantly constitute our nuclear world. At the same time, such knowledge, standards and policies have been deployed to discount numerous accounts of survivor experience and deny them the *hibakusha* status and relief.

In this chapter, I examine these divergent visions of the bomb's consequences, held and posited in the politics of survivor status and assistance, by featuring three key cases of contention: *hibakusha*'s effort to receive the "A-bomb disease" sufferer status; *hibaku taikensha*'s struggle

26 Kyoko Sato

for *hibakusha* status; and the demand for *hibakusha* status by those exposed to the bomb's fallout, "black rain." I argue that the contestation over who counts as a victim and to what they are entitled is significant not only for the recognition of trauma and the allocation of care and resources but also in understanding the post-war development of Japan's nuclear governance. Ultimately, the ongoing disputes over the categories and claims of *hibakusha* have been a site of struggle over the characterisation of what the bomb has done—to what effect and for how long. It is about what the "nuclear" is and how we have lived with, and are to live with, its legacy.

In undertaking this analysis, I build on the insight that the technical is also political and moral. That is, that medical and legal classification of human beings is never simply a matter of mobilising technical knowledge but also exercising power and privileging particular visions of society. Classificatory systems valorise some worldviews and suppress others (Bowker and Star, 1999), revealing a moral order (Douglas, 1966; Durkheim, 1995), and the categories of people are both consequential in and constitutive of social order. Furthermore, identities as categories of experience and signification are always historically contingent and variable, the products of a dialectical interplay between the social and the individual (Scott, 1991; Jenkins, 1996). Similarly, the nuclear *itself* is not a fixed category. Cultural meanings of the bomb and nuclear energy are variable across contexts and over time (Hilgartner et al., 1982; Weart, 1988; Gamson and Modigliani, 1989; Jasper, 1990); so, too, are the technical understandings of the damage caused by atomic bombs (Eden, 2004). Gordin (2007) argues that the bomb's "special status" was constructed *after* Japan's surrender—it was not self-evident until the bomb was dropped on two cities, even among the politicians, military officers and scientists involved in its development and deployment (also see Malloy, 2012).

Addressing the variability of the nuclear at an even more fundamental level, historian Gabrielle Hecht (2006) discusses divergent "nuclearity," showing that the degree to which a nation, program, technology or material counts as "nuclear" is not purely a technical matter but an issue of ontology. Science and Technology Studies (STS) scholars Jasanoff and Kim (2009), for their part, illustrate different visions of society imagined and pursued through the development of national nuclear programs, arguing that the technical and the social (for instance, normative visions of society) are co-produced in "sociotechnical imaginaries." Building on these insights, I contend that categorisation of survivors of the bomb is a powerful arena of nuclear ontologies and imaginaries, in which the bomb's meaning is performed, contested, reproduced and revised. Put differently, policy categories and criteria are political, but they are also highly performative, projecting and reinforcing embedded ideas about the bomb, radiation and nuclear technology in ways that affect subsequent nuclear politics and

What the bomb has done   27

governance. They have affected not only the lives of survivors, but also the ways the effects of radiation are understood and contested after the Fukushima disaster. Furthermore, through the politics of survivor status and relief, particularly through legal cases, new discoveries and counter-expertise were made, especially after the 2011 Fukushima disaster.

Hibakusha identity

Despite the wide and international recognition of the term *hibakusha*, A-bomb survivor identity has never been straightforward or self-evident. Given the history of censorship and press code during the Occupation, societal stigma and public indifference to survivors' suffering, and uncertainty of both the amount of exposure and its long-term effects, individual identification as *hibakusha* or A-bomb victim took place in intricate, deeply personal and diverse manners even after many survivors rejoiced at the 1957 establishment of the Law Concerning Medical Treatment for Victims of the Atomic Bombs.

In her exploration of the politics of remembering the bomb, anthropologist Lisa Yoneyama (1999) further complicates such identification by examining the dialectical nature of memory and survivor identities. Medicolegal frameworks of *hibakusha* assistance that define who legitimate survivors *are*, for instance, significantly shape survivor narratives, compelling them to translate personal, embodied experience into a calculus of measurable damages and distance from the hypocenter. Official certification has also allowed survivors to develop political identity, individually and as a collectivity, and pursue expanded relief measures—even though such endeavors entail a risk that diverse survivor subjectivities will be reduced to a singular objective of world peace and the nuclear weapons ban. Yoneyama identifies these and other persistent clashes between universalist memories of the bomb that center anonymous humanity and more specific remembrance from local and individual subjects. Survivors' testimonial practices, she argues, serve as one avenue to chip away monolithic and standardising historical knowledge ("the regime of truths") in which they are embedded: survivors can exercise their agency by taking on multiple subjectivities—as victim, *hibakusha*, witness and storyteller—and speaking not only about the experience of the bomb but also about the diverse lives they have since lived. This chapter adds to such complex dynamics the role played by scientific knowledge of radiation in dividing survivors, validating some experiences of the bomb and rejecting other claims to acknowledgement, redress and identity.

Some scholars advocate a notion, "global *hibakusha*," to underscore how the experience of damage from nuclear technology is shared beyond Hiroshima and Nagasaki. The concept of global *hibakusha* encompasses victims of nuclear tests, accidents and exposure to radioactive materials

28 *Kyoko Sato*

at mines, plants and other sites, and allows us to explore common mechanisms through which the voices of radiation victims have been suppressed (Takahashi and Takemine, 2006; Jacobs, 2014). This follows the emergence in the late 1970s of the use of ヒバクシャ, *hibakusha* written in *katakana* (phonetic Japanese characters used for foreign words), and *hibakusha* in English, to include victims of other *hibaku* (被曝)—that is, exposure to *radiation* as opposed to the original 被爆, exposure to the *bomb* (Takemine, 2016).[4] Crucially, the concept of global *hibakusha* is meant to universalise the category of *hibakusha* while attending to local specificities. By gathering radiation-exposed people worldwide into a much broader category, scholars and activists have aspired to bring together scattered knowledge and experiences in order to improve our understanding of radiation's effects on human health and the environment.

Effects of radiation and the politics of knowledge

While the legal status *hibakusha* largely hinges on the idea of unique damages caused by exposure to the bomb's radiation, scientific knowledge on radiation's effects has been marked by uncertainty and contestation, as is evident in the fierce, ceaseless decade of debates over the 2011 Fukushima disaster's implications.

Much expertise on radiation's effects on human health comes from the extensive data collected by the Atomic Bomb Casualty Commission (ABCC), an American body set up in Hiroshima in 1947 and Nagasaki in 1948 to study the bomb's effects on survivors. ABCC remained under US control even after the Occupation ended in 1952, and the immensely political nature of its research, especially the influence of Cold War politics, has been well chronicled. The Commission collected and analyzed data on victims in Japan not to treat and cure them, but to better understand the biological effects of radiation and identify the capacities and limits of the bomb's damages (Nakagawa, 1991; Lindee, 1994; Takahashi, 2012). The Japanese government fully cooperated with this research, hewing to US nuclear strategies in the name of contributing to the imminent nuclear age (Sasamoto, 1995). Historian Susan Lindee (1994) argues that the ABCC's notorious "no treatment" policy embodied and reinforced US assertions about the legitimacy and morality of its use of the bomb: The United States did nothing wrong and does not have to provide medical care to the survivors. In ABCC's studies, the genetic and somatic effects of the bomb's radiation were understood in statistical terms and made "real" via academic papers, rather than the actual bodies of survivors (Lindee, 1994). In particular, their focus on the effects of radiation from the first minute after the detonation, disregarding residual radiation including fallout, originated in and reinforced the US framing of an atomic bombing as an instant matter that was spatially and temporally bounded (Sawada, 2007; Takahashi, 2012;

What the bomb has done 29

2009). Even the Commission's longitudinal studies on about 120,000 people who lived in Hiroshima and Nagasaki (94,000 *hibakusha* and 27,000 "non-*hibakusha*"; "Life Span Study," or LSS) and about 77,000 offspring ("Genetic Studies") considered external exposure to radiation only on the basis of individual location and shielding conditions at the time of detonation. Internal exposure via residual radiation and fallout, which was suspected even then to have multiple, variegated, and unfolding effects, was not included in the research objectives. Ultimately, the ABCC studies generally concluded that, except for severely irradiated survivors, exposure to lower dose led to only a minor elevation on cancer rates and there were no known, significant genetic effects on the children of survivors.

These ABCC findings have remained influential: they have been institutionalised in various national and international standards, making it difficult for later studies to succeed in challenging, destabilising and revising them. For instance, the data collected by the ABCC and its successor, the Radiation Effects Research Foundation (RERF, founded in 1975 with joint funding from Japan and the United States), was used as the evidentiary basis for civilian and nuclear-worker radiation safety standards developed by the International Commission on Radiological Protection (ICRP).[5] Challenges to the ABCC findings, including studies by UK and US physicians and occupational epidemiologists as early as the 1950s, have been suppressed, stifled or delegitimised as they have been compared, unfavorably, to the large, longitudinal ABCC data set. In the case of studies on Chernobyl survivors, which challenged the ABCC findings on radiation's genetic effects, their findings were portrayed as the product of politically suspect "Soviet" sciences (Goldstein and Stawkowski, 2015; Brown, 2019).

Today, ABCC/RERF research is still globally deemed the gold standard for understanding radiation's health effects. Its findings shaped the criteria not only for assessing individuals' *hibakusha* status but also for determining evacuation zones and evaluating radiation injury claims after the Fukushima disaster, despite well-known critiques of its design. Scholars have pointed out that the study's data collection only started in 1950, therefore the resulting knowledge could only cover those who survived the bomb for at least five years, not those who died earlier. Further, the ABCC's control groups, those 27,000 "non-*hibakusha*," had, very likely, also been exposed to radiation, therefore skewing statistical significance for any differences between the groups' health outcomes.[6]

Japan's *Hibakusha* assistance regime

At present, to be officially recognised as *hibakusha* by the Japanese government and receive an Atomic Bomb Survivor's Certificate, one has to meet at least one of the following criteria: presence in the specified

30   *Kyoko Sato*

areas at the time of bombing; entrance into the specified area within two weeks of the bombing; direct contact with radioactivity at the time of the bombing or afterward by handling numerous bodies, helping survivors and other rescue activities; and status as the embryo or fetus of a person who met one of these criteria at the time. Additionally, the Japanese government recognises some *hibakusha* as "sufferers of A-bomb diseases" when their conditions require current medical care and are directly traceable to radiation exposure (meeting a threshold for what they call "radiation attributability").

According to the Ministry of Health, Labor, and Welfare, as of March 2021, there are 127,755 *hibakusha* certificate-holders in Japan, with the average age at 83.94 years.[7] They are eligible for free medical checkups, government coverage for most medical expenses and in most cases monthly health-related allowances at ¥34,970 ($300 plus). There are also 6,978 authorised A-bomb disease sufferers, who are eligible for a much larger "Special Medical Care Allowance," currently set at ¥142,170 (around $1,300) per month.[8]

This system, as noted earlier, is the product of more than 60 years of history rife with incremental changes that resulted from accumulated knowledge—often gained through survivor lawsuits—and persistent survivor activism. The original framework to aid those suffering from the exposure to the bomb was established in the 1957 law, 12 years after the bombing. Survivors and activists speak of the post-war decade of general neglect and silence as the "10 years of void" (空白の１０年), during which survivor aid efforts were ad hoc, local and small in scale. They came in the form of municipal research, foreign and domestic donations, and free or reduced medical care at certain clinics and hospitals. Notably, during the Occupation, the public representation of the bombings and their devastation was prohibited, which contributed to the public's ignorance and indifference regarding the plight of survivors, especially outside Hiroshima and Nagasaki Prefectures.

In the mid-1950s, survivors came together and began mobilising more extensively and systematically, as the anti-nuclear movement started spreading rapidly in response to the "Bikini Incident." In March 1954, a Japanese fishing boat, the Lucky Dragon No. 5, and its crew were exposed to nuclear fallout from the US testing of a hydrogen bomb on the Marshall Islands' Bikini Atoll. Encouraged by the ensuing nationwide movement against nuclear weapons, A-bomb survivors' mobilisation grew into the 1st World Conference against Atomic and Hydrogen Bombs. Held in Hiroshima in August 1955, this conference provided many survivors their first significant opportunity to gather, sharing their pain and struggle with each other and with the general public in Japan and beyond. They left energised to intensify local efforts to organise as survivors. At the second World Conference, held in Nagasaki in 1956, *Nihon Hidankyo* (the Japan Confederation of A- and H-Bomb Sufferers

What the bomb has done 31

Organisations) formed to lead the mobilisation calling for medical and financial support, directly contributing to the enactment of the 1957 *hibakusha* law. Since then, *Hidankyo* has represented and worked for survivor interests as their central organisation, with more than 40 locally based member organisations.

From its founding, *Hidankyo* has consistently demanded aid in the form of state compensation specifically for Japan's war responsibilities. After the Occupation ended in 1952, Japan passed the Law on Relief of War Victims and Survivors to provide state compensation to military personnel and civilian workers injured or killed on duty. As the Bikini Incident drew public attention and its victims received "consolation" money through bilateral negotiations and a so-called Full Settlement (see Takahashi, 2012 and this volume), survivors were motivated to seek relief. They were encouraged by the rise in public awareness of harms of radiation and nuclear weapons but frustrated by the contrasting lack of support for A-bomb victims (Naono, 2011). Thus, at *Hidankyo's* inaugural meeting in August 1956, they called for a ban on nuclear weapons and a law to aid victims as state compensation (Tanaka, 2006).

The aid framework created with the 1957 law was welcomed by many survivors, though it did not address either of these two key goals. It was, in fact, quite removed from the reality and needs of survivors. In the original framework, 200,984 survivors who were in Hiroshima City, Nagasaki City and some of their vicinities at the time of the bombing were certified as *hibakusha*. Over time, additional provisions were introduced for "special *hibakusha*," those who were close to the hypocenter (first 2 km, then 3 km) and those who entered the area after the bombing (first within three days, then two weeks). The 1968 Law Concerning Special Measures for the Victims of the Atomic Bombs brought *hibakusha* monthly allowances, depending on such factors as their age, income, medical conditions and need for home care. Meanwhile, both the officially designated geographical area of impact and the slate of diseases for which assistance could be obtained were expanded. Age and income limits were loosened. The distinction between special *hibakusha* and other *hibakusha* was abolished. Importantly, non-Japanese survivors of the bomb became eligible for *hibakusha* status and medical care in the late 1970s. In 1994, two laws were integrated under the Law Concerning Assistance for the Victims of the Atomic Bombs (the "*hibakusha* relief law*").

Survivor organisations and their advocates' persistence lay behind many of these changes. Since the 1950s, they have collected millions of petitions to support the aid law and recognise the Japanese state's responsibility and need to provide aid as compensation; conducted surveys on the conditions and needs of survivors; fashioned and submitted official appeals to the government; and provided various assistance to survivors.

32   *Kyoko Sato*

One key development came in the 1970s, when a deported Korean survivor illegally entered Japan to seek medical care for his illnesses. When his application for *hibakusha* status was rejected, he sued Fukuoka Prefecture and the Ministry of Welfare. In 1978, the Supreme Court ruled in this survivor's favor, arguing that the 1957 law did not require Japanese nationality for establishment of *hibakusha* status or a claim on its provisions. Further, the ruling asserted, *hibakusha* could not be considered responsible for the damages from the bomb, which was brought about by war—that is, by an action of the Japanese state. The landmark decision, which opened doors of survivor relief to non-Japanese survivors, was also interpreted as a legal admission that the system of survivor aid was, for all intents and purposes, a form of state compensation, rather than a type of social security that might be reserved for tax-paying Japanese nationals (Tanaka, 2006).

In 1980, however, that understanding was countered and denied by an advisory panel to Japan's Welfare Minister, the Roundtable Committee for Fundamental Issues regarding Measures for Atomic-Bomb Victims, or *Kihonkon*.[9] First, the *Kihonkon* report argued that under the emergency of war people need to *endure the sacrifice generally*, whether damages from the A-bomb or from fire-bombings. Second, existing relief measures for A-bomb survivors were based on their unique sacrifices, due to radiation's health effects. These ideas suggested that further state compensation was unnecessary—even unfair, since fire-bombing victims were not receiving such aid. Taken together, in order to justify the existing relief framework (relief provided to A-bomb survivors but not to others, and as social security, not as state compensation), this report presented a principle of shared wartime sacrifice and based the whole *hibakusha* aid regime in radiation's effects on health (Takemine, 2008). The third main precept emphasised in the report was that designation of the areas exposed to radiation required a strictly "scientific and rational basis."

The 1980 *Kihonkon* report has been a significant roadblock to the expansion of survivor status and assistance. Recently, media outlets and activists have critically scrutinised the deliberations and negotiations behind the report, as the meeting minutes—initially withheld by the Ministry—and other notes came out, including those made available during the "black rain" lawsuit. The analysis of these documents revealed, for instance, the deliberate intervention of the Welfare Ministry in order to put the "brakes" on the idea of *hibakusha* relief as state compensation.[10] Panelists had internally discussed concerns about the financial burden of expanded relief and fears that healthy survivors were exploiting the system (more on this report below). Their recommendations in the 1980 report are said to have helped delay the establishment of the updated and unified *hibakusha* relief law until 1994, even shaping its content so as to avoid framing aid as compensation.

As the criteria were expanded and more people became willing to apply, the number of *hibakusha* certificate holders peaked in 1980 at 372,264, then began a long decline as *hibakusha* died, year by year. In the fiscal year 2016–2017 (April to March), 322 new applications were submitted; 111, or 34%, were approved.[11] Aging survivors are still applying as they become less concerned about the prejudice against *hibakusha* and find themselves in more urgent need of medical support. They face considerable challenges, as each passing year makes it harder to prove their whereabouts in August 1945. Witnesses are aging and passing away, and after 76 years, documents are becoming harder to find.

A-bomb disease sufferers: "Your cancer has nothing to do with the bomb's radiation"

For decades, one key area of contention has been the low rate of recognition for survivors as "A-bomb disease" sufferers, eligible for the sizable monthly "special" medical care allowance. In March 2017, 8,169 survivors, or 4.96% of *hibakusha* certificate holders, fell into this category. The small ratio actually indicates a dramatic *increase* from a decade or so prior. In 2006, just 0.87%, or 2,280 out of 259,556 *hibakusha*, had this status. The increase resulted from dozens of lawsuits including group lawsuits filed in 2003 and thereafter, which helped expand the inclusion criteria.[12]

Since the system's start, the approval rate for A-bomb disease sufferer status steadily declined, discouraging applications. Between 1985 and 2004, the number of A-bomb disease sufferers remained stable at about 2,000, despite application increases, indicating that the number of new approvals each year roughly equaled the number of those who lost the status (by dying or being cured of their symptoms). According to Hideo Gochi, a doctor who has long served survivors in Hiroshima and supported their lawsuits, the stability in the ranks of approved A-bomb disease sufferers suggests that budgetary concerns dominate the issuance of A-bomb disease sufferer status—which explains why two people of similar age, symptoms, and distance from the hypocenter might have different application outcomes (Gochi, 2007). The criteria, particularly "radiation attributability," are both strict and ambiguous; those whose applications were rejected rarely got any substantive explanation, and the details of the criteria only came to public light through the legal process.

Before group lawsuits, individual *hibakusha* filed suit demanding the reversal of denials for A-bomb sufferer status, beginning in 1969. The first plaintiff lost, with both district and high courts rejecting his claim on "radiation attributability" for his spine conditions, but subsequent suits saw plaintiffs able to demonstrate that their conditions (cataracts, paralysis, low white blood cell counts and liver problems) met the attributability and medical care requirements for certification. In particular,

34 *Kyoko Sato*

in three lawsuits (filed in 1987, 1988 and 1999), the government's simple and reductionist approach to ruling out radiation as a source of many survivors' serious illnesses was censured by the courts.

Despite the legal development, the government did not loosen the restrictions on A-bomb disease sufferer status. Instead, in 2001, the state introduced an even more standardised and reductionist approach, the "probability of causation" or PC doctrine. In determining A-bomb disease qualification, PC was mechanically calculated for each disease, based on the sex, age of exposure, and presumed dose of radiation. The new model was so strict it would have excluded the survivors who won A-bomb sufferer status in a Supreme Court ruling just the year before. Should a survivor have multiple diseases, each disease was to be independently evaluated with regard to the PC, as opposed to being scored as a package. Further, in estimating the amount of radiation exposure, this calculation drew on the Dosimetry System 1986 (DS86), and 10% of PC was commonly used as the threshold for status cutoff.

DS86 was created in collaboration between US and Japanese scientists and their governments as an improvement over earlier systems, Tentative 1957 Doses (T57D) and Tentative 1965 Doses (T65D). While T57D and T65D were based on data from the US Nevada Test Site in the late 1950s and the early 1960s, DS86 was created using a large-scale simulation model of the bomb. Like its predecessors, however, DS86 has been widely critiqued for only accounting for the initial radiation dose, overlooking residual radiation and fallout, and for considering gamma and neutron radiation, but not alpha and beta particles (if ingested, the latter can continue to harm the body internally). Together, critics contend, these features led to underestimates of internal exposure (Sawada, 2015). Such dose-estimate systems have been incorporated into influential studies, including the ABCC's LSS. They have also constituted a major barrier to survivors seeking A-bomb disease sufferer certification.

Starting in April 2003, a series of group lawsuits representing 306 survivors were filed at 17 district courts throughout Japan. In their proceedings, plaintiffs criticised the mechanistic imposition of PC and its basis in flawed and outdated dose estimation systems. They called for a more holistic evaluation protocol that might take into consideration such factors as the applicant's health at the time, immediate symptoms, circumstances of exposure and the possibility of internal exposure to radiation via food, water and dust.

As the survivors began and continued to win these cases, the government introduced new criteria to include "proactive authorisation" for certain A-bomb disease sufferer applicants in 2008. Proactive authorisation extended to applicants who had cancer or four other specified conditions, provided they met certain other conditions (such as the distance from ground zero, the timing of entry into the affected area, and their length of stay in such an area). In the meantime, DS86 was replaced by its revised version, DS02, which retained the same limitations. In August 2009, Prime Minister Taro Aso agreed with *Hidankyo* leaders on a resolution to the lawsuits: the government would set up a fund to resolve plaintiffs' grievances and commit to regular meetings on protocol improvements between Welfare Ministry officials and *hibakusha* representatives. Documented as a "note of confirmation," these official measures were welcomed by plaintiffs, advocates, and *hibakusha* activists. The group suits were soon considered resolved. Yet only a few meetings took place, and the revised criteria (published in December 2013) did not reflect the accumulated insights into survivors' experiences that had been evident in the series of rulings leading up to the "resolution."

Frustrated by this obstinance, activists filed another series of group lawsuits. Dubbed the "No More *Hibakusha*" lawsuits, these were filed to pursue A-bomb disease sufferer status for about 130 survivors. Thus far, a majority of these plaintiffs have defeated the government in court and obtained the A-bomb disease sufferer status. Still, some victims lost their cases. Others are still in progress. And too many have passed away.

Hibaku taikensha in Nagasaki: "You have experienced *hibaku*, but are not *hibakusha*"

Again, the official rationale behind *hibakusha* aid was that the A-bomb was different from other bombs, due to the unique health consequences of radiation. *Hibakusha* are eligible for general medical care, under the logic that radiation exposure has made them more susceptible to diseases and injuries which, in turn, are more difficult to heal and more likely to lead to recognized A-bomb diseases than diseases and injuries in the rest of the population. In Nagasaki, as mentioned above, the area initially designated in 1957 as radiation affected is not a circle (as in Hiroshima), but an oval carved according to the borders of the administrative units (such as villages). Given that distance from ground zero has been used as a primary factor in determining radiation exposure, the oval created a discrepancy by which people at a similar distance from the hypocenter in Nagasaki were variously approved and denied *hibakusha* status.

In 1974 and 1976, the government assigned specific areas surrounding the oval as a zone for limited aid. Those who were in this zone at the time of the bombing were deemed "provisional" (*minashi*) *hibakusha*, eligible for a medical check-up, and if they develop one of the designated illnesses, for full *hibakusha* status. In 2002, a new system was created so as to provide some care, albeit limited, for another new category of survivors: "*hibaku taikensha*," those who were within 12 km from the hypocenter but not within the specified areas for *hibakusha* or provisional *hibakusha*. Curiously, to qualify for this status, one was required to live within the 12-km-radius zone at the time of application as well as at the time of exposure. In 2005, the residency requirement was broadened to

36   *Kyoko Sato*

include the entirety of Nagasaki Prefecture, but the covered conditions were limited to mental illnesses and accompanying conditions.

This move to emphasise mental care for *hibaku taikensha* was spurred by research conducted by Nagasaki City from 1999 to 2000. The study surveyed those who lived outside the areas designated as affected by the bomb (where one might qualify for *hibakusha* status), finding many had PTSD and other psychological symptoms. Since 1995, when Japan suffered both the Great Hanshin-Awaji Earthquake and the sarin attacks on Tokyo's subway system, PTSD had gained public attention and scholarly interest. Further research, conducted in 2001, thus sought to compare the population with a control group (those who moved to the area after 1950), confirming that residents outside the "affected areas" had, in fact, suffered lasting psychological difficulties originating in their experience of the bomb (Kim et al., 2009). Both studies assumed these residents were not exposed to a level of radiation that contributed meaningfully to physical problems, but that trauma from the A-bomb and fear and anxiety about radiation exposure—the "subjective *hibaku* (exposure) experience"—led to ongoing psychological challenges.

These "*taikensha*" have fought for *hibakusha* status in the courts since 2007. Many have experienced known symptoms of radiation exposure, from loss of hair, white spots on the skin and diarrhea immediately after the bombing to cancer, leukemia and cataracts later in life. They testify to various activities that may have subjected them to internal exposure to radioactive materials, such as eating plants, drinking water, playing amid fallout and picking maggots off of severely irradiated victims. The collection of their testimonials is tellingly titled, "Defined as *Hibaku Taikensha*: The Outcry of *Hibakusha*, Testimonials 67 Years after the War: Internal Exposure." Expert witnesses and scholars have helped the *taikensha* make their case.[13] For instance, particle physicist and *hibakusha* Shoji Sawada surmises, in his 2010 expert opinion, that fallout likely spread to a wider area than the current system accedes via mushroom clouds and rain; a lack of data, he insists, is not sufficient evidence to conclude a lack of radioactive fallout.

In an impactful February 2016 decision, the Nagasaki District Court ruled that ten of 161 survivors in the suit at hand be issued a *hibakusha* certificate. It could be presumed, the ruling stated, that these plaintiffs had been subject to the bomb's radiation in excess of a total of 25 mSv annually; the plaintiffs had calculated the level of exposure using a 1945 study by the US research unit and presented the dose limit as ten times more than average annual dose of background radiation, 2.4 mSv. The court accepted the plaintiffs' data and argument about radiation exposure outside the designated area, considering dosages of radiation in individual cases and destabilising the dominant criteria for the *hibakusha* status—namely where you were, especially in terms of which municipal units, at the time of detonation. It rejected the other claims, which argued

What the bomb has done   37

that survivors suffered radiation exposure by ingesting irradiated materials. In December 2018, less than two years later, the Fukuoka High Court overturned the granting of the *hibakusha* status to the ten survivors in this suit, pointing to an "overestimation" of radiation exposure in the US study. The Supreme Court upheld the Fukuoka High Court's decision in a November 2019 ruling.

Another, earlier lawsuit came to an unsuccessful end in December 2017, when the top court upheld the lower court's decision denying another 387 plaintiffs' claims to *hibakusha* status, because these survivors had been outside the designated oval area, even though they had been within 12 km of ground zero. Essentially, both courts affirmed the state's claim that, according to current scientific knowledge, those who were outside a 5 km radius of the hypocenter at the time of bombing could not suffer physical damage directly traceable to radiation exposure in the 1945 bombing of Nagasaki.

Exposed to black rain: "You were in a light rain area, you are not *Hibakusha*"

Immortalised in Masuji Ibuse's 1965 novel *Kuroi Ame* (Black Rain) and Shohei Imamura's 1989 film adaptation of it, the soot-filled rain that fell hours after the bombs has become another major topic of contention in *hibakusha* certification. Many survivors were exposed to the rain, even outside the initially designated *hibaku* zones, and developed acute and delayed symptoms of radiation exposure. As it became evident that the rain had been caused by the detonations and likely contained radioactive materials, the Japanese government declared certain areas of Hiroshima where it rained as an eligible "special exposure" zone. In the mid-1960s, *hibakusha* certificates began being granted, yet survivors and their supporters considered the boundaries of special exposure zone arbitrary in light of survivors' experience. In 1976, the government designated another special area, an oval of about 19 km north-south and 11 km east-west; those who were inside this perimeter were deemed "provisional" *hibakusha*, entitled to receive free medical checkups, and, if they developed one of the certified diseases, became eligible for *hibakusha* status. This particular area was one considered to have endured a heavy rain after the bomb (rather than a light rain), on the basis of a 1953 map made by meteorologist Michitaka Uda's team, which surveyed the area by interviewing residents from August to December in 1945.

This designation, which excluded many who had been doused by the black rain, was not consistent with many residents' memories. As the boundaries between the heavy/light rain areas cut through communities, they divided victims into *hibakusha* and non-*hibakusha*. It was a controversial demarcation. In 1978, survivors started getting together to share the experiences and memories of their exposures among themselves.

38   Kyoko Sato

Then in 1987, a new map was presented. Meteorologist Yoshinobu Masuda spurred demands for a revision of the special exposure zone with a report showing an affected black rain area twice the size of the one on Uda's 1953 map. The Welfare Ministry refused to revisit the issue, but Masuda continued his research, collecting testimonials from residents, and published a second map in 1988. In this map, the area affected by black rain was far less neatly shaped and measured *four* times larger than the area identified by Uda's map. The public was demanding further inquiry, and the 1980 *Kihonkon* report's emphasis on a "scientific and rational basis" for determining survivor assistance hemmed in authorities. They could not ignore the Masuda map's possible implications. Hiroshima Prefecture and Hiroshima City created an expert committee to review earlier research, including analyses of radioactive materials in soil and roofing tiles, meteorological simulations, and chromosomal aberrations in residents' DNA. In 1991, the committee nonetheless concluded that no scientific evidence could be established to indicate radiation affected human health in the map's expanded area of black rain. Without any further interviews or collections of epidemiological information, the "lack of scientific evidence" was used to deny the map created by survivor testimonials.

Both survivor mobilisation and scholarly research on black rain's range, radioactivity, and health effects continued in the face of official unwillingness to expand the *hibaku* area and the narrow, absolutist barrier of "scientific and rational basis" conceptualised by courts and committees. Research on residual cesium-137 in soil samples collected three days after the bombing and other pieces of evidence affirmed again that Masuda's map more accurately showed the black rain area than Uda's (Shizuma et al., 1996). After more research on soil samples, surveys of residents and further meteorological simulations again pointed to much larger areas of radiation exposure via fallout,[14] Hiroshima Prefecture, Hiroshima City and seven other municipalities became swayed, petitioning the national government to expand the zone of *hibakusha* status and benefits. The Welfare Ministry set up another panel to study this request, then concluded in 2012 that it would not change the area of black rain.

In 2015, 64 plaintiffs filed a group lawsuit with the Hiroshima District Court to demand *hibakusha* status. Their lawyers included a team with experience of winning survivors *hibakusha* and A-bomb disease sufferer statuses. They had substantial knowledge of the bomb and radiation's health effects, as well as extensive networks of doctors, researchers, and activists ready to offer their expertise. The suit emphasised not only the scientific basis for the expanded area of black rain but also the significance of internal exposure from ingestion or absorption of radioactive materials from water, air and food. It had, at this point, been four years since the Fukushima disaster, and the public was far more aware of the dangers of internal radiation exposure. In this post-2011 context, the legal team had an explicit understanding of the connections between the A-bomb's legacy and post-Fukushima radiation politics. The lawsuit also helped uncover historical documentation revealing the factors shaping Japan's existing survivor assistance regime. Notably, further details behind the 1980 *Kihonkon* report became available, and sociologist Masae Yuasa's analysis (2019) of them showed the patently political nature of the panel deliberation.[15] For instance, the panel's deliberations were intent on putting the "brakes" on the expansion of exposure zones, and references to the need for a "scientific and rational basis" were kept intentionally abstract in light of conflicting expert views regarding the legitimacy and scientific soundness of the existing system.[16]

In a landmark decision issued on July 29, 2020, the Hiroshima District Court ruled in favor of the plaintiffs (expanded, since 2015, to 84 survivors, aged 75–96). The court ordered the city and the prefecture to grant *hibakusha* status, recognising the evidence of a larger area of black rain than officially demarcated, the uncertainty of such boundaries, the possibility that each plaintiff's symptoms were traceable to radiation exposure, and importantly, the possibility of internal exposure to radiation having relevant health effects. Initially, both Hiroshima City and the Prefecture indicated they would not appeal. A week after the 75th anniversary of the bombing of Hiroshima, however, both joined the national government in filing an appeal. In July 2021, the Hiroshima High Court upheld the 2020 decision and Prime Minister Yoshihide Suga decided not to appeal. By this historic victory with significant implications for the future of survivor politics and radiation governance, 15 plaintiffs had died.

Different visions of the bomb, different worlds

Since the 1957 law set the framework, the history of A-bomb survivor relief measures has been one marked by constant struggle. The government has tried to minimise changes to the system, particularly expansions of eligibility criteria for survivor claims, and survivors and their supporters have sought recognition, rights and redress through program improvement and expansion.

For many survivors, the bombing certainly happened 76 years ago, but its aftermath had never concluded. To them, concerns about radiation are a constant buzzing presence. Many have lived with its effects, even if others have moved on. The act of seeking an official or expanded status is difficult for anyone; those seeking recognition today are generally elderly and have experienced trauma alongside other mental and physical effects since WWII and the all-too-bright dawn of the nuclear age. To fight the government, over and over again, entails personal resolve, political engagement, and a willingness and capacity to challenge existing technical knowledge (medical, legal, scientific) within the possibly chaotic reality of

40 *Kyoko Sato*

their own physical existence. It is remarkable that survivors, officially certified or otherwise, continue the struggle. Many of these survivors experienced Fukushima as an enormous shock; some were motivated by Fukushima to renew and recommit to survivor politics as their mission. Many survivors see their work as a collective effort to uncover the truth of the bomb and protect the future from further nuclear tragedies. Determined, organised efforts by survivors contributed to the historic enactment of the Treaty on the Prohibition of Nuclear Weapons, which went into force in January 2021.

In contrast, the Japanese government has treated the bombs as something that happened in the past, whose unfortunate legacy it still has to attend to. It does not seem to concern itself with what is beyond its narrowly defined policy framework, let alone admissions of war responsibility, which could transform the nation's historical narratives and identity. It has not signed or ratified the Treaty as it remains under the US "nuclear umbrella." The official stance has persistently presented the effects of the bomb's radiation as calculable, knowable and containable, both temporally and spatially. These epistemic approaches originated at a time when knowledge on radiation was even more limited than today, and they have endured despite copious criticism, counter-evidence, and advancements in knowledge that challenge them. In fact, regarding the bomb's radiation as manageable has been crucial for Japan's nation-(re)building via nuclear energy and its reliance on the US nuclear umbrella—and also for the ambition some leaders have had to become a nuclear weapons power. Likewise, transnational radiation protection regimes (such as ICRP, UNSCEAR; see Boudia, this volume) and their abstracted, standardised knowledge—which Japan has drawn on—come hand in hand with the way nuclear technology pervades the world; they are co-produced (Jasanoff, 2004). For instance, just like in Japan, such knowledge prevailed over more intimate local knowledge in post-Chernobyl Belarus, often making harms of radiation invisible (Kuchinskaya, 2014). A world that would seek to produce and value diverse knowledges and take good care of global *hibakusha* might not have been as full of nuclear sites as our world.

The politics of survivor classification and relief is one key site where the dominant nuclear ontology and imaginary become challenged. Since Fukushima, similar conflicts are being replayed in the contestation surrounding low-dose radiation exposure in the region. Again, the government and many experts quickly considered the nuclear disaster sufficiently resolved, dismissing the public's concerns as "radiophobia." Meanwhile, residents, farmers, fishers, workers, and consumers were left to live with invisible, slow violence and the unfolding potentiality of the vast amount of radiation that has become embedded in the region's landscape. More hopefully, however, just as the aging A-bomb survivors have continued to learn about the bomb, radiation, and the politics of knowledge and standardisation, numerous Japanese and world citizens are critically examining

What the bomb has done 41

existing expertise and governance approaches engaging in the production of counter-expertise and alternative visions. Nuclear catastrophe's aftermath is everlasting; so, too, it appears, is the fight over how we all live in the irrevocably nuclear world.

Notes

1 The research for this chapter was partly supported by the National Science Foundation's grant: Award No. SES-1257117, "The Fukushima Disaster and the Cultural Politics of Nuclear Power in the United States and Japan." I would like to thank survivors and their supporters for sharing their experience, knowledge, and documents. I am also grateful to the volume's co-editors and contributors (especially Kate Brown, Angela N. H. Creager, and Hiroko Takahashi), as well as Norma Field, Mark Gardiner, and Magda Stawkowski, for their helpful comments on an earlier draft.
2 City of Nagasaki (n.d.). Jigyo no Jisshi Jokyo ni Tsuite. Available at: http://www.city.nagasaki.lg.jp/heiwa/3010000/3010100/p002227.html [Accessed June 28, 2021].
3 *Bura bura* is an onomatopoeia for wandering around or idling away. Physician and *hibakusha* Shuntaro Hida (2013) and many other doctors who treated survivors have attested to how common severe chronic fatigue was among them. Survivors with severe chronic fatigue were often condemned as lazy.
4 These two *hibaku* are phonetically identical in Japanese, but are written using different Chinese characters, signifying different meanings. Also see Ogata, Y. (1991). *Hiroshima Peace Media Center, The Chugoku Shimbun.* Available at: http://www.hiroshimapeacemedia.jp/?page_id=25627 [Accessed June 28, 2021].
5 ICRP makes radiation protection recommendations on the basis of scientific evidence provided by the United Nations Scientific Committee on the Effects of Atomic Radiation (UNSCEAR), which evaluates data and research on radiation's effects. ABCC research is one of the most significant sources.
6 For critiques of the design of ABCC data, see Alice Stewart's work (referenced in Goldstein and Stawkowski [2015]; Brown [2019]; Wing et al. [1999]; and Sawada [2007]).
7 Ministry of Health, Labor, and Welfare (n.d.). Hibakusha-su, Heikin Nenrei. Available at: https://www.mhlw.go.jp/stf/newpage_13411.html [Accessed on June 30, 2021].
8 Ministry of Health, Labor, and Welfare (n.d.). Genbakusho Nintei ni Tsuite. Available at: https://www.mhlw.go.jp/stf/genbakusyou.html [Accessed on June 30, 2021].
9 The panel is well known as "*Kihonkon*"（基本懇）, an abbreviation of 原爆被爆者対策基本問題懇談会.
10 Okamoto, G. (2017). Hibakusha eno Kokka Hosho, Kyu Koseisho Shokuin ga Kakudai Kenen no Memo. *Asahi Shimbun,* October 2. Available at: https://digital.asahi.com/articles/ASK9N5DH7K9NUTIL033.html [Accessed June 30, 2021]; Hashimoto, M. (2010). "Juninron" ni Iron Dezu, "Hibakusha Pinpin Shiteiru Hito mo Ooi" tono Hatsugen mo. *Tokyo Shimbun,* August 1.
11 Yamada, N. (2017). Hibakusha Techo: Kofu Sanwari Domari, Sakunendo Shinsei 322 ken. *Mainichi Shimbun,* August 5. Available at: https://mainichi.jp/articles/20170805/k00/00m/040/126000c [Accessed June 28, 2021].

42   Kyoko Sato

Both the number of new applications and the ratio of issuance have declined: from 47% (335 issued out of 719 applications) in 2013–2014 to 42% (244 out of 582) in 2014–2015 to 42% (183 out of 436) in 2015–2016.

12 Japan allows lawsuits filed by multiple plaintiffs, but does not have a legal procedure for US-style class action (except for the recovery of consumer property damages).

13 Iwanaga, C., ed. (2012). *Hibaku Taikensha to Sareta Hibakusha no Sakebi: Sengo 67-nenme no Shogen: Naibu Hibaku*. Nagasaki.

14 See two reports that compiled the latest scientific studies on the fallout from a variety of disciplinary approaches: Hiroshima "Black Rain" Radioactivity Study Group (2010); Aoyama and Oochi (2011).

15 This was submitted as an expert opinion by the plaintiffs of the "Black Rain" group lawsuit.

16 Only one of the seven committee members was familiar with radiation's health effects and the existing evaluation process, and he explicitly denied anything other than initial, direct radiation exposure near the hypocenter as relevant to health. Furthermore, as members struggled with the uncertainty of expertise highlighted by specialists on radiation's effects on health, a Welfare Ministry official suggested that a reference to a need for scientific basis, rather than specific scientific basis, would suffice to support or reject the current system or its expansion.

References

Aoyama, M., and Oochi, Y., eds. (2011). *Revisit The Hiroshima A-bomb with a Database: Latest Scientific View on Local Fallout and Black Rain*. Hiroshima: Hiroshima City.

Bowker, G., and Star, S. (1999). *Sorting Things Out: Classification and Its Consequences*. Cambridge, MA: MIT Press.

Brown, K. (2019). *Manual for Survival: A Chernobyl Guide to the Future*. New York: Norton.

Douglas, M. (1966). *Purity and Danger: An Analysis of Concepts of Pollution and Taboo*. London: Routledge.

Durkheim, E. (1995). *Elementary Forms of Religious Life*. New York: Free Press.

Eden, L. (2004). *Whole World on Fire: Organizations, Knowledge, and Nuclear Weapons Devastation*. Ithaca, NY: Cornell University Press.

Gamson, W., and Modigliani, A. (1989). Media Discourse and Public Opinion on Nuclear Power: A Constructivist Approach. *American Journal of Sociology*, 95(1), pp. 1–37.

Gochi, H. (2007). *Genbakusho: Tsuminaki Hito no Tomshibi o Tsuide*. Kyoto: Kamogawa Shuppan.

Goldstein, D., and Stawkowski, M. (2015). James V. Neel and Yuri E. Dubrova: Cold War Debates and the Genetic Effects of Low-Dose Radiation. *Journal of the History of Biology*, 48(1), pp. 67–98.

Gordin, M. (2007). *Five Days in August: How World War II Became a Nuclear War*. Princeton, NJ: Princeton University Press.

Hecht, G. (2006). Nuclear Ontologies. *Constellations*, 13(3), pp. 320–331.

Hida, S. (2013). *Hibaku to Hibaku: Hoshasen ni Makezu ni Ikiru*. Tokyo: Gantosha Renaissance.

Hilgartner, S., Bell, R., and O'Connor, R. (1982). *Nukespeak: Nuclear Language, Visions, and Mindset*. New York: Random House.

Hiroshima "Black Rain" Radioactivity Study Group. (2010). Current Status of Studies on Radioactive Fallout with "Black Rain" due to the Hiroshima Atomic Bomb. Available at: http://www.hisof.jp/01publication/0301BlackRain2010.pdf [Accessed June 28, 2021].

Jacobs, R. (2014). The Radiation That Makes People Invisible: A Global Hibakusha Perspective. *The Asia-Pacific Journal, Japan Focus*, 12(31:1). Available at: https://apjjf.org/2014/12/31/Robert-Jacobs/4157/article.html [Accessed June 23, 2021].

Jasanoff, S., ed. (2004). *States of Knowledge: The Co-Production of Science and Social Order*. London: Routledge.

Jasanoff, S., and Kim, S. (2009). Containing the Atom: Sociotechnical Imaginaries and Nuclear Power in the United States and South Korea. *Minerva*, 47, pp. 119–146.

Jasper, J. (1990). *Nuclear Politics: Energy and the State in the United States, Sweden, and France*. Princeton, NJ: Princeton University Press.

Jenkins, R. (1996). *Social Identity*. London: Routledge.

Kim, Y., et al.(2009). Hibaku Taiken no Motarasu Shinriteki Eikyo ni Tsuite. *Seishin Shinkeigaku Zasshi (Psychiatria et Neurologia Japonica)*, 111(4), pp. 400–404.

Kuchinskaya, O. (2014). *The Politics of Invisibility: Public Knowledge about Radiation Health Effects after Chernobyl*. Cambridge, MA: MIT Press.

Lindee, S. (1994). *Suffering Made Real: American Science and the Survivors at Hiroshima*. Chicago, IL: University of Chicago Press.

Malloy, S. (2012). "A Very Pleasant Way to Die": Radiation Effects and the Decision to Use the Atomic Bomb against Japan. *Diplomatic History*, 36(3), pp. 515–545.

Nakagawa, Y. (1991). *Zoho Hoshasen Hibaku no Rekishi: Amerika Genbaku Kaihatsu kara Fukshima Genpatsu Jiko made*. Tokyo: Akashi Shoten.

Naono, A. (2011). *Hibaku to Hosho: Hiroshima, Nagasaki, soshite Fukushima*. Tokyo: Heibon-sha.

Nixon, R. (2013). *Slow Violence and the Environmentalism of the Poor*. Cambridge, MA: Harvard University Press.

Sasamoto, Y. (1995). *Beigun Senyoka no Genbaku Chosa: Genbaku Kagaikoku ni Natta Nihon*. Tokyo: Shinkansha.

Sawada, S. (2007). Cover-up of the Effects of Internal Exposure by Residual Radiation from the Atomic Bombing of Hiroshima and Nagasaki. *Medicine, Conflict, and Survival*, 23(1), pp. 58–74.

Sawada, S. (2015). Kakuheiki to Genpatsu de Yugamerareta Hoshasen Hibaku no Kenkyu. In: A. Kimura and H. Takahashi, eds., *Kakujidai no Shinwa to Kyozo*. Tokyo: Akashi Shoten, pp. 53–72.

Scott, J. (1991). The Evidence of Experience. *Critical Inquiry*, 17(4), pp. 773–797.

Scott, J. (1999). *Seeing Like a State: How Certain Schemes to Improve the Human Condition Have Failed*. New Haven, CT: Yale University Press.

Shizuma, K., et al. (1996). 137Cs Concentration in Soil Samples from an Early Survey of Hiroshima Atomic Bomb and Cumulative Dose Estimation from the Fallout. *Health Physics*, 71, pp. 340–346.

Takahashi, H. (2009). One Minute After the Detonation of the Atomic Bomb: The Erased Effects of Residual Radiation. *Historia Scientiarum*, 19(2), pp. 146–159.

Takahashi, H. (2012). *Fuuin sareta Hiroshima, Nagasaki: Bei Kakujikken to Minkan Bouei Keikaku*. Tokyo: Gaifusha.

Takahashi, H., and Takemine, S., eds. (2006). *Hibakusha to Sengo Hosho*. Tokyo: Gaifusha.

Takemine, S. (2008). "Hibakusha" toiu Kotoba ga motsu Seijisei: Horitsujo no Kitei o Fumaete. *Ritsumeikan Heiwa Kenkyu*, 9, pp. 21–30.

Takemine, S. (2016). Discourse Analysis of "Hibakusha" Adopted at NGO International Symposium on the Damage and After-Effects of the Atomic Bombing of Hiroshima and Nagasaki. *Meisei Daigaku Shakaigaku Kiyo*, 36, pp. 101–113.

Tanaka, T. (2006). Ichinichi demo Hayaku Engo Gyosei Kaikaku o-Genbakusho Nintei Sosho. In: H. Takahashi and S. Takemine, eds., *Hibakusha to Sengo Hosho*. Tokyo: Gaifusha, pp. 25–36.

Weart, S. (1988). *Nuclear Fear: A History of Images*. Cambridge, MA: Harvard University Press.

Wing, S., Richardson, D., and Stewart, A. (1999). The Relevance of Occupational Epidemiology to Radiation Protection Standards. *New Solutions*, 9(2), pp. 133–151.

Yoneyama, L. (1999). *Hiroshima Traces: Time, Space, and the Dialectics of Memory*. Berkeley, CA: University of California Press.

Yuasa, M. (2019). "Kuroi Ame" Hibakusha no Nintei o Habamu "Kagakuteki Gouritekina Konkyo." Paper presented at the 2019 Meeting of the Peace Studies Association of Japan, held in Fukushima, June 2019.

2 Optics of exposure

Joseph Masco

The military nuclear age has proliferated forms and intensities of exposure since 1945, linking how we see to what is in our bodies to planetary-scale transformations in the environment. Exposure, for the purposes of this chapter, is therefore a material as well as conceptual condition, a way of thinking about how technological revolution is apprehended and embodied and the ways it comes to violently remake the world. Conceptually, "exposure" is a remarkably expansive term. The *Oxford English Dictionary* offers four general meanings: (1) a state of having no protection from something harmful (severe weather, a financial loss, toxicity); (2) the revelation of a secret (publicity in a positive or negative key); (3) the action of exposing a photographic film to light (as in motion picture and still photography); and (4) the direction a building faces (that is, an outlook or perspective). A politics of exposure must then account for both material conditions and anticipations, linking visual culture to a public sphere to political orientations via some kind of violent relation.

A fully rendered exploration of exposure also has a way of exploding time/space relations. One can identify and follow the specific trajectories of material life in the industrial/nuclear age (i.e., radionuclides, carbon, synthetic chemicals), attending to the way such materials organise the complexity of the world through individual injury (for example, Fortun, 2012; Agard-Jones, 2013; Shapiro, 2015). This technique reveals internal structural conditions (across race, economy, gender and geopolitics), and does so because of the longevity of such materials in relation to an expanding collective future (Murphy, 2017). That is, all life on planet earth in the twenty-first century lives in the fallout, the lag, of twentieth century exposures of nuclear, petrochemical and synthetic chemical regimes (Masco, 2020). How, then, might we approach the atomic bomb as a mechanism of planetary exposure, attending to the nuances of vector and domain, tracking its visual life, affective terrain and embodied affects?

A crucial aspect of exposure, as a phenomenon, is that it brings the external world inside the body with complex effects and futurities, blurring any easy distinction between metabolism and milieu. For example, just to look at the bomb is to create an internal optical circuit

DOI: 10.4324/9781003227472-2

46 *Joseph Masco*

involving light, chemistry and psychology, but one that paradoxically allows the world to appear to the subject as *externalised* (see Figure 2.1). Light exposure here operates inside the head but projects an experience of separation from, even objectification of an outside world. The atomic bomb pushes well past this basic logic of vision: it can stun the eye, via dazzle, or burn it via flash-blindness. The flash can also create an afterimage that lingers long after the atomic light has passed creating an out-of-order temporal experience of the material world—a visual derangement. These are psychological as well as biological processes, shaping experiences of the event via the vulnerability and limitation of the human sensory apparatus.

Moreover, in the US context, the atomic bomb has always been embedded in regimes of secrecy and expertise, making a core project of the early nuclear age the effort to remake citizens as nuclear subjects. Exposing citizens to highly selected images of "the bomb" became a central mechanism for establishing US nuclear nationalism and coordinating a mass public notion of nuclear destruction as a controlled, necessary and even righteous marshalling of the ultimate tool of dominance (Oakes, 1994; Masco, 2014). Indeed, after Hiroshima and Nagasaki, the atomic bomb becomes a multigenerational technoscientific project in the United States, as well as a national propaganda campaign and a constant destabiliser of democratic order (Masco, 2006; Wills, 2010). In the United States, nuclear secrecy supersedes or suspends democratic practice as a basic condition, rendering a world-changing violent technology only visible, only subject to public debate via its traumatic after-effects.

One way into this world-making (in terms of technical infrastructures, political imaginaries and military power) but also perversely world-breaking (in terms of health and the environment, concepts of everyday life and the future) order is to attend to its photochemistry, to track the chemical emulsions that enable the bomb to be imaged and made into a technopolitical form. For the atomic bomb is, right from the start, as much a project of photography as nuclear science. The timing and fusing mechanisms for the first atomic device detonated in New Mexico on July 16, 1945 also organised a vast photographic experiment, one that synchronised the plutonium implosive array with a multitude of still and motion picture cameras. Thus, nuclear exposure in its first act is simultaneously material, photochemical and psychosocial. After the wartime strikes on Hiroshima and Nagasaki, US weapons laboratories detonated some 215 nuclear devices into the atmosphere and underwater between 1945 and 1963, creating planetary-scale exposures from radioactive fallout emanating from ground zero events linking the US Southwest to the Marshall Islands to Alaska. This "test regime," as it was paradoxically known, fused settler colonial violence to nuclear colonialism to Cold War geopolitics through unprecedented sequential acts of violence.

Optics of exposure 47

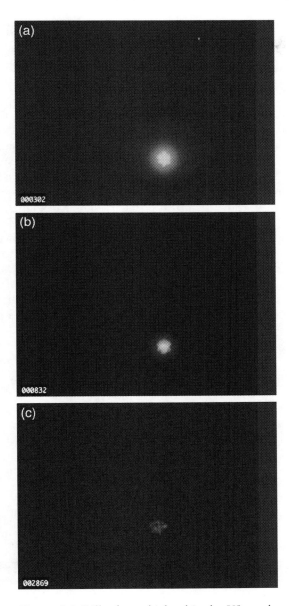

Figure 2.1 Stills from high altitude US nuclear detonation. Courtesy Lawrence Livermore National Laboratory.

Each US atmospheric detonation was also a major photographic experiment, ultimately creating a vast archive of still images and millions of feet of motion picture film. This filmic register was created as proof of

48 Joseph Masco

experimental success and for weapons design purposes, but photography also was used to establish the conceptual building blocks for the nuclear age itself. Importantly, the visual register for the US nuclear project is almost exclusively a product of the atmospheric test period, 1945–1963, an 18-year period in which each photograph or filmic sequence reference a real-world act of nuclear violence marked officially as an "experiment." Out of a massive total archive of nuclear photography, a small subset of images, selected for ideological purposes, were heavily publicised to the American public (Masco, 2014; 2008). All others were controlled via official classification, allowing a highly curated set of photographic and filmic images to stand in for the entire nuclear event, even as radioactive exposure, imperceptible to the eye, was launched into the biosphere and planetary future with each and every detonation (see Figure 2.2).

In what follows, I explore three interconnected domains of nuclear exposure: in Section I, I discuss the collaborations in photochemistry between weapons scientists and Kodak engineers to create mechanisms and techniques for imaging the atomic bomb. In Section II, I discuss how the human body was remade via these same explosive and photochemical experiments in ways that explode the biological future. And in Section III, I consider the legacy of twentieth-century nuclear nationalism within a geology of media as an ongoing form of planetary exposure.

Section I

In August of 1945, employees at the Kodak film production facility in Rochester, New York discovered widespread fogging and spots on undeveloped film stock, ruining some of their core commercial products. A scientific investigation inside the company found that paper materials from two separate cardboard plants located in Indiana and Iowa were somehow contaminated with an "artificial radioactive element," leading to the damaged film stock. Kodak officials concluded that radioactive fallout from an unknown source inside the continental United States was to blame—and it was an increasing threat to their business. Thus, within weeks of the first nuclear detonation in New Mexico, and while news of the atomic destruction of Hiroshima and Nagasaki was still being revealed in US media reports, Kodak had already documented that nuclear events were not local but hemispheric, that invisible contaminates from fallout could produce unanticipated material effects, and that photochemistry was a highly sensitive register of the nuclear revolution.

The second continental nuclear detonation conducted at the newly opened Nevada Proving Grounds in January 1951 raised further concerns within Kodak. Officials registered "hot snow" and additional product damage at the campus in Rochester, some 2,500 miles from the detonation site. In an internal company report, Kodak concluded that "airborne radioactive particles could find their way into sensitised photographic materials at any stage

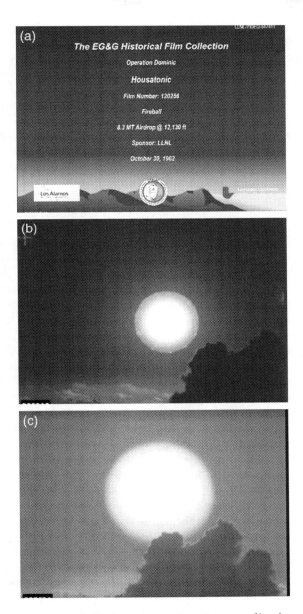

Figure 2.2 Stills from restored nuclear test film from Operation Dominic. Courtesy Lawrence Livermore National Laboratory.

of the manufacturing operation and cause defective product." The company ultimately threatened to sue the federal government over damage caused to their industry by expanding US nuclear national security programs.

50 Joseph Masco

In response, the Department of Defense (DOD) and Atomic Energy Commission (AEC) made an astonishing concession, particularly given the secrecy around US nuclear weapons development and the mounting paranoia about nuclear spies in the anti-communist McCarthy era: Kodak was given advanced warning of each US nuclear test and updated maps of expected fallout patterns across the United States (which were not shared with the public).

The DOD/AEC provisions enabled Kodak to shift production schedules in accommodation of the US nuclear development program—to coordinate their commercial activities to the rhythms of US nuclear detonations. Kodak officials, however, remained worried about the viability of their core products in the nuclear age. By 1960, Kodak had established a widespread monitoring system for radioactive fallout within its distributed production complex, including installing air sensors and Geiger counters to continually test atmospheric conditions at Kodak Park in Rochester. Kodak paper mills adopted protocols involving laying x-ray film between sheets of production paper to test for fallout damage. Today, we would call the production and protection of Kodak film stocks a "critical infrastructure," as photographic film was a vital resource for American technoscience, economy and military power. Securing its "pulp, board and paper" stock, while ensuring the viability of photochemical emulsions of expanding range and sensitivity was a vital mid-century project at Kodak and for the AEC. Overcoming this vulnerability further integrated the company into the broader industrial infrastructure supporting nuclear weapons science.

Kodak was already deeply connected to the US military, providing over a million square feet of film to the war effort in 1945 alone (more than five times the total amount sold to civilian photographers). The expanding needs of surveillance photography in wartime brought together experts in camera design and chemists specialising in photographic emulsions to solve a vast set of problems with aerial photography. Reconnaissance planes flying at high speed, night-time photography and the need for reliable and fast film processing in the field all pushed for the development of new imaging technologies. For example, Kodacolor Aero Reversal film (which offered fast field development and some 3D imaging capability) and Tri-X Aero Panchromatic film (used for night photography lit by flash bombs) were invented at Kodak for the US military in 1941. The Aero Reversal film was marketed after the war to civilians as Kodacolor and Ektacolor film. Put differently, the massive expansion in civilian photography at mid-century, now coded in the still highly saturated colors of Kodak photographic and slide film, was, in part, a product of a US military collaboration during World War II.

This long-running commercialisation of military imaging technologies at Kodak only accelerated during the era of atmospheric nuclear detonations, early satellite systems and the moon missions: indeed, between

Optics of exposure 51

1935 and 1962, Kodak created and marketed some 777 different color film stocks while building a vast set of highly specific emulsions tailored to the defense department and space programs. When US nuclear testing moved underground in 1963 under the terms of the Limited Test Ban Treaty, Kodak created thin, ultra-strong chemical emulsions for satellite photography and specialty film stocks for Apollo Mission's moon photography (that is, photochemistry suitable for the extreme heat and cold of the launch and re-entry cycles as well as zero gravity). It is impossible to overestimate the cultural impact of Kodak imaging in this era: Kodak emulsion chemists created a vast new infrastructure for American historical memory, one tied to the specific qualities of Kodacolor and Kodachrome film stocks (Feser, 2019).

A primary engine of this technological revolution in imaging (and integration into military industrial development) was the difficulty of photographing nuclear events. These posed unprecedented technical challenges. A nuclear detonation, for instance, produces light that is more than ten times brighter than the midday sun, operating across some 12 orders of light magnitude. The high dynamic range photochemical film stocks of the mid-twentieth century could only capture about three orders of magnitude, and so nuclear phenomena were never more than partially accessible by film. Complicating matters, of the key physical properties of a nuclear detonation—blast, heat and radiation—heat and radiation could not be captured by, but could destroy cameras. The core technology for recording nuclear events therefore could document only a fragment of this violent and complex physical process. Photography captures just a temporal slice of a nuclear event that produces measurable effects over a great time and distance, injecting materials like plutonium, cesium and strontium, some with half-lives in the tens of thousands of years, into the biosphere. Thus, while the photographic record of 1945–1963 is the primary mechanism for engaging nuclear events in the United States, it is also highly limited as a technical index of a more complex, and unfolding, reality. The visual archive of nuclear detonations is a vital, but always partial record, even before the ideological project of narrative film started to repurpose selected scientific photography for different publics (Masco, 2008).

For weapons scientists, photography was crucial right from the start in making calculations about the power of the explosion, measuring yield by studying the blast radius and mushroom cloud formation. The timing and firing mechanisms for each nuclear device were integrated into the photographic array, allowing a simultaneous triggering of bomb and cameras. The array, itself, involved a wide range of cameras and film stocks aimed at different parts of the nuclear sequence (see Figure 2.3). Starting in 1947, technical photography, timing and firing were run by Edgerton, Germehausen and Greir (EG&G), a company formed by Harold Edgerton and his MIT colleagues. The scientific photography

52 Joseph Masco

Figure 2.3 Still and motion picture cameras used during early nuclear testing at the Bikini Atoll. Source: US National Archive and Records Administration.

EG&G produced was used at Los Alamos and later Livermore for weapons research, but it was also provided to Lookout Mountain Laboratory, an Air Force film studio set up in Hollywood in 1947 to make documentary subjects for both classified and public audiences (see Figure 2.4; Hamilton and O'Gorman, 2018). These companies created the visual archive of the military nuclear project in the United States: EG&G created tens of thousands of scientific films, the vast majority of which remain classified, stored in national laboratory archives and on military bases to this day. Lookout Mountain Laboratory re-purposed a small portion of that footage for as many as 6,000 narrative documentary films, made mostly for classified audiences.

Though devoted to improving the military capacities of the nuclear state, it is important to underscore that public understandings of nuclear effects derive largely from EG&G and Lookout Mountain Laboratory's work, which in non-classified form represents a highly selective and strategic deployment of photography for US propagandistic purposes. These images now circulate detached from their foundational ideological projects in nuclear nation-building and tend to stand-in for the entirety

Optics of exposure 53

Figure 2.4 Film credits for EG&G and Lookout Mountain Laboratory. Source: Nuclear Testing Archive (NTA).

of nuclear effects. Seventy-five years into the military nuclear age, that is, public understandings of the bomb remain tied to images produced and selectively released in the mid-twentieth century, even though we have

54   Joseph Masco

much greater knowledge about the ongoing health and environmental effects of atmospheric nuclear detonations (for example, National Research Council, 2006).

I find emulsion chemistry fascinating, both in its technical terms and because Kodak and other film companies maintained compartmentalised secrecy around their formulas to rival that of the nuclear complex itself. Kodak built a classified wing on its Rochester campus just for the Department of Defense. It was off-limits to employees not formally cleared by the DOD or AEC. The formulas for key emulsions were also broken into parts and distributed to different sections of Kodak Park for protection, a register of the constant industrial espionage waged by major film companies through the twentieth century. Because Kodak's processing technology was proprietary and treated as top-secret, the exposed film for each of the 106 (atomic and thermonuclear) detonations conducted at the Marshall Islands, for example, needed to be sent to Rochester for processing and development. A special Air Force transport would fly the mass of exposed film to Rochester after each detonation, returning the processed film to Los Alamos and Livermore for scientific study. I have collected exhilarating narratives from young weapons scientists tasked with escorting the hastily collected footage from atoll test sites to New York via the latest high-speed jets. They discuss bearing witness not only to the linked technological revolutions of nuclear weapons science and photography but also describe experiencing a profound global collapsing of time and space. Nuclear testing made the world seem smaller with each detonation.

Photographic emulsions are a petrochemical medium, which is a material form of congealed time. A form of fossil record, photography has the capacity to freeze time in a still image, or to speed time up or slow it down in the form of a motion picture. Each type of film is made out of layers of emulsion chemistry designed to capture specific intensities of light and to calibrate speed, contrast, and grain. For example, the Kodachrome film that creates such vibrant colors involves five layers of emulsion, each designed to capture a specific color range: the top layer is a blue-sensitive emulsion (containing a yellow dye to absorb any blue light from traveling through the matrix), followed by a clear gelatin interlayer. The middle layer is green-sensitive layer, followed by another gelatin interlayer and a final red-sensitive emulsion. When exposed, each layer records its specific negative image. Read as a visual stack, these emulsions render a wide palette of colors. For nuclear weapons photography, the layering of emulsions also solved a temporal problem; thicker compound emulsions were engineered to cover the radically different light intensities of a nuclear event. Peter Kuran (2006: 56–57), who has consulted with the DOD on restoring the scientific photography from early Cold War nuclear tests, has revealed that one of EG&G's key achievements was the creation of an "extended range" or XR color film that could capture a longer range of light. The chemistry involved "three panchromatic layers": cyan recorded the brightest aspect of the blast, magenta the intermediate brightness and yellow served as a highspeed layer. Thus, emulsion chemistry was used to sequence light in relation to shifts in visual intensity and therefore to capture more of the nuclear event, albeit in unnatural colors.

Atmospheric nuclear detonations were often conducted in the early morning, in full darkness. EG&G sought to solve the resulting problem of photographically capturing a radical shift from total darkness to ultra-extreme light intensity via photochemistry, establishing a set of basic principles for high speed and color photography that would soon revolutionise commercial photography. Put directly, commercial cameras (those using photochemical film but also early digital devices) rely on technical insights first made in the era of photographing nuclear detonations. This means that the American public largely understands the bomb via photographic imaging and that weapons science changed photography itself: The bomb is literally embedded within everyday imaging and communication technologies, from film and photography to computers and the internet.

Exposure in this case is technoscientific, an attempt to record as much visual information as possible from nuclear events that resist full capture or representation; it excludes other domains of meaning, from indigenous dispossession to worker sacrifice to global contamination. The visual archive of atmospheric nuclear detonations, despite these profound limitations, remains a central mechanism for constituting the "nuclear referent"—for communicating the potential of the bomb and the coordinates of nuclear power and fear across generations. The still mostly classified US nuclear archive also represents the most expensive film project in human history. Trillions of dollars have been spent to build and deploy and visually document the atomic bomb. But the archive is exceptional beyond its representation of massive photographic experiments and technological innovation; each act documented in the archive is a real-world event with planetary-scale consequences. The exposure of photochemical emulsions to nuclear light thus constitutes simultaneously a laboratory, an archive and an extraordinarily detailed record of extreme violence. It is an unprecedented, as well as insufficient but necessary, visual anchor for maintaining nuclear awareness in a twenty-first century era that is still massively committed to the atomic bomb but also filled with political projects to push it away from collective thought, or alternatively, to keep it hidden from public view.

Section II

The science of photochemical exposure remains a key translator of the early nuclear age, a central means of transforming nuclear physics into

56 *Joseph Masco*

immutable mobiles, texts that can travel and be repurposed within a wide range of narrative structures. But nuclear detonations create problems for vision: the exploding bomb can damage the observing eye, creating temporary or permanent flash-blindness. Thus, just as EG&G and Kodak sought to open the bomb up photographically via emulsion chemistry, the Air Force sought to insulate its pilots from the nuclear flash, creating a human body that could be imagined immune to visual damage during nuclear war. Here, exposure is recognised to be literally blinding, demonstrating the foundational vulnerability of the human form.

Lookout Mountain Laboratory made a highly aestheticised nuclear war training film for US Air Force pilots in 1960. *Nuclear Effects During SAC Delivery Missions* was made to re-assure pilots of the safety of their planes throughout a nuclear bombing run. The film relies not only on the exceptional technical photography of nuclear effects from EG&G but also deploys animation (created by former Disney animators) to detail nuclear war using an idealsed American small town as the target. It has a dual effect: training pilots to conduct nuclear bombing runs while simultaneously demonstrating the vulnerability of American towns to nuclear attack. The film begins with EG&G technical photography demonstrating how a bomber rides out the shock wave of a nuclear blast in flight, then moves into animations reassuring pilots that, from the point of view of "your aircraft," nuclear warfare is ultimately safe provided the right precautions are taken (see Figure 2.5).

If EG&G and Lookout Mountain Laboratory were worried about how to create the proper filmic exposures to study the exploding bomb, the AEC/DOD had another concern about the biological health of its workforce, mobilising a different filmic register of exposure that was more individualised and incremental. From the first nuclear detonation in July 1945, US nuclear workers were required to wear photochemical film badges called dosimeters to record radiation exposure. Deploying dental film made largely by Kodak, filmic dosimeter badges were first only worn when entering radiation exclusion areas. After 1957, all workers at the Nevada Test Site and other nuclear facilities wore color-coded dosimeter badges every day, exchanging them for new ones on a monthly basis (see Figure 2.6). The AEC, and then the US Department of Energy, collected, tested and stored these dosimeter badges across the Cold War period. By the end of the Cold War and nuclear testing in 1992, this filmic archive constituted several million individual monthly records of worker exposures.

Just pause for a moment to consider this unique photochemical archive of US nuclear nationalism: the dosimeter archive indexes radiation exposures from the workers closest to nuclear production, recording the sheer force of nuclear science and militarism in a month-by-month archive of worker bodies over 47 years. The dosimeter badge is a technology capable of registering radiation exposures of many different

Optics of exposure 57

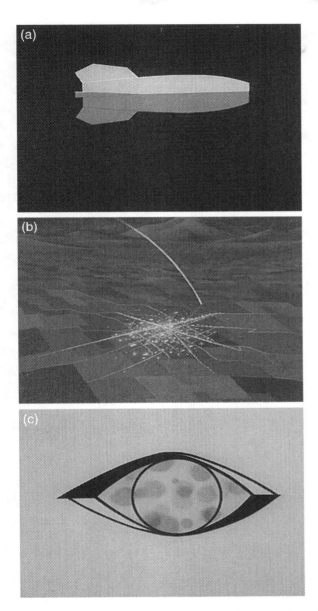

Figure 2.5 Animation of air force nuclear attack and flash-blindness from *Nuclear Effects During SAC Delivery Missions*. Source: Nuclear Testing Archive (NTA).

58   Joseph Masco

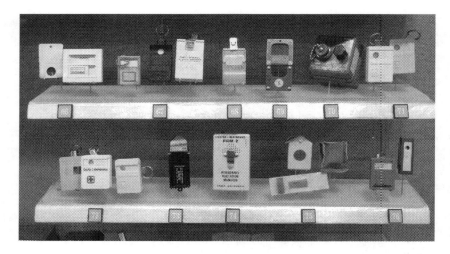

Figure 2.6 Dosimeter film badges exhibit at the Atomic Testing Museum. Photograph by author.

kinds, capturing modes of injury that play out on a vast range of timescales and intensities in embodied form, offering a portrait of fast and slow violence (Nixon, 2011).

In practice, dosimeter badges were collected once a month, providing a cumulative exposure reading for a 30-day period. If a worker received, or was suspected to have received, a radiation dose above a designated level, he or she was suspended from further potential exposures for a designated amount of time. Thus, any effort to understand photographic exposures during the test program necessarily involves the biological as well as mechanical. Every nuclear detonation was not only an experiment in weapons science and photochemistry, but also an acknowledged experiment in human biology. As the years marched on and the bombs were detonated, the camera operators working for Lookout Mountain Laboratory and EG&G all wore dosimeter badges, entering their employee hours into a regime of retrospectively calculated injury, tracking monthly exposures, and projecting health consequences into an unknown future.

The National Research Council (2006) has concluded that no level of radiation exposure is "safe," yet the occupational logics of US weapons science rely on a logic of accumulation and threshold. Shannon Cram (2015) has studied the abstracted statistical body at the center of such administrative judgments at the Hanford site (which converted uranium into the plutonium that is at the core of most US nuclear weapons from WWII through the Cold War), unpacking a startling lack of recognition of race, gender, or age differences in the statistical model. She calls the resulting idealised nuclear worker a "productive fiction" necessary to the biometric logic of the nuclear industry. It works to normalise low-level radiation exposure, to construct an aura of workplace safety, and to absolve the state of responsibility for all but extreme health events (also Brown, 2019).

Today, the Cold War dosimeter archive is housed at the Nevada National Security Site (formerly the Nevada Test Site). It is kept at a low temperature to prevent decay. The smell of millions of pieces of aging film is reportedly overwhelming. So, too, is the constant risk of fire posed by chemical breakdown in the emulsions. Still, the archive is crucial. Its data is used today in litigation over health effects from Cold War-era nuclear production, providing a way for workers to try to document exposures on the job and access the limited terms of a congressionally mandated reparations program. A major report by McClatchy News in 2015 offered a startling overview of the human costs to nuclear workers (not exposed citizens) involved in the US nuclear program since 1943: drawing on dosimeter data and other archives, McClatchy reported over 100,000 documented illnesses and over 33,000 deaths among nuclear workers who received compensation for on-the-job exposures (Hotakainen et al., 2015). Here, exposure is recorded on dosimeter film but also registered in the lag between the event of exposure as registered on a photochemical emulsion and its biological consequences in terms of individual health.

From this perspective, the Cold War was anything but cold, it was more a mix of hot and cold, fast and slow violences mediated and justified by the more immediately terrifying images of nuclear war. The film badges allow for a post-Cold War expansion of biological citizenship (Petryna, 2003) for some nuclear workers while side-stepping the widespread exposures experienced by those not officially monitored by the nuclear state—that is, non-nuclear workers, US residents, and the greater global population (Gallagher 1993, Lindee, 1997). The photochemistry structuring our understanding of the nuclear referent is thus multiple and still unfolding, connecting visual texts to dosimeter records. Photochemical emulsions document that nuclear injury operates on a vast range of vectors and signals complex, ongoing transformations across the biosphere.

Section III

The formal logics of exposure—the official state-based programs to assess nuclear injury—have nonetheless worked to deny the planetary scope of nuclear effects since 1945. Indeed, each nuclear state seeks to restrict the category of "exposed subject" via formal regulation. They require perfect biomedical documentation of injury for inclusion and deploy statistical models that assume a clinical-level control of at-large populations to bolster exclusion. The real-world effects of decades of

60 *Joseph Masco*

nuclear exposure have gone largely without systematic accounting. There is no single mechanism for registering cumulative nuclear state injections of radionuclides into the biosphere since 1945 across nuclear states, projects and technologies. Indeed, there is not even a single radiation exposure metric used uniformly. Thus, within the existing global data there are complex forms of data friction and a host of translation issues that complicate, if not obviate, easy comparative analysis.

One of the most surprising and energetic nuclear debates of recent years has been provoked by geologists, people who care about deep time and the stratigraphic layers of Earth. Since 2009, a formal project in the discipline of geology has been to consider the addition of a new temporal periodisation to the geological time scale of planet earth: the Anthropocene, or the moment when industrial activity became so collectively powerful that it directly affects the Earth system. The formal criteria for this geoscience designation are rigorous: the marker must be artificial, operate on a planetary scale and be long-lasting enough to operate in geological time. The working group on the Anthropocene has agreed (after a wide-ranging debate) that the mid-twentieth century has multiple markers of human activity achieving an intervention into the Earth system on the right planetary scale and in deep geological time. The primary candidate for the Anthropocene designation is the plutonium fallout from above-ground detonation.

Consider Waters et al. (2016) which articulates the various contending radioactive signatures for planetary scale human impacts, singling out plutonium from atmospheric nuclear explosions as the most technically justified marker for the Anthropocene designation. Examining the global distribution of cesium, strontium, and plutonium from atmospheric nuclear explosions in the mid-twentieth century, Waters and his colleagues note that cesium has natural as well as artificial sources (and thus is less than ideal for their purposes), while plutonium stands out as a purely artificial signal:

> Pu-239, with its long half-life (24,110 years), low solubility, and high particle reactivity, particularly in marine sediments may be the most suitable radioisotope for marking the start of the Anthropocene. The appearance of a Pu-239 fallout signature in 1951, peaking in 1963–64 will be identifiable in sediments and ice for the next 100,000 years.

Thus, in all of human activity, the millennia of human attempts to control and change the environment, one signature, one mode of exposure, stands out to contemporary geologists: the plutonium from atmospheric nuclear detonations, distributed globally during the Cold War, and so precisely documented on Kodak film.

A plutonium-based Anthropocene marker has an unusual calibration: the timeline of fallout signals shows peaks in atmospheric distribution from 1952 to 1963, following years of exceptionally active US and Soviet

Optics of exposure 61

nuclear testing. In 1962, for example, the United States and USSR tested nuclear technologies in the atmosphere every other day for the calendar year. The signal drops in 1964, due to the signing of the Limited Test Ban Treaty, which took US—USSR—UK nuclear testing underground. Such calibration offers a shocking specificity to the Anthropocene (for example, in 1952, there were only two nuclear powers, the United States and Soviet Union). And this periodisation elevates not the atomic age, but the thermonuclear age, to a potential geological periodisation.

The crucial insight of the geological working group established in 2009 is that, in the above-ground testing era, just a few nations created a new form of planetary exposure: radioactive fallout from nuclear detonations. It took a lot of work to transform uranium into plutonium—a vast industrial system and decades of labor—and then more labor to use that plutonium in serial atmospheric and underground detonations (Hecht, 2014; Creager, 2015). Many of the worker injuries noted in the last section of this chapter involve the production of plutonium, a specialised commodity that currently has no real use other than in making bombs. The geological review supporting the Anthropocene designation has shown that plutonium fallout is now loaded into the Earth system, where it stands as a clearly artificial and multimillennial signal of human activity on the planet. This makes the scientific film record of US atmospheric detonations a photographic documentation of a radiation exposure at planetary scale (see Figure 2.7).

Thus, we now have a multimodal moment of existential reflection, one linking the historical formation of the concept of existential danger in the form of the mid-twentieth century atomic bomb to the emerging logics of anthropogenic climate disruption today (Masco, 2014). Seventy-five years of existential danger in the form of nuclear war is now challenged by the industrial legacies of petrochemical production (Tsing et al., 2017). But beyond this historical measure, the search for anthropogenic origins, the cumulative legacy of industrial life across nuclear and petrochemical regimes, is being amplified by the continued investment in resource extraction and renewed efforts to build a nuclear complex for a new century. The United States and Russia are working hard to extend nuclear nationalism in the twenty-first century, with the United States planning to spend well over a trillion dollars over 30 years to rebuild its nuclear arsenal (as well as its bombers, missiles and submarines). In reaction, many nation-states are contemplating their own nuclear programs, promising a major expansion of the global nuclear danger. And, at the same time, 120 non-nuclear UN member countries have mobilised to officially ban the atomic bomb—to add it to the list of globally illegal weapons. Clearly, the nuclear referent remains highly fraught: the twenty-first century is filled with new metrics of exposure, even as established nuclear powers recommit to their nuclear complexes while other states attempt to gain them and an international collective

62 Joseph Masco

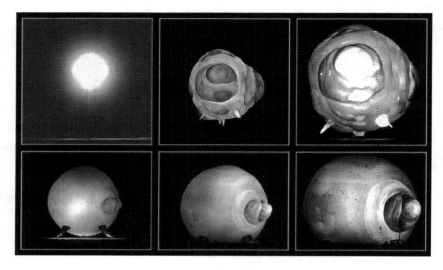

Figure 2.7 Nuclear detonation photographed at millisecond speed. Source: US National Archive and Records Administration.

works to acknowledge and stop the human and nonhuman costs of nuclear weapons once and for all.

Behind each of these projects are hard metrics—technical efforts to think about the past, present, and future dangers of the military nuclear age, detailing specific trajectories, dispersions and temporalities of violence. But let us return, in conclusion, to the photochemistry.

At Livermore and Los Alamos, a major project is now the repurposing of the filmic documentation of above-ground nuclear effects from 1945 to 1963. It is a scientific commitment to extract more technical data from the photochemical archive using current digital technology. The EG&G films are in the process of being scanned and subjected to computer assessment, a formal weapons science effort to calibrate and improve the computer codes necessary to design the next generation of nuclear weapons using the improved yield measurements of historical detonations. High-resolution digital scans and sophisticated computer measurement are resetting the historical record. They have already improved the accuracy of specific Cold War era nuclear yield assessments by as much as 30%. Thus, the photochemistry of EG&G—which created the visual archive for the nuclear age in both a military scientific and public propaganda register—is once again improving US nuclear weapons science and shifting the terms of the collective nuclear future.

To be precise, the nuclear age is now being recoded as *planetary* and *eternal*. As the plutonium from atmospheric nuclear detonations formally enters into geological time, it has collapsed the "nuclear age" into the "Anthropocene." And as the analog film produced by Kodak is digitised, translated into zeros and ones, these exposures enter what Jussi Parikka (2015) calls the geology of media. For Parikka, the digital nuclear age is geological in that computation relies on rare earth materials and digitisation relies on the vast sets of technologies allowing cloud computing (which have anthropogenic environmental consequences). These digital technologies, given the remarkable speed of technological revolution, are soon outmoded, becoming technofossils—that is, the outmoded tech that goes into the landfill (incidentally adding a new layer to Earth's geological record). The analog nuclear photography (made on petrochemical film stock and thus of fossilised time) is becoming digital, and thereby loaded into supercomputers and the vast planetary technical apparatus of nuclear science. From the sensor arrays that measure air, water, and seismic activity for nuclear events to the satellites that watch Earth for nuclear detonations and the early warning systems always looking for the first signs of nuclear attack, the nuclear present is digitally mediated. This evolving technological infrastructure for nuclear war promises to add constant technofossils to the geology of an anthropogenic earth system.

The EG&G films are, in this way, much more than documents of US nuclear weapons development and the first-order expansion of nuclear nationalism. EG&G films are a multi-faceted archive of exposure. They document how specific scientific experiments generated earthly contamination, across landscapes, people and planet. They register, perhaps even in a future legal sense, planetary exposure across photochemical, biological and geological domains. That is, the photochemical archives of films, photographs and dosimeters hold the possibility for the emergence of a new form of accountability for twentieth-century US nuclear nationalism, one equal to the geographical and temporal scope of radioactive contamination itself. For even as those atmospheric nuclear events continue to unfold across bodies, ecosystems and the international system today, the photochemical archive (films, photographs and dosimeters) documents with precision (and ever-increasing digital resolution), a planetary-scale optics of industrial exposure. This raises an important question: how might one now repurpose this photographic archive, not just for new weapons, but for disarmament, or even an entirely new mode of twenty-first century planetary accountability?

References

Agard-Jones, V. (2013). Bodies in the System. *Small Axe*, 17(3), pp. 182–192.
Brown, K. (2019). *Manual for Survival: A Chernobyl Guide to the Future*. New York: Norton.

Cram, S. (2015). Becoming Jane: The Making and Unmaking of Hanford's Nuclear Body. *Environment and Planning D: Society and Space*, 33(5), pp. 796–812.

Creager, A. (2015). *Life Atomic: A History of Radioisotopes in Science and Medicine*. Chicago: University of Chicago Press.

Feser, A. (2019). *Reproducing Photochemical Life in the Imaging Capital of the World*. PhD thesis, University of Chicago.

Fortun, K. (2012). Ethnography in Late Industrialism. *Cultural Anthropology*, 27(3), pp. 446–464.

Gallagher, C. (1993). *America Ground Zero: The Secret Nuclear War*. Cambridge, MA: MIT Press.

Hamilton, K., and O'Gorman, N. (2018). *Lookout America!: The Secret Hollywood Studio at the Heart of the Cold War*. Hanover, NH: Dartmouth College Press.

Hecht, G. (2014). *Being Nuclear: Africans and the Global Uranium Trade*. Cambridge, MA: MIT Press.

Hotakainen, R., Wise, L., Matt, F., and Ehlinger, S. (2015). *Irradiated: The Hidden Legacy of 70 Years of Atomic Weaponry*. Washington, DC: McClatchyDC. Available at http://media.mcclatchydc.com/static/features/irradiated/ [Accessed June 10, 2021].

Kuran, P. (2006). *How to Photograph an Atomic Bomb*. Santa Clarita, CA: VCE.

Lindee, M. S. (1997). *Suffering Made Real: American Science and the Survivors at Hiroshima*. Chicago: University of Chicago Press.

Masco, J. (2006). *The Nuclear Borderlands: The Manhattan Project in Post-Cold War New Mexico*. Princeton, NJ: Princeton University Press.

Masco, J. (2008). Target Audience. *The Bulletin of the Atomic Scientists*, 64(3), pp. 23–31.

Masco, J. (2014). *The Theater of Operations: National Security Affect from the Cold War to the War on Terror*. Durham, NC: Duke University Press.

Masco, J. (2020). *The Future of Fallout, and Other Episodes in Radioactive World-Making*. Durham, NC: Duke University Press.

Murphy, M. (2017). Alterlife and Decolonial Chemical Relations. *Cultural Anthropology*, 32(4), pp. 494–503.

National Research Council. (2006). *Health Risks from Exposure to Low Levels of Ionizing Radiation: BEIR VII Phase 2*. Washington, DC: National Academies Press.

Nixon, R. (2011). *Slow Violence and the Environmentalism of the Poor*. Cambridge, MA: Harvard University Press.

Oakes, G. (1994). *The Imaginary War: Civil Defense and American Cold War Culture*. New York: Oxford University Press.

Parikka, J. (2015). *A Geology of Media*. Minneapolis: Minnesota University Press.

Petryna, A. (2003). *Life Exposed: Biological Citizens after Chernobyl*. Princeton, NJ: Princeton University Press.

Shapiro, N. (2015). Attuning to the Chemosphere: Domestic Formaldehyde, Bodily Reasoning and the Chemical Sublime. *Cultural Anthropology*, 30(3), pp. 368–393.

Tsing, A. Lowenhaupt, Swanson, H., Gan, E. and Bubandt, N., eds. (2017). *Arts of Living on a Damaged Planet*. Minneapolis: University of Minnesota Press.

Waters, C. et al. (2016). The Anthropocene Is Functionally and Stratigraphically Distinct from the Holocene. *Science*, 351(6269), pp. 137–147.

Wills, G. (2010). *Bomb Power: The Modern Presidency and the National Security State*. New York: Penguin.

3 Constructing world order: mobilising tropes of gender, pathology and race to frame US non-proliferation policy

John Krige

> Proponents of an "internationalist" approach envision a world in which *civilized* nations agree on strong norms against the development, acquisition, production, threat, or use of weapons of mass destruction, possibly excepting some residual nuclear capability in the nuclear weapon states. States unwilling to subscribe to these norms, or found to be violating them, would be considered by the others as *pariahs*.
> —Office of Technology Assessment report (US Congress, Office of Technology Assessment, 1993: 30; italics added)

> The bombs that devastated Hiroshima and flattened Nagasaki were not hatched by the "unstable countries" and the "irresponsible minds" of the Third World.
> —Pakistani President Ghulam Ishaq Khan to nuclear scientists and engineers (US Congress, Office of Technology Assessment, 1993: 1, fn. 1)[1]

The successful field-tests of nuclear weapons in Japan in 1945 made for a quantum leap in the construction and consolidation of American global power across the historical arc of the twentieth century. Early efforts to maintain a monopoly over the bomb were, however, shattered by the first Soviet test of a fission weapon in August 1949 (Herken, 1988). The dream of near-unlimited power to shape an American-led world order was pruned back to the pragmatic pursuit of a preponderance of power vis-à-vis friend and foe alike. The global system was reimagined around a two-dimensional strategy premised on the United States maintaining a comparative technological advantage, most notably in the development and deployment of nuclear weapons (Friedberg, 2000). The Cold War confrontation with a rival superpower from a position of nuclear superiority was complemented by collaboration with European allies in an Atlantic community that sheltered under the US nuclear umbrella.

The United States' willingness to take on the "burden of defense" of the free world was nourished by a growing communist threat: the consolidation

DOI: 10.4324/9781003227472-3

Constructing world order 67

of Stalinist control over his "satellite" states in Europe in the late 1940s, the "loss" of China in October 1949 and the outbreak of the Korean war in June 1950. In the NSC-68 paper, Paul Nitze warned the State Department's Policy and Planning Staff in April 1950 that the US was confronted by an enemy that, "unlike previous aspirants to hegemony, is animated by a new fanatic faith, antithetical to our own and seeks to impose its absolute authority over the rest of the world." The implications were all that more dangerous because, "with the development of increasingly terrifying weapons of mass destruction every individual faces the ever-present possibility of annihilation should the conflict enter the phase of total war."[2] The Republic if not civilisation itself was in danger. Soviet communism coupled with Soviet nuclear weapons did not only pose a threat to life and property, but it also posed a threat to everything that America stood for.

The origins of the Cold War remain contested among diplomatic historians. One strand in that debate is particularly interesting here. It is an approach that embeds the "construction" of the Soviet threat, and the justification for the massive re-engineering of American society and of world order to meet that threat, in historically rooted cultural assumptions of US exceptionalism. For Walter Hixon, a leading proponent of this school of thought, US "foreign policy flows from the cultural hegemony affirming "America" is a manly, racially superior and providentially destined beacon of liberty, a country which possesses a special right to exert power in the world" (Hixson, 2002: 1). Joseph Nye, former Dean of the Kennedy School of Government at Harvard University, has taught us that power can be soft (i.e., exercised through the attraction of a nation's education or culture) or hard, as expressed in force (Nye, 2004). Madeleine Albright, President Bill Clinton's Secretary of State from 1997 to 2001, did not hesitate to advocate the use of the latter, not as a means to an end, but because it was constitutive of who "we are." As she put it in a television interview in 1998, "If we have to use force, it is because we are America, we are the indispensable nation. We stand tall and we see further than other countries into the future" (Albright, 2013: 18–19). National identity predicated on American exceptionalism, on its capacity to "see further than others," justifies the use of force as a manly virtue that uses nuclear weapons to express "hard power," weapons that—in the words of one National Security Council advisor—are "irresistible" for defense intellectuals, "because you get more bang for the buck," particularly when "releasing 70 to 80 percent of our megatonnage in one orgasmic whump" (Cohn, 1987: 693).

It is easy to dismiss this phrasing of American identity as little more than a sleight of hand—as a biased, overly simplistic, highly selective conceptualisation of the complex cultural formation that is "America" and its expression in the permanently contested field of foreign relations. It becomes harder to dismiss when we search for the elements that

68 John Krige

constitute something as elusive as "national identity" in the language and behavior of US leaders and senior policymakers in moments when their imagined futures are challenged by *others*. Hixon argues that the manly, racially superior values enshrined in US exceptionalism are expressed by leaders in moments of "psychic crisis." Such crises, I suggest, infuse attempts to construct a world order stabilsed by American technological superiority in nuclear weapons. As early as 1956, John Foster Dulles, President Dwight D. Eisenhower's Secretary of State, was emphasizing to the German Minister for Atomic Affairs that it was "appalling to contemplate a multiplicity of uncontrolled national atomic developments leading to multiplying atomic weapons programs" (Krige, 2016: 1). John F. Kennedy raised the stakes soon after he took office in 1961. Kennedy "was haunted by the feeling that by 1970, unless we are successful (in curbing proliferation), there may be ten nuclear powers instead of four, and by 1975, fifteen or twenty" (what became known as the Nth country problem) (Gavin, 2012: 7).

Indeed, it is striking that US policymakers were, from the late 1950s on, entrapped in what Benoit Pelopidas describes as a "nuclear straitjacket," an attitude that "frames the requirements of national security as a binary choice between nuclear security guarantees from an ally and the quest for an independent nuclear deterrent" (Pelopidas, 2015: 73). US policymakers were "appalled," even "haunted" by what Jayita Sarkar calls "a sort of Murphy's Law of 'nuclear fatalism': if a country can build nuclear weapons, then it most certainly will" (Pelopidas, 2011: 73; Sarkar, 2013). Deep-rooted fears of losing the control over a world order in which Allied security was "guaranteed" by the United States brought to the surface attitudes and values that were rarely shown but were taken for granted among the elite—at least, to judge by the ease with which they expressed them in verbal and written communications during moments of "psychic crisis." By mobilizing tropes of gender, race and pathology to dismiss the nuclear aspirations of others, US policymakers sought to justify denying them nuclear weapons that threatened to destabilise an American-led regime of world order to contain the Soviet threat.

The reactions to their exceptionalist claims were intense because the stakes were high, and the challenge was formidable. "One is nuclear or one is negligible." Thus did a French Minister of Defense define the significance of nuclear weapons in 1962. They promised to restore some of France's past grandeur, now tarnished by its decaying colonial rule. The lure of nuclear weapons was not merely strategic. They were also markers of modernity, protectors of national sovereignty, potent symbols of national pride and desirable luxury fetish commodities (Biswas, 2014). In 1965 Pakistani Prime Minister Zulfiqar Ali Bhutto promised that his people would "eat grass and leaves" to pay for a nuclear bomb should India build one first.[3] The first of five of Pakistani nuclear tests on May 28, 1998—undertaken in response to Indian tests earlier that

Constructing world order 69

month—led to enthusiastic street celebrations throughout the country. The date was henceforth celebrated annually as the Day of Greatness and National Science Day. The leaders of the technical project claimed that it had "boosted the morale of the Pakistani nation by giving it an honorable position in the nuclear world."[4] Reactions abroad included condemnation by the European Union and economic sanctions by the United States, Japan and the International Monetary Fund. US negotiators tried to get Pakistan to sign the Comprehensive Nuclear-Test-Ban Treaty and the Treaty on the Non-Proliferation of Nuclear Weapons. They failed.

The proliferation of populist conceptions of national identity in many countries, built on racist, xenophobic conceptions of the "other," and the physical violence it legitimates, is a stark reminder of the power of discourse to shape relations between "us" and "them." We are all aware of the racist Orientalism of the high colonial period, in which the Orient was presented as the mirror image of the West: "we" are rational and disciplined, "they" are impulsive and emotional; "we" are modern and progressive, "they" are slaves to traditional practices and routines; "we" are compassionate and honest, "they" are treacherous and devious. Such representations do not merely drive discourse; they legitimate interventionist policies in the name of maintaining a "civilised" world order and bringing to heel the irrepressible forces of an irrational other. They subtend the exercise of power to maintain a hierarchical relationship of putative supremacy between the "advanced" West and the "backward" rest. What matters for us here is that the structure of the non-proliferation regime constructed after World War II was also defined by these binaries (Abraham, 2016; Biswas, 2014; Costigliola, 1997; Gusterson, 1999; Walker, 2000; 2012). Such stark divisions provided a dominant mode of discourse for dealing with the nuclear ambitions of some developed and most developing countries. They were not only enshrined in the 1968 Treaty on the Non-Proliferation of Nuclear Weapons that formally restricted nuclear weapons to the five countries that already had them at the time (the United States, the USSR, the UK, France, and the PRC)—what India characterised as a system of "nuclear apartheid." They were also drawn upon by the Washington policy-making elite to make sense of the nuclear ambitions of some of their Western allies, especially those that did not want to toe the Washington line. The lens provided by contrasting the rational and responsible "us" with the emotive and unpredictable "them" did not "determine" US foreign policy in nuclear matters. It was rather a subterranean resource to be drawn on at times of "psychic crisis," a shared language that helped make sense of "their" behavior and how to deal with it.

I must stress that, in criticizing US policymakers for dismissing the nuclear aspirations of others in demeaning terms, I am not trying to turn their language against them or justify the acquisition of nuclear weapons by the countries they have othered. Rather I want to suggest that this

70   *John Krige*

language actually provokes the proliferation that Washington wants to curb. The neo-colonial power relations embedded in this rhetoric fosters a resentful nationalism that can find expression in the active pursuit of nuclear weapons by nuclear have-nots eager to re-establish an equilibrium with the nuclear haves. It produces the backlash described in the case of Pakistan. It drove the resentment of Libyan President Muammar Ghadafi when he said that: "We should be like the Chinese—poor and riding donkeys, but respected and possessing an atomic bomb" (Maddock, 2010: 8). It leads the people of Iran, angered by Washington's "incendiary rhetoric" to argue that "as a great civilisation with a long history, Iran has a right to acquire a nuclear capability" (Takeyh, 2006: 58). If having nuclear weapons is defined as a marker of "civilisation" and a condition for being "respected" by nuclear weapons states, it is but a short step for non-nuclear weapons states to seek them.

Late in the 1950s, the French Defense Minister told *Le Monde* that "it is impossible for France to give up the bomb.... It would give up its rank of world power" (Vaïsse, 2007). This "rank" went along with branding "Third World" countries that aspired to it as inferior and untrustworthy. The hierarchical power relationships that are intrinsic to a nuclear-based world order will only be dismantled when the leading nuclear weapons states stand by the terms of the Treaty on the Non-Proliferation of Nuclear Weapons that many of them designed and fulfill their commitments to take serious steps toward disarmament. Just the opposite is happening.

Dealing with proliferation in Europe

During the 1950s, the Eisenhower administration actively promoted nuclear power for civilian purposes. The initiative aimed to counter the negative political fallout caused by the dispersal of radioactive debris throughout the weapons test grounds in the Pacific, and indeed throughout the globe. In his December 1953 "Atoms for Peace" speech before the UN General Assembly, Eisenhower offered to make the fissile material needed for research and power reactors available to friendly countries. By the end of 1960, shortly before he left office, the US Atomic Energy Commission had signed no fewer than 37 bilateral agreements with "friendly" countries including Argentina and Vietnam, Brazil and Cuba, Iran and Israel, and South Africa and Spain. Neither India nor Pakistan was on the list.

This policy was beset with proliferation risks from the get-go: indeed, what Itty Abraham calls the "ambiguity" of nuclear programs—particularly the dual-use, civilian/military dichotomy of so much nuclear technology—destabilised the American-led nuclear world order from the dawn of the nuclear age (Abraham, 2016; Hecht, 2006). Its foundations were further eroded by the conflict of interest between states wanting to control the flow of nuclear materials and knowledge, and capitalist business interests, wanting to exploit the putative commercial opportunities of nuclear power.

To resolve this contradiction, each bilateral agreement came with an elaborate, built-in system of safeguards and inspections. Recipients of American nuclear fuel were explicitly forbidden from diverting this fissile material, as well as any nuclear technology or knowledge provided by western powers, to military purposes.

Proliferation fears did not completely preclude nuclear sharing with allies. Throughout the 1950s, Eisenhower battled against a recalcitrant Congress to share nuclear weapons technology with the British. Congressional arguments that London was lax on security and that nuclear sharing legitimated undesirable proliferation were sidelined by the Sputnik shock, however. Eisenhower argued that the United States was now fighting a total Cold War. To counter the Soviet threat, the United States had to engage more substantially with its technologically advanced allies. The highly restrictive Atomic Energy Act of 1946 was amended in 1958 to allow for cooperation with countries that had made "substantive progress" with their weapons programs; the language was specifically framed to open the floodgates of nuclear knowledge sharing with the UK but not with France (Baylis, 2001).

Although the United States was willing to provide some nuclear fuel to France, it did all it could to thwart the country from obtaining an effective nuclear weapon.[5] This was partly because the French, and President de Gaulle in particular, were simply not prepared to follow the American line "blindly," as one French minister explained. The difference with Britain—and the difference in the US's approach to nuclear sharing—was made clear in an internal memo to George Ball, Undersecretary of State in the Kennedy administration:

> The real reason we do not share with the French is that we do not trust them—as we do the British. We are fearful that they will trigger us into a nuclear war, since they, unlike the British, follow a foreign policy of their own making... What control has our cooperation with the British given us as regards UK use? The basic answer of course is that when we and the UK differ the British align themselves with us. When we and the French differ, the French go their own way.[6]

This French penchant for going their own way reinforced US stereotypes about the country and its leaders being driven by irrational and childish fears, in contrast with the more level-headed and cooperative British. Diplomatic historian Frank Costigliola has analyzed these attitudes in some depth. "With varying and probably unknowable degrees of intentionality," he writes, "US officials used language that depicted

72   John Krige

difficult allies as beings that were in some way diminished from the norm of a healthy heterosexual male: sick patients, hysterical women, naive children, emasculated men" (Costigliola, 1997).

This was made evident in US disappointment over the *Assemblée nationale's* refusal to ratify the convention for a European Defense Community (EDC) in August 1954. The plans for the EDC required each member state, France and Germany in particular, to relinquish national sovereignty over the deployment of their armed forces. The EDC was appealing to its advocates because it abolished national armies, integrating them into a supranational structure intended to contain German militarism and nationalism. It was "acceptable" to Bonn, but anathema to Paris: "if the US found military integration such a good idea," mused French leader Charles de Gaulle, "why does she not merge with Mexico and Canada and [the] South American countries." French resistance to the EDC plan was parsed as "wayward, unreflecting, illogical," as symptoms of "high fever" in the "weak sister" of the Western alliance, which needed "shock treatment" and "sound therapy." It was symptomatic of French "delusions of grandeur," of de Gaulle's tendency to "punch above his weight."

Many in the United States never could accept that there were rational grounds for France's quest for autonomy, for de Gaulle's determination to secure his sovereignty over key areas of national policy like defense, and for his realpolitik approach to the strategic balance of power. "Would the United States risk New York to save Paris," he liked to ask, rhetorically insisting that France must take control of its own defense and develop a nuclear strike force able to "tear the arm off the Russian bear" (Krige, 2016). Bob Schaetzel of the US State Department simply could not see it: "The fundamental point," he wrote, "is that the French are motivated by a desire to recover status in the world which they feel, either rightly or wrongly, is a function of nuclear weapons production capability" (Krige, 2008). Security could not possibly be a dominant French concern; status, the search for grandeur was what mattered, and those misguided French believed that that was only possible if the country had nuclear weapons.

Note that the French government had not yet taken the decision to embark on a weapons program when Schaetzel wrote this passage. The French President, Guy Mollet, was not even in favor of building one. For Schaetzel, it was enough that the French had a robust civilian nuclear program and that some of its military and political figures wanted to build a bomb: if they could, they would, he surmised. Schaetzel framed a policy to cripple any such initiative. Realizing that France's nuclear resources (money, trained manpower, industrial capacity) were strained at the time, the United States strongly encouraged France to join a new supranational organisation called Euratom, alongside the other members of the Six that established the European Economic Community in 1958. Joining meant that Paris would devote the limited resources it had to a civilian European nuclear power program rather than to nuclear weapon. The United States would offer material aid and financial support to a program that constrained the French in a non-military atomic energy organisation, snuffing out their quest for an independent nuclear deterrent. As Schaetzel explained, to deal with France's irrational urge for weaponry, "our basic strategy is not to hit the French directly but rather to envelop them." Committing their resources to a regional program in Euratom "should make increasingly difficult the disengagement of the scientists and technical people from one country to work on separate, national military projects." A major civilian nuclear power program would also "tax to the utmost the industrial and technical resources of the Six nations," possibly stalling all the members' weapons programs (Krige, 2008).

The French were sometimes aware of US efforts to parse their behavior in gendered and pathological terms so as to trivialise their concerns. In fact, they filed an official complaint about a 1953 editorial in *Life* magazine that portrayed the actions of the French government as a bedroom farce, a stage-show complete with a can-can chorus oblivious to the Cold War conflicts on their own continent (Costigliola, 1997). More often than not, though, rather than challenging the gendering of their behavior, the French deployed tropes of colonial subordination against other countries to (successfully) strike a favorable chord with US authorities.

Washington's policy-making elite of the 1950s had no monopoly on the mostly unspoken, yet systematic assumption of racial superiority to justify US exceptionalism. European powers could do so too. One striking case in point is the European demands that Euratom's use of nuclear fissile material provided by the US Atomic Energy Commission be exempt from external inspection to ensure that it was used exclusively for civilian purposes (i.e., the demand for self-inspection).

> As Schaetzel explained, the Europeans felt they should be on a par with the United States, the United Kingdom, and the Soviet Union, none of which was obliged to allow international inspectors to nose around their nuclear installations. Anything else would be demeaning.

A primary motivation of all the European communities has been to attain a position of political and economic equality with the United States and the Soviet Union. In view of this driving force any arrangement which places any of the communities in a subordinate or what might be called a "colonial" status vis-à-vis the US or particularly the UK is incompatible with this primary objective of the Europeans and therefore unacceptable to them (Hecht, 1998; 2012; Krige, 2008; 2016; Pelopidas, 2012).

For the Six member states of Euratom, self-inspection was at once an affirmation of regional sovereignty, a sign of the esteem in which the United States held supranational institutions like its own, and a marker which differentiated Europe from the rest of the non- or not-yet nuclear

74   John Krige

powers. It was of course ironic that, as one State Department official pointed out, the United States had lectured under-developed countries only a few months earlier at the UN on the "overriding necessity of international verification" of their civil nuclear programs. The British trenchantly surmised that allowing Euratom self-inspection "would be used by the Soviets to confirm their propaganda thesis that major western powers draw a distinction in practice between white, colonial states of Western Europe (which as here are allowed to police themselves) and colored countries of the near East, Africa and Asia, which cannot be trusted to do so and must be subjected to internal inspection and controls which actually are a subtle means of maintaining colonial domination and penetration of industrial secrets".

It was not propaganda, of course. The Soviets had touched a raw nerve. Technological rivalry lay at the core of the early Cold War, with nations measuring their status as great powers along an axis with space programs and nuclear capabilities at the top of the scale. Independent access to space was, as General Aubinière recognised, an obligatory complement to an independent nuclear weapons program. Aubinière, who piloted France's missile program, was more self-conscious than most regarding the implications of colonial power of which he was an instrument—the French, after all, tested their bombs and rockets in Algeria in the early 1960s (Osseo-Asare, 2019). For Aubinière, "space technology touches so many disciplines that to neglect it would signify for our peoples, formerly masters of the world, a decadence and underdevelopment and an unacceptable economic servitude, no matter whence it comes" (Krige, 2014: 233). The new "masters of the world" did not quite see it that way. For Eisenhower, the pursuit of an independent nuclear deterrent by France was symptomatic of de Gaulle's "Messiah complex, picturing himself as a cross between Napoleon and Joan of Arc" (Maddock, 2010: 142). Alternatively arrogant and victimised, effeminate and deluded, emotional and irrational, countries whose nuclear policies were driven by nationalism or shaped by non-alignment were an ever-present thorn in the side of Washington. In this context, it's no wonder that, as Jayita Sarkar has shown, France and India worked comfortably together, sharing space and nuclear knowledge and technology denied them by the self-styled responsible and rational global hegemon for fear that they would drag the world into Armageddon (Sarkar and Bouyssou, 2014; Sarkar, 2015).

The "psychic crises" precipitated by destabilizing moments in the nuclear relationships between the United States and European countries were resolved in Washington by dismissing the "other" as irrational, prey to the uncontrolled excesses of female behavior, amplified by racial tropes. In fact, as the British pointed out as regards Euratom's demand for self-inspection, the distinction between "white colonial states" and "colored countries" offered a *shared* language to manage anxieties in

Constructing world order 75

Washington and in Paris as policymakers struggled to sustain hierarchical structures of power in a rapidly decolonising world.

Devising policies to deal with proliferation in "Developing Countries"

On October 16, 1964, the People's Republic of China (PRC) successfully tested its first atomic device in an underground explosion. Kennedy and his National Security Adviser McGeorge Bundy had been willing to consider a pre-emptive strike on the Chinese nuclear complex before it matured. They also thought of working along with Soviet leader Nikita Khrushchev to "Strangle the baby in the cradle" (Burr and Richelson, 2000). Kennedy's death and Khrushchev's fall from power pre-empted this option.

The Johnson Administration approached the test in more measured terms. They concluded that it posed no immediate security threat to the region or to the United States itself but could not forbear describing people at the site of the PRC test as celebrating like savages "in some sort of orgiastic, ritual sort of way" (Maddock, 2010: 271). Anticipating an "inevitable" domino effect, Johnson quickly convened a high-level committee chaired by Wall Street lawyer and former Deputy Secretary of Defense, Roswell Gilpatric, to examine all aspects of US proliferation policy and assess the likely effects of China's test on international relations. Liberal use was made of racial tropes to emphasise the dangers of irrational forces overwhelming the carefully crafted system of world order. Staff papers warned that Beijing's bomb could create a "widespread feeling that nuclear weapons, now in the hands of the yellow man, can be in the hands of brown and black men. This attitude may reverberate back to the white countries and speed up spread among them" (a reference to West Germans' argument that, if "colored" peoples could do so, they too had the right to produce nuclear weapons). And who knew where the downward spiral would end as nuclear technology became better understood and simplified? Strategist Hermann Kahn warned in 1961 that, before the decade was out, with the kind of technology at hand, "it may literally turn out that a Hottentot, an educated and technical Hottentot it is true, would be able to make bombs" (Maddock, 2010: 7). An American official wondered in 1959 why there was any point in buying an American 50KW research reactor "for pygmies" at the University of Lovanium in what was then the Belgian Congo (Osseo-Asare, 2019: 81). Eisenhower had anticipated this terrifying scenario. It was folly to equip a "savage" foe with nuclear weapons. Deterrence only worked when both sides viewed the nuclear dilemma responsibly and rationally. Thus Asian, African and Latin American states that lacked the full capacity to make reasoned judgments could not be trusted with the ultimate weapon (Maddock, 2010).

76   *John Krige*

The proliferation of nuclear weapons beyond the responsible industrialised countries of the global North could also have dramatic economic consequences. A staff member working on the Gilpatric report surmised that the Chinese explosion might encourage the dispossessed to demand a redistribution of wealth around the globe, so upsetting the post-colonial world order. As the draft paper put it, "any major trend of nuclear capabilities among the populous, non-white nations of the earth would greatly strengthen their hands in attempting to gain an even greater share of the earth's wealth and opportunity" (Maddock, 2010: 242). Curbing nuclear proliferation was imperative not only to stop the "Third World" flexing its muscles but also to stop impoverished nations harboring any illusions about the redistribution of global wealth to their advantage.

The US State Department moved quickly to deal with the possible impact of the Chinese test on the region. Several years prior, it had suggested that, to offset the loss of prestige felt by India if China "beat it to the [nuclear] punch," it might be desirable for the US government to assist the Indian nuclear program. This move was vetoed at once by Secretary of State Dean Rusk who objected that it "would start us down a jungle path" (into the dangerous wilds populated by Third World savages?), "from which I see no exit." Countries like India, which pursued what John Foster Dulles called an "immoral" policy of non-alignment, were managed by policymakers who displayed what Eisenhower called a "feminine hypersensitiveness" and an "emotional" instability (Maddock, 2010: 89). It was essential to keep them well away from nuclear weapons. Now, with the Chinese test a *fait accompli*, the dread that India would seek a bomb had to be cashed in pro-active policies to deal with regional instability. Homi Bhabha, who had spent 20 years building a major nuclear program in the country, called for help with an accelerated effort to compensate for the tilt toward Beijing. Challenging government policy committed to peaceful use of nuclear technology, he used unrealistic data for both the cost and time to completion to argue that a bomb could be built in as little as 18 months, with American help. His pleas fell on deaf ears, and his energetic pursuit of the nuclear weapons path came to an abrupt halt with his untimely death in 1966 (Perkovich, 1999).

Vikram Sarabhia proposed an alternative solution. Where Bhabha only had his nuclear cards to play, Sarabhai could capitalise on his prior links with NASA to secure US support for an advanced Indian space program. Sarabhai was firmly convinced that the technological infrastructure required for a space program would provide invaluable knowledge and industrial experiences furthering the overall development and modernisation of India. In a probably apocryphal remark, he is said to have dismissed charges that a poor country like India could not afford a space program: India needed a space program *precisely because* it was poor. In the early 1960s, Sarabhia had collaborated with NASA to establish a sounding rocket range at Thumba, in the state of Kerala, under the auspices of the UN (Sounding rockets rise vertically to a height of about 150 miles and are used to probe the properties of the upper atmosphere and ionosphere). Now he would exploit American fears that India would embark on a nuclear weapons program to secure support for a major space effort. As he put it in a message to the US State Department in October 1966, "there was some pressure within India to build a nuclear bomb, and to deflect this pressure India needed to do something else to demonstrate an advanced scientific capability" (Krige, 2016: 85). NASA Administrator James Webb picked up the ball, writing to Undersecretary of State for Political Affairs, U. Alexis Johnson. Through cooperation with India on space projects, Webb suggested, "some Indian energies might also be diverted from concern with nuclear weapons development, the more so perhaps as the success of [such a program] contributed to India's prestige in Asia" (Krige, 2016: 85).

The correlation between the conquest of space and the performance of national identity and prestige in the 1960s was spelled out by Kennedy's Defense Secretary, Robert McNamara. McNamara believed that

> All large scale space programs require the mobilization of resources on a national scale. They require the development and successful application of the most advanced technologies. Dramatic achievements in space therefore symbolize the technological power and organizing capacity of a nation. It is for reasons such as these that major achievements in space contribute to national prestige. (Krige, 2016: 84)

To US officials, it seemed that India was less concerned about security than about bolstering its image as a modern nation in the eyes of its own people, of "Third World" partners, and as leader of the non-aligned movement. From this perspective, nuclear and space programs were interchangeable: by encouraging the latter at the expense of the former, perhaps the United States might help secure India's status as a democratic model of a modernizing nation and channel its "energies" down non-bellicose paths.

Matters proved more complex. Sarabhai was determined not to become dependent on foreign suppliers for key nuclear technologies. An "indigenous" program would enable India to escape a neo-colonial technological trap. At the same time, he realised that rocket launchers used in space programs bore a family resemblance to missiles: there was a dual-use dimension to both the key technologies for nuclear power and space exploration that limited the kind of help the US could provide. Inevitably, Sarabhai's request for a license to build a highly reliable American Scout rocket as a technological "substitute" that would divert

78   John Krige

Indian "energies" away from nuclear weapons was rejected (Krige et al., 2013). The United States assumed that, by sharing key dual-use technologies with a foreign government, it would catalyze the inevitable rush to develop a nuclear weapon and missile delivery system.

The very same mindset that shaped US relations with "brown men" informed their dealings with "yellow men." Japan (like Germany) was forbidden to develop nuclear weapons by the terms of the post-war agreements devised by its victors. In September 1966, the Arms Control and Disarmament Agency noted that "A significant program of space cooperation directed toward enhancing Japan's space capabilities can have beneficial nuclear non-proliferation activities by bolstering her prestige, demonstrating her worldwide and regional scientific prowess and affirming US involvement with that nation" (Krige, 2016: 85). Space cooperation was broadly favored in Japan, where public opinion was deeply hostile to nuclear weapons, if not to nuclear power. A dispatch from Tokyo to Washington in November 1964, shortly after the PRC's test, indicated that the Japanese "Prime Minister would like very much to see a satellite orbited by Japan as a counter to Beijing's achievement." The argument was repeated two years later by Yasuhiro Nakasone, a member of the Japanese Diet and a space enthusiast: "Advanced nations today are symbolized by science and technology, particularly atomic energy and space development. ... If China should launch an artificial satellite into space ahead of us," he continued, "the sense of hopelessness of the Japanese will be so great that no one has the heart to see it" (Krige, 2016: 85).

India conducted what it defined as an underground PNE of its own in May 1974 (Perkovich, 1999). In doing so, it formally violated no international treaties. Its aims, it claimed, were those that had animated peaceful underground explosions ever since Edward Teller had loudly promoted their benefits for moving massive amounts of earth quickly and efficiently. All the same, most commentators saw it as an inexorable step on the road to developing an independent nuclear deterrent. In a flight of fancy fueled by "worst-case" imaginings, a secret NATO assessment of the state of India's nuclear program suggested at the time that the "Indians may consider installing nuclear devices at strategic points near their border with China" so achieving a strike capability that required "little further development of the device exploded" and no delivery system (Sarkar, 2013: 325). A few months later, US Secretary of State, Henry Kissinger, attempted to discredit Indian claims to having detonated a peaceful nuclear explosion (PNE) by claiming that, unlike the Americans, their scientists and technical personnel were not competent to control the chain reaction in the reactor's core with sufficient precision to draw a clear line between a PNE and a bomb test (Sarkar, 2013). India *had* the bomb, he insisted, and it was foolish or deceitful to deny that fact.

Concluding remarks

> We're going to do it. I'm going to destroy the goddam country, believe me. I mean destroy it if necessary.... By a nuclear weapon, I mean that we will bomb the living bejeezus out of North Vietnam.... A nuclear bomb, does that bother you? ...I just want you to think big, Henry, for Christ's sake.
>
> —Nixon-Kissinger exchange transcript, around midnight
> April 15, 1972 (Gavin, 2012: 116).

> If we wanted to fight a war in Afghanistan and win it, I could win that war in a week. I just don't want to kill 10 million people. Does that make sense to you? I don't want to kill 10 million people. I have plans on Afghanistan that, if I wanted to win that war, Afghanistan would be wiped off the face of the Earth. It would be gone. It would be over in—literally, in 10 days. And I don't want to do—I don't want to go that route.
>
> —Donald Trump, speaking in the Oval Office with
> Pakistani President Imran Khan beside him, July 22, 2019.[7]

This chapter draws on a small but rich body of literature that highlights a persistent characterisation of those who challenged or flaunted "rational" American nuclear policy as infantile, effeminate, racially inferior or pathological—in short, irrational and irresponsible. It draws on cultural analyses of deep currents that shape US foreign policy, currents that I have suggested surface at times of "psychic crisis." They are called upon whenever US policymakers (and not only they), recognizing the lethal power of nuclear weapons and, seeking to build a world order under American leadership to control their proliferation, are challenged by states that refuse to be bound by their norms.

For the first two decades of the Cold War, US policymakers sought to discredit and delegitimate those governments that did not align with the broad lines of American foreign policy. An attempt was made to stabilise the situation with the signature of the (discriminatory) Non-proliferation Treaty in 1968 and the later establishment of a number of multilateral organisations to manage the global diffusion of chemical, biological, and nuclear weapons. The discursive field shifted with the fall of the Berlin wall. The anti-communist struggle gave way to the threat from "rogue states." The first Gulf War (1990–1991) forced Western powers to acknowledge that "Iraq had successfully evaded the provision of virtually every extant non-proliferation regime. Iraq had succeeded in testing and weaponizing both chemical and biological weapons, improving the range of its Scud missiles, and undertaking a covert nuclear weapons development program."[8] President George H.W. Bush made controlling the proliferation of WMDs the centerpiece of his new grand strategy for the

80   John Krige

United States (Cupitt, 2000). A new binary system was constructed to distinguish between those who respected "civilised" norms and the "pariahs" who violated them, notably Iran, Iraq, Libya and North Korea.

It would be idle to think that we have moved beyond these discursive registers today. They are revealed in the systemic racism that is woven into the structural fabric of American and West European systems and societies and manifested in spontaneous expressions of quotidian White privilege. They have taken hold in nationalist right-wing movements. They are unashamedly used by dictatorial leaders in the ascendancy all over the globe. The people of the United Kingdom elected as their Prime Minister a man known for his mendacity, who is openly homophobic, who speaks of women as "fickle" and "collapsing with emotions," of Black children as "piccaninnies" with "watermelon smiles," and of Muslim women in burqas as "letter boxes" dressed like bank robbers.[9] Boris Johnson imagines transforming Britain into Singapore on the Thames, and hoped for help from an American president who made unabashed use of gender, race and pathology to stigmatise not only those who disagreed with him but entire communities of American citizens and non-White foreign nationals. Together with Russia's Vladimir Putin, Donald Trump and Boris Johnson spread divisive rhetoric to support racist ideologues in France and in Italy, and to destroy the European Union from within. Far from being in decline, the tropes of gender, race and pathology that legitimated the post-war construction of a regime of nuclear apartheid are vibrant and viral at the national and the international levels, whether they are leveraged to justify building border walls to keep invading "rapists" and "killers" from Mexico out of the United States or to justify punitive international measures against "rogue states" (Brown, 2010).

The whiff of war is still in the air, notwithstanding renewed efforts to de-escalate tensions in the Middle East. "To Stop Iran's Bomb, Bomb Iran," wrote John Bolton in *The New York Times* on March 26, 2015 (Bolton would serve as Trump's National Security Adviser from 2018 to 2019). Bolton dismissed the Obama Administration's approach to foreign policy, which at the time included largely invisible efforts like attacking the Iranian enrichment program with a computer virus (Stuxnet) that sent its centrifuges spinning out of control (with little or no blowback from the international community). Bolton wrote that the United States did not need "palpable proof, like a nuclear test," for him to state categorically that "Iran's steady progress toward nuclear weapons has long been evident" and that allowing it to continue without aggressive intervention would trigger a nuclear arms race in the Middle East.

Tensions with North Korea also run high. Trump called Kim Jong-un a "maniac" and a "madman." In his first address to the UN General Assembly in 2017, the new President was unambiguous: "The United States has great strength and patience, but if it is forced to defend itself or its allies, we will have no choice but to totally destroy North Korea.

Rocket Man [Kim Jong-un] is on a suicide mission for himself and for his regime." When the North Korean leader warned that he had a nuclear button on his desk, controlling missiles that could strike the American mainland, Trump famously tweeted in reply: "I too have a Nuclear Button, but it is a much bigger & more powerful one than his, and my Button works!" This affirmation of male superiority and dominance using barely concealed phallic imagery resonates with the everyday discourse "in the rational world of defense intellectuals" described by Carol Cohn (1987). It was here directed against a putatively irrational Asian "other" whose elimination from the face of the Earth would be justified by liberating the surviving citizens of "his depleted and food starved regime" from the tyranny of a "bad dude."

Trump also outlined his plan for dealing with ISIS/Daesh at several political rallies: "bomb the shit out of them." At his direction and just three months into his presidency, on April 14, 2017, he authorised the use of a single MOAB (the so-called Mother-of-all-Bombs) to demolish a complex of tunnels in Afghanistan. With an explosive power equivalent to 11 metric tons of TNT, this 30-foot-long, 21,600-pound, GPS-guided munition was the largest non-nuclear bomb ever used in combat. Estimates put ISIS militant casualties somewhere between 30 and 100. The United States not only has biggest nuclear button in the world, but it also has the biggest non-nuclear bomb in the world.

Shortly before he took office Trump promised to "strengthen and expand" the US's nuclear capability in order to "outmatch" and "outlast" any competitors in a nuclear arms race. The administration's Nuclear Posture Review, released during the election cycle in February 2016, not only vowed to maintain the upgrade to the existing nuclear arsenal promised by Barack Obama but also to extend the range of its weaponry. It also indicated that Trump planned to "broaden the circumstances under which the United States would consider the first use of nuclear weapons," in the words of Kingston Reif, Director of Nonproliferation Policy at the Arms Control Association.[10] Boris Johnson is following suit. In March 2021, he increased the cap on Trident nuclear warheads by over 40%, from 180 to 260, signaling that Brexit Britain is back as an "independent" global nuclear power. As arms agreements tumble and nuclear powers rearm, how long will it be before Nixon's challenge is on the cards again? "A nuclear bomb, does that bother you? ... I just want you to think big, Henry, for Christ's sake."

Notes

1 The OTA report cited *The Pakistan Times*, May 26, 1992, pp. 1–2. For the original reprint of the speech, see JPRS-TND-92-017, June 3, 1992.
2 "National Security Council Report, NSC 68, 'United States Objectives and Programs for National Security'," April 14, 1950, History and Public Policy

82 *John Krige*

Program Digital Archive, US National Archives. Available at: http://digitalarchive.wilsoncenter.org/document/116191 [Accessed June 2, 2021].

3 Anderson, J., and Khan, K. (1998). Pakistani Politicians Rallying Cry: "Let Them Eat Grass." *The Washington Post.* June 11, 1998. Available at: https://www.washingtonpost.com/archive/politics/1998/06/11/pakistani-politicians-rallying-cry-let-them-eat-grass/cf5f99c0-b9da-41ef-9de4-42b5eccec255/ [Accessed June 10, 2021].

4 Sublette, C. (2001). "Pakistan's Nuclear Weapons Program–1998: The Year of Testing." Nuclear Weapon Archive. Available at: https://nuclearweaponarchive.org/Pakistan/PakTests.html [Accessed June 2, 2021].

5 Which is not to say that it succeeded in doing so. The deep deficiencies in the French program developed without US assistance in the 1960s were evident in the 1970s when Kissinger changed tack and offered US help to upgrade the *force de frappe*–see Krige (2016: 149–167), for a detailed account.

6 "Memorandum by Edward Biegel, Bureau of Western European Affairs, 'WE Answers to the Ball Questionnaire'," May 28, 1962, History and Public Policy Program Digital Archive, National Archives, Record Group 59, Bureau of European Affairs. NATO and Atlantic Politico-Military Affairs, Records Relating to NATO, 1959–1966, box 7, Ref 12 Nuclear France 1962. Obtained and contributed by William Burr and included in NPIHP Research Update #2. Available at: https://digitalarchive.wilsoncenter.org/document/110244 [Accessed June 2, 2021].

7 White House (2019). "Remarks by President Trump and Prime Minister Khan of the Islamic Republic of Pakistan Before Bilateral Meeting" [transcript]. July 22, 2019. Available at: https://trumpwhitehouse.archives.gov/briefings-statements/remarks-president-trump-prime-minister-khan-islamic-republic-pakistan-bilateral-meeting/ [Accessed June 10, 2021].

8 Wallerstein, M. (1998), testimony, U.S. Export Control and Non-proliferation Policy and the Role and Responsibility of the Department of Defense, Hearing before the Committee on Armed Services, US Senate, 105th Congress, July 9, Washington, DC: Government Printing Office, 2.

9 Bienkov, A. (2019). Boris Johnson Called Gay Men "Tank-Topped Bumboys" and Black People "Piccaninnies" with "Watermelon Smiles." *Business Insider.* June 9, 2020. Available at: https://www.businessinsider.com/boris-johnson-record-sexist-homophobic-and-racist-comments-bumboys-piccaninnies-2019-6 [Accessed June 10, 2021].

10 Arms Control Association, "A Critical Evaluation of the Trump Administration's Nuclear Weapons Policies" [transcript] July 29, 2019. Available at: https://armscontrol.org/events/2019-07/critical-evaluation-trump-administrations-nuclear-weapons-policies. [Accessed June 10, 2021].

References

Abraham, I. (2016). What (Really) Makes a Country Nuclear? Insights From Nonnuclear Southeast Asia. *Critical Studies on Security*, 4(1), pp. 24–41, DOI: http://doi.org/10.1080/21624887.2015.1121727.

Albright, M. (2013). *Madam Secretary: A Memoir.* New York: Harper Perennial.

Baylis, J. (2001). Nuclear Exchange: Laying the Foundations of the Anglo-American Nuclear Relationship. *Diplomatic History*, 25(1), pp. 33–61.

Biswas, S. (2014). *Nuclear Desire: Power and the Postcolonial Nuclear Order.* Minneapolis, MN: University of Minnesota Press.

Brown, W. (2010). *Walled States, Waning Sovereignty.* Cambridge, MA: MIT Press.

Burr, W., and Richelson, J. (2000). Whether to 'Strangle the Baby in the Cradle': The United States and the Chinese Nuclear Program, 1960–64. *International Security*, 25(3), pp. 54–99.

Cohn, C. (1987). Sex, Death and the Rational World of Defense Intellectuals. *Signs*, 12(4), pp. 687–718.

Costigliola, F. (1997). The Nuclear Family: Tropes of Gender and Pathology in the Western Alliance. *Diplomatic History*, 21(2), pp. 163–183.

Cupitt, R. (2000). *Reluctant Champions: U.S. Presidential Policy and Strategic Export Controls, Truman, Eisenhower, Bush and Clinton*. New York: Routledge.

Friedberg, A. (2000). *In the Shadow of the Garrison State: America's Anti-Statism and its Cold War Grand Strategy*. Princeton, NJ: Princeton University Press.

Gavin, F. (2012). *Nuclear Statecraft: History and Strategy in America's Atomic Age*. Ithaca, NY: Cornell University Press.

Gusterson, H. (1999). Nuclear Weapons and the Other in the Western Imagination. *Cultural Anthropology*, 14(1), pp. 111–143.

Hecht, G. (1998). *The Radiance of France: Nuclear Power and National Identity After World War II*. Cambridge, MA: MIT Press.

Hecht, G. (2006). Nuclear Ontologies. *Constellations*, 13(3), pp. 320–331.

Hecht, G. (2012). *Being Nuclear: Africans and the Global Uranium Trade*. Cambridge, MA: MIT Press.

Herken, G. (1988). *The Winning Weapon: The Atomic Bomb in the Cold War, 1945-1950*. New York: Knopf.

Hixson, W. (2002). *The Myth of American Diplomacy: National Identity and U.S. Foreign Policy*. New Haven, CT: Yale University Press.

Krige, J. (2008). The Peaceful Atom as Political Weapon. *Historical Studies in the Physical Sciences*, 38(1), pp. 5–44.

Krige, J. (2014). Embedding the National in the Global: US-French Relationships in Space Science and Rocketry in the 1960s. In: N. Oreskesand and J. Krige, eds., *Science and Technology in the Global Cold War*. Cambridge, MA: MIT Press, pp. 227–250.

Krige, J. (2016). *Sharing Knowledge Shaping Europe: U.S. Technological Collaboration and Nonproliferation*. Cambridge, MA: MIT Press.

Krige, J., Long Callahan, A., and Maharaj, A. (2013). *NASA in the World: Fifty Years of International Collaboration in Space*. London: Palgrave Macmillan.

Maddock, S. (2010). *Nuclear Apartheid: The Quest for American Atomic Supremacy from World War II to the Present*. Chapel Hill, NC: University of North Carolina Press.

Nye, J. (2004). *Soft Power: The Means to Success in World Politics*. New York: Public Affairs.

Osseo-Asare, A. (2019). *Atomic Junction: Nuclear Power in Africa After Independence*. Cambridge: Cambridge University Press.

Pelopidas, B. (2011). The Oracles of Proliferation. *The Nonproliferation Review*, 18(1), pp. 297–314. DOI: http://doi.org/10.1080/10736700.2011.549185.

Pelopidas, B. (2012). French Nuclear Idiosyncrasy: How it Effects French Nuclear Policies Towards United Arab Emirates and Iran. *Cambridge Review of International Affairs*, 25(1), pp. 143–169.

84 John Krige

Pelopidas, B. (2015). The Nuclear Straightjacket: American Extended Deterrence and Nonproliferation. In: S. von Hlatky and A. Wenger, eds., *The Future of Extended Deterrence: The United States, NATO and Beyond*. Washington, DC: Georgetown University Press, pp. 73–105.

Perkovich, G. (1999). *India's Nuclear Bomb: The Impact of Global Proliferation*. Berkeley, CA: University of California Press.

Sarkar, J. (2013). India's Nuclear Limbo and the Fatalism of the Nuclear Non-Proliferation Regime, 1974–1983. *Strategic Analysis*, 37(3), pp. 322–337. DOI: http://doi.org/10.1080/09700161.2013.782662.

Sarkar, J. (2015). "Wean Them Away from French Tutelage": Franco-Indian Nuclear Relations and Anglo-American Anxieties during the Early Cold War, 1948–1952. *Cold War History*, 15(3), pp. 375–394.

Sarkar, J., and Bouyssou, R. (2014). Compatriotes de l'atome? La coopération nucléaire franco-indienne, 1950-1976. *Critique internationale*, 63(2), pp. 131–149. DOI: http://doi.org/10.3917/crii.063.0131.

Takeyh, R. (2006). Iran Builds the Bomb. *Survival: Global Politics and Strategy*, 46(4), pp. 51–63.

US Congress, Office of Technology Assessment. (1993). Proliferation of Weapons of Mass Destruction: Assessing the Risks, OTA-ISC-559 (Washington, DC: Government Printing Office, August 1993). Available at: https://ota.fas.org/reports/9341.pdf [Accessed June 10, 2021].

Vaïsse, M. (2007). Jacques Chaban-Delmas, ministre de la Défense nationale (novembre 1957-mai 1958). In: B. Lachaise, ed., *Jacques Chaban-Delmas en politique*. Paris: Presses Universitaires de France, pp. 99–110.

Walker, W. (2000). Nuclear Order and Disorder. *International Affairs*, 76(4), pp. 703–725.

Walker, W. (2012). *A Perpetual Menace: Nuclear Weapons and International Order*. London: Routledge.

4 The Nuclear Charter: international law, military technology, and the making of strategic trusteeship, 1942–1947[1]

M. X. Mitchell

On the hot, humid morning of January 31, 1944, nearly 600 Marshall Islanders assembled on the beach of Majuro Atoll to watch as the United States Navy shelled their lands. Although a clandestine US Marine landing party learned overnight that the Japanese military had departed almost two years earlier, the message arrived too late to stop the assault. The bombardment went on for 20 minutes or so. When it ended, Islanders met US forces on the shore. An officer posted a legal notice proclaiming in Japanese and English that the atoll was now under US martial law. Majuro Atoll had been liberated (Richard, 1957a) (Figure 4.1).[3]

According to US Navy commanders, the invasion of Majuro was bloodless. Islanders had reason to see the situation differently, however, for their bodies, lineages, knowledges, laws, and politics were tautly knotted in the atoll's sandy soil and emerald lagoon. Majuro was kin. The people cared for and about their atoll. They belonged (and still belong) to Majuro. Harm to Majuro was harm to them.

The invasion of Majuro opened a new beachhead of colonial encounter between Marshall Islanders and the United States. As a Marshallese saying explains, "Majuro mejen armij"—Majuro is the eyes of the people. The atoll itself bears witness (Walsh, 2003: 237). In 1944, it became one of the first entry points of the US military into lands held by the Japanese Empire prior to the war. The invasion ushered in a new wave of foreign influence in the Marshall, Caroline, Mariana, and Palau Islands, which stretched over nearly 3 million square miles of the equatorial Western Pacific and had been governed by Japan as the League of Nations' South Pacific Mandate. Throughout the US invasion and occupation, new questions emerged about the fundamental nature of these places and their peoples. Why were they important? To whom did they belong? How could they be known? Who should govern them?

This chapter explores how nuclear politics inflected these questions. In 1945, the United States used Tinian Island in the Marianas as an assembly platform and launch site for the atomic bombings of Japan

DOI: 10.4324/9781003227472-4

86 M. X. Mitchell

Figure 4.1 Original Caption: "Natives of Marshall Islands at time of invasion by American forces. They were happy to see the invading Americans and to come down to the shore in their 'Sunday clothes' to shower Marines, who made a bloodless landing, with gifts." US Navy photograph.[2]

(Gordin, 2007). From 1946 to 1958, the United States used atolls in the Marshall Islands as detonation sites for 67 of its most destructive nuclear weapons and as termini for numerous Intercontinental Ballistic Missiles launches (Smith-Norris, 2016; Hirshberg, 2022). Nuclear blasting and missile targeting in the Marshall Islands became emblematic of the character and extent of the United States' post-war power in Oceania. But before and beneath the shadow of the bomb lies a much more complicated story about US power and its shifting relationships to offshore places, technoscientific tools, international law, and Indigenous peoples.

Nuclear science and technology have entangled with colonialisms from root to branch—across many political jurisdictions, throughout every stage of the fuel cycle, from targeting decisions to biological studies (e.g., Lindee, 1994; Hecht, 2012; Maclellan, 2017). Historians and anthropologists of the US nuclear complex in North America have explored how the weapons program both relied on the dispossession of Indigenous peoples and deepened the marginalisation of Indigenous and racialised communities (Kuletz, 1998; Masco, 2006; Brown, 2013; Voyles, 2015). This chapter traces these dynamics offshore, into Oceania, where the expansion of US extraterritorial power relied heavily on international legal configurations of Islanders' Indigeneity while purporting to turn mainly on technological politics. It explores the shifting entanglements between the international legal status of the former Mandate and its peoples and the materiel politics of US power, from the genesis of plans to invade in 1942 through the designation of the area as the sole United Nations Strategic Trusteeship in 1947 and the concomitant expansion of nuclear blasting. At every stage, US planners approached Islanders' status as Indigenous dependents and the qualities of their difference opportunistically in order to facilitate US aims. The growing embrace of strategic, technopolitical, networked standpoints, however, began to obscure Islanders from view and deepen their marginalisation.

The technological affordances of air power, I suggest, created templates for emerging legal forms of US extraterritorial colonialism. Planners needed to innovate to enable the geographical expansion of US military power while paying lip-service to the Roosevelt Administration's rhetoric on decolonisation, its support of the fledgling United Nations Organisation, and its Atlantic Charter pledges to eschew "territorial aggrandisement." The aesthetics of the air atomic network—the material affordances and constraints of nuclear bombs, their relationships to material technological infrastructures, the emotional reactions they could conjure, and especially the possibilities they opened for recharacterising space-time—played a role in justifying and structuring the United States' post-war power in the former Mandate. Recasting Indigenous places as components of a technological system or network and governing them through the one-of-a-kind international status of "strategic trusteeship" smoothed the way for the United States to expand the offshore areas it governed while claiming it was not "taking territory." The subsequent material entrenchment of US nuclear infrastructure and radioactive contamination in the Marshall Islands materialised these foundational technological lenses and logics.

These shifts had important, interrelated consequences for the character of post-war internationalism, the United States' projection of extraterritorial power, and the changing quantum and qualities of Marshall Islanders' marginalisation. Internationally, strategic trusteeship modified dependent status, typified by the League of Nations mandate system, to meet the needs of US military power. It marked a pivot away from an interwar focus on disarmament (Webster, 2017; Hathaway and Shapiro, 2017), including the mandate system's prohibitions on fortification, by taking a permissive stance towards US militarisation. This was an important part of broader moves during the creation of the United Nations that extended great power influence and incorporated military considerations (Mazower, 2009; Bosco, 2009).

88   *M. X. Mitchell*

For the United States, strategic trusteeship represented a new use of international law and institutions to structure its colonialism and to project its power extraterritorially. This was a distinct shift away from its use of national law to acquire island colonies prior to the war (Coates, 2016). The embrace of trusteeship fractured the short-lived ascendancy of what Lisa Ford (2010: 1–2) has called "perfect settler sovereignty"—the nineteenth century "legal trinity of nation-statehood," which tied together sovereignty, territory, and jurisdiction. Instead of linking these attributes of state power, US planners divided them between the United States and the United Nations in ambiguous and underdetermined ways. During the genesis of this shift, US planners began to take a view of strategic trusteeship that simultaneously focused on the technological instruments of US power and began to exhibit a growing, instrumentalist approach toward international law.

The turn toward technology supported the United States' transformation of the Marshall Islands into a detonating node in the nuclear network and an extraterritorial sink of technogenic harm. Under military legal interpretations of strategic trusteeship, Islanders were collateral to the technological system, not entitled to meaningful consideration or participation where the nuclear complex was concerned. Nuclearisation of the Marshall Islands contributed to deepening dispossessions of Marshallese communities and disruptions of the intimate links between their bodies, communities, and ancestral atolls.

On the beach

"I love my atoll where I was born. Her views and her streets are pretty. I will never leave her because it's my home forever and it is better for me to be there," a Marshallese song exclaimed proudly.[4] "Song of Majuro" encapsulated the deep and abiding connections between Marshall Islanders and their ancestral lands and waters. Islanders' identities as Indigenous peoples had shaped their status under international law and Japan's practices under League of Nations oversight. When the US Navy came ashore at Majuro in 1944, Marshall Islanders' difference—their knowledges, politics, and legalities—played an important role both in the US invasion and in US plans for the future.

Japan's foothold in the Marshall Islands resulted from a calculated campaign for influence in the Pacific during and after World War I. Japan joined the Principal Allied Powers, invading and occupying German-colonised islands in the Northern Mariana, Palau, Caroline, and Marshall Islands beginning in 1914. Following the war, the Japanese Empire retained control of these archipelagos, ancestral homes to numerous Indigenous peoples, as a Class C League of Nations Mandate (Peattie, 1988; Hezel, 1995; Pedersen, 2015).

The mandate system turned on disentangling presumed linkages between territorial colonialism, race and indigeneity, and armed conflict. The system grew out of a need to dispose of the Central Powers' former colonies in the Middle East, Africa, and Oceania at the end of World War I. It operated on the assumption that, as one legal commentator later remarked, "territories inhabited by backward and underprivileged people offer fertile ground for unrest and international struggle."[5] The League's Covenant explained that the mandate system would apply to "peoples not yet able to stand by themselves under the strenuous conditions of the modern world." Governing states selected from among the Principal Allied Powers would foster "the well-being and development" of peoples, thereby "forming a sacred trust of civilisation" (Anghie, 2005; Pedersen, 2015).[6]

The League utilised international law and institutions to deterritorialise the mandates and organise them according to perceived "progress" toward civilisation. In each mandate, a designated state from among the Principal Allied Powers served as the governing authority, tasked with promoting the League's civilising mission. The League's architects agreed that the mandatory powers would not hold territorial sovereignty in these areas, but left open the question of where sovereignty lay—whether with the League itself, the Principal Allied Powers, the mandate's inhabitants, or some combination of the foregoing (Pedersen, 2015). The League further sorted the mandates hierarchically into A, B, and C classifications, ranked in descending order according to perceived stage of development. The C mandates included the Japanese-occupied archipelagos, all of the other German colonies in Oceania, and also German Southwestern Africa. Legal commentators generally assumed that the inhabitants of the C mandates, mainly Indigenous peoples, were so underdeveloped that they lacked the legal capacity to hold any sovereignty interest in their own lands and waters.[7] Mandatory authorities in these places consequently held a de facto degree of power nearly equal in scope to territorial sovereignty (Pedersen, 2015).

The League limited the power of mandatory authorities, however, to militarise the C mandates. Interwar internationalism had, in many ways, focused on the possibilities for law to limit armed conflict (Hathaway and Shapiro, 2017). This included a strong focus on disarmament and regulation of armaments (Webster, 2017). These efforts represented a kind of international legalism in which treaty makers assumed that states would abide by the rules and legal frameworks set forth in international treaty law. Mandatory powers, including Japan, accepted formal prohibitions on fortifying, building military bases, dealing arms, and conscripting inhabitants. Although the United States did not join the League, these limitations fostered US leaders' grudging acquiescence in Japan's control over the region. The United States negotiated further on a bilateral basis during the Washington Naval Conference of 1922, extracting additional legal promises from Japan to limit its naval tonnage in exchange for the United States' pledge not to further fortify its territories in Guam, the Philippines, and Samoa (Peattie, 1988; Hezel, 1995).

Under Japanese rule, Marshall Islanders' ways-of-life and knowledge practices endured in many respects. The Japanese civil administration adopted formally an assimilationist stance toward Islanders, whom they deemed to be racially and legally inferior. Japanese interventions, however, varied in intensity across the Mandate. Marshall Islanders retained a relatively wide degree of leeway to manage local affairs under a loose system of indirect rule, especially on outlying atolls (Peattie, 1988).

Ancestral atolls, therefore, remained at the heart of Marshallese society under Japanese rule. Islanders regarded their atolls and bodies as intrinsically and inextricably tied together, no matter where an Islander was physically located. The land tenure system linked hereditary patterns of rule with flexible legal guidelines for the use and disposition of land and lagoon resources. The system was hierarchical, hereditary, and mainly matrilineal. While paramount chiefs (iroijlaplap) and chiefs (iroij and leroij) held the most expansive rights in land, lineage heads (alabs) and commoners (kajur) belonged to the land and held various kinds of use rights (Stege, 2008). Marshallese land tenure and hereditary authority endured with minor modifications. The Japanese administration tended to enroll local government officials from among Marshallese hereditary authorities, although the power of these officials waned somewhat over time (Peattie, 1988; Poyer et al., 2001).[8]

Marshallese "Indigenous" ways-of-life included Islanders' long-standing practices of adopting and adapting new knowledges and people (LaBriola, 2019). For instance, every atoll had converted to Christianity by the early twentieth century, serving as a catalyst for Islanders' development and widespread adoption of written Marshallese (Jetnil-Kijiner, 2014). Islanders not only maintained traditional Marshallese techniques for building outrigger sailing canoes and navigating them through a unique form of wave navigation (Genz, 2018), they also joined merchant marines and learned to build, pilot, and navigate Western water-craft.[9] Many Islanders married or had children with visitors and outsiders who made their homes in the Islands. Islanders eagerly sought opportunities for travel, work, and education abroad. As a result, a number of Islanders were polyglot, speaking English, Japanese, German, or other regional languages as well as Marshallese (Chave, 1947).

The growing encroachment of the Japanese military and the outbreak of war disrupted these ways of life. Japan's focus in the region began to pivot toward militarisation after it announced its intent to withdraw from the League in 1933. By 1939, it began fortifying the islands of the former Mandate in earnest, developing sea and air bases, and garrisoning troops. Japan used the area to support the 1941 assault on Pearl Harbor in Hawai'i and the invasion of the US territories of Guam and the

Philippines (Peattie, 1988; Hezel, 1995). By 1942, US military officials plotted to wrest the area from Japanese control and to hold it in perpetuity as a part of broader plans to develop US military bases worldwide.[10] The Marshall Islands now lay at the center of conflict. As war deepened, Japanese officials forced Islanders into various kinds of labor away from their home communities, limited Islanders' movements, destroyed watercraft, commandeered local food, limited religious practice, and executed some Islanders suspected of disloyalty. The United States conducted regular bombing campaigns and instituted a naval blockade, further damaging the Islands, injuring Islanders, and limiting resources (Poyer et al., 2001; Richard, 1957a; 1957b).[11] By the eve of the US invasion in 1944, many Marshall Islanders were eager to extract their communities from wartime violence.

US Navy plans for invasion and occupation, meanwhile, had begun to focus on the cultural and legal difference of Indigenous peoples across the former Mandate. The navy's past administration of Guam had been criticised for the harsh repression of the Indigenous Chamorro peoples' rights and culture (Strackbein, 1931).[12] Navy officials and legal consultants saw the former Mandate as a means of bringing the US military into line with international law and practices and as a dress rehearsal for post-war administration of the area.[13] The navy developed a specialised training program for military government officers focused on colonial administration, international law, and the management of Native peoples—a new "technic of military government" that included anthropological, political, and economic expertise.[14]

Concurrently, US Navy planners devised a wartime legal system that would accommodate Indigenous legalities. If Guam provided a cautionary tale, the navy's administration of Samoa seemed to point the way forward. There, colonial governors had protected Indigenous laws and land tenure in ways that navy planners believed facilitated Samoans' acceptance of naval administration.[15] The former Mandate's ambiguous international status, itself a result of Islanders' difference, enabled the creation of a two-tiered legal system that applied different laws to Japanese nationals than to Indigenous communities under military occupation.[16] US Navy policy dictated that "local customs" of Indigenous peoples in the former Mandate be maintained as law, except in cases of military necessity.[17] This arrangement, in part, addressed the mismatch between the many, distinct Indigenous systems of land tenure in the area and Western private property rights that the international laws of military occupation had been designed to protect.[18]

Recognition of Indigenous law furthered US objectives in several other ways as well. Naval operations planners felt preserving local laws might develop goodwill among Islanders, as a "logical and necessary step" toward "furthering the aim of retention of these islands" in the long term.[19] The arrangement also gave invading forces wide flexibility in the taking of land and facilities. Since Indigenous law was always subject to military exception, land could be expropriated. The Hague Conventions also held wide exceptions for seizure and destruction of property in cases of military necessity, but they assumed that most dealings with property would be documented and compensated, and included extensive rules on that process.[20] The stated inapplicability of these regimes to Islanders removed the need to determine whether Islanders' held property rights at all or which groups of Islanders—chiefs, lineage heads, commoners—had a legal stake in a taking. These questions at the intersection of Marshallese land tenure law and Western concepts of property were sticky and complicated dilemmas of colonial administration that navy planners and officers sought to postpone addressing for as long as possible.[21]

To develop leverage for use in future international negotiations with other states, meanwhile, US planners resolved to take, hold, and "improve" the land by developing military infrastructures in areas marked for long-term control. This strategy turned on the primacy of possession and the labor theory value embedded in racialised colonial property regimes, which often regarded Indigenous areas as "empty" and the occupation and transformation of land by invaders as indicia of rights (Bhandar, 2018).[22] Last, the two-tiered system of legal controls removed the need for invading forces to treat Islanders as "enemy aliens," fostering the development of collaborations during the US invasion.[23]

As soon as the US Navy landed in the Marshall Islands, military government officers recruited English- and Japanese- speaking Marshallese boys and men, such as one-time San Francisco resident, Michael Madison, pictured below, to serve as scouts and translators (Poyer et al., 2001). The officers appear to have had little difficulty recruiting anglophone men on Majuro, likely because they arrived with Madison's relatives, scouts Archie and Willie Muller from Makin Atoll in the Gilbert Islands.[24] This kind of ad hoc process repeated itself as members of English- and Japanese- speaking Marshallese communities recruited others within their social circles (Figure 4.2).

Scouts' knowledges supported the navy's campaign across the Marshall Islands. Their deep understandings of atoll and ocean environments enabled safe navigation of ocean and lagoons. Scouts' knowledge of Japanese practices and troop locations facilitated clandestine landings. Under cover of night, scouts went ashore alone, sometimes in combat conditions, to make contact with locals. Scouts' personal relationships and grasps of social dynamics helped them connect US forces with influential community leaders. On Lae Atoll, for example, scouts identified a pastor named Kein as a particularly influential leader. On Wotho Atoll, they sought out a man named Lelet—the former skipper of a missionary schooner. With intimate knowledge of their atolls, Marshallese community members provided valuable intelligence about Japanese positions and movements to American forces. After landing parties departed, men and women used

Figure 4.2 Marshallese scout Michael Madison meets with Islanders during US invasion. US Navy photograph.[25]

cloths and canvases as makeshift signal flags to relay messages to US flight crews. By US Navy officers' own recounting, Marshallese scouts and translators, in cooperation with local communities, provided critical intelligence and assistance.[26]

The US Navy also left much of the responsibility for the safety and well-being of Islanders with community leaders. During the battle of Enewetak Atoll, for example, the two iroij (chiefs), Johannes and Abraham, safely led over 50 Islanders across an active battlefield to take refuge behind American lines and relay important intelligence about Japanese positions.[27] Elsewhere, the navy bypassed a number of Japanese-occupied atolls, leaving those Islanders to fend for themselves. By the navy's own counts, over 2,000 Marshall Islanders—about 20% of the entire Marshallese population at the time—fled by swimming or setting to sea on makeshift watercraft, often under Japanese fire.[28] The US Navy assisted, using overflights to locate evacuees and sent patrol ships to pick them up and bring them to safety (Richard, 1957a; Poyer et al., 2001) (Figure 4.3).

Along numerous axes, then, Marshall Islanders' difference had supported US aims on the water and ground. To some military government

Figure 4.3 Islanders escape from Jaluit Atoll. US Navy photo.[29]

officers, Marshall Islanders' contributions to the war effort demonstrated readiness for a relatively swift grant of self-government.[30] International lawyer and navy officer Eugene F. Bogan explained the situation in the racialised languages of progress that had animated the mandate system and inflected international law: "[Marshall Islanders] are intelligent and in no wise inferior to Europeans…. The people are not 'savage' nor 'coolies' nor 'primitives' nor 'pre-industrialists' and are not to be treated as such. They have an independent spirit and can support and maintain themselves…."[31] Marshallese difference, in this rendering, was not cause for a diminished status.

Perhaps buoyed by these wartime partnerships, some Islanders held out hope for the future of their relationship with the United States. One song at war's end proclaimed, "All our troubles end. Let us be thankful for our joy…. We are under law and freedom."[32] The precise contours of laws and freedom under which Islanders would rebuild, however, remained unclear.

The view from 30,000 feet

In meetings held far away from sandy shores, US military standpoints onto the former Mandate took flight. Technology shaped military strategists'

The Nuclear Charter   95

lens on the former Mandate during high-level discussions of how to effectuate ongoing US control over the area. The 1941 Atlantic Charter, to which the United States was signatory, prohibited national "aggrandizement, territorial or other."[33] But the US Joint Chiefs of Staff and Secretaries of War and the Navy worried that placing the former Mandate into the nascent United Nations trusteeship system would diminish the military's freedom of action.[34] Considering the area from above and in connection to military technologies clarified their approaches to, and justifications for taking and keeping the former Mandate as a US territory. The emergence of air atomic power allowed military leaders to reframe their arguments for annexing it as existential ones, shunting consideration of Islanders or of the racial logics of US colonialism to the side.[35]

For many US policymakers, especially those representing military interests, the former Mandate was proof of the abject failures of international legalism to produce peace and security. The "network of treaties," as Secretary of War Henry L. Stimson, a lawyer, internationalist, and the former US Secretary of State, described it in the spring of 1945, had failed spectacularly in the Pacific.[36] International law alone could no longer form the main foundation of efforts to control armed conflict.

War and Navy Department officials turned to technological networks as a new basis for international peace. Within the navy and the army, technologies of flight—air power—increasingly influenced military strategy (McBride, 2000; Biddle, 2001). US air power theorists, in particular, adapted ideas from systems science as a way of considering linkages between technology and other aspects of strategy (Thomas, 2015). These shifting lenses onto military strategy became apparent in discussions over disposition of the former Mandate. The Joint Chiefs of Staff argued throughout the early 1940s that a global "integrated system of mutually supporting bases for land, sea and air forces" was needed in the Pacific to project US power toward Asia and prevent attacks on US territory.[37] As Secretary of the Navy, James Forrestal clarified, this was not "about isolated bases—pin points—but a system of defense in the Pacific." The entire area covered by the former Mandate constituted a "single military entity" and a "defense network."[38]

Naming the islands of the former Mandate as part of a network or system entailed explicit discussion of the relationship between military technologies and emplaced base facilities. As Stimson emphasised, naval bases could be thought of as a component of military materiel, "as essential as battleships."[39] Army Air Forces planners described the islands as "permanent air craft carriers" (Friedman, 2007: 57). Seen from the standpoint of military strategy, place and technology entwined.

By war's end, atomic weapons deepened these ways of seeing space and added urgency to military calls for US annexation of the former Mandate. Even though the United States was then the sole nuclear-weapons state, US air power advocates like Army Air Forces General

Hap Arnold evoked a terrifying future in which enemies might rapidly destroy an entire US city with a single nuclear weapon (Arnold, 1945; Gordin, 2007). Nuclear weapons collapsed time and space in ways that seemed to place the North American continent under existential threat (Masco, 2014). These depictions of nuclear weapons as exceptional and dangerous influenced War Department plans for a system of bases. Air strategists used this fearsome, but imagined future to argue that the US must increase its capacity for rapid, preemptive strikes against potential aggressors worldwide.[40]

Since atomic weapons could only be delivered in a limited area constrained by the flight ranges of B29 bombers and their fighter escorts, Pacific bases were seen as essential sites for airfields and supporting technological infrastructures.[41] Facilities in the former Mandate would be key to further expanding the reach of US air atomic power in Asia. War Department planners envisioned that the integrated system of land, sea, and air bases and infrastructures—a nuclear network—could be made both flexible and redundant. As long as the United States held enough bases to enable alternative routes of attack, the destruction of any individual site was acceptable. Bases would become fungible, interchangeable parts of the overall network from which nuclear attacks could be launched and at which they could be absorbed.[42]

Characterising the former Mandate as a part of a system of bases or a nuclear network supported military planners' claims that US annexation of the area would be permitted under the Atlantic Charter. The former Mandate's centrality to the technologically enabled projection of US military power, they contended, differed from the more traditional, interrelated colonial pursuits of resource extraction and White settlement (Hanlon, 1998).[43] Annexation of the former Mandate as a system of defense and a nuclear network, while territorial, the Joint Chiefs and others contended, would not constitute "aggrandisement."[44] The Joint Chiefs ominously warned that any formulation of international status in the area that included all of the "attributes of sovereignty" needed by the United States would, "by its very deviousness and apparent cynicism, be far more of a threat to US moral leadership in the United Nations, and would set a bad precedent of tricky legalism..."[45] The statement reflected a distinct hierarchy between military need and law. In this view, international laws, interpreted fulsomely according to their policy aims, would not constrain US military power. Rather, the Joint Chiefs foreshadowed that they would approach legalism as another instrument in the military arsenal. Annexation—the outright taking of territorial sovereignty—they suggested, would therefore provide the best fit between the military's plans and the legal form of control.

This focus on technology concurrently sidelined island communities and minimised discussions about the colonial color lines embedded in US law and politics. Although technopolitical concerns—both military and economic—had fueled and inflected the United States' earlier offshore expansion at the turn of the twentieth century (Adas, 2006; Oldenziel, 2011), policy debates about islands' legal relationships to the US polity mainly focused on people. A series of Supreme Court cases, known as the *Insular Cases*, created the legal framework governing US territorial incorporation. These rulings established a bare floor of constitutional protections for territorial residents while permitting the US Congress to determine the degree of belonging afforded to insular territories and peoples.[46] The *Insular Cases* rested explicitly on logics of racialised difference that US lawmakers used to extend and withhold status based on perceptions of communities' progress toward "civilisation" (Thompson, 2010; Erman, 2019). Island communities chased the shifting cultural qualities of Whiteness—never quite able to arrive and always perceived as being in a regressive state of primitive pastness that precluded their full participation in the US polity (Anderson, 2006; Kramer, 2006). These frameworks operated on similar racialised logics about "progress toward civilisation" as those in play in the mandate system and the United Nations trusteeship system being designed to succeed it (Anghie, 2005; Coates, 2016).

Refocusing discussions about the former Mandate on military technology, from the aerial remove of a systematised, strategic standpoint, reinforced these colonial color lines while purporting to turn on different logics. Put differently, focusing on less overtly racialised, technological concerns eased the process of colonisation and limited consideration of how much political authority island communities should have by mostly erasing Islanders from planning conversations. Yet this move, too, had been made possible by US interpretations about the qualities of Islanders' difference—now embodying almost a complete reversal from lower level, navy military government officers' more favorable assessments of some island communities. A Joint Chiefs of Staff memorandum explained that questions of Islanders' development simply did not merit discussion as a part of debates over annexation versus trusteeship because the "divers tribes and races" were in such a "backward state," they would "be wholly incapable of assuming any independent status or even that of self government at any time in the foreseeable future."[47]

The elevation of technology in the disposition of the former Mandate turned on Islanders' indigeneity while removing them from view. Seen through the scope of a B29 flying 30,000 feet above the Pacific Ocean, the only people who seemed to matter, perhaps the only people who could be seen at all, were the generalised, mainly White, US citizens at risk from imagined future attacks on the continental United States.

Strategising trusteeship

As plans for the UN trusteeship system took shape, US officials from the Departments of State and the Interior worked to synthesise the

98   *M. X. Mitchell*

newfound material vantage point on the Pacific with the developmentalist sensibilities embedded in international law. While the need to militarise the former mandate seemed clear, they felt that outright territorial annexation could not be squared with the Atlantic Charter or with US support of the United Nations. The US delegation to the United Nations developed a new international status, called "strategic trusteeship," that merged technological need with a greater focus on the peoples of the former Mandate and their economic and political development.

Since 1944, prominent international legal thinkers had theorised that the United Nations trusteeship system could stretch to accommodate militarisation in the war-torn Pacific (Pedersen, 2015).[48] During negotiations at the UN organisational conference in San Francisco in 1945, Under Secretary of Interior and adviser to the United States UN delegation, lawyer Abe Fortas, developed the concept of a "strategic trusteeship" (Kalman, 1990; Friedman, 2007). Moving away from the interwar focus on disarmament, this novel international status would instead join militarisation within well-trod ideas about international development. "The trusteeship system would have two great purposes," Fortas wrote,

> "First, that any trust area which is so located that it is strategically important for maintaining the peace and military security should be made available to the nation primarily concerned, to be used as a strategic base; and second, that the political, economic, and social welfare of the inhabitants of all of these areas should be protected and advanced."[49]

Militarisation stood over and above development, but the basic trusteeship concept remained intact. The US delegation to the United Nations ensured that provisions allowing for strategic trusteeships were incorporated into the UN Charter. The Charter provisions permitted militarisation and designated the Security Council, over which the US held veto power, to oversee these areas. Strategic trusteeships, however, would also be subjected to UN Charter provisions requiring the promotion of "political, economic, social, and educational advancement" and the "progressive development toward self-government or independence," as well as to the terms of trusteeship agreements negotiated with the United Nations.[50]

While allowing for trusteeships to serve as a platform for military technology, the hybrid form of strategic trusteeship retained an international legalist sensibility about the power of law to establish boundaries around militarisation. Department of the Interior officials were particularly concerned about the potential for military abuse of trusteed peoples in light of the US Army and Navy's poor track-records in protecting individual rights during pre-war colonial administration and wartime regimes of martial law (Kalman, 1990). Fortas believed that an "international check" needed to be embedded in trusteeship agreements in order to limit meaningfully the potentially harmful effects of US military power on trusteed peoples.[51] Fortas' hopes surrounding the capacity of international law and institutions to constrain military power resonated in light of the Joint Chiefs' warnings that the US would take a technical, instrumentalist approach to maximising its power.

State and Interior officials' approaches to strategic trusteeship also trucked in racialised colonial and imperial politics (Kalman, 1990), but they placed people at the center of discussion. Interior officials even argued (albeit unsuccessfully) that all trusteeship agreements should require ratification by the trusteed peoples themselves and lobbied for culturalist, rather than universalist, models of development to be facilitated by the trusteeship system.[52] These calls amplified Department of the Interior officials' controversial, often romanticised views of Indigenous peoples (Weisiger, 2009). Yet they nevertheless placed peoples, not just military technology, toward the center of plans for the exercise of US power.

Militarisation without more, Fortas felt, was simply not enough to secure international peace. "In an exploding world only a few hours large," he explained in December of 1945, referencing atomic weapons, "armaments … are not a Magna Charta or a World Constitution."[53] International law and economic and political development of dependent peoples were equally as necessary, he urged. Just one month later, Fortas' worries about the impact of atomic weapons on US internationalism took on new meaning. On the same January 1946 day that the UN General Assembly passed its very first resolution calling for the peaceful uses of nuclear energy and the abolition of nuclear weapons, US President Harry S. Truman announced that army-navy Joint Task Force One would undertake a series of atmospheric nuclear detonations at Bikini Atoll in the Marshall Islands.[54]

The Nuclear Charter

The bomb made its public debut in the Marshall Islands during the summer of 1946 as part of Operation Crossroads, a widely publicised media spectacle (Hamilton and O'Gorman, 2019). Nominally, the blast series was designed to test the effects of existing nuclear weapon designs on boats, but the series had far reaching political ramifications (Herken, 1980). Now recharacterising Bikini Atoll as a salvific laboratory for science and technology, the United States materialised arguments about the former Mandate's nuclear associations. Shortly afterwards, the US Joint Chiefs of Staff acquiesced in designating the area as a strategic trusteeship and pivoted toward expanding nuclear blasting.

The location of the Crossroads nuclear blasts in the ambiguous international spaces of Indigenous Oceania was no mistake. Geographical and logistical considerations—proximity to a major US base, weather

100 M. X. Mitchell

patterns, distance from other populated areas—had been the main criteria undergirding military officials' selection of Bikini Atoll (Weisgall, 1994; Vine, 2009), but legal and political considerations also came into play. At alternative sites, such as the Galápagos Islands, occupied by the US military, but claimed by Ecuador, US ability to operate freely hinged on relations with another sovereign state, that is, with another entity that had an equal status under international law.[55] No similar obstacles impeded US power in the former Mandate. Because of the muddled situation surrounding sovereignty, no single state held a strong, unitary counter-vailing claim as against US possession. Islanders, meanwhile, were stateless since the League and the US regarded them as dependent peoples, incapable of holding sovereignty in their own right. They therefore lacked the status to object under international law as well as the practical means to raise a claim. The smoothest path for the United States' projection of its nuclear power hinged on Islanders' existing marginalisation under international law.

Reflecting the Joint Task Force's estimation of Islanders' difference and lack of capacity, neither the ri-Bikini nor other Marshallese leaders were consulted in advance of the decision to site nuclear blasts at Bikini Atoll. They were simply "advised" of US plans in February of 1946, while a navy crew began blasting channels through coral heads in the lagoon (Weisgall, 1994).[56] Navy officials did not document legally the expropriation of Bikini or the forced relocation of its people. This may have been partly because military officials seemed to view the situation as temporary (Weisgall, 1994), but it also spoke to the ongoing ways in which occupying forces regarded Indigenous land tenure as distinct from property rights and approached military necessity very capaciously, even after the war's end.

Press observers and US military public relations officials depicted ri-Bikini dispossession not as a legal event, but as a moral, Christian sacrifice that furthered the advancement of science and technology.[57] Task force officials, members of the press, and even the US President described Bikini Atoll as a laboratory and site of experiment, deepening military associations of Pacific places as technological infrastructure.[58] This was a new call to science and technology, one that added weapons proving, now coded as "experiment," to a prior focus on fortification. That summer, Bikini Atoll became an exploding experimental node in the nuclear network—a site where the violence and mass destruction of the United States' signal weapons system could be offshored, routinised, and rationalised. The process resembled what activist and Crossroads observer Norman Cousins (1946: 16) described as the "standardization of catastrophe."

Onlookers worldwide interpreted the spectacle as bearing directly on negotiations over the United States' international power (Herken, 1980). As scientists detected radioactive material from the blasts in Paris during on-going post-war peace talks, CBS newscaster Lyman Bryson observed that

The Nuclear Charter 101

the "shadow of the atom bomb" was at the "back of every discussion ... unseen, but in the front seat."[59]

Just a few months later, the US announced its intention to retain control of the former Mandate as a United Nations strategic trusteeship. In October of 1946, lawyer John Foster Dulles, then serving as an adviser to the Secretary of State, persuaded the Joint Chiefs of Staff that strategic trusteeship would be the "equivalent of sovereign rights without annexation."[60] President Truman circulated a draft trusteeship agreement in November, which had been devised by the Joint Chiefs of Staff in collaboration with the Department of State.[61]

The agreement recharacterised the entire former Mandate as a strategic area. The document thus limited UN oversight and circumscribed it within the Security Council. The agreement reserved broad rights for the United States to develop military facilities, tempered by some protections for Islanders. The text, however, gave no indication of how tensions between US authority, on the one hand, and obligations to Islanders, on the other hand, might be resolved.[62] Less than one year after Crossroads, and with few changes, the US Trusteeship Agreement was accepted by the UN Security Council and signed into US law (Borgwardt, 2005). President Truman designated the US Navy as the administering agency (Friedman, 2007).

The US military establishment and the newly formed US Atomic Energy Commission (AEC) quickly pivoted to deepen and reproduce associations between strategic trusteeship and nuclear weapons. A US Army legal review of AEC plans to create a proving ground at Enewetak Atoll in the Marshall Islands found "no obstacle of international law or agreement." The memo focused exclusively on the Trusteeship Agreement's authorisation of military facilities, reasoning that a nuclear proving ground was just another kind of military facility. The opinion did not mention Islanders at all or delve into trusteeship provisions purporting to protect them.[63]

This opportunistic reading of the trusteeship agreement reflected an implicit assumption that military or "strategic" powers under trusteeship trumped ones relating to Islanders. The interpretation wrote Islanders out of the trusteeship agreement almost completely. Within just a few months after the trusteeship's creation in 1947, the United States designated Enewetak Atoll as the US Pacific Proving Grounds and relocated its people (Hacker, 1994), again without legal process or meaningful negotiation.

Nuclear technologies now seemed so linked to American governance of the former Mandate that one anthropologist and former US military consultant suggested the area could be called ATTOM—The Atomic Trust Territory of Micronesia (Keesing, 1947). From 1946 to 1951 all atmospheric US nuclear blasting took place in the Marshall Islands. After the creation of nuclear proving grounds in Nevada and until 1958, the US Atomic Energy Commission continued to utilise Enewetak and Bikini Atolls as blast sites for its most powerful nuclear devices. By 1954, US diplomats

102 M. X. Mitchell

argued that nuclear detonations had been a foreseeable use of the trusteeship in light of the preceding Crossroads blasts, conducted during the US military occupation. They suggested that nuclear blasting predicated strategic trusteeship and defined the legal scope of permissible US military activity.[64]

The United States' novel experiment with internationalism had tied nuclear weapons and their deleterious effects materially to a new template of US extraterritorial power exercised through international law and institutions. This was not a settler sovereignty but an unsettled sovereignty in which considerable sovereign power lay with the United States while territoriality and jurisdiction were ambiguously divided between the United States and the United Nations. It was a status in which the risks and harms of massive, pollution-generating weapons could be located offshore, in Indigenous lands and waters. Islanders' international status as Indigenous dependent peoples had created affordances for the US invasion, occupation, and use of the former Mandate for nuclear detonations. The extension of blasting under strategic trusteeship now further marginalised Islanders, complicating possibilities for redress and for participation in governing their ancestral atolls.

Once thought antithetical to modern internationalism, militarisation had become central to it in the post-war Pacific and beyond. Peace, in this rendering, could best be ensured by military materiel, not least nuclear weapons. US military technology had been yoked to the international system. The Atlantic Charter had become nuclear.

Notes

1 Funding for this research was furnished by the William Nelson Cromwell Foundation and Cornell University's Atkinson Center for a Sustainable Future. I am indebted to Haris Durrani, John Krige, Whitney Laemmli, Susan Lindee, Davide Orsini, William Rankin, Tina Stege, audience members at Princeton University's Shelby Cullom Davis Center seminar, and the volume editors for helpful comments.
2 #220644, March 24, 1944, Box 603, RG80, United States National Archives and Records Administration II, College Park, MD.
3 V. F. Grant, Field Report No. 20, April 27, 1944, Folder: Columbia Naval School, Box A96, Philip C. Jessup Papers, Library of Congress Manuscript Division, Washington, DC.
4 Song of Majuro, collected in 1947, Folder 8, Box 52, Series IX: Margaret Chave Fallers Papers, Lloyd A. Fallers Collection, University of Chicago Archive, Chicago, IL.
5 Francis B. Sayre, Legal Problems Arising from the United Nations Trusteeship System, March 1948, Reel 862, Trust Territory of the Pacific Islands Archive, University of Hawai'i at Mānoa, Honolulu, HI.
6 The Covenant of the League of Nations (1919), Article 22.
7 Sayre, Legal Problems Arising from the United Nations Trusteeship System.
8 Interview with Kabua Kabua, June 11, 1953, Folder 021, Box 1, Jack Adair Tobin Papers, Unprocessed Collection, University of Hawai'i at Mānoa Pacific Collections, Honolulu, HI.

The Nuclear Charter   103

9 See, for example, Account of a Man named Rudolph Living in Rita Village on Majuro, Folder 13, Box 52, Chave Papers.

10 See Memorandum for Fleet Admiral Nimitz, JCS Views Regarding Japanese Islands- Resume Of, July 6, 1947, Folder: A14-1, Box 5, Secretary and Under Secretary of the Navy James Forrestal, Correspondence Relating to Meetings of the Top Policy Group, 1944–1947, RG80, National Archives and Records Administration, College Park, MD.

11 Grant, Field Report No. 20.

12 See, e.g., Philip C. Jessup, Notes: Law of Belligerent Occupation—Some Applications of the Hague Rules to Areas of the Pacific, n.d. 1942–1943. Folder: Columbia Naval School, Box A93, Jessup Papers; William Edward Johnson, Comparative Analysis of the American & British Manuals of Military Government & Administration, n.d. 1943–1944. Folder: Columbia University School of Military Government, Box A92, Jessup Papers.

13 See, for example, "Military Government School: Its Alumni Face a Big Test in the Marshalls," Bureau of Naval Personnel Training Bulletin, Issue 14916, March 15, 1944, Folder 4, Box 48, Series V: Educational and Military Training Programs, UA#015 World War II Collection 1933–1956, Columbia University Archives, New York, NY; Captain F.J. Cleary to Captain Harry Pence, July 15, 1944. Folder: Columbia Naval School, Box A92, Jessup Papers; January 29, 1944, Directive for Military Government and Civil Affairs, Kwajalein Atoll. Folder: Columbia Naval School, Box A96, Jessup Papers.

14 "Military Government School: Its Alumni Face a Big Test in the Marshalls"; Philip C. Jessup to Herbert H. Lehman, Department of State, February 28, 1943. Folder: Columbia Naval School, Box A92, Jessup Papers.

15 Philip C. Jessup, Transcribed Excerpt of Annual Report of the Secretary of the Navy for Fiscal Year 1940, n.d. 1943–1944. Folder: Columbia Naval School, Box A94, Jessup Papers.

16 Jessup, Notes: Law of Belligerent Occupation. See note 12.

17 Johnson, Comparative Analysis of the American & British Manuals of Military Government & Administration.

18 Jessup, Notes: Law of Belligerent Occupation.

19 John D. Phillips, The Effect upon Principles and Policies of Military Government of the Type of Territory Occupied, n.d. 1943–1944. Folder: Columbia Naval School, Box A93, Jessup Papers.

20 W. J. Miller, Custody of Enemy Property, October 20, 1943. Folder: Columbia Naval School, Box A93, Jessup Papers; Philip C. Jessup, Preliminary Memorandum on Some Aspects of Military Occupation, July 13, 1942. Folder: Columbia Naval School, Box A94, Jessup Papers.

21 Jessup, Preliminary Memorandum on Some Aspects of Military Occupation; Grant, Field Report No. 20.

22 Robert Lovett, Assistant Secretary for War for Air to Assistant Chief of Air Staff, October 19, 1943; George A. Brownell, Colonel, Army Air Corps to Assistant Secretary of War for Air, Memorandum, February 13, 1945, Box 199, Secretary of War, Office, Assistant Secretary of War for Air, Plans, Policies & Agreements, 1943–1947, Item 3–9, RG107, National Archives and Records Administration, College Park, MD; Grant, Field Report No. 20.

23 Phillips, The Effect upon Principles and Policies of Military Government of the Type of Territory Occupied.

24 Grant, Field Report No. 20.

25 #220843, March 24, 1944, Unidentified atoll, Box 603, RG80, United States National Archives and Records Administration II, College Park, MD.

26 C. S. Lawton, Reconnaissance of Wotho, Ujae, and Lae Atolls, March 15, 1944. Folder: Columbia Naval School, Box A96, Jessup Papers.

27 Francis C. Affeld, Civil Affairs Field Report No. 23, June 29, 1944. Folder: Columbia Naval School, Box A96, Jessup Papers.

28 Caption, #323822, n.d. 1944–1945, Box 2, RG38, National Archives and Records Administration, College Park, MD.

29 i #323822, n.d. 1944-1945,1944–1945, Box 2, RG38, National Archives and Records Administration, College Park, MD

30 W. C. Clarke to Harold Ickes, February 12, 1946. Folder: Pacific Islands, 1946–1948, Box 76, Harold L. Ickes Papers, Library of Congress, Manuscript Division, Washington, DC.

31 Eugene Bogan to Eric Beecroft, December 18, 1945. Folder: Pacific Islands, 1946–1948, Box 76, Ickes Papers.

32 People Coming Together, collected in 1947, Field Notes. Folder 8, Box 52, Chave Papers.

33 August 14, 1941, The Atlantic Charter.

34 Office of Strategic Services, Research and Analysis Branch, Legal Problems Concerning the Status of Japanese Mandated Islands, February 7, 1944. Folder: Columbia Naval School, Box A98, Jessup Papers.

35 For thoroughgoing recounting of many aspects of debates over trusteeship and annexation, see Friedman (2001; 2007; 2009).

36 Minutes of the 11th Meeting of the US Delegation to the United Nations, April 17, 1945, Document 158, Diplomatic Papers, 1945, General: The United Nations Volume I, *Foreign Relations of the United States.*

37 Joint Chiefs of Staff, Memorandum for the State-War-Navy Coordinating Committee, June 16, 1946. Folder: Trusteeships, Pacific Islands, Box: 121, President's Secretary's Files, Papers of Harry S. Truman, Harry S. Truman Library, Independence, MO; See also summary and quotes from 1944–1946 in Memorandum for Fleet Admiral Nimitz, JCS Views Regarding Japanese Islands- Resume Of.

38 Minutes of the 11th Meeting of the US Delegation to the United Nations, April 17, 1945.

39 Minutes of the 11th Meeting of the US Delegation to the United Nations, April 17, 1945.

40 General C. P. Cabell to Joint Chiefs of Staff, Memorandum on Basing, September 14, 1945, Box 199, Air War Plans, Policies & Agreements Papers.

41 US Requirements for Post-War Military Airbases and Rights in Foreign Territory, July 11, 1945, Box 199, Secretary of War, Office, Air War Plans, Policies & Agreements Papers.

42 The Effects of the Atomic Bomb on National Security (An Expression of War Department Thinking), n.d. 1945 or 1946. Folder: Atomic Bomb 1, Box 9b, General Records of the Department of the Navy, Office of Information Subject Files, 1940–1958, RG428, National Archives and Records Administration II, College Park, MD.

43 See, for example, Minutes of the 11th Meeting of the US Delegation to the United Nations, April 17, 1945; Lt. Col. Donald T. Winder, Report on Civil Affairs of the 4th Marine division, February 16, 1944, Folder: Columbia Naval School, Box A97, Jessup Papers.

44 See, for example, Memorandum for Fleet Admiral Nimitz, JCS Views Regarding Japanese Islands- Resume Of.

45 Joint Chiefs of Staff, Memorandum for the State-War-Navy Coordinating Committee.

The Nuclear Charter 105

46 The landmark case is Downes v. Bidwell, 182 US 244 (1901).
47 Joint Chiefs of Staff, Memorandum for the State-War-Navy Coordinating Committee.
48 Philip C. Jessup, The Future of Micronesia, November 20, 1944. Folder: Columbia Naval School, Box A98, Jessup Papers.
49 Abe Fortas, Statement on Trusteeship System, May 12, 1945, Folder 37, Box 163, Series V, MSS 858, Abe Fortas Papers, Yale University Manuscripts and Archives, New Haven, CT.
50 United Nations Charter, Ch. XII.
51 Abe Fortas, Speech, What Should the United States Do About Pacific Bases? February 18, 1946. Folder 33, Box 129, Series III, Fortas Papers.
52 Abe Fortas to Harold Ickes, Memorandum 7, January 9, 1946. Folder 40, Box 163, Series V, Fortas Papers.
53 Abe Fortas, The Art of Living Together, January 1946. Folder 31, Box 129, Series III, Fortas Papers; Abe Fortas to Harold R. Moskovitz, December 12, 1945. Folder 31, Box 129, Series III, Fortas Papers.
54 General Assembly Resolution 1/1, *Establishment of a Commission to Deal with the Problems Raised by the Discovery of Atomic Energy* (January 24, 1946); Minutes of Press Conference Held by Vice Admiral W. H. P. Blandy, January 24, 1946, Box 99, Operation Crossroads Releases and Conferences, RG428, National Archives and Records Administration, College Park, MD.
55 Clipping from *Honolulu Star Bulletin*, June 10, 1946, Kili/Bikini Notebook 11, Robert C. Kiste Papers, Unprocessed Collection, Pacific Collections, University of Hawai'i at Mānoa, Honolulu, HI; Lovett to Assistant Chief of Air Staff, October 19, 1943; Brownell to Assistant Secretary of War for Air, February 13, 1945.
56 H. C. Meade to Senior Military Government Officer, March 1946, reproduced in Notebook 13, Kiste Papers.
57 See, for example, Crossroads Release 13, March 11, 1946, Box 99, Crossroads Releases and Conferences; *Honolulu Star Bulletin*, April 1, 1946.
58 See, for example, Crossroads Release 32, April 1, 1946, Box 99, Crossroads Releases and Conferences; Press Release, Address by Rear Admiral W.S. Parsons Before the AAAS, Boston MA, December 27, 1946. Folder: Atomic Energy (3), Box 9, Navy Office of Information Papers; Statement by President Truman, April 12, 1946. Folder: Atomic Bomb 1945–1946, Box 9a, Navy Office of Information Papers.
59 *New York Times*, Radioactive Matter Found in the Air Above France, August 7, 1946, 2; Columbia Broadcasting System, You and the Atom, Transcript, July 31, 1946. Folder: You and the Atom, Box 9b, Office of Information Subject Files, 1940-1958, RG428, National Archives and Records Administration, College Park, MD.
60 John Foster Dulles, Memorandum to James Forrestal, October 16, 1946. Folder: A14-1 Trusteeship-Dumbarton Oaks-Yalta, Box 5, Secretary and Undersecretary of the Navy Papers.
61 R. L. Dennison to James Forrestal, February 6, 1947. Folder: A14-1 Trusteeship-Dumbarton Oaks-Yalta, Box 5, Secretary and Undersecretary of the Navy Papers.
62 Trusteeship Agreement for the Former Japanese Mandated Islands Approved at the One Hundred and Twenty-Fourth Meeting of the Security Council, S/318, April 2, 1947.
63 Memorandum for the Record, Closed Areas in the Trust Territory of the Pacific Islands, October 15, 1947, Folder 18.12, Weapons Testing—Proving Grounds—Bikini, General, 1946–1952, Box 77, General Records Relating to

106 M. X. Mitchell

Atomic Energy Matters, Office of the Secretary, Special Assistant Secretary of State for Atomic Energy & Outer Space, RG59, General Records of the Department of State, National Archives and Records Administration II, College Park, MD.

64 See Statement by Mason Sears (1954). *Department of State Bulletin,* 31, p. 139.

References

Adas, M. (2006). *Dominance by Design*. Cambridge, MA: Harvard University Press.

Anderson, W. (2006). *Colonial Pathologies: American Tropical Medicine, Race, and Hygiene in the American Colonization of the Philippines from 1898 Through the 1930s*. Durham, NC: Duke University Press.

Anghie, A. (2005). *Imperialism, Sovereignty, and the Making of International Law*. New York: Cambridge University Press.

Arnold, H. (1945). *Third Report of the Commanding General of the Army Air Forces to the Secretary of War, November 12, 1945*. Baltimore, MD: Schneidereith and Sons.

Bhandar, B. (2018). *Colonial Lives of Property: Law, Land, and Racial Regimes of Ownership*. Durham, NC: Duke University Press.

Biddle, T. (2001). *Rhetoric and Reality in Air Warfare: The Evolution of British and American Ideas about Strategic Bombing, 1914–1945*. Princeton, NJ: Princeton University Press.

Borgwardt, E. (2005). *A New Deal for the New World: America's Vision for Human Rights*. Cambridge, MA: Harvard University Press.

Bosco, D. (2009). *Five to Rule them All: The UN Security Council and the Making of the Modern World*. New York: Oxford University Press.

Brown, K. (2013). *Plutopia: Nuclear Families, Atomic Cities, and the Great Soviet and American Plutonium Disasters*. New York: Oxford University Press.

Chave, M. (1947). *Final Report Submitted to the Pacific Science Board of the National Research Council for Work Done at Majuro, Marshall Islands—Summer 1947*. Washington, DC: Coordinated Investigation of Micronesian Anthropology.

Coates, B. (2016). *Legalist Empire: International Law and American Foreign Relations in the Early Twentieth Century*. New York: Oxford University Press.

Cousins, N. (1946). The Standardization of Catastrophe. *Saturday Review,* August 10, p. 16.

Erman, S. (2019). *Almost Citizens: Puerto Rico, the US Constitution, & Empire*. New York: Cambridge University Press.

Ford, L. (2010). *Settler Sovereignty: Jurisdiction and Indigenous People in America and Australia, 1788-1836*. Cambridge, MA: Harvard University Press.

Friedman, H. (2001). *Creating an American Lake: United States Imperialism and Strategic Security in the Pacific Basin, 1945–1947*. Westport, CT: Greenwood Press.

Friedman, H. (2007). *Governing the American Lake: US Defense and Administration of the Pacific, 1945–1947*. East Lansing, MI: Michigan State University Press.

The Nuclear Charter 107

Friedman, H. (2009). *Arguing over the American Lake: Bureaucracy and Rivalry in the US Pacific, 1945–1947*. College Station, TX: Texas A&M Press.

Genz, J. (2018). *Breaking the Shell: Voyaging from Nuclear Refugees to People of the Sea in the Marshall Islands*. Honolulu, HI: University of Hawai'i Press.

Gordin, M. (2007). *Five Days in August: How World War II Became a Nuclear War*. Princeton, NJ: Princeton University Press.

Hacker, B. (1994). *Elements of Controversy: The Atomic Energy Commission and Radiation Safety in Nuclear Weapons Testing 1947–1974*. Berkeley, CA: University of California Press.

Hamilton, K., and O'Gorman, N. (2019). *Lookout America! The Secret Hollywood Studio at the Heart of the Cold War*. Hanover, NH: Dartmouth College Press.

Hanlon, D. (1998). *Remaking Micronesia: Discourses Over Development in a Pacific Territory, 1944–1982*. Honolulu, HI: University of Hawai'i Press.

Hathaway, O., and Shapiro, S. (2017). *The Internationalists: How a Radical Plan to Outlaw War Remade the World*. New York: Simon & Schuster.

Hecht, G. (2012). *Being Nuclear: Africans and the Global Uranium Trade*. Cambridge, MA: MIT Press.

Herken, G. (1980). *The Winning Weapon: The Atomic Bomb and the Cold War, 1945–1950*. Princeton, NJ: Princeton University Press.

Hezel, F. (1995). *Strangers in Their Own Land: A Century of Colonial Rule in the Caroline and Marshall Islands*. Honolulu, HI: University of Hawai'i Press.

Hirshberg, L. (2022). *Suburban Empire: Cold War Militarization in the US Pacific*. Berkeley, CA: University of California Press.

Jetnil-Kijiner, K. (2014). *Iep Jāltok: A History of Marshallese Literature*. M.A. thesis. University of Hawai'i.

Kalman, L. (1990). *Abe Fortas: A Biography*. New Haven, CT: Yale University Press.

Keesing, F. (1947). Administration in Pacific Islands. *Far Eastern Survey*, 16(6), pp. 61–65.

Kramer, P. (2006). *The Blood of Government: Race, Empire, the United States, and the Philippines*. Chapel Hill, NC: University of North Carolina Press.

Kuletz, V. (1998). *The Tainted Desert: Environmental and Social Ruin in the American West*. New York: Routledge.

LaBriola, M. (2019). Planting Islands: Marshall Islanders Shaping Land, Power, and History. *The Journal of Pacific History*, 54(2), pp. 182–198.

Lindee, M. (1994). *Suffering Made Real: American Science and the Survivors at Hiroshima*. Chicago: University of Chicago Press.

Maclellan, N. (2017). *Grappling with the Bomb: Britain's Pacific H-Bomb Tests*. Acton: Australian National University Press.

Masco, J. (2006). *The Nuclear Borderlands: The Manhattan Project in Post-Cold War New Mexico*. Princeton, NJ: Princeton University Press.

Masco, J. (2014). *Theater of Operations: National Security Affect from the Cold War to the War on Terror*. Durham, NC: Duke University Press.

Mazower, M. (2009). *No Enchanted Palace: The End of Empire and the Ideological Origins of the United Nations*. Princeton, NJ: Princeton University Press.

McBride, W. (2000). *Technological Change and the United States Navy, 1865-1945*. Baltimore, MD: Johns Hopkins University Press.

108   M. X. Mitchell

Oldenziel, R. (2011). Islands: The United States as a Networked Empire. In: G. Hecht, ed., *Entangled Geographies: Empire and Technopolitics in the Global Cold War*. Cambridge, MA: MIT Press, pp. 13–42.

Peattie, M. (1988). *Nan'yō: The Rise and Fall of the Japanese in Micronesia, 1885–1945*. Honolulu, HI: University of Hawai'i Press.

Pedersen, S. (2015). *The Guardians: The League of Nations and the Crisis of Empire*. New York: Oxford University Press.

Poyer, L., Falgout, S., and Carucci, L. (2001). *The Typhoon of War: Micronesian Experiences of the Pacific War*. Honolulu, HI: University of Hawai'i Press.

Richard, D. (1957a). *United States Naval Administration of the Trust Territory of the Pacific Islands. Volume 1*. Washington, DC: US Government Printing Office.

Richard, D. (1957b). *United States Naval Administration of the Trust Territory of the Pacific Islands. Volume 2*. Washington, DC: US Government Printing Office.

Smith-Norris, M. (2016). *Domination and Resistance: The United States and the Marshall Islands During the Cold War*. Honolulu, HI: University of Hawai'i Press.

Stege, K. (2008). An Kōra Aelōn Kein (These Islands Belong to the Women): A Study of Women and Land in the Marshall Islands. In: E. Huffer, ed., *Land and Women: The Matrilineal Factor*. Suva: Pacific Islands Forum Secretariat, pp. 1–34.

Strackbein, O. (1931). Our Empire. *The North American Review*, 4, pp. 327–334.

Thomas, W. (2015). *Rational Action: The Sciences of Policy in Britain and America, 1940–1960*. Cambridge, MA: MIT Press.

Thompson, L. (2010). *Imperial Archipelago: Representation and Rule in the Insular Territories under US Dominion after 1889*. Honolulu, HI: University of Hawai'i Press.

Vine, D. (2009). *Island of Shame: The Secret History of the US Military Base on Diego Garcia*. Princeton, NJ: Princeton University Press.

Voyles, T. (2015). *Wastelanding: Legacies of Uranium Mining in Navajo Country*. Minneapolis, MN: University of Minnesota Press.

Walsh, J. (2003). *Imagining the Marshalls: Chiefs, Traditions, and the State on the Fringes of US Empire*. PhD dissertation. University of Hawai'i.

Webster, A. (2017). The League of Nations, Disarmament and Internationalism. In: G. Sluga and P. Calvin, eds., *Internationalisms: A Twentieth-Century History*. New York: Cambridge University Press, pp. 139–169.

Weisgall, J. (1994). *Operation Crossroads: The Atomic Tests at Bikini Atoll*. Annapolis, MD: Naval Institute Press.

Weisiger, M. (2009). *Dreaming of Sheep in Navajo Country*. Seattle, WA: University of Washington Press.

Section II
Pacifying through control and containment

5 Sharing the "safe" atom?: the International Atomic Energy Agency and nuclear regulation through standardisation[1]

Angela N. H. Creager and Maria Rentetzi

In his famous "Atoms for Peace" speech in 1953, US President Dwight Eisenhower advocated that the United Nations establish a new specialised organisation to support applications of civilian atomic energy worldwide, for which the United States and the USSR would contribute to a "bank" of fissionable material (Eisenhower, 1990). Following three years of intense negotiations among 12 countries, the Statute of the IAEA was eventually signed by 81 states on October 23, 1956. The basic objective of the new organisation was "to seek to accelerate and enlarge the contribution of atomic energy to peace, health and prosperity throughout the world."[2] The United States and The Soviet Union were already providing nuclear assistance (starting with radioisotopes) to other countries; the IAEA could expand such programs into the developing world and monitor control over aid recipients. As it turned out, the IAEA never became a repository of fissionable materials. Rather, its function became to promote the peaceful uses of nuclear technologies among its member states while seeking to prevent the diversion of these resources into military development.

From the start, the IAEA's planners emphasised that, as the world's demand for energy increased, many countries would turn to atomic energy.[3] Developed nations hoped to become less dependent on oil imported from the Middle East, especially after the Suez crisis in 1956 (Lekarenko, 2018). The UN and IAEA stoked equally high expectations about the transformative power of nuclear energy in the developing— and decolonising—world. The chairman of the Pakistan Atomic Energy Commission recalled that "commercial nuclear electricity generation seemed around the corner" (Khan, 1987: 7).[4] Indonesia's Minister of State for Research and Technology argued that the transfer of nuclear technologies, which the IAEA initiated through its technical assistance programs to the developing countries, was an integral part of the largest process of nation building (Beck, 1989). As Itty Abraham has observed, access to nuclear technology was a way "to create political legitimacy for the postcolonial state" (Abraham, 2006: 62). Yet the IAEA's provision

DOI: 10.4324/9781003227472-5

112 Angela N. H. Creager and Maria Rentetzi

of nuclear access came with ongoing surveillance. As a Ukranian representative to the negotiations over the IAEA's Statute noted, the agency's safeguard measures kept developing countries under the "yoke of atomic colonialism" (Roehrlich, 2018: 209).

The IAEA remains best known for its efforts in certifying that civilian-intended reactors, technologies and fissionable fuel were not used for covert nuclear weapons programs, above all in the developing world. In this respect, the IAEA aimed at securing the hegemony of the nuclear powers in the name of world peace—which would also ensure that Asian, African, and Latin American nations remained subordinate players in Cold War geopolitics, in a state of "nuclear apartheid" (Maddock, 2014; Krige, "Constructing world order," ch. 3, this book). The IAEA was, after all, the brainchild of the US, which used the agency's international and ostensibly independent status to advance American interests, both national security and commercial. As noted by Jacob Hamblin, accommodating these business interests often worked against the effectiveness of nuclear weapons safeguards, and ultimately, nonproliferation (Hamblin, 2017).

Less attention has been paid to the IAEA's health and safety programs related to civilian applications of nuclear energy, which also entailed oversight of recipient (usually developing) countries. Even the peaceful uses of atomic energy involve possible harm, namely exposure to ionising radiation. In fact, early on the agency used the term "safeguard" to refer to both its monitoring of nuclear weapons development and its setting of radiological safety standards for handling nuclear and radioactive materials.[5] Focusing on the agency's first decade, our paper stresses how the IAEA positioned itself as the dominant supplier of tools and guidelines for radiological protection, despite the presence of other international organisations in this domain. We argue that the IAEA used its unique position as an international organisation to promote the atom on a global scale, to safeguard it by providing standards for use and safety, especially to developing countries in the Global South, and to create a "world nuclear law" that could support the development of nuclear industry.

The IAEA's reputation was built on being a strictly technical organisation, allegedly eschewing politics (Hecht, 2006; Weichselbraun, 2020). Its intended role securing nuclear nonproliferation was technocratic. Until the 1970s (notably until India's first nuclear blast), the agency aimed to verify data provided by states, not investigate them (Weichselbraun, 2020). The IAEA's technocratic approach carried over into its radiological protection regime. Its standardisation of instruments, measuring devices, units of measurement, objects, procedures, and specialised vocabulary was a technical-cum-political enterprise. Functioning as a global metrological and regulatory institution, the IAEA crafted standards on radiation safety alongside a complex network of political activities, rules, laws, and hierarchies. While other international bodies with nuclear profiles, such as

Sharing the "Safe" Atom? 113

Euratom or the European Nuclear Energy Agency, were oriented to industrialised powers, the IAEA was explicitly engaged in development projects, especially in the Global South.[6] Its dissemination of radiological standards was part of a neo-colonial mission of technology transfer. Examining the IAEA's role in the sharing and regulation of nuclear technologies and safety standards contributes to recent studies of atomic energy as an instrument of Cold War diplomacy and development (Hecht, 2011; Mateos and Suárez-Díaz, 2015a; Krige, 2016; Ito and Rentetzi, 2021; Rentetzi and Ito, 2021).

Promoting the atom

On January 13, 1959, Mariano Maggiore, chief of *Italpublic*, an Italian public relations firm focused on the nuclear industry, addressed Lars Lind, chief of IAEA's Division of Public Information. Maggiore's question was straightforward: Was the IAEA interested in "illustrating its activities and its scopes to the large number of European businessmen who will be visiting the Fair"?[7] Founded in 1920, the Milan Fair was a successful, longstanding commercial exhibition representing activities in industry, commerce and agriculture from more than 50 different countries. More than 4 million people attended each year, excepting 1943–1945, when it was suspended amid the war.[8] When it began again in 1946, the Milan Fair heralded the rapid progress of Italian industry, becoming a symbol of post-war economic development. In 1959, it featured its first section dedicated to nuclear energy; *Italpublic* was commissioned to organise Milan's atomic-themed exhibit. The plan was to include all industrial and medical applications of nuclear energy in a single exhibition hall, enabling the numerous companies with a stake in nuclear industry to reach the wider public. "A great propaganda value is to be expected," Maggiore explained to Lind.[9]

The IAEA was, indeed, an obvious participant in the Milan Fair (and client for *Italpublic*). Responding to Maggiore a week later, Lind suggested that, since the IAEA had already displayed an exhibit at the Atoms for Peace Conference in Geneva in 1955, "this could be brought up to date without too much difficulty or cost."[10] Financial constraints would actually mean the IAEA could not formally take part in the Milan Fair. Nonetheless, its Deputy Director General Henry Seligman was invited to give a keynote speech in the theater within the industrial exhibits Pavilion. An international expert on the use of radioisotopes in industry, medicine and agriculture who had worked at Harwell, the United Kingdom's nuclear research laboratory, Seligman was delighted to accept the invitation. He proposed the topic "Uses of Isotopes and Radiation in Industry."[11]

The Milan Fair was neither the first nor the last exhibition at which the IAEA sought to propagate its activities. In 1958, the Agency, along with the UN, participated in the Brussels World's Fair, known as Expo

'58, one of the most remarkable displays of the peaceful uses of atomic energy in the 1950s (Banci, 2009). It seemed "eminently desirable" to Marcelle Napier, the Agency's special media officer, to use Expo '58 as a launch site for the IAEA's first published booklet about its aims and activities. The exhibition was expected, after all, to attract 41 million visitors. Its centerpiece, the massive silver "Atomium," signified the bright future of nuclear energy.[12] That year, voices within the IAEA would suggest the formation of an advisory panel on the "possibility of organising exhibitions."[13] Within two years, the Agency was eagerly responding to repeated requests to distribute information, reach out to the public, and participate in exhibitions around the globe.[14]

Throughout the 1960s, the IAEA worked in various ways to present nuclear energy (in the first instance, provision of radioisotopes) as a means of economic assistance for developing nations. This work included organising surveys on the needs of Member States so as to "decide on the lines of effective aid." In early 1959, an IAEA mission visited Burma, Ceylon, Indonesia and Thailand. The next year another mission visited Greece and several African countries. In all cases, the missions collected information and exchanged ideas on the kind of technical assistance that each country could request (Figure 5.1).[15] The major vehicles, in a literal sense, for promoting the use of radioisotopes were a pair of mobile laboratories that toured Latin America, a couple of European countries, Asia and even Ghana on the African continent.

The mobile radioisotope laboratories were designed by the Oak Ridge Institute of Nuclear Studies and donated to IAEA by the United States on April 29, 1958. As Gisela Mateos and Edna Suárez-Díaz have shown in their remarkable study of the journey of "Unit 2" in Latin America, transporting this mobile lab across landscapes and boundaries was a formidable challenge, illustrating some of the diverse obstacles involved in sharing and showcasing even simple nuclear technologies (Mateos and Suárez-Diáz, 2015a; 2015b; 2019). These mobile units—used to provide basic training tools for radioisotope handling techniques and exhibit the benefits of nuclear energy to IAEA's Member States—were the most celebrated and forward-thinking diplomatic gifts offered to the newly created Agency by the Americans. In fact, presenting them as gifts to the IAEA meant the donated labs required political reciprocity. They paved the way to the fulfillment of three major American aims: (a) to dominate on a global scale the material culture of laboratory work on radioisotope techniques, (b) to maintain an upper hand in the global market of radioisotopes and (c) to promote the Atoms for Peace agenda. Put to propagandistic use, the mobile labs served as exhibition spaces across the globe and inducted young scientists in the developing world to the material culture of American laboratories (Rentetzi, 2021).[16]

This was only one among several programs the IAEA developed to impart expertise and technology. Following a linear model of technology

Sharing the "Safe" Atom? 115

Figure 5.1 Original caption: "Modern methods of prospecting for uranium are being applied in a number of countries and the IAEA in Vienna (Austria) is helping its Member States by technical advice and missions. It is also encouraging research on cheaper methods to recover uranium from low-grade ores and as a by-product from other mineral production. The 1969 technical assistance program will give help in the development of nuclear raw materials to Chile, Ethiopia, Greece, Guatemala, Mexico, Peru and Tunisia. In Tunisia samples are examined in a laboratory." IAEA/No. 1984. IAEA Archives/E0045-003. 1969. Credit: IAEA/Moir.

transfer, nuclear technologies were purportedly transferred from developed countries to developing countries' recipient institutes, finally reaching their end users in local contexts (Mateos and Suárez-Díaz, 2020). In its first decade, the IAEA's technical assistance program was limited to small, short-term projects (lasting less than a year) involving technology transfer and circulation of expertise (Fischer, 1997: 3). In its first year alone, the IAEA announced a fund of around $2 million for more than 200 fellowships, giving young engineers and scientists the chance to visit foreign universities and research institutes around the world.[17] Training young professionals, going into the field to dispense expert advice, donating nuclear equipment and presenting well-designed international exhibitions became some of the most effective instruments used by the IAEA to channel post-war expectations for atomic energy.

116 *Angela N. H. Creager and Maria Rentetzi*

Some three decades later, the IAEA was presented as "catalyst" in accelerating nuclear technology transfer (Beck, 1989).

Radioisotopes and nuclear energy represented one of several technological fronts for fostering economic development, especially in the Global South, during the Cold War.[18] Contributing to the Green Revolution, the IAEA collaborated with the UN's Food and Agriculture Organisation to use new radiation sources such as cobalt-60 for generating new crop strains (Hamblin, 2015).[19] Yet atomic energy presented distinctive and undeniable risks that the IAEA sought to control. Even if nuclear materials and technologies were not diverted toward covert military development, civilian exposure to ionising radiation was a known health hazard.[20]

Safeguards

The scientific understanding of the biological effects of ionising radiation on humans changed significantly in the decades after World War II, raising new questions and stakes for radiological protection. In 1946, exposure to low-level radiation was generally regarded as safe—or at least, its hazards were manageable. But by the mid-1950s, studies of radioactive fallout and waste, in conjunction with ongoing studies of radiation's long-term effects on Japanese atomic bomb survivors, led many scientists to question whether US safety standards for occupational and populational exposures were adequate—even whether the available global scientific knowledge was adequate to set such standards (Divine, 1978: 262–280; Kopp, 1979; Creager, 2015). As Soraya Boudia has shown (Boudia, 2007; Boudia, "in this volume", intergovernmental organisations found themselves grappling with the changing science and politics of exposure in formulating "global risk."

The 1956 report on the Biological Effects of Atomic Radiation (BEAR), released by the US National Academy of Sciences/National Research Council, highlighted these concerns. The experts appointed to the panel were organised into six committees: genetics, pathology, agriculture and food supply, meteorology, oceanography and fisheries, and disposal of radioactive waste. Their cumulative report recommended reducing the maximum cumulative radiation exposure to reproductive cells from 300 to 50 roentgens and limiting the average exposure through age 30 in the population at large to ten roentgens. The geneticists were particularly insistent on the possible hazards of exposure, asserting that there was no lower threshold for risk from ionising radiation. They were unconvinced that US government occupational standards protected workers sufficiently against genetic damage from ionising radiation—and somatic mutations that might lead to cancer (Jolly, 2003; Beatty, 2006). Their views had implications for protecting civilian populations from low-level radioactive contamination, as well as use of X-rays and radioactivity in medicine and dentistry.[21]

Sharing the "Safe" Atom? 117

Thus, at the time the IAEA was established, the perceived risks of radiation were a political as well as a scientific issue. The promulgation of radiological safety standards and education, alongside its promotion of radioactive materials and nuclear technologies for agriculture and medicine, became a prime objective of the IAEA.[22] Working on the assumption that atomic energy *would* be developed, even *should* be developed, and *could* be developed safely, an anti-nuclear position was never on the table. Radiological safety was, the IAEA asserted, key to the inevitable public acceptance of nuclear energy and technologies.

When Lewis Strauss, chairman of the US Atomic Energy Commission (AEC), welcomed representatives of 81 nations at the UN headquarters in New York to work out the final text of the IAEA's Statute on September 20, 1956, he made it clear that the new organisation was to "accelerate the application of the peaceful uses of atomic energy everywhere, reaching the utmost parts of the earth." This development of atomic energy required "safeguards to [both] health and peace." Brazilian Ambassador Muniz supported the US position in his first remarks as the conference's president, arguing that the Agency must maintain the balance between "reality and aspiration." The world-wide peaceful utilisation of atomic energy required a profound change in international relations, Muniz admitted, specifically toward the adoption of a "system of safeguards and controls."[23] In 1959, the new agency stressed:

> One of the basic objectives of the International Atomic Energy Agency has been to ensure that its activities in promoting the peaceful uses of atomic energy do not defeat their own purpose by posing a danger to public health or by harming the interests of the public in any other way. The Agency seeks, on the one hand, to take positive action in developing the uses of atomic energy in peaceful pursuits and, on the other, to institute systems for guarding against any undesirable consequence that might flow from such action.[24]

In other statements, the IAEA more clearly distinguished two kinds of safeguards implicit in their charge—"those which will be designed to prevent the diversion of Agency assistance to military use and those against health and safety hazards."[25] There was a logic in linking these activities: both verification methods and radiological safety monitoring relied on attaining the best possible detection equipment and well-calibrated standards, and together, these roles addressed the major hazards of nuclear power (health and environmental risks from ionising radiation and nuclear weapons proliferation). However, within five years, the term "safeguard" would exclusively refer to policies and procedures for preventing the diversion of fissionable material from civilian to military uses.

In the early days, according to Carlos Büchler, IAEA's first designated safeguards inspector, "safeguards was technically about accounting for nuclear materials and keeping track of their use and whereabouts" (Büchler, 1997: 47–48; see also Roehrlich, 2018). Politically, however, IAEA safeguards were the subject of heated disputes. David Fischer, Director General of IAEA's External Relations and its internal historian, recalls "the Agency's safeguards initially encountered mistrust and resistance, especially from its developing country members, but also from its Soviet bloc and some West European states intent on protecting Euratom" (Fischer, 2007: 8).

Early discussions on the establishment of the IAEA reflected early Cold War tensions and American anxiety about losing nuclear control. Euratom was established by the six member states of the European Community (forerunner to the EU) in the 1950s to safeguard the use of nuclear materials and technologies for peaceful purposes. The agreement signed between the United States and Euratom in November 1958 consequently kept the IAEA's nuclear safeguards from application in most of Western Europe. Meanwhile, the Soviets joined with developing countries, including India, in full-throated opposition to the safeguards and the US-Euratom agreement. Neither suited the Soviets' political interests in Europe, especially its loss of oversight (via membership in IAEA) over the Federal Republic of Germany (Fischer, 1997: 245).

Despite various oppositions, the Agency announced the appointment of the first Director of the Division of Safeguards in July 1958. Pushing ahead, this division was tasked with the development of safeguard standards, methods and policies. Two years later, the Agency's Board of Governors decided to set up a working group of experts to review the provisional principles of these safeguards. The working group was headed by Gunnar Randers, the Norwegian physicist, who served as Sterling Cole's advisor, and the title of its press release, "Atomic safeguards and health protection before IAEA Board," pointed to their dual mandate. In an extended discussion of IAEA's scientific advisory committee in 1959, some members insisted in differentiating the two tasks while others thought that, "as both functions would be carried out together by the same team of inspectors," there was no need for "unnecessary controversy."[26] By its third meeting, the IAEA's scientific advisory committee was expressing concerns about the Agency not being in line with its statutory responsibilities concerning safeguards. Although its Statute emphasised this function, in practice, the Agency seemed only to focus on safety when it came to reactor safety, waste disposal, and liability questions. It invested more heavily, in the early years, in the technical assistance programs—the promotion of the two mobile laboratories, for example—that would spread nuclear knowledge, avoiding hot conflicts by leaving safeguards regarding weapons development and biohazards aside.[27]

Eisenhower supported authorising the IAEA to monitor nuclear weapons development—in part because overseeing its many bilateral agreements was so costly for the United States—but, as mentioned above,

Sharing the "Safe" Atom? 119

the Soviet Union and many developing countries resisted the IAEA's regulatory role, especially its mandated, on-site inspections. The USSR and its allies "succeeded in delaying approval of the first safeguards agreement with Japan in 1959" (Brown, 2015: 47; see also Holloway, 2016). In 1961, Vasilij Emelyanov, the USSR's representative to the Board of Governors and scientific advisory committee, vehemently objected to the use of any Agency funds for research contracts connected with safeguards and their application.[28] In the end, it took a decade—and the Non-Proliferation Treaty in June 1968—before the IAEA consolidated its authority on international verification, including on-site inspections.

In taking on the mantle of health protection, the IAEA had effectively made its monitoring role over their uses of atomic energy more palatable to member states. As Randers advised Cole,

> [T]he prospect of international control carries with it only the promise of inconvenience and unpleasantness for national establishments... the only way to remedy this basic complication is to find possible ways and means of making the system of safeguards and controls attractive by combining them with related services that are highly desirable for both technical and financial reasons from the point of view of national projects.
>
> (as quoted by Büchler, 1997: 48)

It is not by chance that Randers headed the expert panel on the preparation of the first manual of safe practice for radioisotope users in 1958 (see below).[29] Emphasising its "universal importance," the Agency launched the manual alongside technical publications meant as recommendations for all member states.

Yet if the provision of radiological health services was meant to make surveillance of military diversion more acceptable, there remained a divide between the nuclear "haves" and "have nots" in the IAEA's program of radiological protection.[30] Paul C. Szasz, international lawyer at the IAEA, referred to the agency's "tutelage" approach in providing health and safety controls to developing countries (Szasz, 1970: 682). The IAEA would not assume any liability related to its safety measures, although they required each nation signing a Project Agreement with the IAEA to abide by them (Szasz, 1970: 681, 686). As Szasz explained,

> The principal reason why it seems desirable to use the Agency's standards as models is that they are formulated with the help of the collective expertise of the scientifically most developed States of the world, and few small countries can hope to match the effort and knowledge that is mobilized in this task—most of the less developed States lack the manpower to make even a start on the drafting of truly original standards; left to their own devices, they might adopt

120 *Angela N. H. Creager and Maria Rentetzi*

standards that are too lenient and thus dangerous, or too severe and thus restrictive of safe and useful activities.

(Szasz, 1970: 682)

The IAEA established a core of health and safety inspectors for countries receiving reactors, illustrating the early overlap with safeguards against diversion of nuclear materials or technologies into weapons.[31]

The IAEA's expertise in radiological health and safety came with other challenges and opportunities. The Agency made an "initial foray into nuclear safety after an accident at a facility in Vinča, Yugoslavia" (Brown, 2015: 184; Higuchi and Hymans, 2021). The October 1958 accident occurred at the Boris Kidric Institute, colloquially known as the Vinča Institute for Nuclear Sciences, near Belgrade. During an experiment, human error caused the Institute's reactor to reach the critical level. None of the personnel present noticed. A further increase in heavy water elevated the reactor to supercritical. Several instruments that were supposed to monitor radioactivity levels failed. It was only when the staff smelled ozone, owing to the ionisation of the reactor hall's air, that they realised the system was supercritical and manually shut down the assembly. Meanwhile, all six persons operating the reactor had been exposed to high levels of radiation—estimated at 50% of the lethal dose—originating from neutrons and gamma rays. One died within a few days. The remaining five were treated at the Curie Hospital in Paris by Georges Mathé, whose method of marrow transplantation made medical history with this first successful human application (Kraft, 2009).

Right after the accident, physicist Karl Ziegler Morgan and his team from the Oak Ridge National Laboratory reached out to Sterling Cole. The scientists hoped Cole would convince the Yugoslavs to let them perform an experiment at the Vinča Institute to obtain an accurate estimate of the radiation dose received by the workers present during the accident. Given the Cold War political context, the Americans could not risk contacting the Yugoslavs directly; they needed the IAEA to play intermediary. It worked, and in April 1960, Morgan's team was joined by English and French scientists to perform what has been diplomatically termed the IAEA's "Joint Dosimetry Experiment"[32] (IAEA, 1962). It marked the beginning of the Agency's research program in the field of health and safety, through which the IAEA created a space for itself in Cold War nuclear medicine and radiation protection (Higuchi and Hymans, 2021). Over time, the Agency dominated this field, in part by establishing the Joint IAEA/WHO Dose Intercomparison Service for Radiotherapy, a project that offers calibration services to the United Nations Member States even today (Rentetzi, forthcoming). As the radiation protection program acquired a life of its own, ostensibly outside the IAEA proper, it separated from the controversial issue of safeguards against nuclear weapons proliferation. Thus, when on January 3, 1961

Sharing the "Safe" Atom? 121

the Board of Governors approved the Agency's first safeguard system, set forth in the INFCIRC/26 document, health and safety had been removed.[33]

Codifying standards

Although no longer directly connected to safeguards against nuclear proliferation, the IAEA's role in codifying health and safety standards continued and expanded. The Agency was, above all, as a diplomatic and metrological institution, created for establishing standards for its own technical operations and responding to the international demand for cooperation in the nuclear field. The health and safety standards were tied, if indirectly, into the expansion of post-war markets, in that the Agency's on-site inspections aimed to ensure that commerce related to the international nuclear power industry did not increase the chances of nuclear warfare.

Yet, there was an even more political reason for establishing safety standards in the late 1950s. At this time, many member states, in addition to international and regional organisations, were in the process of preparing health and safety legislation. Standardisation was envisioned as a significant practice in furthering IAEA's developing goals of oversight. As it promoted nuclear energy, IAEA hoped to move developing countries onto the path of modernity. "[T]he existence of Agency standards would permit them [member states] to use these standards as models," the Board of Governors argued in the IAEA's first annual report in 1958.[34] In providing and promoting uniform standards, the IAEA worked to project a public image of atomic energy as safe and manageable.

The IAEA's very first technical publication was a booklet entitled *Safe Handling of Radioisotopes*, issued in English on December 15, 1958.[35] It was, in the Agency's words, "a comprehensive handbook of internationally compiled recommendations for users of radioisotopes," covering "organisational, medical and technical aspects of radiation safety practices."[36] A panel of 13 experts from ten different countries—a truly international scientific team of men directed by a diplomatic organisation—collected and reviewed existing manuals and regulations across member states, accepted comments from member governments, and drew on similar work and studies undertaken by other international organisations in order to finally compile its recommendations.[37] The main issues the Agency addressed in this booklet were those involved in the rapidly developing nuclear industry and the medical uses of radioisotopes. Thus, these early guidelines addressed the handling of radioactive materials (from sealed and unsealed sources), radiation safety in medical establishments, and waste collection, disposal, storage and transportation of radioactive materials.

Safe Handling of Radioisotopes was submitted to the IAEA board for approval, and therefore became part of Agency's formal Codes of

122 Angela N. H. Creager and Maria Rentetzi

Practice (Szasz, 1970: 678, 698n62 and n70). However, the recommendations pertained only to "radioactivity surpassing the limit of 0.002 microcurie concentration per gram of material (i.e., 2 microcuries per kilogram), or a total activity of more than 0.1 microcuries in the working area."[38] The Agency did not yet believe levels lower than this required special safety methods, and indeed, most uses, especially therapeutic ones, required exposure to far higher amounts of radiation. Even diagnosis required higher amounts until more sensitive scanning instruments were devised (Creager, 2013, ch. 9). On the question of "safe dose," the Agency reported, "IAEA experts have not presented any new conclusion on this question because this is a matter that should call for separate detailed investigation."[39] In fact, the Agency deferred to the ICRP recommendations on the matter. Interestingly, the IAEA's manual was published shortly after Euratom issued health protection rules for atomic workers; in the press, one writer bemoaned the duplication.[40]

Simultaneous with disseminating safety standards, the Agency worked to increase the commerce in radioisotopes. In spring and summer 1959, IAEA expert panels started to work on guidelines for the transport of radioisotopes and larger quantities of radioactive materials.[41] That same year, it published an *International Directory of Radioisotopes*, prompted by "the growing interest in the use of radioisotopes all over the world"—and certainly by its own aim to spread knowledge about the multifarious uses.[42] The Agency saw itself as the logical clearinghouse for information about the 44 suppliers of radioisotopes, widely viewed as the peaceful fruits of nuclear reactors.

Besides technical and scientific standards, the IAEA joined early efforts to produce international standards regarding civil liability for nuclear damage. Triggered by major nuclear accidents such as the Kyshtym disaster in Russia and the Windscale accident in England (both in 1957), insurance and reinsurance companies were making their way into the nuclear industry. While the Committee of European Insurers established the Committee for the Study of Atomic Risks and sought ways to affect international nuclear legislation, the IAEA became involved in drafting standards on civil liability for nuclear damage (Kyrtsis and Rentetzi, 2021). A panel of legal experts drawn from 16 member states met in 1959 to prepare an international convention on minimum standards, leaving room for national-level legislative action. "Only in this way can we hope to have a convention of world-wide scope" argued the IAEA, recognising that nuclear risks extended beyond all national boundaries.[43]

The IAEA was not the only international body working on reactor liability and transboundary harm. Only a few months after the establishment of the IAEA, the Organisation for European Economic Co-operation founded the European Nuclear Energy Agency (ENEA) to develop nuclear collaboration in Western Europe. The two organisations shared a number of key actors; the Nobel laureate John Cockcroft who

Sharing the "Safe" Atom? 123

chaired the ENEA and was also member of IAEA's Scientific Advisory Committee, a powerful group of leading scientists who influenced the Agency's earlier programs; Sigvard Eklund, chairman of ENEA's study group on experimental reactors during 1960 and IAEA's second Director General appointed a year later in 1961. These close connections led to an early co-operation agreement signed between the two agencies in July 1960 to govern issues of common concern and especially that of the legal regime governing nuclear liability. Although ENEA's first Convention on Third Party Liability (1960) aimed to establish a standard European nuclear liability law, the IAEA was well-poised to produce a legal regulatory framework which could be exported to the developing world, a profitable market for the nuclear industry.[44] Harmonisation of technical and legal standards was critical to the expansion of markets, in the nuclear domain as well as more generally. It is not by chance that the IAEA sought to educate what it called "the atomic lawyers" within the context of its program of advisory services to member states, inviting legal administrators from developing countries and hoping to standardise even the legal frameworks of nations states concerning nuclear issues. As Eklund argued, the "creation of a world nuclear law" is a direction "which must be taken increasingly if the problems are to be met successfully."[45]

Overall, the international regulatory system—technical, scientific and legal—that took shape in the early 1960s was not only a result of the geopolitical division of the Cold War world but also of intense negotiations among the newly created international organisations that elevated nuclear science to a highly diplomatic issue. For example, although primarily a political and diplomatic organisation, the IAEA gradually took the lead from institutions such as the International Committee for Radiological Units (ICRU) and the International Commission on Radiological Protection (ICRP) in promoting radiation protection measures. When these international organisations realised that the IAEA was determined to create a niche within regulatory institutions on radiation protection, they sought compromise. The division of labor was finally decided in 1960: the IAEA would produce codes, but the philosophy would be dictated by the ICRP (Boudia, 2007; see also Vetter, 1966). In the case of nuclear liability, the IAEA sought cooperation with ENEA with which it shared individuals who played key and powerful roles in both agencies. It was at this time that lawyers and nuclear insurers were assuming major roles as backstage ambassadors defining how nuclear energy and expertise was going to be distributed in the developing world (Kyrtsis and Rentetzi, 2021).

The IAEA's oversight was more aspirational than actual (Szasz, 1970: 666). Unlike national atomic energy agencies, the IAEA could not legally enforce its safety standards, as it readily acknowledged.

124 *Angela N. H. Creager and Maria Rentetzi*

> [M]any of the Agency's own research activities are concerned with the establishment of international standards and regulations to govern operations involving radiation and radioactive materials. The importance of these regulatory functions has been widely recognized and will grow further with the rapid development of atomic energy programs in different parts of the world. Although the Agency regulations can be binding only with respect to its own operations or projects carried out under its aegis, their actual impact is much wider.[46]

In addition to issue of enforceability, there were numerous international bodies (not to mention national agencies) working in the domain of radiological safety; in addition to several mentioned above we would add the UN's Scientific Committee on the Effects of Atomic Radiation. Nonetheless, the IAEA was able to attain an authoritative place among them, promulgating safety and legal standards within the post-war nuclear order (Boudia, 2010: 73–98).

Moreover, the IAEA's standards for radiological protection were key bargaining chips with countries seeking nuclear materials. Abena Dove Osseo-Asare's recent account of the development of Ghana's atomic energy program is illuminating in this regard. Just before an IAEA mission to Ghana in 1961, the country's first post-colonial President Kwame Nkrumah and his administration negotiated to receive a reactor from the Soviet Union. Ghana had only been independent from the British Empire for four years, and British officials were stunned by this agreement with the USSR (Osseo-Asare, 2019: 89). But, as Osseo-Asare notes, "the wait for the reactor in Ghana was much longer than anticipated and scientists became increasingly dependent on IAEA demands" (Osseo-Asare, 2019: 110). In order to "request small amounts of fissionable material through the IAEA," Ghanaian officials were required to document adherence to the body's health and safety standards (Osseo-Asare, 2019: 110). In response to Ghana's requests for instrumentation that would help the country adhere to these standards, the IAEA suggested loan of one of its mobile radioisotope laboratories as a more affordable solution than setting up permanent testing stations. The IAEA cast a large, if not unavoidable, shadow over the path to nuclear development, especially for formerly colonised states.

Metrology of the atom

Practices of standardisation have often featured in the geographical or economic consolidation of power (Kula, 1986). International standards for network technologies (railroads, telegraph and electricity), as well as for weights, measures and banking, date back to the nineteenth century (Yates and Murphy, 2019). As Glenda Sluga has observed, the technological infrastructures for energy and transportation, as well as the global commerce they enabled, made "internationalism" appear to early twentieth century observers as an objective feature of modernity. So did the many international organisations that were established, including, after World War II, a proliferation of specialised organisations at the UN (Sluga, 2013).

Within this longer history, the IAEA's activities in standardising radiological protection and nuclear liability can be understood as part of the establishment of global governance in the post-war world. This process of technical standards-setting was, of course, thoroughly political and deeply diplomatic, and far from harmonious. First, the IAEA provided a stage on which the major powers during the early Cold War (especially the nuclear "haves") struggled to establish influence over countries in the developing world and to use inspection provisions to limit each other's military activities. And the contest was also between different international bodies, such as IAEA and Euratom. Second, the IAEA's mandate contained an inherent conflict. As the Director General, Dr. Sigvard Eklund, put it to the United Nations General Assembly on November 22, 1966: "A factor of paramount importance is the dual nature of atomic energy, which is reflected in the dual function of the Agency; not only to promote, but also to safeguard the peaceful uses of atomic energy."[47] As Jacob Hamblin has most recently argued, the agency's unwavering commitment to spread nuclear power in the developing world meant that the goal of non-proliferation was a mirage (Hamblin, 2021).

During the early years of the IAEA, the nuclear power industry was just getting off the ground. But as more and more countries began ordering commercial power reactors, the nuclear industry was a major beneficiary of the IAEA's programs and its role establishing radiological standards. Through its various programs, the agency was promoting not only safe practices but also international trade of nuclear materials and technologies. The globalisation of high-tech industry tends to rely on standards-setting, and the nuclear sector is no exception (Yates and Murphy, 2019). Yet the IAEA was simultaneously responsible for monitoring nuclear weapons proliferation, illustrating that the technology it promoted could never be wholly entrusted to the "market." Rather, its role in codifying and disseminating radiological safety through technical standards and its unwavering support of the growing, multinational nuclear industry remained inextricably linked to the broader geopolitics of the atom.

Notes

1 Funding: This publication is part of the HRP-IAEA project that has received funding from the European Research Council (ERC) under the European Union's Horizon 2020 research and innovation programme (Grant agreement No770548).

126 *Angela N. H. Creager and Maria Rentetzi*

2 Article II of original Statute, IAEA, as quoted by Fischer (1997: 36).

3 Preparatory Commission of the IAEA, "Draft Report of the Preparatory Commission Concerning the Programme and Budget for the First Year of the Agency," June 15, 1957, IAEA/PC/W.45(s), IAEA Archives, Vienna, Austria. Concerning the history of the IAEA, see Fischer (1997); Hecht (2006); Rentetzi (2017); Roehrlich (2018).

4 On the IAEA's role in Pakistan's nuclear development, see Hamblin (2020).

5 As noted almost quizzically by one of the agency's lead lawyers, these are "intermixed in the statutory provisions": (Szasz, 1970: 532).

6 On the uneasy relations between the IAEA and Euratom and the European Nuclear Agency, which became the OECD's Nuclear Energy Agency, see Fischer (1997: ch. 4).

7 Mariano Maggiore to Lars Lind, January 13, 1959, I/320, IAEA Archives, Vienna, Austria.

8 Orio Vergani and Gustavo Montanaro, 1959, The Milan Fair, booklet, vol IV, I/320 Milan 1958–1970, IAEA Archives, Vienna, Austria.

9 Mariano Maggiore to Lars Lind, January 13, 1959, I/320, IAEA Archives, Vienna, Austria.

10 Lars Lind to Mariano Maggiore, January 20, 1956, I/320, IAEA Archives, Vienna, Austria.

11 M. Franci to Henry Seligman, March 13, 1959, I/320, IAEA Archives, Vienna, Austria; Henry Seligman to M. Franci, March 17, 1959, I/320, IAEA Archives, Vienna, Austria.

12 Marcelle Napier to Paul Jolles, January 9, 1958, Memorandum, I/300-3, IAEA Archives, Vienna, Austria.

13 Vladimir Migulin, "Possibility of organizing exhibitions," June 27, 1958, I/320, IAEA Archives, Vienna, Austria. Migulin, deputy director general of the department of training and technical information, suggested in a document he shared with Sterling Cole, the agency's Director General and the deputy directors of other departments, to set up this panel following the advice of Hubert de Laboulaye, Deputy Director General of the Department of Technical Operations.

14 See, for example, D. Morgan, Head of the Department of Biology, Adisadel College, Ghana, to Lars Lind, IAEA, January 29, 1960, I/320, IAEA Archives, Vienna, Austria.

15 See, for example, Survey in South-East Asia (1959). *International Atomic Energy Agency Bulletin*, 1(2), pp. 5–8; Atomic Survey in Africa and Greece (1960). *International Atomic Energy Agency Bulletin*, 2(4), pp. 10–15.

16 "USA offers two mobile radioisotope laboratories to IAEA," April 29, 1958, PR 58/14, IAEA Archives, Vienna, Austria.

17 "IAEA announces more than 200 fellowships for atoms for peace training," May 7, 1958, PR 58/15, IAEA Archives, Vienna, Austria.

18 For example, the agricultural chemist Peter Hague Nye was hired by the IAEA to use radioisotope techniques in soil research in Latin America after having an extended experience of working at the British Colonial Office in Ghana and a big part of West Africa (Greenland et al., 2011). Nye's case is not unique. See, for example, Atomic Energy in Africa (1967). *International Atomic Energy Agency Bulletin*, 9(2), pp. 5–14.

19 The IAEA was also advocating use of high-intensive radioactive sources like cobalt-60 for food irradiation (Zachmann, 2011).

20 The issue of "diversion" of nuclear assistance to military uses was itself complex and often ambiguous (Abraham, 2006). The IAEA had an early interest in radiation protection first of all for its own employees (Rentetzi, 2017).

Sharing the "Safe" Atom? 127

21 Commercial uses of X-rays were also implicated (Duffin and Hayter, 2000).
22 In addition, the IAEA's determination as to what counted as "nuclear" affected the implementation of non-proliferation safeguards as well as worker safety in uranium mining (Hecht, 2014).
23 "Conference on the Statute of the IAEA," September 20, 1956, pp. 13, 96–97, IAEA/CS/OR.1, IAEA Archives, Vienna, Austria.
24 Legal Protection Against Nuclear Damage. (1959). *International Atomic Energy Agency Bulletin*, 1(1), pp. 15–16, on 15.
25 A Year of Expansion. (1959). *International Atomic Energy Agency Bulletin*, 1(3), pp. 2–6, on p. 4.
26 Press Release, "Atomic safeguards and health protection before IAEA Board," January 21, 1960, PR 60/4, IAEA Archives, Vienna, Austria. See also Press Release, March 10, 1958, PR 58/7, IAEA Archives, Vienna, Austria; Press Release, "Appointment of Director of Division of Safeguards of the IAEA," July 23, 1958, PR 58/25, IAEA Archives, Vienna, Austria; Scientific Advisory Committee, "Official Record of the Second Meeting," August 20, 1959, SAC/OR.2, IAEA Archives, Vienna, Austria.
27 Scientific Advisory Committee, "Official Record of the Second Meeting," January 20, 1960, SAC/OR.3, IAEA Archives, Vienna, Austria.
28 Scientific Advisory Committee, "Official Record of the Second Meeting," June 29, 1961, SAC/OR.6, IAEA Archives, Vienna, Austria.
29 "Manual of Safe Practice in the Use of Radioisotopes," PR 58/21, IAEA Archives, Vienna, Austria; "IAEA issues international manual on radiation protection," December 4, 1958, PR 58/36, IAEA Archives, Vienna, Austria.
30 The language of nuclear "haves" and "have-nots" was used by India's Homi Bhabha (Roehrlich, 2016).
31 The IAEA's program for health and safety inspection was replaced by a voluntary system in 1976 (Fischer, 1997: 184).
32 Rentetzi, M. (2015). *Getting the Radiation Dose Correct: The Politics of Radiation Dosimetry and the Role of the IAEA.* Unpublished paper presented at History of Science Society Annual Meeting, San Francisco, California.
33 "The Agency's Safeguards," March 30, 1961, INFCIRC/26, IAEA Archives, Vienna, Austria.
34 "IAEA first annual report of the Board of Governors to the General Conference" covering the period from October 23, 1957, to June 30, 1958, GC (II)/39, IAEA Archives, 34.
35 Now accessible on the IAEA's website under "Superseded Standards and Obsolete Standards." Available at: http://ns-files.iaea.org/standards/superseded-safety-standards.pdf [Accessed June 8, 2021].
36 IAEA Publishes First Health and Safety Manual. (January 1959). *Bulletin of the International Atomic Energy Agency*, 24.
37 Press Release, "IAEA issues international manual on radiation protection," December 4, 1958, PR 58/36, IAEA Archives, Vienna, Austria.
38 "IAEA Publishes First Health and Safety Manual," (January 1959). *Bulletin of the International Atomic Energy Agency*, 24.
39 Safety with Isotopes. (1959). *International Atomic Energy Agency Bulletin* 1(1), pp. 11–12, 19.
40 The unnamed writer for "Atomic World" was quoted in "Safety with Isotopes" (1959), 19.
41 A Year of Expansion (1959). *International Atomic Energy Agency Bulletin*, 1(3), pp. 2–6, on 5. By 1960, regulations had been recommended by these panels (IAEA, 1961: 9).

128 Angela N. H. Creager and Maria Rentetzi

42 Guide to Radioisotopes. (1959). *International Atomic Energy Agency Bulletin*, 1(3), p. 26.
43 "Civil Liability for Nuclear Damage," December 30, 1960, GOV/INF/47, IAEA Archives, Vienna, Austria. See also Daston (2017).
44 The OEEC European Nuclear Energy Agency (1961). *International Atomic Energy Agency Bulletin*, 3(3), pp. 23–26; Developing Nuclear Law (1968). *International Atomic Energy Agency Bulletin*, 10(3), pp. 3–8.
45 Training the Atomic Lawyers (1968). *International Atomic Energy Agency Bulletin*, 10(3), p. 9.
46 Legal Protection Against Nuclear Damage (1959). *International Atomic Energy Agency Bulletin*, 1(1), p. 15.
47 IAEA's Dual Function (1967). *International Atomic Energy Agency Bulletin*, 9(1), pp. 3–6, on 3.

References

Abraham, I. (2006). The Ambivalence of Nuclear Histories. *Osiris*, 21, pp. 49–65.
Banci, S. (2009). *Turkish Pavilion in the Brussels Expo '58: A Study on Architectural Modernization in Turkey during the 1950s*. PhD dissertation. Middle East Technical University.
Beatty, J. (2006). Masking Disagreement among Experts. *Episteme: A Journal of Social Epistemology*, 3(1), pp. 52–67.
Beck, E. (1989). The Role of the IAEA as Catalyst in Accelerating Technology Transfer. In: *International Atomic Energy Agency Yearbook*. Vienna: International Atomic Energy Agency, pp. A1–A5.
Boudia, S. (2007). Global Regulation: Controlling and Accepting Radioactivity Risks. *History and Technology*, 23(4), pp. 389–406.
Boudia, S. (2010). *Gouverner les risques, gouverner par le risque. Pour une histoire du risque de la société du risque*. Habilitation à diriger des recherches. Université de Strasbourg.
Brown, R. L. (2015). *Nuclear Authority: The IAEA and the Absolute Weapon*. Washington, DC: Georgetown University Press.
Büchler, C. (1997). Safeguards: The Beginnings. In: *International Atomic Energy Agency: Personal Reflections, A Fortieth Anniversary Publication*. Vienna: International Atomic Energy Agency, pp. 45–52.
Creager, A. (2013). *Life Atomic: A History of Radioisotopes in Science and Medicine*. Chicago: University of Chicago Press.
Creager, A. (2015). Radiation, Cancer, and Mutation in the Atomic Age. *Historical Studies in the Natural Sciences*, 45(1), pp. 14–48.
Daston, L. (2017). What Is an Insurable Risk? Swiss Re and Atomic Reactor Insurance. In: N. Viggo Haueter and G. Jones, eds., *Managing Risk in Reinsurance: From City Fires to Global Warming*. Oxford: Oxford University Press, pp. 230–247.
Divine, R. (1978). *Blowing on the Wind: The Nuclear Test Ban Debate, 1954–1960*. New York: Oxford University Press.
Duffin, J., and Hayter, C. (2000). Baring the Sole: The Rise and Fall of the Shoe-Fitting Fluoroscope. *Isis*, 91(2), pp. 260–282.
Eisenhower, D. (1990). *Atoms for Peace: Dwight D. Eisenhower's Address to the United Nations*. Washington, DC: National Archives and Records Administration.

Fischer, D., ed. (1997). *History of the International Atomic Energy Agency: The First Forty Years, A Fortieth Anniversary Publication.* Vienna: International Atomic Energy Agency.

Fischer, D. (2007). Nuclear Safeguards: The First Steps. *International Atomic Energy Agency Bulletin*, 49(1), pp. 7–10.

Greenland, D., Tinker, P., and Kirk, G. (2011). Peter Hague Nye: September 16, 1921–February 13, 2009. *Biographical Memoirs of Fellows of the Royal Society*, 57, pp. 315–326.

Hamblin, J. (2015). Quickening Nature's Pulse: Atomic Agriculture at the International Atomic Energy Commission. *Dynamis*, 35(2), pp. 389–408.

Hamblin, J. (2017). "A Glaring Defect in the System": Nuclear Safeguards and the Invisibility of Technology. In: R. Popp, L. Horovitz, and A. Wenger, eds., *Negotiating the Nuclear Non-Proliferation Treaty: Origins of the Nuclear Order*. London: Routledge, pp. 203–219.

Hamblin, J. (2020). Aligning Missions: Nuclear Technical Assistance, the IAEA, and National Ambitions in Pakistan. *History and Technology*, 36(3–4), pp. 437–451.

Hamblin, J. (2021). *The Wretched Atom: America's Global Gamble with Peaceful Nuclear Technology*. New York: Oxford University Press.

Hecht, G. (2006). Negotiating Global Nuclearities: Apartheid, Decolonization, and the Cold War in the Making of the IAEA. *Osiris*, 21, pp. 25–48.

Hecht, G., ed. (2011). *Entangled Geographies: Empire and Technopolitics in the Global Cold War*. Cambridge, MA: MIT Press.

Hecht, G. (2014). *Being Nuclear: Africans and the Global Uranium Trade*. Cambridge, MA: MIT Press.

Higuchi, T., and Hymans, J. (2021). Materialized Internationalism: How the IAEA Made the Vinča Dosimetry Experiment, and How the Experiment Made IAEA. *Centaurus*, 37, DOI: http://doi.org/10.1111/1600-0498.12358.

Holloway, D. (2016). The Soviet Union and the Creation of the International Atomic Energy Agency. *Cold War History*, 16(2), pp. 177–193.

IAEA. (1961). *Regulations for the Safe Transport of Radioactive Materials*, Safety Series 6, STI/PUB/40. Vienna: International Atomic Energy Agency.

IAEA. (1962). *The Vinca Dosimetry Experiment*, Technical Reports Series 6, no. 92-0-125062-2. Vienna: International Atomic Energy Agency.

Ito, K., and Rentetzi, M. (2021). The Co-Production of Nuclear Science and Diplomacy: Towards a Transnational Understanding of Nuclear Things. *History and Technology*, 37. DOI: http://doi.org/10.1080/07341512.2021.1905462.

Jolly, J. (2003). *Thresholds of Uncertainty: Radiation and Responsibility in the Fallout Controversy*. PhD dissertation. Oregon State University.

Khan, M. (1987). 1957–1987: Development through Global Co-Operation. *International Atomic Energy Agency Bulletin*, 29(3), pp. 7–10.

Kopp, C. (1979). The Origins of the American Scientific Debate over Fallout Hazards. *Social Studies of Science*, 9(4), pp. 403–422.

Kraft, A. (2009). Manhattan Transfer: Lethal Radiation, Bone Marrow Transplantation, and the Birth of Stem Cell Biology, ca. 1942–1961. *Historical Studies in the Natural Sciences*, 39(2), pp. 171–218.

Krige, J. (2016). *Sharing Knowledge, Shaping Europe: US Technological Collaboration and Nonproliferation*. Cambridge, MA: MIT Press.

130 Angela N. H. Creager and Maria Rentetzi

Kula, W. (1986). *Measures and Men*. Princeton, NJ: Princeton University Press.

Kyrtsis, A., and Rentetzi, M. (2021). From Lobbyists to Backstage Diplomats: How Insurers in the Field of Third Party Nuclear Liability Shaped Science Diplomacy. *History and Technology*. 37(1) pp. 25-43.

Lekarenko, O. (2018). The United States-EURATOM Agreement of 1958: The Cold War Impact. *Diplomacy & Statecraft*, 29(3), pp. 432–454.

Maddock, S. (2014). *Nuclear Apartheid: The Quest for American Atomic Supremacy from World War II to the Present*. Chapel Hill, NC: North Carolina University Press.

Mateos, G., and Suárez-Díaz, E. (2015a). Clouds, Airplanes, Trucks and People: Carrying Radioisotopes to and across Mexico. *Dynamis*, 35(2), pp. 279–305.

Mateos, G., and Suárez-Diáz, E. (2015b). *Radioisótopos itinerantes en América Latina: Una historia de ciencia por tierra y por mar*. Mexico City: Universidad Nacional Autónoma de México.

Mateos, G., and Suárez-Díaz, E. (2019). Technical Assistance in Movement: Nuclear Knowledge Crosses Latina American Borders. In: J. Krige, ed., *How Knowledge Moves: Writing the Transnational History of Science and Technology*. Chicago: University of Chicago Press, pp. 345–367.

Mateos, G., and Suárez-Díaz, E., eds. (2020). Development Interventions: Science, Technology and Technical Assistance. *History and Technology*, 36(3–4), pp. 293–474.

Osseo-Asare, A. (2019). *Atomic Junction: Nuclear Power in Africa after Independence*. Cambridge, UK: Cambridge University Press.

Rentetzi, M. (2017). Determining Nuclear Fingerprints: Glove Boxes, Radiation Protection, and the International Atomic Energy Agency. *Endeavour*, 41(2), pp. 39–50.

Rentetzi, M. (2021). With Strings Attached: Gift-Giving to the International Atomic Energy Agency and US Foreign Policy. *Endeavour*, 45, 100754.

Rentetzi, M. (forthcoming). Building up the "Global Experiment": IAEA's Early Attempts to Standardize Radiation Dosimetry. *NTM Journal of the History of Science, Technology and Medicine*.

Rentetzi, M., and Ito, K. (2021). The Material Culture and Politics of Artifacts in Nuclear Diplomacy. *Centaurus*, 63(2), 233–243.

Roehrlich, E. (2016). The Cold War, the Developing World, and the Creation of the International Atomic Energy Agency (IAEA). *Cold War History*, 16(2), pp. 195–212.

Roehrlich, E. (2018). Negotiating Verification: International Diplomacy and the Evolution of Nuclear Safeguards, 1945–1972. *Diplomacy & Statecraft*, 29(1), pp. 29–50.

Sluga, G. (2013). *Internationalism in the Age of Nationalism*. Philadelphia, PA: University of Pennsylvania Press.

Szasz, P. (1970). *The Law and Practices of the International Atomic Energy Agency*. Vienna: International Atomic Energy Agency.

Vetter, H. (1966). Nuclear Medicine—A New Discipline. *International Atomic Energy Agency Bulletin*, 8(2), pp. 7–13.

Weichselbraun, A. (2020). From Accountants to Detectives: How Nuclear Safeguards Inspectors Make Knowledge at the International Atomic Energy Agency. *Political and Legal Anthropology Review*, 43(1), pp. 120–135.

Yates, J., and Murphy, C. (2019). *Engineering Rules: Global Standard Setting Since 1880*. Baltimore, MD: Johns Hopkins University Press.

Zachmann, K. (2011). Atoms for Peace and Radiation for Safety—How to Build Trust in Irradiated Foods in Cold War Europe and Beyond. *History and Technology*, 27(1), pp. 6590.

6 From military surveillance to citizen counter-expertise: radioactivity monitoring in a nuclear world

Nestor Herran

In March 2015, a radioactivity monitoring station of the Swedish Defense Research Agency (FOI) detected a peak of the radioisotope iodine-131. The measures, confirmed by other stations in Finland, pointed to an accidental release somewhere in Russia. In January 2017, similar peaks were detected in several European countries, again pointing to a Russian source, and in February 2017, a US Air Force WC-135 Constant Phoenix plane equipped with radiation sensors was deployed to Norway to investigate a mysterious spike in radiation. Another peak, involving ruthenium-106, was revealed in late 2017, and the Russian Weather Bureau acknowledged that it came from the Mayak nuclear reprocessing and isotope production plant.

These incidents, like similar warnings around Fukushima, are a reminder of the relevance and ubiquity of environmental radioactivity monitoring networks throughout the modern world. Established by nation-states (such as the American RadNet) or international institutions (such as the European EURDEP or the International Monitoring System run by the Comprehensive Nuclear-Test-Ban Treaty Organization, CNTBTO), these infrastructures have an increasingly prominent place in the nuclear global landscape.

However, the history of these networks and their role in the configuration of the nuclear world is a quite underexplored topic. What were the motivations behind their establishment? Which actors and institutions played a relevant role in their creation and maintenance? How the measurements they provided were mobilised in debates on nuclear risks? In order to answer these questions, I examine their history since the establishment of the first monitoring programs in the late 1940s. This history reveals that their development has been driven by at least four different (and sometimes competing) agendas. The most fundamental one is typically military, associated with the implementation of military nuclear surveillance systems. Exemplified by the wide CNTBTO network, it continues to be central even after the end of the Cold War. In the mid- and late-1950s, a second agenda, related to the assessment of global nuclear risks, appeared amidst the controversy regarding nuclear tests

DOI: 10.4324/9781003227472-6

Radioactivity monitoring 133

fallout. Intertwining military and civil institutions, this configuration contributed to the public visibility of radioactive fallout as well as its construction as a manageable problem. Following a similar logic, a third layer of monitoring networks was implemented starting in the 1960s alongside the extension of nuclear power stations. These both served to oversee potential problems and to preempt liability claims resulting from foreseeable accidental releases of radioactivity. These initially modest monitoring networks were expanded after the Chernobyl disaster in 1986 to appease public fear and distrust of nuclear technology. The parallel emergence of alternative, citizen-based monitoring networks, constitutes the fourth and last agenda, in direct tension with the previous one, which has aided to foster recent participative dynamics that promote transparency. Public participation emerged as key elements for the legitimation of the nuclear complex.

The military origin of environmental radioactivity monitoring

Environmental radioactivity was known since the early twentieth century, but no systematic monitoring program was established until World War II, when the United States military decided to assess the state of German nuclear operations. In late 1943, General Leslie Groves, head of the Manhattan Engineering District and responsible for US nuclear intelligence operations, charged Luis Alvarez, a MIT-trained physicist, with the task of developing a system to detect nuclear activities by measuring radioactivity released into the environment (Ziegler and Jacobson, 1995). The method focused on the detection of xenon-133, a rare isotope released by the operation of nuclear reactors, by using detectors mounted in US and British A-26 aircraft. These monitoring activities, carried out in the fall of 1944, confirmed that Germany did not yet have an advanced nuclear program.

After the nuclear bombing of Hiroshima and Nagasaki, the US military developed other methods for monitoring nuclear blasts at a distance. Sonars, seismographs and Geiger Muller radiation counters were tested and compared as part of the Operation Fitzwilliam, carried during the Sandstone nuclear tests in the Marshall Islands in spring 1948. The results showed that the detection of environmental radioactivity was the most promising technique for long-range surveillance. Thereafter, the Central Intelligence Group (the institutional predecessor of the Central Intelligence Agency, or CIA) unified all monitoring activities under a single umbrella group called AFOAT-1 (Air Force Deputy Chief Staff of Operations, Atomic Energy Office, Section One), which took charge of monitoring all aspects of the US nuclear cycle, from uranium mining to stockpiling fissionable materials to nuclear testing. By combining its detection

134 Nestor Herran

capabilities with those of a similar network implemented by the United Kingdom, the system was able to detect the first Soviet nuclear test on August 29, 1949.[1]

In the 1950s, the US military improved the reliability of this monitoring network by checking its own nuclear tests in the Pacific using a diversity of methods: radiological analysis of air and precipitation aided in determining the composition of the bomb, the detection of electromagnetic pulses helped ascertain the time of explosion, analysis of sound waves was used to calculate the yield of the bomb, and seismic measurements determined the location of the test (Richelson, 2006: 113). Monitoring environmental radioactivity was also developed as part of systems aimed at the early detection of nuclear attacks, such as those implemented by the Federal Civil Defense Administration (FCDA) since 1951. In 1956, these systems were integrated into the Radiation Alert Network (RAN), a network of stations aimed at detecting nuclear attacks on the United States and providing alerts on radiation fallout.[2]

Knowledge gained in the early nuclear tests constructed fallout into a measurable object and a key element in military strategy. Nuclear strategists wondering about nuclear war scenarios asked themselves how many nuclear bombs could be used before the effects of fallout became an important health issue. In order to answer this question, the US military undertook the secret project dubbed Gabriel, whose first report, circulated in 1951, concluded that nuclear explosions released strontium-90, a radioisotope particularly dangerous to human life. Chemically similar to calcium, it is assimilated by the bones and becomes an *internal* source of damaging radiation. In the mid-1950s, the AEC expanded fallout studies under the direction of atomic chemist and AEC Commissioner Willard F. Libby. His project, codenamed Sunshine, collected samples of air, water, soil, milk and human bone in the United States and abroad, and can be considered as the first global survey of radioactive environmental contamination (Eisenbud, 1990; Masco in this volume).[3]

Early environmental radioactivity monitoring was carried under military secrecy, keeping fallout concerns out of public attention. However, the situation abruptly changed in 1954 with the development of thermonuclear bombs and the onset of the controversy that arose after the "Castle Bravo" nuclear test. Considered the very first global environmental controversy (McCormick, 1989), it emerged after the miscalculated test of a hydrogen bomb carried in March 1954 in the Marshall Islands, which spread nuclear fallout over hundreds of square kilometers. The population of nearby atolls received high radiation doses, as did the crew and cargo of a Japanese fishing boat called the Lucky Dragon No. 5. Public outcry in Japan was considerable, leading to the creation of a unified Japanese Council against Atomic and Hydrogen Bombs, which was able to gather more than 35 million signatures on petitions calling for a ban on nuclear weapons (Higuchi, 2018). The pacifist movement seized the public concern about the tests, and non-aligned countries mobilised it as a stark example of Western powers' disregard for the health of human populations. India's first minister, Jawaharlal Nehru, was one of the most outspoken critics of nuclear tests. In April 1954, Nehru requested a "standstill agreement" on nuclear testing as a first step toward disarmament, pointing out that "Asia and her peoples appear to be always nearer these occurrences and experiments, and their fearsome consequences, actual and potential" (Jones, 2010: 202).[4] Confronted with the perspective of issue taken up by UNESCO's scientific committees, the United Nations General Assembly took action and, in December 1955, it approved the establishment of a research body of scientists and diplomats, the United Nations Scientific Committee on the Effects of Atomic Radiations (UNSCEAR).[5]

Counting among its membership representatives of 15 states, including the trio of nuclear powers (the United States, the Soviet Union, and the United Kingdom), UNSCEAR was the first international institution devoted to the regulation of nuclear affairs, predating the creation of the International Atomic Energy Agency (IAEA) (Fischer, 1997; Roehrlich, 2016). UNSCEAR also established the first open international effort for the monitoring of environmental radioactivity, which materialised in the first global map of fallout-produced Sr-90. Drawn as part of the first UNSCEAR report to the UN Assembly in 1958 (UNSCEAR, 1958), the map was based on data obtained from 350 stations worldwide, most of them part of the pre-existing American infrastructure, including the worldwide network of 122 stations put in place by the US Weather Bureau in 1955 to track the fallout from the Castle Bravo tests.[6]

The fallout controversy added a second, non-military layer of environmental monitoring programs, bringing environmental radioactivity monitoring into the daylight. Measurements of environmental radioactivity were incorporated into political debates over nuclear proliferation. In the United States, public anxiety over fallout led to the declassification of the data obtained in the Sunshine project in 1956, and the establishment of complementary Sr-90 surveys, such as the High Altitude Sampling Program (HASP), carried by the US Air Force (Friend, 1961).[7] Public distrust of the government also led to counter-expertise initiatives, the first examples of citizen-based monitoring of radioactivity. For example, the Consumers Union conducted a national study of Sr-90 concentrations in milk, which was published in the 1960s in the magazine *Consumer Records*, and the Greater St. Louis Citizens' Committee for Nuclear Information started a survey of Sr-90 in children's teeth (Lutts, 1985).

The fallout controversy contributed to the institutional displacement of environmental radioactivity monitoring from the military to the health domain: from 1959, the RAN network, established as part of the civil defense operation, was transferred to the jurisdiction of the US

136 *Nestor Herran*

Department of Health, Education, and Welfare. A decade later, in 1973, it merged with other measuring networks (the Air Surveillance Network, the Pasteurised Milk Network, the Interstate Carrier Drinking Water Network, and the Tritium Surveillance System) to form the Environmental Radiation Monitoring System (ERAMS). Counting with 68 monitoring stations and working under the responsibility of the Environmental Protection Agency (Aston, 2012), the ERAMS network was assimilated into the current RadNet network in 2005.

The rise of European radioactivity monitoring

As in the United States, the first European initiatives for the monitoring of environmental radioactivity were related to the military. In 1958, the United Kingdom contributed 19 monitoring stations' data (from 6 stations in the British Islands and 13 overseas) to the previously discussed Anglo-American military surveillance network. Norwegian stations, such as those at Tromsø and Bodø, were also part of the US military monitoring network surveilling Soviet Union nuclear tests. When the fallout controversy erupted, Norway put to use an additional 12 stations run by the Norwegian Defense Research Establishment (FFI) to measure radioactivity in dust and precipitation through daily measurements of air and snow samples. These measurements were complemented by monthly measurements of sea water, fish, milk and foodstuffs, as well as occasional animal and human tissue tests, carried out by the Directorate of the Fisheries and the Institute of Marine Research in collaboration with Norwegian universities (Bergan, 2002; Skogen, 2003).

France, which counted with an advanced national nuclear program and was already developing its own atomic bomb, established by 1957 a network of 15 monitoring stations in continental France along with at least one more station in Tahiti. In 1958, this surveillance network was able to detect and determine the causes of the Sellafield accident and to survey British nuclear tests in the Pacific.[8] In southern Europe, Italy implemented a surveillance network of 17 measuring stations, five of them run by the meteorological service of the Italian Air Forces and three by the Nuclear Research Centre for the Armed Forces (CAMEN).[9] Sweden used 18 stations for the measurement of airborne radioactivity by the late 1950s, 13 of which were run by the Institute of Radiophysics (RFI) and 5 by the National Defense Research Institute (FOA). Both RFI and FOA also monitored radioactive material in dust, precipitation, soil, vegetation, milk, and foodstuffs. Germany, banned from most nuclear research until 1955, had ten monitoring stations run by the German Weather Service (DWD). This reliance on weather services instead of military stations also occurred in other countries with relatively small monitoring networks, such as Ireland (Irish Meteorological Service, 1957; Kelleher, 2017).[10]

Radioactivity monitoring   137

As in the United States, fallout controversies led European countries to develop national monitoring initiatives, which were complemented and partially coordinated by the new nuclear international institutions emerging from the Atoms for Peace initiative. Between 1955 and 1960, a myriad of international expert committees related to radiation protection were established in response to growing concerns about the effects of radioactivity on human health (Boudia, 2008), which in some cases led to the development of monitoring networks or field programs to assess environmental radioactivity. In 1958, for example, the IAEA and the World Meteorological Organization (WMO) established the Global Network of Isotopes in Precipitation (GNIP) to monitor fallout from thermonuclear tests. From 1961 to the present, this network has gathered samples of precipitation and sent them to the IAEA's Isotope Hydrology Laboratory in Vienna to detect and monitor changes in the concentration of deuterium, oxygen-18, and tritium in rainfall. In the mid-1960s, these measurements revealed an important increase in tritium traced to the last American and Soviet atmospheric nuclear tests, conducted before the implementation of the Partial Test Ban Treaty (PTBT) in 1963 (Erikson, 1965).

At the same time, legislation and treaties were implemented at the national and international scale to regulate the use of nuclear technology, which also gave ground to monitoring initiatives. Euratom, signed in Rome on March 15, 1957, is a good example (Helmreich, 1991; Dumoulin et al., 1994; Krige, 2008; 2016). One of the first articles of this treaty indicated that signatory countries had to "establish uniform safety standards to protect the health of workers and of the general public and ensure that they are applied."[11] Indeed, it included provisions for the establishment of regular measuring of environmental radioactivity in European countries. In particular, Article 35 stated, "each member state shall establish the facilities necessary to carry out continuous monitoring of the level of radioactivity in the air, water and soil and to ensure compliance with the basic standards." This was accompanied by the indication that "the Commission shall have the right of access to such facilities; it may verify their operation and efficiency." Yet Article 36 required that member states "periodically communicate information on the checks referred to in Article 35 to the Commission so that it is kept informed of the level of radioactivity to which the public is exposed,"[12] implying that keeping the Commission informed by submitting regular radioactivity measurement data would obviate the need for more hands-on interventions.

The European Nuclear Energy Agency (ENEA) became one of the main vehicles for the implementation of the aforementioned directives.[13] Created by the Organization for European Economic Co-operation (OEEC) in February 1958, ENEA took one of its first actions in this sense by establishing a Health and Safety Committee (HSC) to develop recommendations for radiation protection against the hazards of ionising radiation that

138   *Nestor Herran*

member countries could apply in their own national legislation.[14] Working together with the International Commission on Radiological Protection (ICRP), the HSC thus implemented in 1959 standards for radiation protection norms in the OEEC countries (Marcus, 2008).

In relation to environmental radioactivity, the HSC's first actions were directed at compiling information about the OEEC member countries' ongoing monitoring. Einar Saeland, director of the ENEA, delegated this task to his compatriot Thorleif Hvinden in June 1958. Research director of the Norwegian Defense Research Institute (FFI) and an expert in the field of fallout deposition, Hvinden requested data from UNSCEAR, the IGY radiation monitoring program, and the Scientific Working Party of the NATO Civil Defense Committee, and he visited European countries, such as Sweden, Denmark, Holland, Germany, and Norway to examine their extant monitoring networks (Marcus, 1997). In his communications, Hvinden justified the collection of data "in view of the 'international' nature of radioactive contamination," which made it "desirable to have a common reporting system." The creation of this system, initially based on collaboration among existing facilities, would not only respond to the fear raised by nuclear testing, but also help the extension of nuclear energy in Europe, he wrote:

> [It] is desirable to make routine measurements of natural and artificial radioactivity in air, precipitation, soil, plants, seawater, food, animals and humans, to learn about the level before nuclear activities start or accidents happen, to be able to take necessary protective steps if contamination due to activities or incidents should reach hazardous levels, and to be able to allay unreasoned apprehensions. A well-organized monitoring system will also be essential for the evaluation of economic claims in connection with nuclear activities in general or special accidents.[15]

In June 1959, Hvinden presented his report, "Measurements of Environmental Radioactivity in the OEEC Countries," to the HSC. In the introduction, he reiterated that implementation of nuclear technology naturally implies the "manipulation of considerable quantities of radioactive materials" in activities such as extraction, enrichment, reprocessing, disposal, production and transport, and this process would result in the regular exposure of workers and nearby populations to radiation "in the course of normal operations as well as in cases of accident." Thus, international radiation protection regulations were necessary "to keep the external radiation level and the concentration of radioactive material in air, in food and drink, below certain maximum permissible values" and required local authorities' constant surveillance and reporting of radiation levels at each nuclear reactor or nuclear installation. That radioactive pollution is mobile, and monitoring requires the coordinated exchange of information

Radioactivity monitoring 139

between countries necessitated, in turn, the standardisation of methods of measurement and conversion factors. With such endeavors, the HSC could gather and provide international data "for [the] scientific evaluation of how radioactive materials reach men."[16]

Radioactivity monitoring and the nuclear industry

For the ENEA, environmental radioactivity monitoring had a third motivation. Beyond military surveillance and the management of nuclear test fallout concerns, the coordination of measures was supposed to be an essential element for the extension of the nuclear industry throughout Europe. However, the idea of establishing a European-wide network for the monitoring of environmental radioactivity lost momentum after the implementation of the PTBT and the extinction of the fallout controversy. This dip in enthusiasm can also be related to the signing in July 1960 of the Paris Convention on Third Party Liability in the Field of Nuclear Energy, which limited the liability of nuclear installation operators in case of accidental release of radioactivity. Monitoring of environmental radioactivity continued to be developed locally or nationally or under specific programs of international nuclear institutions.

At a global scale, the UNSCEAR continued to produce reports each four or five years after the mid-1960s,[17] and the GNIP program run by the IAEA to collect data on light radioisotopes in precipitation, but the focus gradually moved from fallout assessment to the establishment of data set for hydrological studies (Hamblin, 2009).[18] Indeed, after a first stage of expansion (from 155 stations in 1963 to 221 stations in 1965), the network dwindled: by 1987, it collected data from just 151 stations.[19] In Europe, the only systematic international monitoring program was led by the Euratom's Joint Nuclear Research Center at Ispra (Italy), which measured radioisotopes strontium-89, strontium-90 and cesium-137 in air, rain, milk and fish. The Center produced yearly reports of local measurements from 1960, expanding in 1977 to include data from stations in the nine European Economic Community member states.[20] Another seven reports were issued, including data from around 25 stations in Western European countries, until the restructuring of the service after the Chernobyl accident in 1986. The list of stations and laboratories included in these surveys reveal the absence of a coordinated strategy among European countries, which relied on very diverse approaches to monitoring. Most states reported a diversity of institutions, from meteorological laboratories to military centers, nuclear establishments, and health and hygiene services, while others had dedicated services, such as the *Service Central de Protection Contre les Rayonnements Ionisants* (SCPRI), established by the French government in 1956.[21]

By the late 1970s, important advances in instrumentation, combined with the cessation of atmospheric nuclear tests (China performed its last in October 1980) allowed for a significant reduction of atmospheric fallout activity worldwide.[22] As a result of this attenuation, the detection of accidental emissions became more precise. In the 1950s, nuclear accidents such as the Kyshtym disaster (1957) could go undetected—in that case, it would only be known in Western Europe after the revelations of a Soviet dissident in 1976 and confirmed by the careful reading between the lines of Soviet radioecology literature (Trabalka et al., 1980). By the early 1980s the situation had changed dramatically: new germanium detectors were able to detect radioactivity in the order of the micro-Becquerel per cubic meter and allowed the development of long-distance "early alert" systems associated. For example, a series of peaks in environmental radioactivity detected in northern Europe in 1983 spurred the creation of an informal system of data-exchange between scientists from Germany, Finland, Sweden, Norway and Denmark. Called the "ring of five," this group has since provided a system of early alerts regarding radiological accidents.[23]

On April 27, 1986, the monitoring system at Forsmark, a Swedish nuclear station in the north of Stockholm, detected a sudden peak in radioactive fallout. It was one of the first indications in the West that Reactor 4 in Chernobyl's nuclear complex had exploded.[24] The Chernobyl accident tested the reliability of European networks and their ability to communicate radioactive hazards to the public. In France, for example, the director of the SCPRI, Pierre Pellerin, was accused of minimising or denying the effects of the "Chernobyl radioactive cloud." Noting the degree of difference among the discourses emanating from national monitoring systems after the accident, international organisations undertook to create centralised databases. In October 1986, the IAEA approved the Convention on Early Notification of a Nuclear Accident, which encouraged states to communicate nuclear accidents from which the "release of radioactive material occurs or is likely to occur and which has resulted or may result in an international trans-boundary release that could be of radiological safety significance for another State."[25] Under this convention, each state must, as soon as possible, report to the IAEA the apparent or confirmed accident's time, location, nature and other data essential for assessing the situation. Before the year's close, Euratom adopted a resolution on community arrangements for the early exchange of information in the event of a radiological emergency (resolution 87/600, December 14, 1987). This included the obligation that member states "inform the Commission, at appropriate intervals, of the levels of radioactivity measured by their monitoring facilities in foodstuffs, feeding stuffs, drinking water and the environment."[26] This was the basis for the 1988 creation of the Radioactivity Environmental Monitoring program by the European Commission (EC) at the Ispra Joint Research Centre. Aimed at collecting fallout measurements produced in countries of the European Community, this project constituted

Radioactivity monitoring 141

the Radioactivity Environmental Monitoring data bank (REMdb), which included some radioactivity measurements in Eastern European countries from a similar database set up by IAEA.[27]

A participative turn?

As happened during the nuclear fallout controversy, the Chernobyl crisis fostered a more critical attitude toward nuclear technology. In some countries, communication failures fueled public mistrust of data presented by the authorities, stimulating the emergence of counter-expertise initiatives. As I have mentioned, the French SCPRI's results and methodology were challenged, and citizens organised into groups like the CRIIRAD, the Commission for Independent Research and Information on Radioactivity (*Commission de Recherche et d'Information Indépendantes sur la Radioactivité*), which aimed to provide independent measurements of environmental radioactivity (Topçu, 2013). Established in 1989, the CRIIRAD set up independent monitoring groups across France and called for international coordination among similar groups (Topçu, 2013).[28] Since that time, the CRIIRAD's activities have evolved beyond the evaluation of the Chernobyl accident; it now gathers data on all aspects of the nuclear cycle, from the impact of uranium mining and milling in Africa (Hecht, 2012) to the monitoring of all types of nuclear installations, such as power stations, reprocessing plants, military plants, nuclear research centers and hospitals. However, its reliance on non-governmental funding circumscribes the scope of these initiatives to small-scale, local measurements.

In comparison, data dragnet behemoths such as the International Monitoring System (IMS) provide the public with abundant data on environmental radioactivity. Established in 1996 in the framework of the Comprehensive Nuclear-Test-Ban Treaty Organization (CTBTO), the IMS counts with 80 radionuclide stations among its 337 facilities, combining seismic, hydro-acoustic and infrasound technologies into a global alarm system aimed to detect "rogue" nuclear tests. Due to its global extent, it is not surprising that the CTBTO network became the main source of data about the global spread of radioactivity from the Fukushima nuclear accident on March 11, 2011. The first detections of radionuclides such as iodine-131 and cesium-137 came only one day after the accident, recorded at the Takasaki CTBTO monitoring station in Japan. Within three days, radioisotopes were detected in eastern Russia and on the west coast of the United States. One month later, the network was able to trace—in detail—the global spread of radioactivity from Fukushima.[29]

As had happened with the Chernobyl catastrophe, the Fukushima disaster brought nuclear controversy to new methods of public engagement in relation to environmental radioactivity. In addition to destroying the

142 *Nestor Herran*

reactors at the Fukushima nuclear station, the tsunami that followed the earthquake damaged 95% of the region's nuclear monitoring stations. The provisional monitoring stations installed by the government and commercial operators in the area (TEPCO) did not provide estimates of radioactivity releases until two weeks after the accident. In reaction, citizens took it upon themselves to volunteer to measure the radiation affecting their bodies. Groups of Japanese people built crowdfunded Geiger counters in a citizen-science project called Safecast, which recorded 45 million measurements using open-source detectors (the DIY model bGeigie Nano), publishing them in real-time through an open database under Creative Commons licensing for four years following the accident.[30] Armed with these data, activists confronted the Japanese government and challenged the official data, pointing out discrepancies of up to 30% between the citizen and government networks.[31] This case, as it happened with the early American citizen initiatives on fallout or the CRIIRAD counter-expertise, provide an ironic turn from the secretive, top-down character of early radioactivity monitoring. Its appropriation by groups of citizens constitutes a profoundly subversive action, as technologies of surveillance and monitoring activities traditionally accompanied and legitimated the concentration of power in big organisations.

However, as happened with controversies on the impact of nuclear accidents on human health, the validity and relevance of data collected by citizen initiatives has been questioned and confronted with the more massive and comprehensive reading produced by governmental institutions. It is maybe too soon to be certain whether citizen initiatives to monitor global radioactivity will pose a significant challenge to nuclear establishments. However, it is undeniable that citizen-science has contributed to the "participative-deliberative turn" of nuclear establishments (Sundqvist and Elam, 2010), which increasingly work to encourage public participation as a way to maneuver around public concerns regarding nuclear technology. In this sense, it will be no shock when future controversies over nuclear technology involve weighing the legitimacy of competing metrics and networks and the management of the data produced by official and unofficial watchdogs.

Notes

1 The network included four dedicated BW-29 squadrons for air-sampling and stations along the Pacific, from Northern Alaska to the Philippines, and Atlantic coasts of the United States. The strategic importance of gathering intelligence about Soviet nuclear activities easily circumvented the limitations imposed by the 1946 McMahon Bill, which otherwise prevented the exchange of "American" nuclear information with foreign countries. See Goodman (2007: 43–46).

2 The extent of these early networks was not negligible. The federal government acquired instruments for these systems for a value of $1.5 million in 1955,

almost $4 million in 1957 and more than $20 million in 1962. Federal Emergency Management Agency (1986). *Radiological Instruments: An Essential Resource for National Preparedness*. Publication CPG 3-1. Available at: https://www.hsdl.org/?view&did=456492 [Accessed June 15, 2021].

3 AEC (1956). *Worldwide Effects of Atomic Weapons: Project Sunshine*, August 6, 1953. Santa Monica, CA: Rand Corporation. Available at: https://www.rand.org/content/dam/rand/pubs/reports/2008/R251.pdf [Accessed June 15, 2021]. The monitoring of radioactive fallout was not only based on health concerns, but industrial ones, as it responded to complaints from the National Photographic Manufacturers Association and some producers of photographic films, whose production chains were affected by radioactive fallout.

4 Trumbull, R. (1954). Nehru Proposes Atom "Standstill" Pending UN Curb. *New York Times*. April 3, 1954. Available at: https://www.nytimes.com/1954/04/03/archives/nehru-proposes-atom-standstill-pending-u-n-curb-asks-powers-with.html [Accessed June 15, 2021].

5 On the role of UNSCEAR in delaying the implementation of a test ban, see Boudia (2007), Hamblin (2007), and Higuchi (2018). For a discussion on its connection to other international cooperation endeavors in radioprotection, see Hamblin (2006). For the networks, see Herran (2014).

6 The US Weather Bureau network, established under the direction of meteorologist Lester Machta, coordinated measurements obtained from 39 stations in the continental United States and 14 overseas locations; 23 overseas stations operated by the Air Weather Service; 31 stations from the State Department; 3 operated by the Navy and the Coast Guard; and 2 by the Atomic Bomb Casualty Commission. The Canadian Meteorological Service and the Canadian Atomic Energy Commission cooperated, providing data from ten more stations (List, 1955), while the Military Sea Transport Service in the Pacific Ocean performed daily measurements based on gummed film stands.

7 Between August 1957 and June 1960, this survey collected 3,700 air samples at more than 70,000 feet (around 20,000 meters) of altitude in a meridian-sampling corridor to measure stratospheric concentrations of fallout (particularly Sr-90) from nuclear tests. Data obtained allowed meteorologists to estimate the stratospheric residence times of fallout and model the mechanisms and rates of transfer within the stratosphere and from the stratosphere to the troposphere.

8 *Division of international affairs, Memorandum of conversation. Discussion with Dr. Yves Rocard, French physicist*, February 26, 1958. NARA archives, box 490, folder 21.33.

9 Of the remaining nine stations, seven were part of the Italian contribution to the International Geophysical Year, the National Committee for Nuclear Research, and Ferrania, a private photography company.

10 The Irish Meteorological Service carried routine airborne measurements of radioactivity in precipitation and dust since 1957 in the stations of Dublin and in Valentia. Aiming at detecting fallout from nuclear weapons tests with GM counters, the system was nonetheless unable to detect radioactivity from the Windscale accident, as the increase of the levels of radioactivity detected in October 1957 were attributed to nuclear testing.

11 Article 2b of the *Treaty Establishing the European Atomic Energy Community*, March 25, 1957. Other articles related to radiation protection are Articles 30–33 in Chapter 3, which dealt with radiation protection and safety standards, and Articles 34–38 in the same chapter, which concern environmental radioactivity.

144 *Nestor Herran*

12 *Treaty Establishing the European Atomic Energy Community*, March 25, 1957, Chapter 3, Articles 35 and 36. For an analysis of the practical implications of these articles, see Janssens (2004).

13 ENEA's main objective was to promote nuclear co-operation among OEEC countries and encourage the development and use of nuclear energy for peaceful purposes. Its founding members were the 17 OEEC countries: Austria, Belgium, Denmark, France, Germany, Greece, Iceland, Ireland, Italy, Luxembourg, the Netherlands, Norway, Portugal, Sweden, Switzerland, Turkey, and the United Kingdom. Canada and the United States were associate members. In 1972, the ENEA was renamed Nuclear Energy Agency (NEA) "to reflect its growing membership beyond Europe's boundaries." Available at: https://www.oecd-nea.org/ [Accessed March 30, 2020].

14 It was not until June 1958 that the ENEA launched a second project: the building of a reactor in Halden (Norway), conceived as a space for training and exchange of information on reactor technology among different national nuclear programs. On the early history of the HSC, see Métivier (2007).

15 T. Hvinden to E. Saelund, *Memorandum. OEEC Monitoring Programme. Survey of Existing Radiation Monitoring Programmes in the OEEC Countries, with Recommendations on Coordinated OEEC Monitoring and Reporting System.* Historical Archives of the European Union, Florence. Work of the Sub-Committee of Health and Safety. NUC 79.

16 The Hvinden report also provides a detailed survey of existing radioactivity measuring stations in OEEC countries and measuring data from 1959. Fifteen national radioactivity monitoring networks and 144 stations are included, with France boasting the densest network, followed by Sweden, then Italy. The report includes tables with measurements of airborne radioactivity, settled dust, and precipitations and an annex with recommendations. *Measurement of Environmental Radioactivity in the OEEC Countries. Provisional Report Prepared by the Secretariat of the European Nuclear Energy Agency.* Historical Archives of the European Union, Florence. Work of the Sub-Committee of Health and Safety, NUC 79.

17 The UNSCEAR Reports were issued in 1958, 1962, 1964, 1966, 1969, 1972, 1977, and 1982, published as part of the official records of the United Nations. Since 1964, they included data on carbon-14.

18 The focus on hydrology is characteristic of the IAEA's increasing involvement in agricultural research as part of the so-called "green revolution."

19 The GNIP counted by 155 stations in the period 1953–1963; 221 in 1964–1965; 212 in 1966–1967; 177 in 1968–69; 164 in 1970–1983; and 151 in 1987. See the reports *Environmental Isotope Data*, number 1 to 9, published by the IAEA in 1969, 1970, 1971, 1973, 1975, 1979, 1983, 1986 and 1990, respectively.

20 Commission of the European Communities. (1977). *Results of Environmental Radioactivity Measurements in the Member States of the European Community for Air-Deposition-Water (1973-1974), Milk (1972-1973-1974)*. Luxembourg: Office for Official Publications of the European Communities.

21 In July 1994, le SCPRI was renamed *Office de protection contre les rayonnements ionisants* (OPRI), and in 2002 it merged with the *Institut de Protection de Sûreté Nucléaire* (IPSN) to become the current *Institut de Radioprotection et de Sûreté Nucléaire* (IRSN).

22 China and France continued to perform atmospheric nuclear tests until 1980 (50 tests between 1960 and 1974 by France and 22 tests between 1964 and 1980 by China), which is only a fraction of the more than 400 tests performed by the United States and the Soviet Union until 1962.

23 The informal status of the "ring of five" is stressed in public communications. However, the mailing list is notably maintained by the FOI.
24 According to Mould (2000), an American spy satellite in orbit over the Soviet Union also detected the explosion incidentally. Three days after the explosion, images of the Landsat 5 were also used to confirm the accident at the Chernobyl nuclear plant.
25 IAEA (1986). Convention of Early Notification of a Nuclear Accident. Available at: https://www.iaea.org/sites/default/files/infcirc335.pdf [Accessed May 31, 2021].
26 The resolution is available at: https://eur-lex.europa.eu/legal-content/EN/TXT/PDF/?uri=CELEX:31987D0600 [Accessed May 31, 2021].
27 The first collection of data was published in 1989 in two volumes: Raes, F., Graziani, G., Grossi, L., Marciano, L., Piers, D., Pedersen, B., Stanners, D., and Zarimpas, N. (1989). *Radioactivity Measurements in Europe after the Chernobyl Accident. Part I: Air.* Luxemburg: Commission of the European Communities. Available at: https://op.europa.eu/en/publication-detail/-/publication/ca9207fc-1490-4dbc-832d-35e206a9264f/language-en/format-PDF/source-search [Accessed June 15, 2021]; Graziani, G., Raes, F., Stanners, D., Pierce, D., Holder, G. (1991). *Radioactivity Measurements in Europe after the Chernobyl Accident. Part 2: Fallout and Deposition.* Luxemburg: Commission of the European Communities. Available at: https://op.europa.eu/en/publication-detail/-/publication/ebf6ce9a-89d2-4ca7-812b-c8a91234cb77 [Accessed June 15, 2021].
28 CRIIRAD call for an alternative monitoring system appeared in Tsuji, K. (1989). Global Network of Citizen Groups Monitoring Radioactive Contamination Proposed. *Nuclear Monitor*, 323–324. Available at: https://www.wiseinternational.org/nuclear-monitor/323-324/global-network-citizen-groups-monitoring-radioactive-contamination-proposed [Accessed June 15, 2021].
29 Additionally, CTBTO seismological stations were able to detect the earthquake preceding the flooding of Fukushima and helped the Japanese authorities to issue tsunami warnings. A colloquium on the CTBTO role in early warning and monitoring in the Fukushima disaster was held in Vienna on March 9, 2012: *CTBTO Past and Future Contributions to Emergency Preparedness: Fukushima Case Study*, summary available at https://www.ctbto.org/verification-regime/the-11-march-japan-disaster/one-year-after-fukushimathe-ctbtos-contributions/ [Accessed May 31, 2021].
30 Bonner, S., Brown, A., and Cheung, A. *The Safecast Report*. Available at: https://safecast.org/downloads/safecastreport2015.pdf [Accessed June 15, 2021].
31 On Safecast results, see Brown et al. (2016). A comparison of Safecast and official contamination data is available in Hultquist and Cervone (2018). See also the Safecast blog (https://blog.safecast.org).

References

Aston, K. (2012). *Detection, Modeling and Assessment of Radiological Conditions: An Analysis of a Radiological Preparedness Program*. PhD thesis. San Diego State University.

Bergan, T. (2002). Radioactive Fallout in Norway from Atmospheric Nuclear Weapons Tests. *Journal of Environmental Radioactivity*, 60, pp. 189–208.

Boudia, S. (2007). Global Regulation: Controlling and Accepting Radioactivity Risks. *History and Technology*, 23(4), pp. 389–406.

146 *Nestor Herran*

Boudia, S. (2008). Sur les dynamiques de constitution des systèmes d'expertise scientifique: le cas des rayonnements ionisants. *Genèses*, 70, pp. 26–44.

Brown, A., Franken, P., Bonner, S., Dolezal, N., and Moros, J. (2016). Safecast: Successful Citizen-science for Radiation Measurement and Communication after Fukushima. *Journal of Radiological Protection*, 36, pp. S82–S101.

Dumoulin, M., Guillen, P., and Vaïsse, M., eds. (1994). *L'énergie nucléaire en Europe: des origines à Euratom*. Bern: Peter Lang.

Eisenbud, M. (1990). *An Environmental Odyssey: People, Pollution, and Politics in the Lie of a Practical Scientist*. Seattle, WA: University of Washington Press.

Erikson, E. (1965). An Account of the Major Pulses of Tritium and their Effects in the Atmosphere. *Tellus*, 17, pp. 118–130.

Fischer, D. (1997). *History of the International Atomic Energy Agency: The First Forty Years*. Vienna: International Atomic Energy Agency.

Friend, J., ed. (1961). *The High Altitude Sampling Program, Report DASA-1300*, Volume 1. Available at: https://apps.dtic.mil/sti/pdfs/AD0267616.pdf [Accessed May 31, 2021].

Goodman, M. S. (2007). *Spying on the Nuclear Bear: Anglo-American Intelligence and the Soviet Bomb*. Stanford: Stanford University Press.

Hamblin, J. (2006). Exorcising Ghosts in the Age of Automation: United Nations Experts and Atoms for Peace. *Technology and Culture*, 47(4), pp. 734–756.

Hamblin, J. (2007). "A Dispassionate and Objective Effort": Negotiating the First Study on the Biological Effects of Atomic Radiation. *Journal of the History of Biology*, 40(1), pp. 147–177.

Hamblin, J. (2009). Let There be Light… and Bread: The United Nations, the Developing World, and Atomic Energy's Green Revolution. *History and Technology*, 25, pp. 25–48.

Hecht, G. (2012). *Being Nuclear: Africans and the Global Uranium Trade*. Cambridge, MA: MIT Press.

Helmreich, J. (1991). The United States and the Formation of Euratom. *Diplomatic History*, 15(3), pp. 387–410.

Herran, N. (2014). Unscare and Conceal: The United Nations Scientific Committee on the Effects of Atomic Radiation and the Origin of International Radiation Monitoring. In S. Turchetti and P. Roberts, eds., *The Surveillance Imperative: Geosciences during the Cold War and Beyond*. Basingstoke, UK: Palgrave MacMillan, pp. 69–84.

Higuchi, T. (2018). Epistemic Frictions: Radioactive Fallout, Health Risk Assessments, and the Eisenhower Administration's Nuclear-test Ban Policy, 1954–1958. *International Relations of the Asia-Pacific*, 18(1), pp. 99–124.

Hultquist, C., and Cervone, G. (2018). Citizen Monitoring during Hazards: Validation of Fukushima Radiation Measurements. *GeoJournal*, 83, pp. 189–206.

Irish Meteorological Service. (1957). *Measurements of Radioactivity of Precipitation, Settled Dust and Airborne Particles in Ireland in 1957*. Dublin: Department of Transport.

Janssens, A. (2004). Environmental Radiation Protection: Philosophy, Monitoring and Standards. *Journal of Environmental Radioactivity*, 72, pp. 65–73.

Jones, M. (2010). *After Hiroshima: The United States, Race and Nuclear Weapons in Asia, 1945-1965*. Cambridge UK: Cambridge University Press.

Radioactivity monitoring 147

Kelleher, K. (2017). Radiation Monitoring in Ireland—The Impact and Lessons Learned from Nuclear Accidents. *Radiation Environment and Medicine*, 6(2), pp. 49–54.

Krige, J. (2008). The Peaceful Atom as Political Weapon: Euratom and American Foreign Policy in the Late 1950s. *Historical Studies in the Natural Sciences*, 38(1), pp. 5–44.

Krige, J., ed. (2016). *Sharing Knowledge, Shaping Europe: US Technological Collaboration and Nonproliferation*. Cambridge, MA: MIT Press.

List, R. (1955). *World-Wide Fallout from Operation Castle Bravo*. Washington, DC: Weather Bureau, United States Department of Commerce.

Lutts, R. (1985). Chemical Fallout: Rachel Carson's Silent Spring, Radioactive Fallout, and the Environmental Movement. *Environmental Review*, 9(3), pp. 210–225.

Marcus, F. (1997). *Half a Century of Nordic Nuclear Co-operation: An Insider's Recollections*. Copenhagen: Nordgraf.

Marcus, G. (2008). The OECD Nuclear Agency at 50. *Nuclear News*, 51(2) (February), pp. 27–33.

McCormick, J. (1989). *Reclaiming Paradise: The Global Environmental Movement*. Bloomington, IN: Indiana University Press.

Métivier, H. (2007). *Cinquante ans de radioprotection. Rapport commémoratif du 50ème anniversaire du CRPPH*. Issy-les-Moulineaux: AEN/OCDE.

Mould, R. (2000). *Chernobyl Record: The Definitive History of the Chernobyl Catastrophe*. Bristol UK: Institute of Physics Publishing.

Richelson, J. (2006). *Spying on the Bomb: American Nuclear Intelligence from Nazi Germany to Iran and North Korea*. New York: Norton.

Roehrlich, E. (2016). The Cold War, the Developing World, and the Creation of the International Atomic Energy Agency (IAEA), 1953–1957. *Cold War History*, 16(2), pp. 195–212.

Skogen, E. (2003). *Fra Forsvarets forskningsinstitutts Historie*. Virkninger av kjernevåpen. Available at: https://publications.ffi.no/nb/item/asset/dspace:6101/FFIs-historie-nr5.pdf [Accessed May 31, 2021].

Sundqvist, G., and Elam, M. (2010). Public Involvement Designed to Circumvent Public Concern? The "Participatory Turn" in European Nuclear Activities. *Risk, Hazards and Crisis in Public Policy*, 1(4), pp. 203–229.

Topçu, S. (2013). *La France nucléaire. L'art de gouverner une technologie contestée*. Paris: Seuil.

Trabalka, J., Eyman, L., and Auerbach, S. (1980). Analysis of the 1957-1958 Soviet Nuclear Accident. *Science*, 209(4454), pp. 345–353.

UNSCEAR (1958). *Report of the United Nations Scientific Committee on the Effects of Atomic Radiation*. General Assembly, thirteenth session. Supplement no. 17 (A/3838). New York: United Nations. Available at: https://www.unscear.org/docs/publications/1958/UNSCEAR_1958_Report.pdf [Accessed June 15, 2021].

Ziegler, C., and Jacobson, D. (1995). *Spying without Spies: Origins of America's Secret Nuclear Intelligence Surveillance System*. Westport, CT: Praeger.

7 Making the accident hypothetical: how can one deal with the potential nuclear disaster?

Maël Goumri

> Atomic power can cure as well as kill. It can fertilize and enrich a region as well as devastate it. It can widen man's horizons as well as force him back into the cave.
>
> —Alvin M. Weinberg, nuclear physicist, testimony to
> the US Senate Commission on Atomic Uses, December 1945

Geneva, 1955. The first international conference of the Atoms for Peace program took place on the shores of Lake Geneva. Initiated by US President Dwight D. Eisenhower in 1953, Atoms for Peace was created, with UN patronage, to promote all the peaceful uses of nuclear technology over the world, and the conference signaled an energetic optimism. Industrial achievements, mostly American, were exhibited for the first time, harbingers of a massive use of promising energy. As the historian John Krige (2006) has shown, this was not simply a question of using a new source of energy but enabling the advent of affluence across societies, in which energy would be so cheap that the electricity meters could simply disappear. It was a far cry from the image of destruction and devastation that had gripped the world a decade earlier and seemed to signal a radical change in the trajectory of the atom.

Since the very development of nuclear power industry, the destructive potential of the atom has been made concrete. The transition from experimentation to the commercial exploitation of the atom between the 1950s and 1970s was accompanied by numerous reflections on the new risks generated by the use of nuclear energy. Of course, destruction was not the purpose of civilian technologies, but accidents, experts cautioned from the start, could occur. In particular, nuclear physicists cautioned that nuclear energy raised a new form of risk, and plant designers worked to imagine the damages that an accident might cause. This is why, at the Geneva conference, a small session addressed the issue of reactor safety, in conjunction with the issues of "industrial hygiene" and "radiation protection." Jean Bourgeois, head of the French subcommittee

DOI: 10.4324/9781003227472-7

Making the accident hypothetical 149

on reactor safety, suggested that, "Technical precautions are such that the probability of such an accident is extremely low, while the most pessimistic assumptions lead to extremely high damage, so that the product approaches the undetermined form 0 X ∞."[1] Thus, amid participants' enthusiasm for an expansion of peaceful nuclear applications, the proceedings of the conference reveal that, even then, mastering risk was also a good business practice: the consequences of an accident affecting public opinion could shut down the nascent industry.[2]

Proponents appeared truly challenged by the effort to master this new form of risk. As experts claimed that an accident was extremely unlikely, the development of nuclear energy aimed not at rendering such accidents impossible but minimising the risks to an economically acceptable level. During the same session that included reactor safety, C. Rogers McCullough, representing the Advisory Committee for Reactor Safety of the US Atomic Energy Commission (AEC) said plainly: "Of course, absolute safety is not possible and what is really meant in connection with reactor hazards is the minimization of hazards until one has an acceptable calculated risk."[3] Promising a quick and massive expansion of nuclear technology in 1955 meant promising that a still brand-new technology, full of unknowns, was a hurdle; this new type of risk and the impossibility of absolute safety challenged the nuclear industry and regulation. Five years prior, the AEC had taken a more cautionary tone: "The situation confronting the Atomic Energy Commission is one in which the danger of building and operating these devices must be weighed against the need for advancement of the technology of the field."[4] The 1945 bombings had left a deep impression, as Paul Boyer writes in *By the Bomb's Early Light* (2005), and scientists, business interests, and policymakers understood that they would need to be serious about safety if the non-military use of atomic power was to gain social acceptance. Development of nuclear power relied on the premise of safely operated power plants (Topçu, 2013), and that raised a host of debates about what constituted a sufficiently adequate level of safety in order for a proposed facility to move forward. Throughout the 1960s and 1970s, the expression "how safe is safe enough?" would be deployed regularly in the rhetoric of both supporters and detractors of nuclear expansion.

This chapter aims to examine nuclear engineers' working practices and strategies to minimise the risks related to civilian uses of atomic energy. How can nuclear energy be considered safe, in spite of its potential for destruction? How do we envision to live safely amid the new nuclear risk? While the focal case is French, it reveals nuclear development in relationship with other countries, as nuclear safety is, without question, an international domain. Understanding the French case is impossible without looking to the way nuclear safety has been treated in other countries and in the US particularly because of the transnational dimension of nuclear safety. As knowledge and standards circulated across world

150 *Maël Goumri*

borders, the United Stated and the United Kingdom were quickly joined by other governments, including France, in drafting and assessing early regulatory regimes. This case also reveals the national particularities of safety management, including reactions to notable accidents including Three Mile Island in 1979, which led to divergences—sometimes large ones—in various country's national positions on the future of nuclear energy.

On the hypothetical

The promoters of nuclear energy, by the 1970s, had tried to spread a rhetorical change: they did not speak of nuclear accidents as impossible but "hypothetical." To this day, engineers and experts use the term "hypothetical accident" as they consider eventualities that are not *supposed* to occur—the reactors were designed to prevent accidents—yet certainly *could* occur. "Hypotheticality" was theorised in 1974 by West-German nuclear physicist Wolf Häfele, who participated in and led nuclear energy programs in the Federal Republic of Germany.[5] In designating the particularity of nuclear risk, Häfele theorised:

> Subdividing the problem can lead only to an approximation to ultimate safety. The risk can be made smaller than any small but predetermined number which is larger than zero. The remaining "residual risk" opens the door into the domain of "hypotheticality." ...The strange and often unreal features of that debate, in my judgement, are connected with the "hypotheticality" of the domain below the level of the residual risk.
>
> (Häfele, 1974: 314)

Clearly, Häfele had enormous confidence about the improbability of a nuclear accident yet remained aware of the destructive potential. Experts could not totally exclude the possibility of a nuclear disaster but hoped to demonstrate that it was sufficiently unlikely in order to gain social acceptance. Häfele had provided, with the notion of "hypotheticality," a way to downplay risk and allay fear so that the nuclear industry might flourish.

But how can experts actually consider nuclear accidents hypothetical? The low number of large, severe accidents does not allow nuclear experts to assess nuclear safety only through first-hand experience. They develop a large range of concepts and tools to assess nuclear safety and to demonstrate that accident probability is low enough to be considered near impossible. I propose a retracing of the technical and social work needed to allow engineers, relying on a combination of technical features, representations, confidence and expertise, to render the accident "hypothetical." I also explore the material and institutional infrastructures implemented to deal with the risk of accidents as citizens, countries and

Making the accident hypothetical 151

anti-nuclear movements increasingly considered any nuclear danger socially unacceptable. I argue that nuclear experts and engineers framed the "accident" to inspire trust in efficient prevention. Despite uncertainty, nuclear energy's champions downplayed possible damage as hypothetical.

Three early stages in the age of nuclear energy help disentangle this shift. The first section will thus cover the emergence of nuclear energy as an *engineering project*. The second corresponds to the *industrialisation* of nuclear energy, as big projects were met by growing public contestation worldwide. And the third stage opened when the unexpected core-meltdown at Three Mile Island, PA, on March 28, 1979 spurred a new urgency around the concurrent needs to consider the probability and impact of severe accidents and to save—indeed, expand—the industry in which they occurred.

Defining a safe design: technical challenge of the early atomic age

After WWII, nuclear safety organisations sprang up in the main nuclearised countries, mostly linked to military nuclear applications. In the United States, the Atomic Energy Act (McMahon Act) signed by President Harry S. Truman in 1946 created the AEC to continue research initiated during the war. Toward the development of future munitions as well as peaceful applications, the AEC set up a Reactor Safeguards Committee by 1947. The body, charged with evaluating nuclear safety and hazards, was merged with the Industrial Committee on Reactor Location Problems (created in 1950) after the 1954 (new) Atomic Energy Act, forming the Advisory Committee for Reactor Safeguards (ACRS). In France, the AEC's correlate, the Commissariat à l'énergie atomique (CEA), formed in 1945, dealt with safety problems within the "*sous-commission de sûreté des piles*" (sub-committee for reactor safety) following the model of the United States and United Kingdom. This CEA subcommittee was specifically assembled to advise the French government on best practices for avoiding nuclear accidents without hampering nuclear development (Foasso, 2007).

In the international sphere, matters of safety were particularly discussed with regard to the development of civilian nuclear energy. After the launch of Atoms for Peace, the nearly two-week long first international Geneva conference in 1955 explored the potential of such peaceful applications of nuclear energy. This event helped establish a shared vision of a technical (Del Sesto, 1993) and political (Krige, 2010) utopia marked by the swift development of peaceful nuclear applications. The atomic future was posed as being so bright as to justify the new risks it created. In Session 6.2, "Reactor Safety and Location of Power Reactors," the Geneva Conference assessed the possibility, in terms of probability and consequences, of a nuclear accident. The American delegation concluded:

152 *Maël Goumri*

> We believe that useful electric power in large quantities can be generated by nuclear reactors. It is our concern that rapid progress shall be made but that enough caution be observed so that no catastrophic event will delay the fruition of reactor development.[6]

Their approach aimed to inspire confidence in reliable design, clearing a serious hurdle to the industrial development of nuclear power. The AEC had initially decided that nuclear reactors (particularly those dedicated to research and development uses) be located only in uninhabited areas for safety (Mazuzan and Walker, 1985) but, as the attendees in Geneva pointed out time and again, nuclear reactors would need to be sited close enough to large cities to provide electricity.[7]

At this point, the problem of safety—like the promise of limitless cheap energy—was expressed in economic terms. What could constitute an adequately safe design that would control the risk of accident, drastically reduce costs so that the effort of atomic energy was both profitable and competitive (understanding that profits would be affected by transportation costs should reactors be too remote), and realise the hoped-for atomic future? General Electric representatives in Geneva reported:

> To achieve the economic advantage of locating nuclear power reactors close to large communities, it is essential that the potential environmental radiation hazards be unequivocally eliminated. At the present time, it seems certain that inherently safe reactors can be constructed. Even if there is still a minute possibility of serious reactor accident, release of radioactive material to the environs can be prevented by a protective envelope, of which a large steel sphere is one feasible form.[8]

That is, as promoters promised a low probability of accident, they also began planning for and communicating the assurance of efficient containment of potential releases.

The issue of location is rooted in the specific American regulation of nuclear applications and the development of AEC accountability in the 1950s. To control the risk of accidents in civilian facilities, the AEC Reactor Safeguards Committee (later, the ACRS) decided in 1950 to pursue the isolation policy set for the WWII-era Manhattan Project. The committee stated, "It is unfortunate that our experience in the operation of nuclear reactors to date is small and the hazards to human life which may result from accident or faulty operation are believed to be great."[9] The authors noted, by way of example, how the early development of motor vehicles disrupted various aspects of life in New York City, and they proposed a very restrictive policy nicknamed the "rule of thumb." It required the establishment of an "exclusion distance," assessed through modeling a huge release of radioactivity from an uncontained reactor.

Making the accident hypothetical 153

The exclusion radius was calculated with the formula "R = 0.01 √ P," in which P is the reactor's full power (Okrent, 1978: 2–8). But in the mid-1950s, the ACRS sidestepped these regulations to allow the installation of light water reactors at Shippingport and Indian Point, sites too close to populated areas to comply with the American "rule of thumb." The ACRS concluded that these facilities' specific designs ensured the efficient containment of radionuclides in the event of an accident. As projects were examined on a case-by-case basis, the ACRS rejected the implementation of small reactors proposed for the perimeters of mid-size cities using no formal criteria but the experts' judgment (Okrent, 1981).

Later in the decade, AEC regulation staff began working on formal site criteria under the leadership of Dr. Clifford Beck. Guidelines released in 1961 more specifically determined that the exclusion area for a nuclear energy project must be calculated by considering a maximum acceptable human exposure of "doses of 25 rem whole body and 300 rem to the thyroid" (Okrent, 1978: 2–2) should an accident occur. This hypothetical accident, called the Maximum Credible Accident, was now a primary "focus of siting evaluation." (Okrent, 1978: 2–2) Designers now had to prove to the ACRS that the Maximum Credible Accident occurrence for any given facility would have no catastrophic consequences on the population or the environment and that any accident of lower intensity must be contained in this "envelope" (to further minimise consequences). This set of regulations was called "10 CFR PART 100."

Obviously, this calculation involved a fundamental problem: how to determine what constitutes the Maximum Credible Accident (MCA). University of California in Los Angeles (UCLA) physicist David Okrent, an ACRS member, explained that the notion of "credibility" was assessed by considering the number of potential *simultaneous* failures:

> In general, accidents would be considered credible if their occurrence might be caused by one single equipment failure or operational error, though clearly some consideration must be given to the likelihood of this failure or error. It has been suggested that this criterion might be extended to the assignment of decreasing probabilities to accidents which would be occasioned only by 2, 3 or more independent and simultaneous errors or malfunctions, with the possibility that accidents requiring more than 3 or 4 such independent faults would be considered incredible.
>
> (Okrent 1978: 2–1)

This distinction between credible and incredible, although well-discussed by experts, allowed regulators to sort out possible accidents, paying more attention to the most likely and ignoring the most improbable. Like all typologies, this would have irreversible material consequences—in this case, on the siting and design of nuclear reactors.[10] Even for its

154 *Maël Goumri*

authors, the concept of an MCA remained admittedly imperfect. In presenting this new approach at the nuclear congress in Rome in June 1959, Dr. Beck argued,

> it is inherently impossible to give an objective definition or specification for 'credible accidents' and thus the attempt to identify these for a given reactor entails some sense of futility and frustration and, further, it is never entirely assured that all potential accidents have been examined. (quoted in Okrent, 1978: 2–31)

However, the "Maximum Credible Accident" became the ground basis of the licensing process. It took the name of "design-basis accident" and the designers needed to take them into account in the reactor's design. The "design-basis accident," if it occurs, must not lead to significant consequences thanks to adequate safety features.

In 1957, the AEC published a study out of the Brookhaven National Laboratory in Long Island, "Theoretical Possibilities and Consequences of Major Accidents in Large Nuclear Power Plants." also known as WASH-740 report. It focused on the potential consequences of a major accident and enlightened legislative debate over the Price Anderson Act, which would determine the liability level of nuclear operators. as well as insurance and compensations for victims of nuclear accidents. In the words of French sociologist Sezin Topçu, this was a way to "organise the irresponsibility" (Topçu, 2014) and foster private investment. In 1960, the Paris convention adopted the same principle, greenlighting European development of the nuclear industry despite its potentially unknowable and immeasurable consequences (Daston, 2016; Kyrtsis and Rentetzi, 2021). This report included a section headed, "A Study of Possible Consequences if Certain Assumed Accidents, Theoretically Possible but Highly Improbable, Were to Occur in Large Nuclear Power Plants," in which experts again asserted: "The probability of occurrence of publicly hazardous accidents in nuclear power reactor plants is exceedingly low."[11]

Under this regulatory scheme, scientists first determined the worst possible accident that could occur at a given nuclear power plant, regardless of probability. That choice spurred a major change in the way nuclear accidents were conceived. To this point, experts had considered that the main risk was a reaction runaway event, called a *reactivity accident*. Now they added that a Loss Of Coolant Accident (LOCA) followed by a core meltdown was the one case in which a large quantity of radionuclides would be released, because the molten core could alter the containment materials.[12] Nevertheless, designers and regulators continued to consider containment the best approach to coping with a LOCA and largely left uncalculated the potential for a core meltdown to alter and amplify the spread of nuclear fallout.

Making the accident hypothetical   155

At the same time, a severe nuclear fire that occurred at Windscale in the United Kingdom on October 10, 1957 led to major changes in the United Kingdom's Atomic Energy Agency (AEA). At the second Atoms for Peace Conference in 1958, the AEA put forward a formalised containment philosophy later known as the "method of barriers."[13] This system relies on three independent, nested barriers: fuel cladding, reactor core vessel, and containment building. Each should be able to contain and reduce radioactivity even in case of leakage (a core meltdown damaging the cladding or a fuel fire), using a Russian doll set-up.

The first period of nuclear development led to the implementation of various infrastructures meant to overcome the hypothetical nuclear disaster that threatened the commercial exploitation of atomic energy. The hypotheticality of a nuclear accident had been established on two assumptions: the probability was low enough to be acceptable and the consequences of any accident would, thanks to careful design, be "containable." However, the massive spread of nuclear energy in the mid-1960s and its mounting public contestation contributed to a reframing such that, in addition to technical arguments, risks to the public had to be taken into account.

Demonstrating that the accident is hypothetical to experts and public

In the mid-1960 and the 1970s, the technical precautions that experts considered efficient enough to master the risk of nuclear accidents and sufficient to convince nuclear technicians could no longer satisfy the fast-growing anti-nuclear contingent. According to historians George T. Mazuzan and Samuel J. Walker, the changes in US regulation policies throughout the 1960s aimed to enhance public confidence in the AEC and its regulatory process (Mazuzan and Walker, 1985: 373). Therefore, the AEC decided not to substantially change its policies in terms of licensing, but to develop new processes of requiring proof of safe design, notably via experiments.

In the early 1960s, Dr. Beck, a North Carolina State University nuclear physicist and AEC member, had, for instance, investigated the interaction between water and zirconium. In the mid-1960s, the AEC came around to the idea that safety should be empirically demonstrated in tests like these, rather than continue to rely exclusively on calculations. But the first "semi scale" experiments performed at Idaho Falls National Laboratory to prepare for the Loss of Flow Test (LOFT) program and the WASH-740 report update showed that the Zirconium-water chemical reaction might be highly exothermic and, should a temperature of 1205°C be exceeded, lead to a major, uncontainable core meltdown (Okrent, 1981).

A few years later, the construction of the LOFT testing station at Idaho National Engineering Laboratory (INEL) was completed. Its scientists

156   *Maël Goumri*

were permitted to perform experiments on core degradation in the event of a meltdown. Preliminary tests indicated that the Emergency Core Cooling System (ECCS) was not as reliable as had been assumed. Designers and regulators proposed a new strategy: enhancing the reactor's ability to reduce the leakage of radioactive material in case of damage. Frank Reginald Farmer, head of the Safeguard division of the Authority Health and Safety Branch of the United Kingdom's AEA made the proposal at the 1967 IAEA symposium on Reactor Siting and Containment, saying:

> Mr. Hake suggested that containment is required to meet a situation when the control system fails. For this event, it is very difficult to decide the course of the accident, taking into account molten fuel metal/water reactions and associated shock forces. It is precisely for this event that the value of containment is in doubt. There are other alternatives to containment, which have a comparable combination of availability and effectiveness. In the United Kingdom, we have shown that suitably designed suppression ponds will reduce iodine in the steam-gas mixtures by a factor of 30-300, and the availability of a pond is very good.[14]

Clearly, there were limits to the "design-basis accident" (determined with the MCA) regulatory approach to ensuring safety, and uncertainties concerning containment strategy continued to stymie the expansion of the nuclear industry.

Nonetheless, the exportation of reactors helped the US disseminate the risks inherent to reactor design in that country. Like most capitalist nuclearised countries, France was an importer of these American reactors. In 1969, after a huge competition between the French CEA and the state-owned electricity company, the Ministry of Energy abandoned the CEA's proposed gas-graphite reactor and instead adopted a light water reactor design using American technology (Hecht, 1998). The French American company *Framatome* bought licensed technology for a Westinghouse pressurised water reactor to aid the fast development of nuclear energy, importing US safety regulations alongside the technology. However, by the end of 1972, the Ministry of Industry SCSIN decided to launch a commission led by the safety department of the CEA to determine general standards for nuclear safety in France. The CEA's *Départment de Sûreté Nucléaire* (DSN) proposed "principles to be studied for the definition of accidents," particularly "*beyond design*-basis accidents," (worser accidents than the MCA) to prepare possible new regulations and emergency plans. Industrialists, such as *Framatome's* subcontractor (Groupement Atomique Alsacienne Atlantique—GAAA), pushed back:

> The approach proposed in this worksheet does not seem to us to be the best because it seems to make an arbitrary separation between

Making the accident hypothetical   157

accidents taken into account for the design and *beyond design*-basis accidents. This arbitrariness has the disadvantage of always leaving open the list of accidents to be taken into account for design.[15]

In a subequent letter, *Framatome* added:

> We are opposed to taking into account beyond design basis accidents. The manufacturer must carry out an installation where safety is guaranteed on the basis of a coherent list of accidents, drawn up in agreement with the safety organisations, and for which the installation is designed and dimensioned. The rule of the game must be set at the start: the manufacturer must work within a precise framework. The so-called "beyond design basis" accidents might become accidents taken into account for design.[16]

During a February 28, 1975 meeting, an array of French manufacturers reaffirmed that "the study of beyond design basis accidents should not, in [our] opinion, influence the design."[17] Apparently, industrial interests wanted to rely as much as possible on American criteria and practices rather than any stronger French restrictions.

The CEA's *Département de Sûreté Nucléaire* (DSN) launched construction on the Phébus Research Reactor in Cadarache in order to obtain experimental data on accidental situations (LOCA, in particular). The government hoped to address uncertainties about the ECCS's efficiency, following the efforts of other countries.[18] From the outset, though, the Phébus Research Reactor's construction was doomed. The CEA was under too much pressure to cut costs, and a competing research reactor, CABRI, which would study power excursions for CEA-designed fast breeder reactors, was an important focal project.[19] To ensure industrial funding, the first program, Phébus LOCA, was a compromise between DSN and the industry meant to "convince" Électricité de France (EDF) that it was necessary to study core degradation phenomena *beyond design*-basis accidents.[20] Before the Three Mile Island accident, EDF refused to support research on fuel behavior in beyond-design conditions, so the Phébus LOCA program studied fuel and zirconium cladding behavior, within design limits, at 1205°C (not coincidentally, the value determined by the US Nuclear Regulatory Commission [NRC]) to verify the validity of reference temperature without studying fuel behavior in a *beyond design*-basis situation.

At the same time, public communication was based on probabilities estimated by experts without using experimental data. Safety assessments based on the experts' judgment of "probability" were highly contested by independent experts from anti-nuclear organisations including the Union of Concerned Scientists (founded by Massachusetts Institute of Technology scientists in 1969). In 1972, facing criticism, the

158   *Maël Goumri*

AEC commissioned an ambitious study to assess the risk of a severe accident and its potential consequences in the United States from Professor Norman Carl Rasmussen, an MIT nuclear physicist. A team of 50 high-level experts worked full time, under Professor Rasmussen's supervision, to provide a nuclear accident probability assessment that was more "realistic" than the WASH 740 report study, which dealt with extreme accidents regardless of probability. The team borrowed from business school research, adopting the "event trees method" to consider both the reliability of systems and the probability of failures (Keller and Modarres, 2005; Esselborn and Zachmann, 2020). The final Rasmussen Report, released in 1975, challenged the MCA approach and demonstrated that the likeliest scenarios leading to a core meltdown were those involving multiple failures—the ones considered *incredible* in the 1960s. The study also emphasised the role played by human factors in the level of risks and demonstrated that the risk of core meltdown was higher than experts had previously claimed.[21] The AEC estimated that the probability of a large release of fission products (affecting 100 or more people) was around 10^{-9}, per reactor year, which meant a 1 in 100 million chance that any given reactor might experience such an accident in any given year. Comparing nuclear risks to other industrial and natural risks, the report concluded that nuclear risk was by far the lowest, excepting the risk of meteorite strike.[22]

The Rasmussen Report's ostensible demonstration of nuclear safety was not without controversy. The Union of Concerned Scientists prepared a counter-report, the Kendall Report, which deemed the AEC executive summary partial and unfair (Rip, 1986). The Kendall Report alleged that the probability of ECCS failure, reported at 10^{-1} per reactor year in the Rasmussen Report (for a 1 in 10 chance of failure), was even higher, taking into account data from the first LOFT test on ECCS performed at Idaho Falls (Ford, 1986). The United States commissioned another official report, this time to reevaluate Rasmussen. The resulting Lewis Report critiqued and revoked the Rasmussen Report's executive summary in January 1979 (Okrent, 1981).

While West Germany also decided to establish its own probabilistic safety assessment, France never launched such studies. EDF retained the main conclusion that "Risks incurred by the public due to nuclear power plants are, by far, lower than risks of other kinds," favorably comparing nuclear risks with the risks of natural, technological, and daily life occurrences like car accidents and deeming them, thus, socially acceptable.[23] EDF pointed out that the probability of core meltdown was higher than in its previous studies (6.10^{-5} per reactor year in Rasmussen, versus 10^{-6} per reactor year in the studies performed by EDF). It also noted that core meltdown was more likely after a *small* break in the primary circuit (8.10^{-5} per reactor year) than after a *large* one (5.10^{-5} per reactor year). EDF assumed then, from a technical standpoint, its

Making the accident hypothetical   159

assessment of risk was both more realistic and more pessimistic about human-factor data. Accordingly, EDF concluded that the core meltdown probability (6.10^{-5}) was "extremely reasonable" given the existing margin and human-factor improvements that could be achieved in the expansion of nuclear power.[24]

This report, prepared by the Probability Safety Assessment Department, did not, however, reflect consensus among EDF members. Some even pointed out weaknesses in the safety evaluations published in the report. Still, the organisation concluded that the risk of major accident was low enough that structural modifications or important R&D programs in France should not be delayed over that potential.

When the unexpected accident happens: believing that major accidents are hypothetical

On March 28, 1979, at 4 am, a technical failure exacerbated by human error caused a core meltdown at Three Mile Island, PA. Nearly half the reactor core melted, shocking the nuclear industry worldwide. Not only was this a once "unthinkable" scenario, but it was also a resounding disqualification of existing precautionary measures and the MCA. Contrary to what was foreseeable when the reactor was designed, the Three Mile Island accident was the consequence of *multiple* failures.[25] For Charles Perrow, a sociologist of organisations and member of the Kemenny investigation commission, this accident came about, in part, because technical complexities rendered individual operators unable to master every step involved in operating a nuclear power plant. Perrow dubbed Three Mile Island a "normal accident" (Perrow, 1981; 1984) in that organisational characteristics lead to *normal accidents*. The nuclear industry was, to Perrow, a prime example in which a complex organisation experiences normal accidents, because the complexity of operating an entire power plant was beyond the understanding of any single individual, thereby compounding the possible errors leading to and in reaction to nuclear accidents.

In the United States, President Jimmy Carter responded to the Three Mile Island crisis by commissioning an investigation into its causes. The resulting Kemenny Commission Report recommended reinforcing effective control of the NRC over the nuclear industry and strengthening the complementary role of ACRS. Further, it advocated better training for nuclear operators and better management of maintenance operations in order to mitigate the possibility that another small failure should, in a domino effect, result in a serious, multifaceted accident like Three Mile Island. Emphasising that this accident's consequences for the public, given the low level of radioactivity leaked from the plant, had been limited (Walker, 2004), the Kemenny Commission's report concluded that "if the country wishes, for larger reasons, to confront the risks that

160 *Maël Goumri*

are inherently associated with nuclear power, fundamental changes are necessary if those risks are to be kept within tolerable limits" (Walker, 2004: 210–211).

Weathering massive public attacks, the NRC decided to launch its own investigation commission, the "TMI 2 Lessons Learned Task Force." It would be chaired by Mitchell Rogovin and accompanied by a freeze on all nuclear development projects until its conclusions were published. Neither Congress nor the NRC set a formal moratorium on nuclear energy (Temples, 1982), but the NRC set a pause in the issuance of licenses—a *de facto* moratorium (Walker, 2004; Wellock, 2021). After the Three Mile Island accident, and despite efforts toward safety and the reassuring conclusions of both Congress and the NRC, Reactor 2 was not replaced. New NRC requirements were deemed too expensive and the tarnished image of nuclear power too controversial; a slump in electricity demand settled the issue. The NRC's director, who worked to reassure the public during the Three Mile Island crisis, announced that the cleanup would take less than four years, helping things return to normal. But because of the costs and complexity of the cleaning process, the reactor was *never* cleaned up and *never* restarted. The second reactor at Three Mile Island (Unit 1) was finally shut down in September 2019.

In contrast, in France, neither the government nor the CEA considered reducing or delaying the use of nuclear energy. The Three Mile Island incident was reported in French media, and authorities declared that French reactors and operators were different enough to rule out such an accident in France. The CEA and SCSIN nevertheless sent groups of experts to the United States to gather technical information. After examining the accident, the French advisory expert group (*Groupe Permanent*) concluded that this accident did not challenge French safety principles, though it drew attention to the human side of nuclear operation and crisis management.[26]

This view of the Three Mile Island accident was certainly debated at the highest level of the CEA, particularly within the direction committee. The military division said it "defeated the concept of a reference accident," while the CEA General Administrator assumed that the French nuclear "safety philosophy was not deficient."[27] The CEA minimised the consequences of the Three Mile Island incident and decided that no major change should be made to the French standards:

> The fundamental principles of safety, the principle of barriers and what the Americans call "defence in depth," are not being challenged. We knew that safety analysis will always be unable to predict everything, including human errors, and the ultimate backup measures are there to deal with unexpected situations. It is therefore necessary to maintain this global concept of safety.[28]

Making the accident hypothetical   161

The French Academy of Sciences asserted that the major damage caused by the accident in Pennsylvania had been due to a failure in public communication: the "psychological" aspects of both operation and crisis were, the Academy believed, poorly managed by American authorities.[29] The design was excellent and a state-owned, centralised company like EDF was a major advantage to the French authorities in implementing the lessons learned from the accident going forward.

However, the political consequences of the Three Mile Island accident worried both the CEA and the French Ministry of Industry. An accident's *political* fallout could affect the entire nuclear industry. Thus, because it would impose a moratorium on the opening of new nuclear facilities, these two bodies criticised a proposal to create an international regulation body for the harmonisation of safety practices.[30] The head of CEA even publicly deplored the US and German delegations to the June 1979 G7 summit in Tokyo, which argued for more international nuclear regulation.[31] France's strong pro-nuclear position in this moment may be connected to the second oil crisis in 1979, which urged the further development of new European energy sources (Bonneuil and Fressoz, 2016). Nuclear promoters, particularly in France, managed to again demonstrate the improbability of another accident such as Three Mile Island by decoupling this abnormal situation from a disaster with long-term impacts. The accident, they insisted, actually revitalised the promises of nuclear energy by showing first that, even in a beyond-design accident, efficient containment could prevent total disaster, and second that this abnormal event had simply pointed out design and operations weaknesses that could be fixed. With this discursive twist, nuclear promoters chose to present the accident as an important contribution to enhancing the safety of nuclear technology.

Conclusion

Making the accident hypothetical was a specific way to control the risk of severe nuclear accidents—an impossibility according to normal accident theory. The risk that was initially considered exceptional, with the image of a nuclear bomb in the background, was reframed as "hypothetical" by promoters of *civilian* nuclear reactors who needed to boost the social acceptability of nuclear energy.

As I have shown in this chapter, three major strategies were employed. First, technological reliability was declared "inherently safe" given adequate design. This safe-by-design strategy was borrowed from chemical industries, which saw their first large accidents in the 1950s and 1960s. (Kletz, 1999; Boudia and Jas, 2014) It became a common way to claim control over risks in the United States (Boudia and Jas, 2013) in the 1970s. Second, the champions of nuclear industry determined the "acceptable" consequences of a potential accident on the basis of exposure norms (called

162   Maël Goumri

radioprotection norms) developed by the International Commission on Radiological Protection (Boudia, 2008), even as others protested that there were no acceptable radiation risks. Third, to validate project designs, designers and experts adopted an approach based on the safety assessment of consequences on the assumed MCA of each facility.

The response to the exceptional nuclear risk is a combination of conventional practices meant to master the new risks and the contestation by extensively considering the likeliest accidents but leaving aside far riskier "hypothetical accidents." The risk has been technically controlled and decoupled from its inherent political dimension (Douglas and Wildavsky, 1983; Perrow, 1984; Beck, 1992). This technological approach is strongly linked to the risk assessment analysis performed by nuclear experts, without consulting the public or taking contestation into account. Because the public has been generally considered "ill-informed" and unable to take part in technological decisions, we can see that the management of nuclear accidents via preemptive regulation in design and siting actually exemplifies the deficit model characteristic of twentieth-century politics. Making the accident hypothetical means dealing with virtual accidents, which fosters confidence in preventive measures, despite the material consistency of nuclear risks.

Notes

1 Bourgeois, J., Costes, C., Henri, C., Segot, C. and Lamrial, G. (1962). Problème de sécurité des réacteurs de puissances à uranium naturel modérés au graphite et refroidis au gaz. In: *Reactor Safety and Hazards Evaluation Techniques, Proceedings of the Symposium on Reactor Safety and Hazards Evaluation Techniques* (IAEA, Vienna, May 14–18), volume 2, pp. 151–168: 152. Translated by the author.
2 Dietrich, J. (1956). Experimental Determination of the Self-Regulation and Safety Operating Water-Moderated Reactors. In *Proceedings of the International Conference on the Peaceful Uses of Atomic Energy* (United Nations, Geneva, August 8–20, 1955), volume 13, p. 88.
3 McCullough, C., Mills, M., and Teller, E. (1956). The Safety of Nuclear Reactors. In *Proceedings of the International Conference on the Peaceful Uses of Atomic Energy* (United Nations, Geneva, August 8–20, 1955), volume 13, pp. 79–87.
4 Atomic Energy Commission, "Summary Report of reactor Safeguard Committee," Technical Information division, ORE, Oak Ridge WASH-3, 1950, pp. 1–2.
5 I would like to give warm thanks to Stefan Esselborn of TUM München for this very useful reference.
6 McCullough et al., The Safety of Nuclear Reactors, p. 87.
7 Question of Mr. Went of The Netherlands to Mr. McCullough (USA), discussion of session 6.02. In: *Proceedings of the International Conference on the Peaceful Uses of Atomic Energy*, volume 13, p. 126.
8 Parker, H., and Healy, J. (1956). Environmental Effects of a Major Reactor Disaster. In: *Proceedings of the International Conference on the Peaceful Uses of Atomic Energy*, volume 13, p. 106.

Making the accident hypothetical 163

9 AEC (1950). WASH-3 Summary Report of Reactor Safeguard Committee, Technical Information Division, ORE, Oak Ridge TN, pp. 1–2.

10 The material implication and consequences of classification has been extensively studied by Science and Technology Studies (see, for example, Bowker and Star, 1999; Busch, 2013).

11 AEC (1957). WASH-740 Report, Theoretical Possibilities and Consequences of Major Accidents in Large Nuclear Power Plants, p. 3. Available at: https://www.osti.gov/servlets/purl/4344308 [Accessed June 23, 2021].

12 WASH-740 Report, Theoretical Possibilities, p. 3.

13 Farmer F., Flechter P., and Fry T. (1958). Safety Consideration for Gas Cooled Thermal Reactors of the Calder Hall Type. In *Proceedings of the Second United Nations International Conference on the Peaceful Uses of Atomic Energy* (United Nations, Geneva, 1–13 September 1958), volume 11. p. 197.

14 *Containment and Siting of Nuclear Power Plants: Proceedings of a Symposium* (IAEA, Vienna, April 3–7, 1967), pp. 91–92.

15 Lettre de réaction aux Fiches DSN de GAAA, January 8, 1975, p. 6, FAR 08, IRSN archives, Fontenay-aux-Roses, France Translated by the author.

16 Lettre de réaction de Framatome aux Fiches du DSN, January 27, 1975, FAR 08, IRSN archives, Fontenay-aux-Roses, France Translated by the author.

17 Compte rendu de la réunion du groupe de travail Réglementation technique générale des réacteurs, February 28, 1975, p. 3, FAR 08, IRSN archives, Fontenay-aux-Roses, France Translated by the author.

18 Note Dg PSN 73-467 du délégué à la Mission Protection et Sûreté Nucléaires à Monsieur l'Administrateur Général, septembre 19, 1973, p. 1, FAR 08, IRSN archives, Fontenay-aux-Roses, France.

19 Note Dg PSN 73-467 du délégué à la Mission Protection et Sûreté Nucléaires à Monsieur l'Administrateur Général, septembre 19, 1973, p. 6, FAR 08, IRSN archives, Fontenay-aux-Roses, France.

20 Interview with a retired CEA-IPSN engineer, by the author.

21 EDF's first studies anticipated a general risk of core meltdown of approximately 10^{-6} per reactor year, while the Rasmussen Report assessed it at a level of 6.10^{-5} per reactor year (*Note Technique* SEPTEN E-SE/SN 74-36 (written by L. Prouteau); *Analyse du rapport Wash 1400 du Professeur Rasmussen sur la Sûreté des Réacteurs Nucléaires*, 7 novembre 1974, FAR 08, IRSN archives, Fontenay aux Roses, France.

22 NRC (1975). WASH-1400, Reactor Safety Study (NUREG 75/014).

23 *Note Technique* SEPTEN E-SE/SN 74-36, Prouteau, *Analyse du rapport Wash-1400*.

24 *Note Technique* SEPTEN E-SE/SN 74-36, Prouteau, *Analyse du rapport Wash-1400*.

25 NRC (June 21, 2018). Backgrounder on the Three Mile Island Accident. Available at: https://www.nrc.gov/reading-rm/doc-collections/fact-sheets/3mile-isle.html [Accessed June 19, 2021].

26 Note Institut de Protection et de Sûreté Nucléaire, Études Faites par le Département de Sûreté Nucléaire, June–November 1979, p. 3, FAR 08, IRSN archives, Fontenay-aux-Roses, France.

27 Groupe CEA, *Compte Rendu du Conseil de Direction du 14 Mai 1979, 15/05/1979*, Chrono IPSN 2930c/CEA41, FAR 08, IRSN archives, Fontenay-aux-Roses, France.

28 Pierre, T. (1979). Description de l'accident de Three Mile Island (update of the first report of April 10, 1979), pp. 13–14, FAR 08, IRSN archives, Fontenay-aux-Roses, France. Translated by the author.

164 Maël Goumri

29 Académie des Sciences, Rapport institué à la suite de l'accident survenu à la Centrale de Three Mile Island, September 18, 1979, FAR 08, IRSN archives, Fontenay-aux-Roses, France.
30 Groupe CEA, Compte rendu du conseil de direction du 14 mai 1979.
31 Letter from the Directeur Général of the Direction générale de l'énergie et des matières premières of the Ministry of Industry, François de Wissocq, Lettre DGEMP/A N°290, May 7, 1979, FAR 08, IRSN archives, Fontenay-aux-Roses, France.

References

Beck, U. (1992). *Risk Society: Towards a New Modernity*. London: Sage.
Bonneuil, C., and Fressoz, J. (2016). *The Shock of the Anthropocene: The Earth, History, and Us*. London: Verso.
Boudia, S. (2008). Sur les dynamiques de constitution des systèmes d'expertise scientifique: le cas des rayonnements ionisants. *Genèses*, 70, pp. 26–44.
Boudia, S., and Jas, N., eds. (2013). *Toxicants, Health and Regulation Since 1945*. London: Pickering & Chatto.
Boudia, S., and Jas, N., eds. (2014). *Powerless Science? Science and Politics in a Toxic World*. New York: Berghahn Books.
Bowker, G., and Star, S. (1999). *Sorting Things Out: Classification and Its Consequences*. Cambridge, MA: MIT Press.
Boyer, Paul. (2005). *By the Bomb's Early Light: American Thought and Culture At the Dawn of the Atomic Age*. Chapel Hill: University of North Carolina Press.
Busch, L. (2013). *Standards: Recipes for Reality*. Cambridge, MA: MIT Press.
Daston, L. (2016). What Is an Insurable Risk? Swiss Re and Atomic Reactor Insurance. In: N. Haueter and G. Jones, eds., *Managing Risk in Reinsurance: From City Fires to Global Warming*. Oxford: Oxford University Press, pp. 230–247.
Del Sesto, S. (1993). Qu'il était beau l'avenir de l'énergie nucléaire. *Culture Technique*, 28, pp. 66–83.
Douglas, M., and Wildavsky, A. (1983). *Risk and Culture: An Essay on the Selection of Technological and Environmental Dangers*. Berkeley, CA: University of California Press.
Esselborn, S., and Zachmann, K. (2020). Nuclear Safety by Numbers: Probabilistic Risk Analysis as an Evidence Practice for Technical Safety in the German Debate on Nuclear Energy. *History and Technology*, 36(1), pp. 129–164. DOI: http://doi.org/10.1080/07341512.2020.1766916.
Foasso, C. (2007). L'Expertise de la sûreté nucléaire en France: un point de vue institutionnel et technique. *La Revue Pour L'Histoire du CNRS*, 16. DOI: http://doi.org/10.4000/histoire-cnrs.1549.
Ford, D. (1986). *Meltdown: The Secret Papers of the Atomic Energy Commission*. New York: Simon & Schuster.
Häfele, W. (1974). Hypotheticality and the New Challenges: The Pathfinder Role of Nuclear Energy. *Minerva*, 12(3), pp. 309–301.
Hecht, G. (1998). *The Radiance of France: Nuclear Power and National Identity after World War II*. Cambridge, MA: MIT Press.
Keller, W., and Modarres, M. (2005). A Historical Overview of Probabilistic Risk Assessment Development and Its Use in the Nuclear Power Industry: A Tribute

Making the accident hypothetical 165

to the Late Professor Norman Carl Rasmussen. *Reliability Engineering & System Safety*, 89(3), pp. 271–285. DOI: http://doi.org/10.1016/j.ress.2004.08.022.

Kletz, T. (1999). The Origins and History of Loss Prevention. *Process Safety and Environmental Protection*, 77(3), pp. 109–116.

Krige, J. (2006). Atoms for Peace, Scientific Internationalism, and Scientific Intelligence. *Osiris* 21(1): 161–181.

Krige, J. (2010). Techno-Utopian Dreams, Technopolitical Realities: The Education of Desire for the Peaceful Atom. In: M. Gordin, H. Tilley and G. Prakash, eds., *Utopia/Dystopia: Conditions of Historical Possibility*. Princeton, NJ: Princeton University Press, pp. 151–176.

Kyrtsis, A., and Rentetzi, M. (2021). From Lobbyists to Backstage Diplomats: How Insurers in the Field of Third Party Liability Shaped Nuclear Diplomacy. *History and Technology*, 37(1), pp. 1–19. DOI: http://doi.org/10.1080/07341512.2021.1893999.

Mazuzan, G., and Walker, S. (1985). *Controlling the Atom: The Beginnings of Nuclear Regulation, 1946-1962*. Berkeley, CA: University of California Press.

Okrent, D. (1978). On the History of the Evolution of Light Water Reactor Safety in the United States. Available at: https://www.nrc.gov/docs/ML0906/ML090630275.pdf [Accessed June 23, 2021).

Okrent, D. (1981). *Nuclear Reactor Safety: On the History of the Regulatory Process*. Madison, WI: University of Wisconsin Press.

Perrow, C. (1981). Normal Accident at Three Mile Island. *Society*, 18(5), pp. 17–26.

Perrow, C. (1984). *Normal Accidents: Living With High-Risk Technologies*. New York: Basic Books.

Rip, A. (1986). The Mutual Dependence of Risk Research and Political Context. *Science & Technology Studies*, 4(3/4), pp. 3–15.

Temples, J. (1982). The Nuclear Regulatory Commission and the Politics of Regulatory Reform: Since Three Mile Island. *Public Administration Review*, 42(4), pp. 355–362. DOI: https://doi.org/10.2307/975979.

Topçu, S. (2013). *La France nucléaire: l'art de gouverner une technologie contestée*. Paris: Seuil.

Topçu, S. (2014). Organiser L'irresponsabilité? *Écologie & Politique*, 49, pp. 95–114

Walker, J. (2004). *Three Mile Island: A Nuclear Crisis in Historical Perspective*. Berkeley, CA: University of California Press.

Wellock, T. (2021). *Safe Enough? A History of Nuclear Power and Accident Risk*. Oakland, CA: University of California Press.

8 Governing the nuclear waste problem: nature and technology[1]

Tania Navarro Rodríguez

> [I]f the industry is to expand, better means of isolating, concentrating, immobilizing, and controlling wastes will ultimately be required.
>
> (AEC, 1949: 10)

The quote is from the public report "Handling Radioactive Wastes in the Atomic Energy Program," issued by the United States Atomic Energy Commission (AEC) in December 1949. The document also predicted that the nuclear industry "will develop on a wide scale only if production plants, laboratories, and hospital carry on their operations so that the discharge of radioactive waste does no harm to the surrounding community of plants, animals, and men" (AEC, 1949: 10). Its optimistic assessment suggested that, with further research and experimentation, nuclear waste problems would not prove unmanageable. For example, a safe expansion of these technologies could occur, given a more complete understanding of the permissible doses (tolerance levels); more information about the various biological systems, micro-organisms, higher plants and animals living in environments of low levels of radioactivity; and better methods of concentrating radioactive wastes in air and water (AEC, 1949: 11–12).

More than 70 years later, serious efforts to implement and improve waste-management practices have been made in the United States, France and Sweden, to mention just three nuclear countries with high commitment to the development of solutions to the nuclear waste problem. However, no country has yet reached consensus on a definitive solution for handling radioactive waste. The heated debates regarding how to deal with these hazardous materials play out among social actors including regulatory authorities, scientists and politicians, revealing that effective decision-making concerning nuclear waste management absolutely must consider both technological and political concerns and social, economic and environmental concerns, and a vast body of literature studies controversies over nuclear waste management solutions worldwide (Anshelm and Galis,

DOI: 10.4324/9781003227472-8

Governing the nuclear waste problem 167

2009; Barthe, 2006; Blanck, 2017; D'Agata, 2011; Hadjilambrinos, 1999; Lits, 2015; MacFarlane and Ewing, 2006; Patinaux, 2017; Petit, 1993; Shrader-Frechette, 1993; Walker, 2009). Consider the Yucca Mountain Nuclear Waste Repository in the United States. Approved in 2002 and closed in 2011 under the Obama Administration, this project was highly contested and faced roadblocks with the non-local public, the Western Shoshone peoples upon whose ancestral lands the facility was placed, and a host of politicians (MacFarlane, 2003; MacFarlane and Ewing, 2006). Given the lifespan of radioactive waste, its effects on the environment and its potential hazards to human health (Odum, 1971), these actors variously made plain that decisions taken in the present have consequences extending very far beyond current circumstances; decisions regarding materials on a nuclear time-horizon will impact the lives of future generations over thousands of years.

This chapter studies the choices made by nuclear experts and decision-makers in designing solutions for managing and lowering the impact of radioactive waste. Various sociological studies have focused on the political aspects of technological choices concerning nuclear waste. These studies particularly analyze public action related to the nuclear waste problem and issues concerning public participation, concertation and social inclusion (Barthe, 2003; 2006; Blanck, 2017; Elam et al., 2010; Lits, 2015; MacFarlane, 2003; Parotte, 2018; Walker, 2009). Another body of work attends to controversies over the solutions implemented in different countries to manage nuclear waste (Barthe et al., 2020; D'Agata, 2011; MacFarlane and Ewing, 2006; Patinaux, 2017; Petit, 1993; Shrader-Frechette, 1993). In contrast, this chapter questions the process that leads experts and decision-makers to opt for a partnership bringing together nature and technology in the development of waste-management solutions—and effort dating to the early days of nuclear technology—and situates it within a transnational perspective. Revisiting past and present public decisions made for the management of nuclear waste, I emphasise the paradigmatic shift in which the early concept of waste *disposal* transformed into policy around waste *storage* and the correlated, changing vision of technological action. Waste disposal means to discharge waste in a specific environment with little plan for management thereafter, while waste storage involves efforts to contain waste and its hazards by the implementation of different kinds of barriers and facilities. This change in approach has led to today's focus on isolating radioactivity via containment as a primary, foundational step in the process of responsibly handling nuclear waste.

Based on the analysis of various discourses given by experts at international conferences between 1950s and the early 1970s (Geneva Conferences, Nuclear Energy Agency, International Atomic Energy Agency), my argument fleshes out the hybrid strategy that brings together nature and technology in response to the nuclear-waste problem,

168 *Tania Navarro Rodríguez*

particularly in the case of the development of waste-management solutions to high-level and long lifespan radioactive waste. Nuclear experts materialised this partnership between nature and technology in the 1970s, with the emergence of the concept of deep geological disposal, expecting underground geological materials to act as a barrier protecting humans from the hazards that emerge when technological containment materials inevitably erode. By engaging geological materials as long-term actors in nuclear waste management, nuclear experts extend the realm of technology in the expectation of partnership between the geosphere and the technosphere. In doing so, they imagine and later materialise a new paradigm of waste disposal: no longer will they perpetuate the illusion of the safe dispersion (and consequent dilution) of radioactivity but endeavor to ensure its containment. Shifting from the concept of waste *disposal* to waste *storage* and consequently changing the vision of technological approaches to defanging the radiation threat from dilution to containment only occurred when scientific and social concern around environmental threats and the potential damage to humans accrued from the ever-expanding volume of radioactive waste reached a threshold. Indeed, a better knowledge of nature drove regulatory authorities, scientists and politicians to question waste-management strategies, to recognise technological weaknesses and to look for concrete solutions. Today, the problem of nuclear waste is frequently addressed by experts and decision-makers pushing forward their own ideas about natural and technological barriers and developing a perspective focused on close management. For safety's sake, the diversification of waste-disposal methods and the development of waste-management strategies continue apace, based on the idea of "taking care" of those hazardous materials in order to take care of living beings and systems.

I begin by describing how nuclear experts initially homed in on the possibility of underground burial as a potential way to dispose of nuclear waste. Their work involved various government attempts, particularly in the United States, to move away from sea disposal controversies and environmental concerns. In the late 1950s, experts thus characterised the nuclear-waste problem primarily as a problem of geology. Bringing together geological and ecological expertise, I then consider the process by which such nuclear experts and decision-makers strengthened their vision of ground as a potential sphere ready made for waste-disposal solutions and how this led to a drive to improve man-made barriers. The third section turns to rising awareness of the limitations of such technological containment methods; amid rising concern about the weakness of man-made barriers against hazardous waste, considering the long timescales and economic issues attending this waste, decision-makers reinforced the perspective of a partnership between nature and technology. When containment materials failed, the earth itself would provide the backstop to manage—or at least push-off—the waste problem.

Governing the nuclear waste problem 169

I conclude by examining the first international proposal for a policy of waste-management as a combination of natural and man-made barriers, taking different temporalities into consideration. Of course, the time issue is compounded by the increase in waste load and the varying periods of attention to waste management by experts and decision-makers. When it comes to managing this hazardous material, both prior planning and technology have proven faulty. The choice to site waste locally and pour scientific resources into improving barrier materials—in short, a containment policy—has dominated since the early days of the nuclear era, yet has not come close to solving our collective, global nuclear waste problem.

Ocean or ground?

On September 29, 1957, a huge explosion occurred in the waste disposal area of the plutonium production plant in Mayak, Chelyabinsk, in the USSR. This accident contaminated over a thousand square miles in the Southern Urals with radioactive waste. Several hundred people died. Thousands were evacuated and hospitalised. In this industrially developed region, an extensive area was suddenly a danger zone—it would remain so for decades (Medvedev, 1979). At about the same time, in the United States, a nuclear facility in Hanford, Washington leaked over 500,000 gallons of high-level radioactive waste into the soil. From there, it traveled into the Columbia River and onward to the Pacific Ocean. Hanford remains the most contaminated nuclear waste site in this country, despite massive, costly efforts at cleanup (Findlay and Hevly, 2011; Shrader-Frechette, 1993). And, to be sure, the costs have gone beyond dollars and cents. Both accidents were devastating. The continual reappearance of material problems at the Hanford site and more recent accidents such as the one at the Waste Isolation Pilot Plant in New Mexico[2] (Ialenti, 2018) serve as indicators of just what a leaking repository can mean in economic, natural and social terms, in the past, present and long into the future. Nonetheless, at the time, and despite the already known consequences of these accidents for neighboring populations and for the biosphere, the problem of nuclear waste was neglected by nuclear institutions and governments. It remained a problem to be addressed after calamity, not prevented as a matter of course.

By the end of the 1950s, sea disposal was becoming a topic of debate; experts had begun questioning whether this approach was poor management and unsafe storage of radioactive waste. Sea disposal is what nuclear experts and nuclear institutions call the action of dumping nuclear waste into the sea. It was the first option adopted by nuclear countries for managing radioactive waste: dump it, untreated, into the nearest convenient environment (this could be a river, a lake, a well, the ocean, the air or, if need be, the soil). Throughout the 1940s and 1950s, the United States, the Soviet Union and Britain commonly released their nuclear waste into rivers that flowed onward to the sea. Sometimes, they dumped it directly into the ocean from ships. In 1957, the AEC estimated that, in the United States, "facilities were discharging a volume of more than 8 billion gallons of low-level and intermediate-level liquids annually" (Mazuzan and Walker, 1984: 347). Even solid radioactive waste from weapons, civilian power and research activities associated with radioisotopes, produced by different institutions all over the world, were being dumped into the water. The United States and Britain packaged these hazardous materials into drums, and those drums were offloaded into the ocean from ships (when not buried on-site; Hamblin, 2008). By 1960, the AEC announced that the United States alone "had disposed about twenty-three thousand drums [of nuclear waste] at sites off the Atlantic coast and about twenty-four thousand drums and concrete boxes [containing the radioactive materials] off the Pacific coast" (Mazuzan and Walker, 1984: 346).

For many years, nuclear countries continued to dispose of their solid and liquid radioactive waste using the sea. It did not attract much public attention or press scrutiny. But as the establishment of new atomic energy sites increasingly met resistance from politicians, scientists (specifically those concerned with water pollution) and everyday laypeople, that changed. In the summer of 1959, for example, there was a series of protests against the dumping of low-level solid radioactive waste into the Gulf of Mexico. These public demonstrations opposed a license granted to Industrial Waste to dump "an aggregate of 240 curies and storing materials with a total of no more than 10 curies of radioactivity at one time" (Mazuzan and Walker, 1984: 356). A June 1959 report from the US National Academy of Sciences examined "the feasibility of discarding waste in coastal waters at depths of less than a thousand fathoms" (Mazuzan and Walker, 1984: 359); it amplified and extended the controversies about sea disposal, particularly in its effects on the food chain. If radioactivity was supposed to eventually dilute and disperse through ocean waters, there was the very real possibility that the drums would prematurely rupture in the deep waters. The effects would travel up the food-chain to humans and damage the biosphere in the process. Concern about the impact on humans particularly pushed nuclear experts to consider the relative risks of radionuclide concentration in living organisms and the effects of their transfer through the food-chain (Odum, 1971). By January 1959, the license to continue sea-disposal practices was a controversial issue for nuclear institutions; at a public AEC hearing in Houston, Texas, the speakers decided to adopt a conservative position in consideration of the fact that this practice "could endanger the health of thousands of people who used Gulf waters for food supplies and recreation" (Mazuzan and Walker, 1984: 356). At the same time, critiques of sea disposal were also related to risks incurred by workers

Governing the nuclear waste problem 171

charged with the task of sea-dumping. These workers dumped thousands of tons of radioactive waste into the Atlantic Ocean, often without even the simplest health precautions. This was the case for the crew of the USS Calhoun County, which spent some 15 years following World War II dropping large quantities of nuclear waste into the Atlantic—before being ordered sunk by the Navy in 1963 because it was so dangerously radioactive.[3]

In this context, nuclear experts in international organisations (IAEA, NEA, FAO) directed their efforts toward additional research and development on deep-water and other sea disposal issues. Before adopting a general resolution, these experts argued it was necessary to gain more knowledge about "currents at great depths" (IAEA-UNESCO-FAO, 1960: 251).[4] In addition, their work opened investigations concerning the diversification of waste-disposal methods, particularly by expanding the burial of nuclear waste in the soil.

Which is to say, as controversies on sea dumping were raised, those charged with the disposal of nuclear waste turned their attention to terrestrial disposal methods. At first, this implied surface and sub-surface storage. Deep underground storage would be envisaged some years later, after the particularly long lifespans of highly radioactive waste were recognised and brought into the calculus of containment. By 1963, in the United States, 95% of low-level solid radioactive waste had been buried in the three low-level sites on state-owned land in Nevada, Kentucky and New York (Walker, 2009). As in the early days of the nuclear era, nuclear waste is still dumped into the sea or buried into the land today. Decisions regarding when and which categories of waste material might be dumped or buried are the result of a long process, including confronting sometimes conflicting expert views, public reactions to technological choices and public/political decisions.

Waste problem: between ground and underground

In the early 1960s, research and development work on nuclear waste in international organisations mobilised various scientific disciplines, especially ecology, geology and physical medicine. Investigations in the Ecosystems Theory (Odum, 1971) helped constitute and legitimise ecology as a scientific discipline by highlighting its potential to manage problems involving natural and technological issues. These studies led to the establishment of the field of radioecology, the branch of ecology dedicated to analyzing radioactivity in Earth's ecosystems.

Regarding radioactive waste, radioecological studies particularly showed that residues do not stay put. A large volume of the waste degrades the quality of people's living space and endangers human health. Existing waste management practices for handling gaseous, liquid and solid radioactive waste (including air-cooled reactor operations and

172 Tania Navarro Rodríguez

meteorological surveys for gaseous, reactor cooling water and liquid processing wastes for liquid, and storage and geological disposal for solid) all interact with components of the ecosystem (soil, air, water and/ or biota), hence radioecological knowledge has contributed to nuclear institutions' heuristics regarding when and how different radioactive wastes should be dispersed or contained (Odum, 1971: 467). Angela N. H. Creager, in her work about the history of radioisotopes in biomedicine and ecology, concludes that expertise related to the movement of radioisotopes "furthered the importance of ecosystems to ecological research and offered concrete information about how the government and nuclear industry might manage the growing load of radioactive waste" (Creager, 2013: 378). Knowledge about nature gave new relevance to radioactive-waste problems, especially because public interest in ecosystems cast doubt on the wisdom of leaving the clean-up to nature.

Radioecology investigations pushed forward the development of methods for the elimination of radioactive waste. These studies were primarily produced by AEC scientists during the military nuclear period, and they focused on issues related to irradiation, radioactivity and contamination caused by fallout from atomic weapons, nuclear tests and peaceful nuclear applications. Creager confirms that the development of "domestic nuclear power, and the associated declassification and dissemination of information about reactors, gave Hanford's findings about radioactive waste a new relevance" (Creager, 2013: 374) in the post-war period. Hanford scientists made their findings about nuclear-waste disposal public for the first time at the first International Conference on the Peaceful Uses of Atomic Energy in Geneva in 1955 (UN, 1955).[5] Experts at this conference who presented on nuclear waste problems were essentially geologists or ecologists who had developed their expertise on waste disposal into the ground at Oak Ridge National Laboratory[6] and through the United States Geology Survey. Raymond Nace from the Water Resources Division of the Geological Survey mentioned that, in those days,

> more than 300 non-military reactors are reportedly in operation or soon will be. Probably most of the large ones are in the United States, and this is the reason why much study of waste disposal on the land has been done in the United States. (IAEA-UNESCO-FAO, 1960: 461)

But if land waste disposal was the approach considered most viable by such American specialists as Raymond Nace and Wallace de Laguna, it was also a way they tried to differentiate between the technical and political dimensions of handling nuclear waste. In the words of various scientists from the Oak Ridge National Laboratory during a first international symposium on the disposal of radioactive waste in 1959,

Governing the nuclear waste problem   173

we shall leave the question of ocean disposal and international aspects of the problem to competent authorities in this field, and examine here the possibilities of safe disposal on land, with particular emphasis on the research and development programs now under way in our country. (IAEA-UNESCO-FAO, 1960: 483)

Thus international discussions focused on exploring the soil as a means of disposing of nuclear waste of any kind. According to Nace, the "environment is a key word in the waste problem" (IAEA-UNESCO-FAO, 1960: 460). Following this perspective, the ground can be taken as the only available place for practical disposal, shunting the nuclear waste problem aside so that it becomes "basically a problem for geologists" (IAEA-UNESCO-FAO, 1960: 461). Geology being a science of history and prospection, it was seen as a knowledge source for the development of waste-management solutions that came with two upsides: the "study directly advances knowledge that is needed to cope with waste problems, and most of this knowledge has direct applications in other kinds of water problems" (IAEA-UNESCO-FAO, 1960: 464).

The growing interest in geology was also motivated by institutional choices. Nuclear institutions tended to use what was called interim storage, in the ground, to store and monitor nuclear waste on-site for an undetermined length of time. Favoring land burial as a path to understanding nuclear decay and its environmental effects, this choice reduced sea-dumping and its associated costs, including the expenses related to purchasing containers, transportation to the dock and transportation to disposal points in the sea (Ringius, 2000). In 1959, Joseph Pomarola, French expert at the French Atomic Energy Commission (CEA), estimated the total pecuniary cost of sea disposal at 100,000 francs by cubic meter of waste (IAEA-UNESCO-FAO, 1960: 282). Interim storage, meanwhile, was far more economical, if understood as inherently temporary. It required the use of metallic tanks of recent design on sites presenting suitable geological and hydrological conditions—those thought to best mitigate the unavoidable safety hazards of this operation: potential leakage from materials that remain hazardous for hundreds of years. In that respect, the Hanford accident was a significant moment that helped cast doubt on temporary solutions and exposed a strategic lack of radioactive-waste management. Short-term waste policies looked, more and more, like short-sighted politics. On the other hand, the choice to approach the waste problem from a geological perspective shows that the development of waste-disposal solutions was directly linked to the evolution not of nuclear technology, per se, but of the nuclear industry (Jasper, 1990). Experts were careful to point out that, regardless of the disposal solution adopted, it was unavoidable that choices would need to be made about the risks and rewards of nuclear-power development, and those would require scientific investigation to

174 *Tania Navarro Rodríguez*

guide issues including the future location of nuclear installations, their operation rules, and how these rules would be applied in order to guarantee protection and public security.

The first proposal for the classification of disposal practices was based on the degree of permanency of the practice: interim practices (which "may entail a small to moderate hazard if they are employed only for a short time"), hold-over practices ("Nuclear-energy operations were expected to end or to be curtailed after the war, so the long-term implications of waste disposal received relatively little study. Some of these practices have created potentially hazardous situations and have been, or probably will have to be, changed"), and permanent practices ("that might be continued 'for ever'") (IAEA-UNESCO-FAO, 1960: 464). Experts agreed that three waste-disposal solutions were still applicable: storage (the short-term containment of waste, in an approved manner, prior to collection and disposal), burial underground and sea-dumping. Each remained tethered to the logics of dilution and dispersion, which were established in particular by the AEC's American scientists. Their common link was the use of nature—whether sea or ground—to accomplish the objective of isolating radioactivity from humans and their biosphere.

When the waste environment is not safe enough

The prospects of a rapid expansion of peaceful uses of atomic energy intensified scientific and public concerns about radioactive-waste disposal. In the 1970s, growing international public resistance against nuclear energy development, as well as international ecological movements, exposed the risks associated with the increase of waste mass, poor waste-management practices, as well as explained a complete strategic absence of radioactive-waste management (Shrader-Frechette, 1993). Scientific predictions made in the 1950s and 1960s attempted to discern the production of radioactive waste in the United States by the year 2000 and came to what seems a rather self-evident point: there was a clear correlation between the acceleration of the nuclear industry and the mass production of radioactive waste (IAEA, 1963; Mazuzan and Walker, 1984).[7] These trends were confirmed: the overall volume of low-level waste produced by US commercial and federal sources has increased steadily, more so since the late 1970s (Ringius, 2000). Some countries are now insisting that decisions cannot be made through deferrals; Sweden, for instance, has introduced legislation "obliging a nascent Swedish nuclear industry to find an immediate solution to the waste problem or face the end of nuclear expansion" (Bartheet al., 2020: 2). In other words, new nuclear facilities cannot be sited without firm plans for the safe storage of their inevitable radioactive byproducts.

Nuclear experts responded to rising public concern about nuclear waste by proposing a program to manage hazardous materials. But experts' confidence in the existence of technical solutions to waste problems has drawn a range of criticisms. Environmental movements across counties have questioned, for instance, whether new nuclear reactors should be constructed at all, given that waste disposal is an unavoidable problem of nuclear production (Milder, 2017). The United States became a pioneer in pushing for a comprehensive program dealing with the problem of waste-management, yet at the international level, experts have long recognised that the problem of waste is not limited to science. It is also a problem that extends into politics, public relations and ethics, and so it cannot be addressed via technological innovation alone. In this respect, Jacob Hamblin's work on sea disposal controversies has shown that, while public reactions against sea disposal mostly focus on sea pollution and associated human health hazards, these actions also actively contest the manner in which the nuclear-waste problem has been managed by political bodies (Hamblin, 2008).[8]

Identifying the kind of material—low-level or high-level—is now required of experts investigating the eventual implementation of any waste-management program (Diaz-Maurin and Ewing, 2018). Disposal solutions for low-level waste have developed in two ways. First, experts have sought improved methods for the treatment and handling of large-volume liquid and gaseous wastes prior to discharge. Second, they have undertaken research toward a better understanding of the fate and effects of radionuclides in the environment. The disposal of high-level waste is worth even more intense expert scrutiny owing to the length of time in which such waste remains dangerous to humans and the environment (the radioactive decay time). Temporary containment in tanks is no solution for the disposal of high-level waste, because the potential hazard is far too great to justify a reliance on man-made barriers to prevent leakage into the living environment. In a context of rising public concern with nature preservation, the safety of natural systems (sea, ground, etc.) became a crucial consideration in the development of waste-disposal practices. In the prescient words of various American experts from the Oak Ridge Laboratory, "it is necessary to consider the safety of natural barriers for the final disposal of … waste. And, as an added safety factor, we would reduce their mobility by converting liquid waste to chemically stable solids, if it is economically feasible" (IAEA-UNESCO-FAO, 1960: 483).

Experts aware of the weaknesses of man-made barriers, especially regarding the long timescales of hazards from high-level waste, have therefore turned their attention toward a hopeful investment in technology that might reduce the risks as well as the volume of waste in need of storage.

Different technological processes have been implemented to treat waste and to facilitate its management. According to François Diaz-Maurin and Rodney Ewing, specialists in geological sciences and issues related to the radioactive waste materials, "the different compositions of the waste experience different types of treatment and conditioning (e.g., reprocessing, vitrification, incineration) which, in turn, modify the properties of the waste" (Diaz-Maurin and Ewing, 2018: 3). One such process has been developed with the objective of concentrating liquid waste to its minimal volume (this concentration process, however redundant it may sound, actually became paradigmatic in all subsequent waste-management operations). Other technological searchers have looked at processes for the conversion of liquid wastes to solid forms, considered less risky to transport and bury and easier to contain within the earth. The first industrial solidification technique in this vein, vitrification, was pioneered by the French in 1969 at a pilot-plant in Marcoule. A third aim of those pursuing waste-management technology has been to improve the storage methods themselves. The performance of storage tanks, for example, has been called into question. Because some storage tanks are built several feet below ground, it seems evident that we must review and improve such tanks, particularly with scientific knowledge gained through the Hanford incident. Different types of storage tanks were designed according to "variations in the volumes and compositions of the wastes to be stored, in the environmental conditions of the different storage sites, and in engineering judgment factors" (IAEA, 1963: 23). As one can understand, there are multiple interactions between the engineered and geological barriers defining the containment strategy of different repository concepts (Diaz-Maurin and Ewing, 2018).

It is not only a concern for nature and worry over the recognised weakness of man-made barriers that drive this technological endeavor but also economic considerations. In December 1959, staff at the Divisions of Reactor Development and Licensing and Regulation prepared an analysis of land disposal. In it, they argued that land burial "appeared to be cheaper and more convenient" than sea disposal (Mazuzan and Walker, 1984: 366). The reduction of waste volume, as mentioned above, was cited as a way to maximise storage capacity and, in turn, reduce monitoring and transportation costs. They also emphasised that all estimations of long-term nuclear waste approaches must include the costs of surveillance, waste processing or transfer and replacement facilities. The report estimated, in 1959 dollars, that the costs of land burial of low-level waste requiring no special protective measures was "$5.15 per drum" (Mazuzan and Walker, 1984: 367). However, according to some General Electric experts and to the Hanford Atomic Products Operation, the overall costs of waste storage facilities in the United States in the 1960s was between "$0.47 to $2.66 per gallon" (IAEA, 1963: 23). It appears difficult to get an idea of the total costs of the management of radioactive waste: these competing estimates, for instance, refer to different types of waste and units of measure. The total costs of storing radioactive waste must be calculated with consideration

Governing the nuclear waste problem   177

for *future* capital and operating expenses—predictions that, at the time, were hindered by a lack of available data. Today, however, it does not seem any easier to calculate or obtain reliable data about the costs of nuclear-waste management in different nuclear countries. One indication of the potentially enormous, compounding expense of land disposal can be found in the manipulation and depollution costs at the Hanford site; a 2019 news article reported, "This year the nation is spending about $2.5 billion on managing and cleaning up the Hanford site."[9]

The emerging understanding of the operational aspects of waste disposal has led experts to adopt an expanded perspective regarding waste handling, informed by lessons learned in countries' various approaches to resolving such problems. With data from the United States, the United Kingdom, Germany, France and India, experts now conceptualise two main approaches for the disposal of these materials. Now, *waste treatment*, which involves technical and chemical processes to reduce waste volume and modify its form joins *waste disposal* and *waste storage* within interim storage and within geological formations (including salt formations and deep bedrock).

In spite of efforts made to establish a program to handle nuclear waste by clarifying and improving technical approaches to waste disposal, it appears that nature continues to play a central role in isolating radioactivity from humans and the environment. Experts, therefore, advise an integrated approach that uses waste treatment and waste disposal as complementary endeavors. Rather than committing to choosing the better of these options in each case, we may understand this shift as the collective realisation and acknowledgement of the limits of technological solutions of containment against the need to moderate the role of nature in containing hazardous wastes. In other words, the decision to coalesce around "design with nature" solutions to managing radioactive waste has strengthened over time. It is now seen as the only possible answer to the waste problem.

Barrier implementation policies

In the 1970s, the extent of the waste problem was becoming an unavoidable consideration. Future oriented nuclear-industry backers sought the development of "final storage" units to allay critiques of new nuclear installations. Governments in the United States, Sweden, France and elsewhere introduced criteria for the development of nuclear power plants that attempted to force industry to innovate effective solutions for the disposal of the radioactive waste that a proposed facility was expected to produce. To some extent, though, this is a siloed view: dealing with radioactive waste must be a concern for all countries, whether or not they develop nuclear products, because the effects of such waste are inarguably global. Nuclear waste accidents and waste-disposal controversies have

178   *Tania Navarro Rodríguez*

demonstrated that many of the proposed solutions for dealing with radioactive waste could in fact push risks even further outward, beyond the natural drift of waste through water and air, especially onto vulnerable populations and their environments. The risks introduced by waste-disposal solutions involve timescales that are ill-fit to even deliberative political processes; these problems, as seems the case regarding high-level waste in particular, will continue to evolve as isotopes and containment materials decay and humans change environments and landscapes through all their activities.

Because of the limited feasibility of waste-storage facilities as well as inherent conditions relating to chemical releases into the atmosphere and waterways, international cooperation has become central to defining nuclear waste management policy and creating an ultimate disposal solution for high-level waste. Based on current knowledge, international experts at the Fourth International Conference of Atoms for Peace in Geneva, 1971, devised what was then a future policy for the long-term management of radioactive waste. Yves Sousselier and Jacques Pradel, members of France's CEA, took charge of the report. So as to update radioactive waste-management practices in Europe, the conference took place at the same time as a pilot committee was founded in the European Nuclear Energy Agency (ENEA), of which Sousselier was also a participant.

The main objective of the waste-management proposal was to set up guidelines for the selection of the most appropriate disposal method according to the category of waste being disposed of. A change of terminology meant that *waste disposal* was replaced by the term *waste storage*. Changes in terms like this are important for historical analysis—they help mark changes in perspective. Thus, we see at this moment that views of waste management in general were malleable. It was established by this report that, before proceeding to final storage, those charged with disposing of such waste must demonstrate that their chosen solution did not present any risks; if the proposal could not be confirmed in such a way, it must also include a plan for the possibility of waste retrieval in the future. The report indicated further that it was important that nuclear actors, even when pressed by economic consideration, choose the best method for the type of waste produced, avoiding any bigger potential safety concerns known to present.

A new radioactive waste-management strategy emerged from this policy-storage proposal. On the one hand, the basis for the development of a concept for *waste storage* was formulated. The main point was to clarify that using nature and technology together was the only way to work through high-level waste problems in the future. The strategy established the treatment of liquid waste through a solidification process, then, after a proper period, the separation of fission products and transuranic elements, the conditioning of fission products in order to store them in final geological storage (or, in the case of transuranic elements, into any geological

Governing the nuclear waste problem 179

formation). On the other hand, the new strategy recognised the different roles ensured by different geological barriers. The barrier is supposed to guarantee the containment of radioactivity in different ways: physical containment, containment from the outside and containment regarding radioprotection rules. It should also ensure that waste remains inaccessible (particularly important because waste is hard to guard over long periods). More precisely, deep geological disposal emerged and was strengthened as a preferred choice combining natural and technological barriers to cope with highly radioactive waste dangers. This concept was discussed at length during the international symposium regarding the Underground Disposal of Radioactive Waste, held in Otaniemi, Finland, in 1979. Organised by IAEA and NEA, this symposium saw experts agree on deep geological disposal as "the most feasible option for ... safe disposal" (IAEA/NEA, 1979: Foreword).

Conclusion

More than 40 years have passed since Sweden engaged in a deep geological repository project, the Spent Fuel Repository.[10] The license granting SKB permission to start the construction of a repository remains contentious to this day, as do two other advanced projects led by France (Cigéo),[11] and Finland (ONKALO).[12] In 2019, in the United States, the Nuclear Regulatory Commission presented a project to build a temporary waste installation to store 210,000 tons of nuclear waste, some highly radioactive, in Texas and New Mexico,[13] but met almost immediate criticism; because this is a zone where oil extraction and hydraulic fracking are intensively practiced, the geological barrier is understood as already damaged. In 2021, Japan revealed its proposal to discharge more than one million tons of contaminated water from the ruined Fukushima Daiichi nuclear power station into the ocean. Neighbors including China and South Korea, and a number of scientists immediately expressed their opposition, considering this "extremely irresponsible." But other scientists as well as the International Atomic Energy Agency say, "the risks are likely to be minimal if the release is carried out as planned."[14] It appears that the historical decision to pursue "designed with nature" solutions to managing nuclear waste raises a responsibility issue. Questions arise around who is or shall be responsible for handling nuclear waste problems: the producers of waste or society at large, whose demands for nuclear technologies to support the modern way of life obviously spurs the production of such waste?

Despite long-standing efforts by nuclear countries such as the United States, Sweden and France, despite the development of nuclear waste management policies, there is still no firm consensus regarding how to safely deal with nuclear waste. Various approaches to waste management over time have revealed many weaknesses and limitations endemic

180 *Tania Navarro Rodríguez*

to technological solutions, while the accelerated development of the nuclear industry has simultaneously increased the urgency of addressing health and environmental concerns. The idea of "taking care" of nuclear waste has again shifted the paradigm of waste disposal: no longer can we cling to the illusion of a safe dispersion of radioactivity. We must aim at containment. But as different experiences of deep geological repositories show, solutions developed according to this paradigm are constantly challenged by the obligation to publicly demonstrate safety. On a nuclear timescale, *safety* remains, in many ways, unknowable.

Notes

1 I owe particular thanks to book editors and all participants to workshop "Living in a Nuclear World: Order, Knowledge, and Normalisation" for their useful comments to preliminary versions of this chapter.
2 In August 2016, the direct costs and indirect costs of clean-up of WIPP were estimated to exceed US $2 billion. Vartabedian, R. (2019). Nuclear Accident in New Mexico Ranks among the Costliest in US History. *Los Angeles Times.* Available at https://www.latimes.com/nation/la-na-new-mexico-nuclear-dump-20160819-snap-story.html [Accessed June 16, 2021].
3 Tampa Bay Times (2013). USS Calhoun County Sailors Dumped Thousands of Tons of Radioactive Waste into Ocean. Available at: https://www.tampabay.com/news/military/veterans/the-atomic-sailors/2157927/ [Accessed June 16, 2021].
4 This work was made public in particular during the "Scientific Conference on the Disposal of Radioactive Wastes" sponsored by the International Atomic Energy Agency and the United Nations Educational, Scientific and Cultural Organization, with the Co-operation of the Food and Agriculture Organization of the United States Nations, and held at the Oceanographic Museum in the Principality of Monaco, on November 16-21, 1959.
5 In the volume IX of proceedings of this conference, two parts were devoted to the nuclear waste issue.
6 This laboratory is operated by Union Carbide Corporation for the US Atomic Energy Commission.
7 In its report on the biological effects of radiation in 1956, the National Academy of Sciences estimated that "by the year 2000 the United States would accumulate 2.4 billion gallons of high-level liquid waste, mostly from commercial reactors producing electricity" (Mazuzan and Walker, 1984: 348). Additionally, at the symposium *Treatment and Storage of High-level Radioactive Wastes,* held by IAEA in October 1962, experts estimated that the US could have generated approximately 36 million gallons and 300 million gallons by the year 2000 (IAEA, 1963: 5).
8 Some of the problems highlighted by Hamblin are the relation between safety and the role played by threshold values to setting policies and justifying them publicly, the biological effects of radiation (opposing health physicists and oceanographers), the role of radioactive waste in cold war international relations, and the relationship between radioactive waste and environmental policy making.
9 Cary, A. (2019). Hanford Cleanup Costs Triple. And that's the "Best Case Scenario" in a New Report. *Tri-City Herald.* Available at: https://www.tri-

cityherald.com/news/local/hanford/article225386510.html#storylink=cpy [Accessed June 1, 2021].

10 SKB (n.d.). A Repository for Nuclear Fuel that Is Placed in 1.9 Billion Years Old Rock. Available at: http://www.skb.com/future-projects/the-spent-fuel-repository/ [Accessed June 16, 2021].

11 ANDRA (n.d.). Protéger des Déchets Radioactifs les plus Dangereux. Available at: https://www.andra.fr/cigeo [Accessed June 16, 2021].

12 Positiva (n.d.). Repository in ONKOLO. Available at: https://www.posiva.fi/en/index/finaldisposal/researchandfinaldisposalfacilitiesatonkalo.html [Accessed June 16, 2021]. Available at: http://www.posiva.fi/en/final_disposal/onkalo#.Wv2n8cjLhE4 [Accessed 1 June 2021].

13 Available at: https://www.lemonde.fr/energies/article/2019/08/20/etats-unis-bataille-en-sous-sol-entre-dechets-nucleaires-et-industrie-petroliere_5500917_1653054.html [Accessed June 20, 2021].

14 Nogrady, B. (2021). Scientists OK Plan to Release One Million Tonnes of Waste Water from Fukushima. *Nature*. DOI: https://doi.org/10.1038/d41586-021-01225-2.

References

AEC. (1949). *Handling Radioactive Wastes in the Atomic Energy Program*. Washington, DC: U.S. Atomic Energy Commission.

Anshelm, J., and Galis, V. (2009). The Politics of High-level Nuclear Waste Management in Sweden: Confined Research Versus Research in the Wild. *Environmental Policy and Governance*, 19(4), pp. 269–280.

Barthe, Y. (2003). Le recours au politique ou la problématisation politique "par défaut." In J. Lagroye, ed., *La Politisation*. Paris: Belin, pp. 475–492.

Barthe, Y. (2006). *Le pouvoir d'indécision: la mise en politique des déchets nucléaires*. Paris: Economica.

Barthe, Y., Elam, M., and Sundqvist, G. (2020). Technological Fix or Divisible Object of Collective Concern? Histories of Conflict over the Geological Disposal of Nuclear Waste in Sweden and France. *Science as Culture*, 29(2), pp. 196–218.

Blanck, J. (2017). *Gouverner par le temps. La gestion des déchets radioactifs en France, entre changements organisationnels et construction de solutions techniques irréversibles (1950-2014)*. PhD thesis. Institut d'études politiques de Paris.

Creager, A. (2013). *Life Atomic: A History of Radioisotopes in Science and Medicine*. Chicago: University of Chicago Press.

D'Agata, J. (2011). *About a Mountain*. New York: W. W. Norton & Company.

Diaz-Maurin, F., and Ewing, R. (2018). Mission Impossible? Socio-Technical Integration of Nuclear Waste Geological Disposal Systems. *Sustainability*, 10(4390), pp. 2–39.

Elam, M., Soneryd, L., and Sundqvist, G. (2010). Demonstrating Safety – Validating New Build: The Enduring Template of Swedish Nuclear Waste Management. *Journal of Integrative Environmental Sciences*, 7(3), pp. 197–210.

Findlay, J., and Hevly, B. (2011). *Atomic Frontier Days: Hanford and the American West*. Seattle, WA: University of Washington Press.

Hadjilambrinos, C. (1999). Toward a Rational Policy for the Management of High-Level Radioactive Waste: Integrating Science and Ethics. *Bulletin of Science, Technology & Society*, 19(3), pp. 179–189.

182 Tania Navarro Rodríguez

Hamblin, J. (2008). *Poison in the Well: Radioactive Waste in the Oceans at the Dawn of the Nuclear Age*. Rutgers, NJ: Rutgers University Press.

IAEA. (1963). *Treatment and Storage of High-level Radioactive Wastes*. Vienna: IAEA.

IAEA/NEA. (1979). *Underground Disposal of Radioactive Wastes. Proceeding of a Symposium vol. 1 and 2*. Vienna: IAEA/NEA.

IAEA-UNESCO-FAO. (1960). *Disposal of Radioactive Wastes II*. Vienna: IAEA.

Ialenti, V. (2018). Waste Makes Haste: How a Campaign to Speed Up Nuclear Waste Shipments Shut Down the WIPP Long-Term Repository. *The Bulletin of the Atomic Scientists*, 74(4), pp. 262–275.

Jasper, J. (1990). *Nuclear Politics: Energy and the State in the United States, Sweden, and France*. Princeton, NJ: Princeton University Press.

Lits, G. (2015). *La gestion des déchets hautement radioactifs belges à l'épreuve de la démocratie. Contribution à une sociologie des activités décisionnelles*. PhD thesis. Université Catholique de Louvain.

Mazuzan, G., and Walker, S. (1984). *Controlling the Atom: The Beginnings of Nuclear Regulation, 1946-1962*. Berkeley, CA: University of California Press.

MacFarlane, A. (2003). Underlying Yucca Mountain the Interplay of Geology and Policy in Nuclear Waste Disposal. *Social Studies of Science*, 33(5), pp. 783–807.

MacFarlane, A., and Ewing, R. (2006). *Uncertainty Underground: Yucca Mountain and the Nation's High-Level Nuclear Waste*. Cambridge, MA: MIT Press.

Medvedev, Z. (1979). *Nuclear Disaster in the Urals*. London: Angus & Robertson.

Milder, S. (2017). *Greening Democracy: The Anti-Nuclear Movement and Political Environmentalism in West Germany and Beyond, 1968-1983*. Cambridge, UK: Cambridge University Press.

Odum, E. (1971). *Fundamentals of Ecology*. Philadelphia, PA: Press of W. B. Saunders Company.

Parotte, C. (2018). *L'Art de gouverner les déchets hautement radioactifs*. Liège: Presses Universitaires de Liège.

Patinaux, L. (2017). *Enfouir des déchets nucléaires dans un monde conflictuel. Une histoire de la démonstration de sûreté de projets de stockage géologique, en France (1982-2013)*. PhD thesis. Ecole des Hautes Études en Sciences Sociales, Paris.

Petit, J. (1993). *Le stockage des déchets radioactifs: perspective historique et analyse sociotechnique*. PhD thesis. École Nationale Supérieure des Mines, Paris.

Ringius, L. (2000). *Radioactive Waste Disposal at Sea: Public Ideas, Transnational Policy Entrepreneurs, and Environmental Regimes*. Cambridge, MA: MIT Press.

Shrader-Frechette, K. (1993). *Burying Uncertainty: Risk and the Case against Geological Disposal of Nuclear Waste*. Berkeley, CA: University of California Press.

UN. (1955). *Proceedings of the 1st International Conference on the Peaceful Uses of Atomic Energy*. Geneva: United Nations.

Walker, S. (2009). *The Road to Yucca Mountain: The Development of Radioactive Waste Policy in the United States*. Berkeley, CA: University of California Press.

Section III
Normalising through denial and trivialisation

9 Trivialising life in long-term contaminated areas: the nuclear political laboratory

Soraya Boudia

Even the repeated claims about the safety of nuclear technology tacitly assume that the danger exists while asserting that it can be overcome, there is no longer any doubt that nuclear power is dangerous. In the 35 years after the very public birth of the nuclear age, announced by the devastation of the cities of Hiroshima and Nagasaki in 1945, the United States, the Soviet Union, Great Britain, France and China have conducted over 2,000 nuclear tests, 543 of them atmospheric.[1] More recently, nuclear reactor accidents including those in Chernobyl in 1986 and Fukushima in 2011 have contaminated vast areas for the foreseeable future. Scientists have learned that highly contaminated production sites such as Hanford in the United States and Mayak in Russia will remain hazardous for thousands of years, like the long list of sites used for stocking nuclear waste around the world.

But, as this chapter aims to show, nuclear power is not *just* a hazardous technology. It has long been a political laboratory for designing and testing various ways of managing industrial and environmental hazards. This situation is directly related to the cascade of problems that nuclear technology has created in the past 75 years. Since its sudden public emergence in the form of a bomb of unprecedented lethality, the list of technological, health, environmental and political dangers, and fears relating to nuclear technology has grown steadily to include planetary war, the health consequences of atomic tests, major industrial accidents, multiple forms of pollution, the risks of transporting fissionable materials, occupational hazards and radioactive waste issues.

The political history of nuclear power is also related to its particular circumstances as a strategic technology developed for and expanded by the military and energy sectors. Nuclear professionals have developed a culture and skillset around managing the variety of risks associated with nuclear activities; they develop action plans of generic and generalisable procedures and gather data. Given their sector's exceptional resources, various social actors including experts (engineers, physicists, chemists, biologists, doctors, psychologists, sociologists), administrators and politicians have been mobilised for, against, and in relation to nuclear technology.

DOI: 10.4324/9781003227472-9

186 Soraya Boudia

Lastly, nuclear energy is a political laboratory because it has been a highly contested technology from shortly after its inception. It has been targeted by an ever-renewing variety of critical mobilisations, including international pacifist movements opposing nuclear arms and the prospect of total war as early as the late 1940s. In the mid-1950s, protests expanded to exposing the effects of nuclear fallout from atmospheric testing (Wittner, 1993; 1997) and drawing focus to military activities and the major risks posed to humanity worldwide. The anti-nuclear movement of the 1970s extended critiques of the various technological, environmental and health risks of the nuclear industry in the context of environmental movements, while also rejecting the technocratic, centralised and authoritarian model of governance sustaining nuclear power (Nelkin and Pollak, 1981; Jasper, 1990). This criticism rebounded after Chernobyl and Fukushima accidents, denouncing the catastrophic consequences of a dangerous industry (Topçu, 2013a).

Nuclear power thus offers a particularly stimulating field for those studying how hazardous technologies are scientifically and politically framed and managed over the long term. This chapter aims to characterise the variety of rationales at work in the governance of nuclear hazards. It focuses on how scientific experts, public authorities and industries conceive, design and manage the wide range of potential dangers and specifically addresses the problem of radioactive contamination. Mobilising recent scholarship on the government of hazardous technologies and several case studies (Pestre, 2014), I distinguish three successive approaches to governing nuclear hazards: government through containment, government through risk and government through adaptation (Boudia and Jas, 2019).

While these approaches developed successively, they did not replace or displace the prior; all three now coexist, blended according to the problems they are intended to solve. As a result, nuclear governance is characterised by a vast array of instruments and practices tailored to overcoming the sector's various crises and critiques. This accumulated toolkit has come out of what can be described as a "sedimentation" of practices, instruments and discourses rather than the development of best practices. It has cemented what we now see as inherent contradictions and tensions between the various approaches and tools that have been used to characterise, delimit and manage risks for the past 75 years. In turn, the sedimentation has become a source of *new* risks for the nuclear industry, especially concerning the legitimacy of its model and its ability to manage, both publicly and internally, the pursuit of nuclear development despite the exorbitant (and wholly apparent) economic and environmental costs.

Containing the hazards of nuclear power

A large body of research has examined the effects of the radioactive contamination of atomic bombs on the body and the environment, especially in Hiroshima and Nagasaki. The violence of the detonations and the immediate destruction was joined by another, slower form of violence (Nixon, 2011)—the secrecy imposed on research findings on the victims, who were studied like human guinea pigs (Lindee, 1994; 2016). In the mid-1950s, the framing of and debate over the nuclear hazards of radioactive fallout all occurred in the shadow of the nuclear bomb. The scale of the destruction in Hiroshima and Nagasaki, once unthinkable, became a point of reference and comparison for all nuclear risks, from major incidents to low-dose exposures to radioactivity.

The result was a specific form of governance for nuclear power risk, distinct although similar to the governance of other high-risk technologies. The exceptionality (and sometimes the exceptionalism) of nuclear power (Hecht, 2012) stems from several factors. Even today, its high risk sets it apart. Since the late 1940s, nuclear institutions have deeply invested in the promotion of nuclear power in order to improve its public image, which has been associated with death since the bombings in Hiroshima and Nagasaki (Strasser, 2006). The promotion of civil uses of nuclear power was also driven by post-war economic concerns: access to new energy sources in times of economic recovery and colonial independence was a paramount concern for many countries in the mid-twentieth century and beyond, so the public and politicians were not unreceptive to this rhetorical and technological shift (Hecht, 1998).

What makes the governance of nuclear hazards exceptional? For one thing, the establishment of a specific risk management insurance system. As in other industrial sectors, the actors involved in the developing field of nuclear power had to manage the constant tension between technical mastery, economic profitability and health and environmental protection. Nuclear science developed under more tense and controversial conditions than other hazardous technologies. In need of heavy investments, nuclear power's promoters regularly struggled to convince private companies of its potential profitability, particularly as compared to the oil industry. But investors were reluctant to risk capital on a sector with such potentially high liabilities from accident-related compensation and the need to repair or rebuild damaged facilities. By the late 1950s, however, a specific insurance scheme was developed for nuclear power that would govern its future development. Designed to reassure industrialist investors, the Price-Anderson Nuclear Industries Indemnity Law was passed in the United States in 1957 and adopted in European countries in the 1960s, limiting the liability of private industry by ensuring state coverage of nuclear harm (Daston, 2017).

Nuclear exceptionalism is furthermore characterised by institutionally distinct ways of coordinating expertise and regulation with its own production and control system. The nuclear world has gradually built a specific system to manage the hazards it generates. Very early, nuclear risk management was organised into three areas of expertise and activity: security,

188 Soraya Boudia

which aims to protect against criminal and unauthorised acts (espionage, sabotage); nuclear safety, which includes all the technical provisions and organisational measures relating to the design, construction and operation of power plants; and radiation protection, which corresponds to a set of measures designed to ensure the protection of the population and workers from ionising radiation (Boudia, 2007; Foasso, 2012).

Third, the governance of nuclear hazards is characterised by a tension between national prerogatives (in a field where sovereignty is central) and the internationalisation of expertise in technological hazards. Internal expertise in the nuclear industry is far more internationalised than in other sectors, due to its high technicality and the level of financial investment required. The special status accorded to nuclear hazards, their global scale and their long-term consequences—all decried by a range of critical movements—contributed significantly to the construction of these transnational organisations.

The internationalisation is the most advanced in the field of radiation protection. Since the late 1950s, norms for regulating ionising radiation developed on an international scale in a system of committees with converging and intertwining activities. The first actor in this system was the International Commission on Radiological Protection (ICRP), which coopted scientists into the committee in charge of making recommendations for national regulations and codes. The second actor was the United Nations Scientific Committee on the Effects of Atomic Radiation (UNSCEAR), an assembly of official representatives from 15 countries. It was responsible for collecting and organising all information about ionising radiation levels of all origins, natural or otherwise, and studying its possible effects on mankind and the environment. In addition to these committees, a pair of inter-governmental agencies, the International Atomic Energy Agency (IAEA) and the European Atomic Energy Community (Euratom), were created. Between 1950 and 1960, doctrine and recommendations for protection from ionising radiation were developed in a complex struggle among these international authorities (Boudia, 2007).

Nuclear governance has several unique features, yet it also shares many similarities with the governance of other industrial hazards. Since its development in the 1950s, the civil nuclear industry has appropriated and adapted the discourses and methods of industrial hazard management in constant development since the nineteenth century, pushing their logic to extremes. The governance they promote is dominated by the idea of mastery: control of dangerous techniques made possible through the design of reactors, control of contaminant flows and their effects through technical emission standards and exposure limit values, and/or by simply concentrating hazardous activities in limited geographical zones (Boudia and Jas, 2019).

Consequently, the development of nuclear power has involved much work and discussion relative to the design parameters of reactors, where power plants should be installed, possible kinds of accidents and how to remedy them, and exposure standards. The dominant discourse of mastery manifests differently in each of the three sectors for managing the hazards of nuclear power: nuclear safety, nuclear security, and radiation protection. Despite such variations, containment and zoning became the central concepts framing the governance of nuclear hazards (Goumri and Navarro-Rodriguez, in this volume). This is reflected in debates over geographical confinement and site selection, as some experts argued that nuclear power plants should be kept away from human-inhabited areas, while others, concerned with cost reduction, preferred installations close to existing infrastructure and successfully lobbied for another type of containment: the technical containment of reactors. A safety doctrine developed around nuclear facilities' mandated installation of multiple containment barriers, such as ducts surrounding radioactive materials and primary cooling circuits, chambers, and buildings, all of which might avoid nuclear accidents as well as the possible harms of ongoing normal operations at these facilities. Standards for exposure and radioactive effluent output as well as procedures for operations and work organisation were intended to complement and complete these technical measures and help guarantee that risk was "negligible." But asserting a doctrine of mastery is not the same as *having* total mastery of a hazardous technology or the public criticism it draws.

Legitimating high and negligible risks

The nuclear industry likes to promote itself as an industry of technical experts with perfect mastery over the development of its techniques. But in the 1950s, the emerging civil nuclear power industry was not immune to heated controversies over the effects of atmospheric atomic tests, undermining the idea of mastery. Critics pointed to the unpredictable: a simple turn of the wind during a test that leads to the contamination of Japanese fishermen (Takahashi's paper in this volume) or French politicians in the Algerian Sahara. Nuclear hazards constituted a clear global risk, with radioactivity capable of contaminating bodies and the environment worldwide. Experts were pressured to get specific, to prove the safety of radiation exposure and define "negligible risk." The public debate undermined the discourse of risk containment and forced those developing the nuclear industry to build a new way of governing.

In the early 1960s, after the Cuban missile crisis and the 1963 signing of a treaty banning atmospheric and oceanic nuclear weapons tests, controversy and mobilisation opposing atomic testing were on the wane (Balogh, 1991; Boyer, 1994). Military uses of nuclear power became less visible as civil nuclear power, with its energy-producing and medical applications, became the focus of public discourse and research programs. After years of nuclear power proponents' struggle to overcome fallout controversies and convince private industry and policy makers of its profitability, the oil crisis of the early 1970s was a real springboard for nuclearisation in some countries. In the late 1960s, however, many of these countries (including the United States, West Germany, Sweden and France) had also seen the rise of one of the largest social movements to ever challenge an industrial technology. The anti-nuclear movement had a significant impact on discourse, organisation, and risk management methods: this is well illustrated by the controversy around the effects of exposure to low-dose radiation, which helped to undermine the prevailing logic of containment in the governance of nuclear hazards and accelerate the turn to a new regulatory framework that has since been adopted for all environmental health problems.

One issue that would come to the fore at this time was the generalised contamination of the environment by radioactive discharge continuously "spilling" from nuclear plants and the long-term effects of chronic low-dose exposure. The question was not entirely new, as it had been raised in the early 1950s about the effects of fallout from nuclear weapons. But two decades later, the nature of the question had changed: the doses were much lower, and criticism, formerly focused on malfunctions and exceptional situations, widened to include the safety of the nuclear industry under normal operating conditions.

The making of low-dose exposure into a public problem—meaning the development of the controversy and its handling by public authorities—owes much to the American scientist John Gofman and his colleague Arthur Tamplin.[2] In late 1969, Gofman and Tamplin published an exhaustive summary of six years of work funded by the Atomic Energy Commission (AEC) on the links between exposure to low-dose radiation and cancer. They suggested that 10% of all human deaths from cancer were due to the effects of radiation. In the interest of public health, Gofman urged the AEC to lower radioactive effluent emissions thresholds by a factor of 10 (Boudia, 2013).

The AEC immediately moved to deny and condemn Gofman's results. Gofman himself came under attack from the private nuclear industry and the AEC, but far from intimidating him, their reactions strengthened his determination. With the active support of clean-air champion Senator Edmund Muskie and activist lawyer Ralph Nader, Gofman set out to present his team's work in a wide range of public forums. As his anti-nuclear activism grew, Gofman became president of the Committee for Nuclear Responsibility and one of the best-known counter-experts on the health effects of radiation. Amid public controversy and environmentalists' mobilisation, public authorities had little choice but to provide answers.

The AEC's second reaction was to establish committees of experts in an attempt to institutionally channel public controversy, delay decision-making and incorporate a few responses to some of the criticism into

The nuclear political laboratory   191

existing practices. As is often the case, however, the results did not always match their intentions. The National Academy of Sciences (NAS) was asked to conduct a study on low-dose radiation. The NAS committee on Biological Effect of Ionizing Radiation (BEIR) brought together experts from different disciplines, and its report was made public in 1972 (BEIR, 1972). Resulting from work by dozens of inter-disciplinary scientists, the document was internationally accepted as the key reference on the issue. It contained a partial acceptance of Gofman and Tamplin's assertions: the BEIR concluded that 170 mrem per year—the official limit value of radiation dose exposure—caused between 3,000 and 15,000 additional deaths from cancer per year, depending on the dose-effect model used. This recognition breached nuclear industry experts' line of defense, not by condemning past choices, but by revealing the clear choices involved in legislative logic: the emissions threshold had been determined out of industry and political attempts to balance society's demand for cheap nuclear energy with its demonstrable public health risks. The report concluded that it was entirely possible to maintain this balance, but only by increasing the weight apportioned to public health. Armed with this information, the Environmental Protection Agency (EPA) drastically lowered the acceptable norm from 170 to 25 mrem per year.

The third response was an institutional reconfiguration. As a way out of the deep crisis of trust in regulatory institutions, the AEC reformed its radioactivity risk monitoring and controls. While reckoning with the issue of low-dose exposure and facing vocal public concern over nuclear accidents, in 1972 the AEC confidently ordered a large-scale study of the probability and consequences of a wide range of possible nuclear accidents (Goumri, in this volume).[3] The 1974 findings report put the annual risk of a major accident at a nuclear power plant at 1 in 1 billion. The AEC was not happy with this probability, even as low as it was, and a salvo of criticism from experts at the Union of Concerned Scientists and the American Physical Society went even further with the publication of a report questioning how the probability was calculated. Governments began to legally separate nuclear power producers and nuclear risk regulators to sooth mounting public distrust. In the United States, Congress abolished the AEC and divided its responsibilities between the Department of Energy (DoE), in charge of nuclear development, and the Nuclear Regulatory Commission (NRC), in charge of its regulation. This move also responded to two pressing demands from social movements: independent expertise and transparent results.

Lastly, in a move demonstrating the depth of the crisis facing the nuclear industry and its regulatory institutions, experts began to develop a new paradigm for risk governance that would eventually encompass technologies and phenomena beyond nuclear technology. Throughout the 1970s, nuclear power became a real test case for a number of groups

192 *Soraya Boudia*

of experts probing the best ways to regulate a swath of hazardous innovations and technologies (Boudia, 2014). By mid-decade, several US federal agencies had begun working on what they called "risk assessment." They built on efforts begun in the late 1960s (and extending into the early 1980s) by various communities of experts and government agencies including the EPA, the Occupational Safety and Health Administration (OSHA), the Food and Drug Administration (FDA), the National Institutes of Health (NIH), and the National Science Foundation (NSF), in collaboration with NAS and the National Research Council (NRC). The undertaking meant thinking practically about how to define a cross-cutting evaluation and decision-making methodology for activities presenting technological, health, or environmental hazards. By hybridising conceptions and practices embodied in joint institutional work in the United States and Great Britain, the ICRP came to adopt as its guiding principle for radiological protection management an acronym: ALARA (As Low as Reasonably Achievable).

The risk-assessment approach is both a confession and an assertion. It is a confession that "zero risk" does not exist, according to the new formulation of the time. Nuclear power always presents a degree of danger, even during normal operation. But it asserts that serious harm, which cannot be ruled out, is still unlikely—on par with the risks presented by *all* technology. Rather than abandoning these technologies, this approach defines the level of risk that society should be willing to accept. The target is no longer the guaranteed absence of harmful effects, but limiting them to a certain level, defined collectively on the basis of scientific knowledge weighed against that technology's economic and social stakes. In this new way of governing nuclear hazards, different techniques and procedures—risk assessment, cost-benefit analysis, and opinion surveys—are used to define the degree of social acceptability and subsequent mechanisms for stakeholder participation. The aim is to eliminate important adverse effects such as a disaster on the scale of a health crisis or major industrial accident, and if one does occur, to implement compensation and remediation mechanisms, starting with financial compensation to remediate the damage caused.

Risk technologies that aim to ensure socially "acceptable" levels of hazards have never succeeded in building a lasting consensus, however. Anti-nuclear power movements, the Three Mile Island accident, and falling oil prices in the late 1970s weakened the civil nuclear industry in several countries, including the United States and Sweden. The 1986 disaster at Chernobyl paved the way for a new type of governance, and Fukushima put it to the test in 2011. The Chernobyl accident reveals a major break in nuclear risk managers' public discourse and marks a shift in the production of doctrine on the management of radioactive contamination risks.

The age of major nuclear accidents

Chernobyl was the breaking point for any claim of "mastery" over nuclear risk. The loss of control of a reactor, the contamination of a large area and the inability to stop the radioactive cloud at the border all undercut nuclear actors' apparent confidence. Despite attempts to singularise the event, brand it a "Soviet accident," and coordinate the concealment and denial of its devastating consequences (Petryna, 2013; Kuchinskaya, 2014; Davies and Polese, 2015; Brown, 2019), Chernobyl made it clear that major nuclear accidents could no longer be considered extremely rare events at the end of the twentieth century. Twenty-five years later, the Fukushima Daiichi accident unquestionably contributed to the radical transformation of representations of the hazards of nuclear power.

Each of these major accidents came with disastrous environmental and social consequences. Following the Chernobyl accident, an exclusion zone was established in a 30 km radius around the damaged power plant, enclosing some 2,600 km^2 (about the size of Luxembourg). Local residents were unceremoniously evacuated from the villages of Novochepelytchi, Kotcharivka, Kopatchi and especially Prypiat, from which 90,000 evacuees were forced out (Alexis-Martin and Davies, 2017). Fallout was discovered across 150,000 km^2 of Europe, particularly across Belarus, Ukraine and the Russian Federation.[4] A quarter century later, policies were more flexible: Fukushima's exclusion zone changed over time, starting with a 20 km radius and confinement up to 30 km and gradually dwindling until all access restrictions were lifted (Asanuma-Brice, 2015).[5]

Between these two disasters, a new expert discourse on nuclear risk emerged. Today, experts do not deny or downplay the possibility of serious accident; they affirm that accidents may very well happen, and that society must learn to live with this possibility, prepare itself for accidents, and manage the consequences. Moreover, the new discourse emphasises the rehabilitation of "life" in permanently contaminated territories. The contaminated areas around Chernobyl and Fukushima are currently serving as living laboratories in which experts experiment with emerging practices and policies for learning to "live with" lasting radioactive contamination.

Several such projects were implemented with support from the European Commission, nuclear regulatory organisations, organisations for expertise, ICRP, IAEA, the European Nuclear Energy Agency (NEA), and French, Belarusian, Swiss, Norwegian and Japanese national authorities. At their helm are a handful of French experts and one central figure, Jacques Lochard.

This trained economist's professional trajectory is notable for his multiple connections to bodies of expertise. Lochard began his nuclear career in 1977, in France's Centre d'Étude sur l'Évaluation de la

194 *Soraya Boudia*

Protection dans le domaine Nucléaire (CEPN), an association with a distinctive status. Indeed, its members are the primary actors in the French nuclear industry, Electricité de France (EDF), the Commissariat à l'énergie atomique (CEA) and the Institut de radioprotection et sûreté nucléaire (IRSN) (CEA).[6] CEPN is both a provider of services benefitting the strategies of its sponsors and a producer of expertise benefitting from European programs mainly funded by Euratom (Hecht, 1998; Topçu, 2013a). Lochard would serve as CEPN's director from 1989 to 2016, overlapping with his tenures as President of the French Society of Radiation Protection (SFRP) from 1997 to 1999, Executive Officer of the International Radiation Protection Association (IRPA) from 2000 to 2012, and chairman of the Committee on Radiation Protection and Public Health (CRPPH) of the NEA from 2005 to 2009. He became a member of Committee 3 of the ICRP in 1993 and vice-chair of the main commission in 2013, positions he still holds today. He is also currently Professor at Nagasaki University, affiliated with Atomic Bomb Disease Institute at the Department of Health Risk Control and Visiting Professor at Hiroshima University's Graduate School of Biomedical and Health Sciences.

In the mid-1990s, Lochard and some fellow CEPN members began to investigate the dynamics of crises following nuclear accidents. At the time, the playbooks available for managing such situations were extremely limited; Lochard's team worked on developing new modalities destined to favor the return of normalcy, as indicated in one of their programmatic publications: "Because there have been very few accidents, knowledge is limited about the acceptability criteria of post-accident situations involving radiation. In the case of [the] Chernobyl accident, for example, the use of classical risk perception concepts (Slovic, 2000) does not really help to understand the development of post-accident crisis" (Lochard and Prêtre, 1995: 23). With CEPN members including Thierry Schneider and Gilles Hériard Dubreuil (Director of Mutadis, a consulting firm specialising in the management of the social dimensions of risk), Lochard insisted that a new initiative must go beyond making accidents socially acceptable (Lochard and Schneider, 1992) and even attempt "to rehabilitate living conditions based on a strong involvement of the local population both to assess the situation and to seek ways of acting together" (Hériard Dubreuil, 2006: 54). The complexity of problems woven into any nuclear accident, they argued, invalidated classic political and social responses, especially regulatory approaches to risk management, and demanded "the search for new forms of governance" (Hériard Dubreuil, 2006: 55). In this, the CEPN was inspired by participative governance technologies integrating stakeholders that are today so popular in European and other international organisations.

From 1996 to 2008, a series of social experiments were conducted in areas contaminated by the Chernobyl accident. The resulting feedback was highly valued by international organisations, especially the ICRP. Financed by European programs and carried out by French institutions in collaboration with Belarusian national and local authorities, the pilot project ETHOS (1996–1998) started in the village of Olmany, 200 km from Chernobyl, before being extended to five other villages in the same district with ETHOS 2 (1998–2001), concerning 90,000 inhabitants in total (Rigby, 2003; Topçu, 2013b; Lochard, 2007). The ETHOS projects were followed by projects titled SAGE (2002–2005) and CORE (2003–2008), which called on the talents of a range of French academic actors from the Institut national d'agronomie de Paris-Grignon (the French agricultural research institute), the University of Technology Compiègne, and the University of Caen, as well as non-governmental organisations such as the Association pour le contrôle de la radioactivité dans l'Ouest (ACRO).

Although the ICRP is not an emergency response organisation, it was fully mobilised following the accident in Fukushima (Lochard et al., 2019). In the autumn of 2011, it took a key role in establishing collaborations among Japanese experts (most significantly Ohtsura Niwa, an ICRP Main Commission member recently appointed special professor at Fukushima Medical University [FMU]), local citizen organisations, French experts from CEPN and the French nuclear regulatory authority (Institut de radioprotection et de sûreté nucléaire [IRSN]). These collaborations were built through visits to affected communities, joint meetings and joint analyses (Schneider et al., 2019). A series of initiatives were organised within six months of the accident. In September 2011, 16 ICRP members participated in the First International Expert Symposium in Fukushima, titled "Radiation and Health Risks," held at FMU and funded by the Nippon Foundation (Asanuma-Brice, 2015; Ribault, 2019). ICRP Committee 4 (chaired by Lochard) organised a visit to the contaminated parts of Belarus, and later that year a small group composed of members of Committee 4, the Main Commission, and an NGO named Radiation Safety Forum Japan initiated dialogue on the rehabilitation of living conditions after the Fukushima accident (Lochard et al., 2019). This dialogue took place in a series of 12 meetings from November 27, 2011 to September 13, 2015, for the most part weekend seminars bringing experts, local authorities, and citizens together to address various consequences of the accident, addressing topics such as the education of children, the management of contaminated products and the role of measurement.

On conclusion of these meetings, an international workshop was held on the Fukushima Dialogue Initiative, followed by eight meetings between 2016 and 2018, organised by local associations and Japanese experts and funded by the Nippon Foundation, while the ICPR remained in charge of organising some local logistics and the participation of its members and foreign guests. This second wave of meetings was organised by civil society

196 Soraya Boudia

and usually held in villages affected by the accident; others were organised under the auspices of ETHOS Fukushima (Ando, 2016) and citizen-science networks (Polleri, 2019).

Rehabilitating life in contaminated areas

In Chernobyl, as in Fukushima, experts shared one dominant idea from the outset: long-term evacuation could not be the favored solution to minimising the risks of radioactive exposure in case of severe accidents. It is not that evacuation is necessarily ill-suited to addressing an immediate danger, but the psychological and social hazards accruing from permanently uprooting people and severing their social ties amplifies the health concerns and economic disruption of the displaced (Tanigawa et al., 2017). Instead, experts have come to promote an "innovative approach" to nuclear accident response, as developed under the ETHOS program (Lochard et al., 2019). The goal is to engage relevant stakeholders to find ways to respond to the challenges of the long-term rehabilitation of living conditions in the affected areas. This approach focuses on several aspects of life in affected zones, each with the same target populations and around the same activities, yet tailored to the specific site. It encourages the involvement of mothers to ensure the protection of children (Kimura, 2016), farmers to improve food quality and rebuild economic production and marketing channels (Sternsdorff-Cisterna, 2018), young people to develop their skills (including through artistic activities) and schoolchildren to define "a kind of practical pedagogy of life in contaminated territories" (Hériard Dubreuil, 2006: 58). The approach was formalised and adopted as a policy for the "protection of populations," emphasising rehabilitation and the establishment of a new, culturally specific "normal." It speaks to the gradual emergence of a new doctrine among regulatory authorities, formalising what is now called the "post-accident" period and presenting it as a normal step in risk and crisis management.

This approach does not try to master risks or minimise their scope. It does not deny the existence of the risk but instead aims to understand and tame it as an everyday reality while presenting life in these contaminated areas as an individual decision. The experts promoting these initiatives are carving out a practical approach that does not attempt to

> force countermeasures on the inhabitants, but on the contrary, respects their choices and to share their doubts. In that sense, experts involved in co-expertise processes have to be empathetic, and to know how to put themselves "at the service of" and certainly not "in place of".... Experts have to acknowledge the complexity of this situation.... Likewise, experts have to show humility by acknowledging the fact that they will never fully understand, as well as the local populations do, the impact that may have a nuclear accident on

The nuclear political laboratory 197

the daily life. In that sense, experts should not place themselves as those who know what to do to protect people and to improve their situation. Their role is rather to recognize that the radiological contamination is not legitimate in their territory, and that the rehabilitation process will be long, tedious and cannot be done without the help of local populations. In other words, they should accept that their duty is not to work for the population but to work with the population.

(Schneider et al., 2019: 266–267)

These experts promote among their peers the adoption of an attitude of humility and highlight the need for a compassionate process concerned with sharing the pain of affected people (Kimura, 2018). They insist on the necessity of working within communities and among residents while acknowledging that each has the freedom to choose whether to stay or leave. The outcome is that people who continue to live in permanently contaminated areas must improve their ability to take care of themselves and enhance their technical and coping skills; they are urged to show "creativity" in managing their daily life as best as possible. These citizens will become their own risk-assessors by learning, for example, to measure radioactivity levels and the dispersion of contamination, often by fetishising the Geiger counter. In this new participatory and inclusive post-accident governance paradigm, the responsibility of the authorities and risk managers is to inform and help individuals craft their *own* knowledge of contamination and strategies for mitigation: mothers can learn to better protect their children, inhabitants can grow and eat their own vegetables, and production and distribution chains can be created and safeguarded. Guidelines are produced and made available for all such activities.

This approach is increasingly formalised in nuclear risk management at the international level and encoded in the radiation protection measures vaunted by the ICRP under the impetus of French actors (ICRP, 2009). Nuclear actors are trying to appropriate and adapt a form of governance that initially emerged in other hazard-management sectors and is based on a logic of adaptation (Boudia and Jas, 2019). Its vocabulary and logics for action in the nuclear sector are thus not entirely new. For instance, "preparedness" receives special attention—a central notion that postulates that extreme events are entirely possible, even probable, and that people must prepare to weather them by designing scenarios and conducting crisis management and simulation exercises. Created in Cold War America to prepare the population to respond autonomously in the event of an atomic attack (Weart, 2012), the "preparedness" approach was widely revived in the United States after the terrorist attacks of September 11, 2001, and then appropriated from the field of national security for use in management of major natural disasters (Collier and Lakoff, 2008; Masco, 2014).

198 *Soraya Boudia*

"Resilience" is another flourishing concept serving as a cornerstone for policies of adaptation. This concept is gradually entering risk and crisis management circles, in the fields of the environment, terrorism and finance (Pelling, 2011; Chandler and Reid, 2016; Bourbeau, 2018). In the case of nuclear accidents, developing resilience means that people living in contaminated areas must learn how to carry on and reinvent themselves despite the difficulties they might face. By highlighting the capacities of individuals and populations, resilience is presented as a very positive solution for solving major environmental and health crises, even by NGOs.

Government through adaptation, as it was promoted following the disasters at Chernobyl and Fukushima, aims to normalise and naturalise major nuclear accidents and the major harm they can cause. Risks are recognised as inevitable and the impacts of disasters thought to be controllable, provided that individuals are prepared and equipped with tools for mitigating the effects of disaster in the short and long terms. This way of governing transfers a significant share of the responsibility for managing deleterious effects onto individuals. Emphasising each person's individual responsibility can even be presented as a liberating solution that empowers individuals in situations for which they are not responsible and over which they have very limited actual control.

The rationales behind the governance of nuclear power hazards have transformed over the 75 years since Hiroshima and Nagasaki were bombed by the United States in World War II. Once operating under a logic of mastery, today's logic emphasises the necessity of adaptation in zones permanently contaminated by major accidents. Defenders of the nuclear industry developed a whole repertoire of justifications and actions to legitimate activities that remain dangerous, no matter how many regulatory and protection measures are adopted. They do not even make convincing people that nuclear sites are safe a priority. Indeed, in a context of aging infrastructure, rising demand for alternative energy sources, and many states' refusal to fund a costly industry, these transformations have made it difficult to convince the public that even regulatory bodies can effectively manage nuclear hazards or their consequences when accidents inevitably occur. Continuing to defend nuclear technologies at the national and international scales may have other functions, beyond simply arguing their effectiveness: keeping the promise of abundant energy in the future, silencing the voices and demands of nuclear opponents and victims, and stalling government efforts to take greater control of the sector or halt certain nuclear activities. The promotion of these modes of government is also addressed to actors within the nuclear sector, in response to the concerns of workers in the sector fueled by repeated and wide-ranging criticism through the years. The discourse that developed on the ground at Chernobyl and Fukushima and actions that were taken at each of these sites reassure

The nuclear political laboratory 199

some of the people in charge that they are able to innovate in managing the risks they once minimised. This repertoire of actions is also a way to internally reassure the sector about its own future, despite its reliance on an intrinsically risky technology.

Notes

1 IRSN (n.d.). Retombées des essais nucléaires atmosphériques. Available at: https://www.irsn.fr/FR/connaissances/Environnement/surveillance-environne-ment/resultats/retombees-tirs-armes-nucleaires/Pages/2-essais-nucleaires-at-mospheriques.aspx#.XmJrmq0lCgQ [Accessed June 2, 2021].
2 Gofman was a PhD student of Glenn Seaborg, whose career had included early work in nuclear chemistry, years as a renowned professor of biology at the University of California, Berkeley, and serving as the medical division head at one of the AEC's largest labs, the Lawrence Livermore National Laboratory.
3 This study was conducted by the MIT Professor Norman Rasmussen. Rasmussen's team consisted of the equivalent of 70 engineers a year and had a budget of $3 million. The report was 3,300 pages long, plus appendices.
4 UNSCEAR (2000). *Sources and Effects of Ionizing Radiation*. New York: UNSCEAR. Available at: https://www.unscear.org/docs/publications/2000/UNSCEAR_2000_Report_Vol.I.pdf [Accessed June 17, 2021].
5 IRSN (n.d.). Fukushima de 2017 à 2020. Fukushima en 2017 et 2018. Available at: https://www.irsn.fr/FR/connaissances/Installations_nucleaires/Les-accidents-nucleaires/accident-fukushima-2011/fukushima-2018/Pages/2-evacuation-accident-nucleaire-fukushima-2018.aspx#.Xk5Bl60lCgQ [Accessed June 2, 2021].
6 The founding members of CEPN are EDF and CEA. In 1993, Cogema became the third member; it changed its name to Areva in 2001, and left CEPN in 2016. IRSN joined the CEPN from its very inception, in 2002.

References

Alexis-Martin, B., and Davies, T. (2017). Towards Nuclear Geography: Zones, Bodies, and Communities. *Geography Compass*, 11(9). DOI: http://doi.org/1 0.1111/gec3.12325.
Ando, R. (2016). Reclaiming our Lives in the Wake of a Nuclear Plant Accident. *Clinical Oncology*, 28, pp. 275–276.
Asanuma-Brice, C. (2015). De la vulnérabilité à la résilience, réflexions sur la protection en cas de désastre extrême: le cas de la gestion des conséquences de l'explosion d'une centrale nucléaire à Fukushima. *Raison Publique*. Available at: https://raison-publique.fr/422.
Balogh, B. (1991). *Chain Reaction: Expert Debate and Public Participation in American Commercial Nuclear Power, 1945–1975*. Cambridge, UK: Cambridge University Press.
BEIR. (1972). *The Effects on Populations of Exposure to Low Levels Ionizing Radiation*. Washington, DC: The National Academies Press.
Boudia, S. (2007). Global Regulation: Controlling and Accepting Radioactivity Risks. *History and Technology*, 23(4), pp. 389–406.
Boudia, S. (2013). From Threshold to Risk: Exposure to Low Doses of Radiation and its Effects on Toxicants Regulation. In: S. Boudia and N. Jas, eds.,

200 Soraya Boudia

Toxicants, Health and Regulation Since 1945. London: Pickering & Chatto, pp. 71–87.

Boudia, S. (2014). Managing Scientific and Political Uncertainty. Risk Assessment in an Historical Perspective. In: S. Boudia and N. Jas, eds., *Powerless Science? The Making of the Toxic World in the Twentieth Century*. New York: Berghahn Books, pp. 95–112.

Boudia, S., and Jas, N. (2019). *Gouverner un monde toxique*. Versailles: Éditions Quea.

Bourbeau, P. (2018). *On Resilience: Genealogy, Logics and World Politics*. Cambridge, UK: Cambridge University Press.

Boyer, P. (1994). *By the Bomb's Early Light: American Thought and Culture at the Dawn of the Atomic Age*. Chapel Hill, NC: University of North Carolina Press.

Brown, K. (2019). *Manual for Survival: A Chernobyl Guide to the Future*. New York: Norton.

Chandler, D., and Reid, J. (2016). *The Neoliberal Subject: Resilience, Adaptation and Vulnerability*. London: Rowman & Littlefield International.

Collier, S., and Lakoff, A. (2008). Distributed Preparedness: The Spatial Logic of Domestic Security in the United States. *Environment and Planning D: Society and Space*, 26(1), pp. 7–28.

Daston, L. (2017). What Is an Insurable Risk? Swiss Re and Atomic Reactor Insurance. In: N. Viggo Haueter and G. Jones, eds., *Managing Risk in Reinsurance: From City Fires to Global Warming*. Oxford: Oxford University Press, pp. 203–247.

Davies, T., and Polese, A. (2015). Informality and Survival in Ukraine's Nuclear Landscape: Living with the Risks of Chernobyl. *Journal of Eurasian Studies*, 6(1), pp. 34–45.

Foasso, C. (2012). *Atomes sous surveillance: une histoire de la sûreté nucléaire en France*. Brussels: Peter Lang.

Hecht, G. (1998). *The Radiance of France: Nuclear Power and National Identity after World War II*. Cambridge, MA: MIT Press.

Hecht, G. (2012). *Being Nuclear: Africans and the Global Uranium Trade*. Cambridge MA: MIT Press.

Hériard Dubreuil, G. (2006). Vivre dans un territoire contaminé? *Revue Projet*, 4(293), pp. 54–59.

ICRP. (2009). *Application of the Commission's Recommendations to the Protection of People Living in Long-term Contaminated Areas After a Nuclear Accident or a Radiation Emergency*. ICRP Publication 111. Annals of the ICRP 39(3). Available at: https://journals.sagepub.com/doi/pdf/10.1177/ANIB_39_3 [Accessed June 17, 2021].

Jasper, J. (1990). *Nuclear Politics*. Princeton NJ: Princeton University Press.

Kimura, A. (2016). *Radiation Brain Moms and Citizen Scientists: The Gender Politics of Food Contamination after Fukushima*. Durham, NC: Duke University Press.

Kimura, A. (2018). Fukushima ETHOS: Post-disaster Risk Communication, Affect, and Shifting Risks. *Science as Culture*, 27, pp. 98–117.

Kuchinskaya, O. (2014). *The Politics of Invisibility: Public Knowledge about Radiation Health Effects after Chernobyl*. Cambridge, MA: MIT Press.

The nuclear political laboratory 201

Lindee, S. (1994). *Suffering Made Real: American Science and the Survivors at Hiroshima.* Chicago: University of Chicago Press.

Lindee, S. (2016). Survivors and Scientists: Hiroshima, Fukushima and the Radiation Effects Research Foundation, 1975-2014. *Social Studies of Science,* 46, pp. 184–209.

Lochard, J. (2007). Rehabilitation of Living Conditions in Territories Contaminated by the Chernobyl Accident: The Ethos Project. *Health Physics,* 93(5), pp. 522–526.

Lochard, J., and Prêtre, S. (1995). Return to Normality after a Radiological Emergency. *Health Physics,* 68(1), pp. 20–26.

Lochard, J., and Schneider, T. (1992). *Réflexions sur l'acceptabilité sociale et conséquences économiques d'un accident nucléaire.* Fontenay-aux-Roses: CEPN, rapport no. 191.

Lochard, J., Schneider, T., Ando, R., Niwa, O., Clement, C., Lecompte, J., Tada, J. (2019). An Overview of the Dialogue Meetings Initiated by ICRP in Japan after the Fukushima Accident. *Radioprotection,* 54(2), pp. 87–101.

Masco, J. (2014). *The Theater of Operations: National Security Affect from the Cold War to the War on Terror.* Durham, NC: Duke University Press.

Nelkin, D., and Pollak, M. (1981). *The Atom Besieged.* Cambridge, MA: MIT Press.

Nixon, R. (2011). *Slow Violence and the Environmentalism of the Poor.* Cambridge, MA: Harvard University Press.

Pelling, M. (2011). *Adaptation to Climate Change. From Resilience to Transformation.* London: Routledge.

Petryna, A. (2013). *Life Exposed: Biological Citizens after Chernobyl.* Princeton, NJ: Princeton University Press.

Pestre, D., ed. (2014). *Le Gouvernement des technosciences.* Paris: Les Éditions de la Découverte.

Polleri, M. (2019). Conflictual Collaboration: Citizen Science and the Governance of Radioactive Contamination after the Fukushima Nuclear Disaster. *American Ethnologist,* 46, pp. 214–226.

Ribault, T. (2019). Resilience in Fukushima: Contribution to a Political Economy of Consent. *Alternatives: Global, Local, Political,* 44(2-4), pp. 94–118.

Rigby, J. (2003). *Principes et processus à l'œuvre dans un projet d'amélioration de conditions de vie dans les territoires contaminés par la catastrophe de Tchernobyl-ETHOS I (1996-1998).* PhD Thesis. Université de Technologie de Compiègne.

Schneider, T., Maître, M., Lochard, J., et al. (2019). The Role of Radiological Protection Experts in Stakeholder Involvement in the Recovery Phase of Post-nuclear Accident Situations: Some Lessons from the Fukushima-Daïchi NPP Accident, *Radioprotection,* 54(4), pp. 259–270.

Slovic, P., ed. (2000). *The Perception of Risk.* London: Earthscan Publications.

Sternsdorff-Cisterna, N. (2018). *Food Safety after Fukushima: Scientific Citizenship and the Politics of Risk.* Honolulu, HI: University of Hawaii Press.

Strasser, B. (2006). *La fabrique d'une nouvelle science: la biologie moléculaire à l'âge atomique, 1945-1964.* Florence: Leo S. Olschki Editore.

Tanigawa, K., Lochard, J., Abdel-Wahab, M., and Crick, M. (2017). Roles and Activities of International Organizations After the Fukushima Accident. *Asia Pacific Journal of Public Health,* 29(2S), 90S–98S.

202 *Soraya Boudia*

Topçu, S. (2013a). *La France nucléaire. L'art de gouverner une technologie contestée*. Paris: Le Seuil.

Topçu, S. (2013b). Chernobyl Empowerment. In: S. Boudia and N. Jas, eds., *Toxicants, Health and Regulation since 1945*. London: Pickering and Chatto, pp. 135–158.

Weart, S. (2012). *The Rise of Nuclear Fear*. Cambridge, MA: Harvard University Press.

Wittner, L. (1993). *The Struggle Against the Bomb. Volume 1. One World or None: A History of the World Nuclear Disarmament Movement through 1953*. Stanford, CA: Stanford University Press.

Wittner, L. (1997). *The Struggle Against the Bomb. Volume 2. Resisting the Bomb: A History of the World Nuclear Disarmament Movement, 1954–1970*. Stanford, CA: Stanford University Press.

10 Continuing nuclear tests and ending fish inspections: politics, science and the Lucky Dragon Incident in 1954

Hiroko Takahashi

On March 1, 1954, the United States conducted a thermonuclear test code-named "Bravo Shot" at the Bikini Atoll in the Marshall Islands. A Japanese fishing boat, the Lucky Dragon No. 5, was 130 km away from the hypocenter, yet its sailors were exposed to radioactive fallout. And Bravo was only the first explosion of the "Operation Castle," one of nuclear test programs that would go on to expose thousands in the Marshall Islands, along with military personnel and fishing boat crew members, to the known dangers of radiation.

It took more than two weeks before the Japanese public learned about the "Lucky Dragon Incident" (known in English as the "Bikini Incident"). Japan's largest daily newspaper, *Yomiuri Shimbun*, broke the news on March 16. Media reported that 23 of the boat's crew were hospitalised with symptoms typical of radiation exposure: nausea, fatigue, burns and hair loss. Naturally, fish from the Pacific, consumed widely in Japan, was contaminated by radioactive fallout; thus, the Japanese Ministry of Health and Welfare began an effort to inspect seafood before it went to market. The program would be shelved by January 1, 1955 as the United States prepared for its next series of nuclear tests and paid some $2 million to the Japanese as a sort of conciliatory measure.

The ten months over which this development unfolded were pivotal to nuclear politics in the two countries and beyond. The negotiations and diplomacy involved significantly shaped subsequent approaches to radiation contamination and protection from US nuclear testing in the Pacific, foreclosing possibilities for later lawsuits, negotiations, and even research on the environmental effects of testing by setting a payout precedent. To this day, both the US and Japanese governments downplay the ongoing damage of radioactive fallout caused by the nuclear testing performed in the Marshall Islands.

The Bikini Incident is the best known of such fallout incidents, but certainly not the only time civilian Japanese fishing crews have been irradiated. Independent research by a high school teacher in Kochi Prefecture, Japan, has uncovered many others. Yamashita (2012) shows

DOI: 10.4324/9781003227472-10

204 Hiroko Takahashi

that crew members of approximately 1,000 boats (many of which were used and reused by different crews throughout the nuclear test period) were affected. None has been compensated.

After the 2011 Fukushima disaster, with renewed attention to the harms caused by atomic radiation, these victims launched a 2016 suit against the Japanese government demanding recognition and compensation. One of the plaintiffs, Ms. Setsuko Shimomoto, spoke on behalf of her father:

> I'm really worried about the situation of radiation exposure caused by the Fukushima Nuclear Power Plant Disaster. I'm concerned that, like my father, people have been exposed to radiation from the disaster. That's why I joined this lawsuit against the Japanese government.[1]

Her concern was reasonable: the Japanese government has almost always tried to minimise the harm of radiation exposure, whether it stemmed from the atomic bombings in Hiroshima and Nagasaki, US testing in the Pacific or domestic nuclear accidents. When, after the Bikini Incident, the National Institute of Radiological Sciences (now the National Institute for Quantum and Radiological Science and Technology) was established in 1957, its longitudinal study of the health outcomes of the Lucky Dragon No. 5 crew members was not an expression of care for their well-being, but a way to gather biological data and evidence (data that, incidentally, was never provided to the crew-members). The same institute used whole-body counters to determine the internal radiation exposure of people at and near Fukushima Daiichi, concluding that their radiation levels were not a matter of concern and testifying to that effect.

This chapter focuses on how the governments of Japan and the United States handled the aftermath of the Bikini Incident and reached a settlement with reverberations today. I analyze documents from the Japanese Foreign Ministry as well as the Central Intelligence Agency (CIA), State Department, Operation Coordinating Board and Atomic Energy Commission (AEC) in the United States to shed light on how the bilateral negotiations unfolded, publicly and privately, culminating in the "full settlement." In its development, scientists played a key *political* role, helping both countries tamp down fears about radiation in order to find an acceptable international agreement while evading the human consequences of their actions. For the United States to continue its nuclear testing with impunity, the very real risk to Japanese fishermen must be hidden, and that meant shutting down the Japanese program to test tuna hauls for radiation. The Japanese government generally went along with the United States, prioritising security alliances as it closed down the tuna testing. Further, as the two countries joined forces to downplay the effects of radiation exposure on human health, their method of settling the Bikini Incident foreclosed other possible avenues of legal recourse for victims. This helped institutionalise official approaches to ignore or underestimate radioactive fallout—which Boudia (2007) has identified as the first *global* health and environmental risk—and render the Lucky Dragon Incident a fully resolved issue.

US denial and trivialisation of radiation's health effects were dominant from the start. Following the US bombings of Hiroshima and Nagasaki, Australian journalist Wilfred Burchett reported in *Daily Express* on "atomic plague" affecting the Japanese survivors in early September 1945.[2] Brigadier General Thomas F. Farrell, Chief of the US War Department's atomic bomb mission, known as the Manhattan Project, then issued a statement denying that radiation could cause such damage. Farrell claimed that the atomic bombs dropped in Japan had been detonated at such a high altitude that little radiation could have reached people on the ground. Those who died later, he insisted, nonetheless died because of injuries from the blast, not residual radiation, radioactive fallout or internal exposure (radiation poisoning) (Takahashi, 2009).

Nine years later, the Bikini Incident would urge another reckoning with radiation and Japanese bodies—and be met with more denials. It did, however, prompt Japan to dispatch its own research vessel, which reported that a shockingly vast area of the Pacific was, in fact, contaminated by radioactive materials. When Aikichi Kuboyama, the chief radio operator of the Lucky Dragon No. 5, died in September 1954, the US AEC remained silent.

Yasushi Nishiwaki, who worked at Osaka City Medical College at the time of the Bikini Incident, traveled in Europe from July to November 1954, raising the alarm about dangerous radioactive fallout measures at 20 separate research sites. One BBC radio presentation he made, on October 28, 1954, was broadcast worldwide, inspiring Joseph Rotblat, a physicist who worked on the Manhattan Project, to tell Bertrand Russell that the Bikini H-bomb had been a "dirty bomb" (Nakao et al., 2015). The following year, on July 9, 1955, Russell released a document titled, "Statement: The Russell-Einstein Manifesto," that proclaimed:

> It is stated on very good authority that a bomb can now be manufactured which will be 2,500 times as powerful as that which destroyed Hiroshima. Such a bomb, if exploded near the ground or under water, sends radio-active particles into the upper air. They sink gradually and reach the surface of Earth in the form of deadly dust or rain. It was this dust which infected the Japanese fishermen and their catch of fish.[3]

The controversy over radioactive fallout in the wake of "Bravo Shot" turned into a public debate that polarised the scientific world (Winkler, 1993). Later scholars writing on the Bikini Incident largely

206 Hiroko Takahashi

focused on fallout controversy in the United States (Winkler, 1993; also Boyer, 1994) and on the relationship between US and Japanese scientists in the post-war period (Higuchi, 2020). The work on this issue, in fact, largely overlooked the politics involved in this scientific wrangling regarding the Incident (Hacker, 1994), and only one scholarly article (Sakamoto, 1994) appears to attend to the governmental ties between the United States and Japan in this period (even then, focusing on the political settlement of just the Lucky Dragon Incident).

By way of an initial corrective, I use this chapter to briefly consider the fallout controversies unfolding in the United States and Japan in this period and to use government documents declassified in response to my FOIA requests to consider the geopolitical implications of the relationship between the two countries. My aim is to explore the connection between human-level damage from radiation and international politics.

I begin with the Japanese government's collaboration on an investigation of the Lucky Dragon No. 5's crew, undertaken by the CIA on orders from AEC chair Lewis Strauss. Then I review how and why the fish contamination inspection program was cancelled by the Japanese government following the November 1954 meeting between US and Japanese scientists and analyze how their respective governments subsequently settled the Bikini Incident. I conclude by considering how government collaboration in the Bikini Incident settlement worked to obscure scientific knowledge on the hazards of radioactive fallout and their direct link to the suffering of humans exposed to it.

The CIA investigation into the Lucky Dragon No. 5

Alongside Hiroshima and Nagasaki, the Bikini Incident is the third notable event in which Japanese citizens were exposed to radiation from nuclear weapons. Yet the Japanese government endeavored not to protect the rights of the survivors and monitor their medical conditions but to strengthen its alliance with the United States, using the Bikini Incident for negotiating leverage. Behind the scenes, the Japanese government complied with US attempts to blame (or at least deflect attention from) the Lucky Dragon No. 5's crew members, investigating their political thoughts and affiliations. The compromise epitomised the way in which the two countries conspired to settle their differences in the Cold War context. The United States tried to stifle anti-nuclear testing movements in Japan with assurances that the tests and occupation of the Marshall Islands were necessary if the superpower was to establish a presence and win the Cold War. And they had the support of the Japanese government; without it, the kind of settlement discussed below would never have come to fruition.

The Lucky Dragon No. 5 was exposed to radiation from the Bravo Shot, the first in a series of six nuclear tests code-named "Operation Castle." The tests were conducted between March 1 and May 13, 1954.

Following the second test, on March 26, AEC Chair Lewis Strauss issued a statement lauding the success of the first and second tests, while admitting that, despite careful preparation, 23 crew members of the Lucky Dragon No. 5, 28 American personnel and 236 residents of the Marshall Islands had been within the fallout zone. He insisted that "None of the American personnel have burns" and that "the 236 natives also appear to me to be well and happy," implying that there was no sign of any testing-related illness even one month after the Bravo Shot. However, he kept secret the research project on people in Marshall Islands, "Project 4.1.: Study of Response of Human Beings exposed to Significant Beta and Gamma Radiation due to Fall-out from High Yield Weapons." Sterling Cole, the chairman of the US Congress Joint Committee on Atomic Energy, speculated that it was not inconceivable that the Lucky Dragon No. 5 crew had entered the experimental site with aims *other* than fishing—that is, the Senator publicly hinted that the boat was actually a spy vessel exposed to radiation after having entered the US-designated "danger zone." Not incidentally, the May 1, 1954, issue of the *Chubu Nippon Shimbun* reported that the Japanese police and the Public Security Investigation Agency had begun looking into the politics of the crew members at the request of the Foreign Ministry. The paper also reported that Foreign Ministry denied requesting or receiving a US request for such an investigation, that it "had no conception of why such an investigation should be deemed necessary," and that "the allegation was totally unfounded."

The Strauss Papers released in 1998 tell a different story. Strauss formally requested that the CIA, using behind-the-scenes help from Japan's Foreign Ministry, investigate the Lucky Dragon No. 5's alleged espionage.[4] The documents show that the main purpose of the investigation, titled "CIA Investigation of Circumstances of Exposure of Fuku Ryu Maru 'Fortunate Dragon' to Hydrogen Bomb Test," was to determine whether or not the Lucky Dragon No. 5 had entered the designated "danger zone" or otherwise intentionally exposed itself to the explosion with the object of making observations, taking instrument readings, or providing evidence for anti-American propaganda.[5]

Due to redactions in the documents, it remains unclear whether the Lucky Dragon No. 5 was actually outside the danger zone.[6] Japan's Foreign Ministry submitted copies of the boat's track charts to the US embassy, and it did so after the Japanese government had made a public announcement that it "had no conception of why such an investigation should be deemed necessary." This indicates that US officials were given a confidential opportunity to analyze the track charts and likely concluded that the Lucky Dragon No. 5 *was* outside what the military considered the danger zone (details of Japan's cooperation and the analysis of relevant information provided by Japan have either been left

208 *Hiroko Takahashi*

unmentioned or deleted from these AEC documents). The report also addresses such questions as: "Was the Japanese doctor in charge of treating the crew politically suspect?"; "Is there any evidence of special instruments having been on board?"; "Is there any evidence of a rendezvous with a Russian vessel before putting into port?"; and "What is the possibility of a substitute vessel having been offered for inspection?" No credible evidence seems to have supported any of these conjectures. As a result, Frank Wisner, Deputy Director of Plans at the CIA, emphasised in a letter to Strauss that the CIA had found no evidence that the Japanese government had withheld any important information from the United States with respect to the Bikini Incident.

To recap: AEC documents reveal that the Japanese government carried out an investigation into the alleged spying activities of the Lucky Dragon No. 5's crew in response to a US request. A subsequent CIA investigation confirmed the reliability of the Japanese conclusion that the Lucky Dragon No. 5 was definitely *not* spying. Thus, despite the Japanese Foreign Ministry's denials to the *Chubu Nippon Shimbun's* reporters, the Japanese and American governments quickly coordinated and cooperated to handle the aftermath of the Bikini Incident and move on.

One important historical note helps explain their coordination. On March 8, 1954, seven days after the nuclear tests in the Marshall Islands began, an agreement titled the "Mutual Defense Assistance Agreement between Japan and the United States of America" was signed. The agreement stipulated that the Japanese government create a Self Defense Force by July 1954, intensifying its cooperation with US Cold War strategies. In the same year, the US established the Foreign Operations Administration (FOA), which, according to President Dwight D. Eisenhower, "to centralize the control, direction, and operations of all foreign economic and technical assistance programs and to coordinate mutual security activities. FOA furnished military, economic, and technical assistance to friendly nations."[7] Using the FOA's budget to provide economic and military aid to "the nations of the free world" allowed the United States to fund Japanese endeavors and further shore up the nations' shared military fates.

Inspection of contaminated fish and radioactive fallout controversy

As mentioned above, the Bikini Incident invoked great fear around radioactive fallout and its potentially global implications. An organised anti-nuclear movement started to form in Japan, the United States and Europe. If nuclear testing was to continue, atomic advocates needed to calm this controversy promptly. The AEC and the US Ambassador to Japan, in particular, tried to influence the trajectory of the fallout controversy in Japan through technical debates and exchanges regarding radiation's effects. That is why everyone was talking about tuna.

Continuing nuclear tests 209

By mid-March of 1954, news of the Bikini Incident and radioactive fallout from US nuclear tests (*"shi no hai,"* or ash of death) had spread among the Japanese public. As the ash dropped into the sea, people feared it was eaten by and subsequently contaminated tuna, a crucial protein in their diets. Thus, the Ministry of Health and Welfare started an extensive inspection of tuna fish by the end of March. Meanwhile, the anti-nuclear movement gained momentum. From November 15 to 19, 1954, the Science Council of Japan in Tokyo organised and hosted the first Japan–US conference on the effects and uses of radioactive substances. Notably, all the US delegates were government-affiliated—most from the AEC.[8] The Japanese participants also included scientists with strong ties to the government.[9] All those present seemed more keenly interested in uses of radioactive substances to promote the nuclear industry than with the influence of radiation on a human body (Takahashi, 2021).

Although the conference was about technical issues being debated among scientists, it had grave political significance. The Bikini Incident was still diplomatically unsettled at the time, so a great deal of political coordination had to take place before the conference could get off the ground. Prior to their arrival in Japan, US participants met with US Ambassador John Allison, a meeting noted in the Operation Coordinating Board Records: "Meeting with Ambassador Allison on Japanese-American Scientists' Meeting in Japan."[10] US delegate and biologist Paul B. Pearson wrote to John C. Bugher, the Director of the AEC's Division of Biology and Medicine, about the content of the meeting, saying that Allison stressed that "this [is going to be] a very important conference from both the diplomatic implications and the scientific assistance to the Japanese." Yet he also noted "there appeared to be some inconsistency in his messages recommending that no top AEC people be sent and the Embassy statement that they considered the conference important." Then, Pearson reported, Allison said

> he recognized this and that his concern was that the conference be kept on a scientific basis and that the representatives from the Commission not be on a level that would discuss policy, particularly as related to the claims of the Japanese for damages from the March 1 incident.[11]

In his diplomatic way, Allison was advising the participants to understand that this was, in fact, a political conference, but everyone needed to stick to the scientific facts and pretend it was not.

On November 16, 1954, after the first day of the conference, the English edition of *Mainichi Shimbun* reported that Walter D. Claus, an AEC scientist, had argued that fish with radiation of up to 500 counts per minute (conducted in accordance with scientific guidelines and at a standard distance of 10cm) were not dangerous for human consumption.[12] This

210   *Hiroko Takahashi*

was a significantly larger permissible count than the 100 counts per minute threshold mandating fish disposal set by Japan's Ministry of Health and Welfare. Four days later, the conference having closed, Pearson sent another letter to AEC's Bugher that attests to the political significance of this one specific assertion:

> One important outcome of the Conference is that the Ministry of Welfare has announced that the present maximum safety limit of 100 counts per minute is probably too low and that they are calling a conference to give this matter further study. This may have important implications regarding the reparations for the losses to the tuna industry.[13]

While Allison and AEC scientists publicly framed their discussion with Japanese scientists at this conference as purely scientific, not political, the science presented (and likely the science not presented) held important political and diplomatic implications. As Pearson reported, Japan's Health Ministry had just publicly judged its safety limit on permissible radiation in edible proteins as "probably too low"—that is, that the tuna testing had been based on an overreaction to the danger of fallout. This concession was an important step in the Ministry's subsequent decisions to terminate their fish inspection program before the year's end. (Takahashi, 2012)

To be sure, the Japanese scientists did not reach consensus around terminating the tuna inspection. Ambassador Allison sent a telegram to Bugher in Washington, DC, on December 27, 1954: "Comments of Japanese Scientists on continuance of inspection have been largely critical. Various prefecture governments have publicly indicated they expected to continue inspections at own expense."[14] In the absence of a federal program, local governments were cobbling together inspection efforts. With this in mind, Allison worked to negotiate with Foreign Minister Shigemitsu around compensation related to the Bikini Incident. Ending the fish inspection policy could minimise the economic damage to Japanese fisheries, but the hasty shift in standards was not based on empirical data. Instead, the US and Japanese governments sought to quell public anxiety or address readily apparent health damage in the interest of advancing US nuclear strategies.

"Ex gratia"

The stage for a swift settlement was set by the Japanese government's decision to terminate its fish inspection program, following the standards suggested by US AEC scientists. The settlement of the Bikini Incident, then, involved blatantly political, behind-the-scenes maneuvering, including covert US intelligence activities and Japanese government officials' attempts to leverage the Incident for the release of war criminals. Much of the highest-level political negotiation was conducted between US Ambassador Allison and Japan's Foreign Minister Mamoru Shigemitsu. Allison, having coordinated with the Operations Coordinating Board (OCB) and under the President's approval, thus brought the US proposal as a representative of American political, military, and psychological policy toward Japan.

The analysis in this section, focused on the process that produced the "full settlement" through the OCB and diplomatic meetings between Allison and Shigemitsu, is based on recently declassified documents. These include documents related to the Allison-Shigemitsu Conference, declassified in 2014 by the US National Archives of Record Administration, as well as documents from Japanese Foreign Ministry, declassified in 2018 by the author's FOIA request.

The OCB was established in the United States in September 1953 as psychological warfare intensified in the Cold War context. It succeeded the Psychological Strategy Board, set up by President Harry Truman on April 4, 1951, and it was, according to Presidential Executive Order 10483, created "in order to provide for the integrated implementation of national security policies by the several agencies."[15] Its tasks included the oversight of covert operations. OCB negotiations were particularly important because they handled intelligence strategies and represented the highest-level coordination among the US Department of State, Department of Defense, CIA, Foreign Operation Administration (FOA) and the President.

In order to sidestep the regular channels, which would have involved a Congressional budgetary review, the negotiations over the amount of direct payments to Japanese parties after the Bikini Incident took place out of the public eye and using, via the OCB, the intelligence budget under the direct orders of President Eisenhower. On October 30, 1954, the OCB agreed to a payment of $1.5 million as compensation for the Bikini Incident. The FOA looked for additional money to increase the payment. On November 22, 1954, FOA Director Harold E. Stassen sent a memorandum to Elmer B. Stats, Executive Officer of the OCB, indicating that President Eisenhower had been informed about "the OCB Japanese Matter" and stood ready to make a formal decision if "a settlement is reached which OCB recommends."[16] This letter is important for understanding this compensation's meaning. Usually, if the United States must pay "compensation" to another country, extensive information and rationale would need to be presented to Congress and approved as part of the federal budget. In the United States, after all, the legislative branch retains what is called "the power of the purse." If the administration wants to use federal funds without gaining this tedious Congressional approval, it needs to turn to "secret money" set aside for clandestine intelligence activities. The FOA at the time had access to undisclosed funds designated for the promotion of anti-communist policy, including economic and military aid to foreign actors; this is the money the OCB planned to use—in the process, keeping a great deal of information about radiation poisoning in the Pacific out of the Congressional record.

Two days after Christmas in 1954, two top officials, Ambassador Allison and Foreign Minister Shigemitsu, sat down in Tokyo to negotiate the terms of the settlement of the Bikini Incident. They exchanged a variety of suggested schemes including direct "compensation for damages caused by nuclear tests in the Marshall Islands," a plan called GARIOA (Government Appropriation for Relief in Occupied Area), an "Agreement on Japan's contribution to the joint defense expenditures" and "Release and parole of war criminals on a larger scale."

Shigemitsu presented a document that indicated his country's willingness to be generally conciliatory in order to strengthen bilateral cooperation with the United States for security and defense (see Figure 10.1).[17] Among this document's proposals, the request that the United States "Release and parole of war criminals on a larger scale" as a sort of friendly gesture between emerging allies was striking, given that Shigemitsu was himself a Class-A criminal who had remained imprisoned until 1950.[18] In fact, many Japanese Class-B and Class-C war criminals were still in prison in Tokyo as the two countries met secretly. It seemed the settlement of the Bikini Incident was just one among various matters under negotiation.

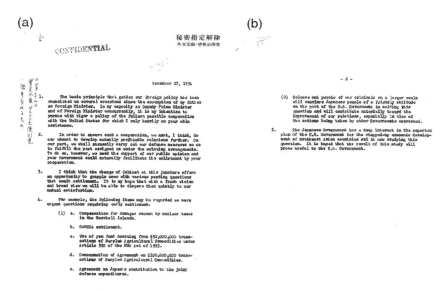

Figure 10.1 Documents on Alison and Shigemitsu Meeting on December 27, 1954, Japanese Foreign Ministry. This document was declassified by request of the author on October 4, 2018.

For his part, Ambassador Allison presented a "Memorandum of Urgent Problems in Japan-United States Relations" listing the following three issues: "Defense Budgetary Problems," "Compensation for Damage Resulting from 1954 Nuclear Tests in the Marshall Islands," and GARIOA.

Allison sent a telegram to the State Department after the meeting, reporting that Shigemitsu had focused on the Bikini compensation matter. They had a detailed negotiation, Allison wrote, in which he informed Shigemitsu that the United States was prepared to pay out $1.5 million. "I also told him that if this was not satisfactory I was prepared to discuss a slight increase, but that any substantial increase would probably have to be approved by Congress and would entail considerable delay and possible unfavorable discussion on the floor in Congress." In response, Shigemitsu asked "if it would not be possible to go up to $2,000,000 as he thought he could obtain agreement at this sum."[19]

After the meeting, on January 4, 1955, the US government paid $2 million to the Japanese government for the Bikini Incident. The US government provided the following note, which the Japanese government accepted:

> I now desire to inform Your Excellency that the Government of the US of America hereby tenders, ex gratia, to the Government of Japan, without reference to the question of legal liability, the sum of two million dollars for purposes of compensation for the injuries or damages sustained as a result of nuclear tests in the Marshall Islands in 1954.... It is the understanding of the Government of the US of America that the Government of Japan, in accepting the tendered sum of two million dollars, does so in full settlement of any and all claims against the US of America or its agents, Nationals and jurisdictional entities for any and all injuries, losses or damages arising out of the said nuclear tests[20].

Officially, the payment was *ex gratia*—a gift, essentially—not compensation. And the Japanese government accepted it as such. The Japanese public, however, interpreted this payment as compensation for damage, paid by the United States, partially because the Japanese government translated "ex gratia" to "*isharyo*," implying compensation for mental damage. This led people to see the payment as an American expression of regret. But crucially, the US note referred to "injuries," "losses" and "damages," but not "casualties" or "deaths." It carefully sidestepped the question of whether these nuclear tests had killed anyone. It was also, crucially, characterised as a payment "in full settlement" regarding "all injuries, losses or damages arising out of the said nuclear tests," and did not include payment for Japanese fishermen who were affected by their presence in the Pacific during US nuclear tests.

214 Hiroko Takahashi

The ex gratia payment was disbursed to the Japanese government, and some went to the owner of the Lucky Dragon No. 5 boat—compensation for the loss of the fish discarded after failing radiation tests as part of the tuna inspection program. A one-time allowance was made for payments to the crew members of this single boat. No other sailors exposed to US tests received funds from the ex gratia payment. None were even recognised as victims by the US or Japanese governments.

Correspondence between an expat living in Japan and an AEC member makes it clear that the scientific conference in November and its effect on the end of tuna inspection set the trajectory of the Bikini Incident's settlement. The day after Allison and Shigemitsu's "full settlement" was announced, on January 5, 1955, William C. Noville, Manager of Tuna Research Foundation's Tokyo Branch, wrote the following to Dr. Willis R. Boss in the AEC's Division of Biology and Medicine:

> The first international conference on radiobiology has apparently influenced the Government (Welfare Ministry) to discontinue the inspection of the tuna landings for evidences of radioactivity.... On December 28, the Cabinet approved such recommendation of the Welfare Minis, Abolition of tuna inspection become effective January 1, 1955.

Noville concluded on a celebratory note: "Congratulations to you and the rest of the boys who helped this event materialize Best regards and Season's greetings."[21] Ending the inspections that proved the poisoning was considered a key achievement by the scientists at the US AEC—it limited liability, foreclosed public evidence, and allowed nuclear testing to continue in the Marshall Islands for the foreseeable future.

Legacy of the Bikini Settlement

Instead of protecting and advocating for its radioactive fallout-exposed people, the Japanese government sought a powerful political and military ally after WWII, collaborating with the Americans to cover over and downplay evidence in the Bravo Shot tests. It supported a CIA investigation of Japanese citizens' political beliefs, as requested by the AEC Chair. And the US and Japanese governments tried to claim the matter, after negotiation of a one-time ex gratia payment, was "fully settled."

For the suffering people, this issue was far from fully settled. From fishermen to residents of Marshall Islands to US personnel, many people were exposed to radioactive fallout from US nuclear tests at Bikini Atoll in 1954. Through the Bikini Incident, people started to know the danger of radioactive fallout, an idea that confirmed—or at least named—the ongoing health problems among survivors of the atomic bombs ostensibly dropped to end the second World War. Thus, the incident became, as discussed in Ran Zwigenberg's chapter in this volume, a turning point in the nascent anti-nuclear movement. At the same time, the arrangement of the "full settlement" allowed both the US and Japanese governments to avoid dealing with the enduring aftermath of radiation exposure in human bodies, to plow ahead with nuclear development and testing without acknowledging their victims. The fact that it was based on scientists' assertions downplaying the gravity of radiation contamination in fish—the major source of fears of radiation in Japan at the time—was an important and insidious step. A not-so-well-known scientific conference, held in Tokyo in late 1954, was critically important to the politics of dealing with the Lucky Dragon/Bikini Incident and the rise of anti-nuclear sentiment.

On February 15, 1955, the AEC issued its first statement concerning the "Bravo Shot." It made no reference to the suffering of people exposed to radioactive fallout, though it obliquely acknowledged the effects of the "ashes of death," or radioactive fallout resulting from a test that involved a surface or near-surface explosion of a thermonuclear weapon. This was followed by an erroneous declaration: "In an in-the air explosion where the fireball does not touch Earth's surface, by the time it has reached Earth's surface, the majority its radioactivity has been dissipated harmlessly in the atmosphere, and the residual contamination is widely dispersed." The AEC presented escaping from the exposure as a feasible proposition: "In an area of heavy fallout the greatest radiological hazard is that of exposure to external radiation, which can be greatly reduced by simple precautionary measures. Exposure can be reduced by taking shelter and by simple decontamination measures."[22]

This 1955 statement confirmed the US stance: it denied the impact of internal exposure to radiation from the Bravo tests or from the residual radiation of the atomic bombs dropped in Hiroshima and Nagasaki. But the Japanese government took a similar stance: neither its laws nor its systems recognised fallout's impacts on the bombs' survivors. As the ensuing six decades have brought more research on fallout, residual radiation and internal exposure of radiation, as scientists have worked to identify the complex ways radiation operates within and damages human bodies, it remains challenging to recognise these realities in efforts aimed at victim relief. Why?

Rather than simply offer direct compensation to those who have suffered, the Japanese government has used the precedent of the "full settlement" in the Bikini Incident to continue to deny history. Those people who suffered black rain from the atomic bomb must sue for recognition as *hibakusha* (see Sato, this volume). Those who suffered the accrual of residual radiation within their bodies must sue for recognition that their sicknesses come from the atomic bomb. Fishermen, victims who worked near Bikini Atoll during the US testing, must attest that their symptoms and sicknesses look like those suffered by the Lucky

216   *Hiroko Takahashi*

Dragon No. 5's crew; on May 9, 2016, they brought suit against the Japanese government at Kochi District Court, and on July 20, 2018, the plaintiffs' appeal was rejected. Even then, the documents on the Bikini Incident were kept classified.

Though the Japanese government claimed the classification was an oversight, it is clear that it took a FOIA request for these documents to be declassified. Even after it declassified the documents, they were moved to the Archives of Foreign Ministry, where I was told, in April 2020, that researchers were not allowed to view the documents until they had been fully screened—a process that would take a year. Only after a request was made by the Chair of the Japanese Diet Affairs committee of the National Democratic Party Kazuhiro Haraguchi, were these made viewable in June. Without his request, the formally declassified documents would have remained functionally classified.

Policy sets precedent. The Japanese decisions to ignore or under-estimate data about radiation and human suffering after WWII, after the Bikini Incident, and even in response to Chernobyl were abundantly evident by the time of the Fukushima disaster in 2011.

The International Commission on Radiological Protection (ICRP) set a 2007 recommendation for the return of residents to radiation contaminated areas at 20mSv per year, and it remains the current standard applied by the Japanese government, though it was not a law when the disaster occurred in March 2011. The standard of 20mSv seems to have been slipped in during the chaotic days following the Fukushima disaster, and the number itself seems to have been based on the experience of Chernobyl—that is, the number was set specifically to reduce the number of government-mandated refugees and, accordingly, limit the burden of compensation payments owed by government or the plant's operator, Tokyo Electric Power Company (TEPCO). It was then debated over the course of 20 meetings (March 13, 2009–January 12, 2011) of the Basic Policy Committee of the Radiation Council of the Ministry of Education, Culture, Sports, Science and Technology. TEPCO retained representation on this committee, meaning that parties dedicated to promoting nuclear power were included in Japan's deliberations over setting standards for radiological protection. It appears to be a clear conflict of interest.

The committee's second interim report proposed the following on "reference levels for public radiological exposure during an emergency":

> With regard to reference levels for the public in an emergency, we deem that the dose proposed by the ICRP (20-100mSv) is an appropriate index for formulating comprehensive strategy as to whether emergency protection measures need to be adopted or not, in optimizing protection, and determining the need for further protection measures. Accordingly, Japan should consider this index

Continuing nuclear tests 217

in establishing plans for protection activity. Standards pertaining to particular protection measures proposed to date in our country (sheltering in place, evacuation, the administration of potassium iodide) can continue to be deemed applicable in making initial determinations as to whether emergency protection measures in emergency should be taken or not.

Even though the recommendations of ICRP 2007 were not reflected in Japanese laws and regulations at the time, this reference level was applied immediately after the Fukushima disaster in 2011.

The adoption of the 20mSv per year standard prompted strong objections. On April 29, 2011, a special advisor to the cabinet who was a professor at Tokyo University and a member of the Basic Policy Committee of the Radiation Council stepped down, stating:

> The application of this standard to infants, young children, and elementary school students is something I find difficult to accept not only from an academic point of view but from the point of view of my own humanity. I am resigning my post as special advisor to the cabinet.

Yasuo Nakagawa, a specialist on the health effects of radiation exposure, writes, "The ICRP imposes radiation exposure on the people and delivers economic and political benefits to the nuclear industry and the ruling class" (Nakagawa, 2011: pp. 89–90). Far from being a charitable organisation working to benefit the public, the ICRP appears to scholars like Nakagawa to be an organisation seeking to permanently impose an even more lenient standard for radiation exposure (10mSv per year) in countries around the world in service of promoting the spread of the nuclear power industry.

Those who experienced the Fukushima disaster were robbed of the rights guaranteed to them under the Japanese Constitution and the Universal Declaration of Human Rights. They were denied "the right to live in peace, free from fear and want." Those who fled from the contaminated areas and were driven from refugee housing rather than receiving compensation and support found that "the right to life, liberty and security of person" has been violated, "the right to an effective remedy" threatened, and "the right to freedom of movement and residence" robbed. To apply the ICRP's nuclear-industry oriented standards to the human lives of the public is, surely, a violation of both documents—and humanity itself.

Notes

1 Personal conversation with the author, December 12, 2019, at the Takamatsu High Court. The author has worked with the plaintiff group by providing a written statement on the historical background of the "full

218 *Hiroko Takahashi*

settlement" of the Bikini Incident, as well as relevant primary documents such as "Alison-Shigemitsu conference," which were classified until the author's October 2018 FOIA request. While the plaintiffs' group requested that the author serve as a witness as a historian, the court rejected it on the grounds that the author was not in attendance at the 1954 negotiations.

2 On September 5, 1945, Wilfred Burchett, a correspondent for the *Daily Express*, reported from Hiroshima: "People are still dying, mysteriously and horribly—people who were uninjured in the cataclysm—from an unknown something which I can only describe as the atomic plague." This was one of the few accounts that directly reported on the bombed areas, as the US Occupation banned journalists from visiting Hiroshima and Nagasaki.

3 Website of Pugwash Conferences on Science and World Affairs. Available at: https://pugwash.org/1955/07/09/statement-manifesto/ [Accessed June 27, 2021].

4 Document No.1820: From Frank Wisner to Lewis Strauss, April 29, 1954, Strauss Papers, Herbert Hoover Presidential Library in *The Declassified Documents Catalogue* (1998). Woodbridge, CT: Research Publications. The documents consist of a letter dated April 29, 1954, from the CIA's Frank Wisner, in charge of covert operations, to Strauss, followed by a three-page summary of the investigation into the Lucky Dragon No. 5, and finally a reply from Strauss to Wisner, dated May 7.

5 Document 1820: Wisner to Strauss, 29 Apr. 1954, Strauss Papers, Herbert Hoover Presidential Library in The Declassified Documents Catalogue (1998). Woodbridge, CT: Research Publications.

6 The summary report says:

"US officials did not have the opportunity to check the ship's log, track charts, navigation records, accuracy of navigational instruments, or competency of the ship's navigator, we have not been able to make an estimate of its actual location. However, in addition to the Japanese Government's public announcement that the ship was outside the danger zone, [Sensitive Information Deleted]"

7 Website of US National Archives, Records of US Foreign Assistance Agencies (RG 469) Available at: https://www.archives.gov/research/foreign-policy/related-records/rg-469 [Accessed June 28, 2021].

8 Delegates from the United States were as follows: Dr. Paul B. Pearson, Chief of Biology Branch, Division of Biology and Medicine, US Atomic Energy Commission; Mr. Morse Salisbury, Director of Information Services, US Atomic Energy Commission; Dr. Walter D. Claus, Chief of Biophysics Branch, Division of Biology and Medicine, US Atomic Energy Commission; Dr. Merrill Eisenbud, Director of the Health and Safety Laboratory of the US Atomic Energy Commission's Operation Office in New York City; Dr. W. R. Boss, Physiologist, Division of Biology and Medicine, US Atomic Energy Commission; Dr. John H. Harley, Chief of the Analytical Branch of the Health and Safety Laboratory of the US Atomic Energy Commission's Operation Office in New York City; Dr. Sterling B. Hendricks, Head of the Soil and Water Conservation Branch of the US Department of Agriculture.

9 Delegates from Japan were as follows: Yoshio Hiyama, Professor, Fisheries Institute, Faculty of Agriculture, Tokyo University; Kenjiro Kimura, Professor of Inorganic Chemistry and Dean, Faculty of Science, Tokyo University; Yasuo Miyake, Chief, Geochemical Laboratory, Meteorological Research Institute; Masanori Nakaizumi, Professor and Head of Radiology

Continuing nuclear tests 219

and Chief, Department of Radiology, Medical School, Tokyo University; Eizo Tajima, Professor of Physics, St. Paul's University, Toshima-ku, Tokyo; Fumio Yamazaki, Chief, Applied Nuclear Physics Laboratory, Scientific Research Institute; and others.

10 Morse Salisbury, Director Division of Information Service, AEC, Meeting with Ambassador Allison on Japanese-American Scientist Meeting in Japan, November 2, 1954. File: OCB 091. Japan (File #2) (8)[October 1954-March 1955], White House Office: National Security Council Staff: Papers, Operation Coordinating Board (OCB) Central File Series, The Eisenhower Presidential Library, Abilene, KS.

11 From Paul B. Person to Dr. John C. Bugher, Director, Division of Biology and Medicine, Atomic Energy Commission, Washington, DC, November 1, 1954. File: Organization & Management Japanese-American Conference 1954, Series Title: Division of Biology and Medicine, Radiation Exposure ("Special Case") Inclusive Date: 1945-1962, Entry 316-78-0003 Box 2, Records of Atomic Energy Commission, Record Group 326, National Archives at College Park, College Park, MD.

12 "Japanese-US Scientists Discuss Radiobiology," November 16, 1954. *Mainichi Shimbun.*

13 From Paul B. Pearson to Dr. John C. Bugher, Director, Division of Biology and Medicine, Atomic Energy Commission, Washington, DC, November 10, 1954. File: Organization & Management Japanese-American Conference 1954, Series Title: Division of Biology and Medicine, Radiation Exposure ("Special Case") Inclusive Date: 1945-1962, Entry 316-78-0003 Box 2, Records of Atomic Energy Commission, Record Group 326, National Archives at College Park, College Park, MD.

14 From American Embassy, Tokyo, Japan, to Dr. John C. Bugher, Director, Division of Biology and Medicine, Washington, DC, December 27, 1954. File: Organization & Management Japanese-American Conference 1954, Series Title: Division of Biology and Medicine, Radiation Exposure ("Special Case") Inclusive Date: 1945-1962, Entry 316-78-0003 Box 2, Records of Atomic Energy Commission, Record Group 326, National Archives at College Park, College Park, MD.

15 The OCB consisted of

"(1) the Under Secretary of State, who ... shall be the chairman of the Board, (2) the Deputy Secretary of Defense, who shall represent the Secretary of Defense, (3) the Director of the Foreign Operation Administration, (4) the Director of Central Intelligence, and (5) a representative of the President to be designated by the President"

This quote from Executive Order 10483 by the President available at: https://www.presidency.ucsb.edu/documents/executive-order-10483-establishing-the-operations-coordinating-board [Accessed June 27, 2021].

16 From Harold E. Stassen, Foreign Operation Administration, to Mr. Elmer B. Staats, Executive Officer, Operation Coordinating Board, November 2, 1954. File: OCB 091. Japan (File #2)(8) [October 1954–March 1955], White House Office: National Security Council Staff: Papers, Operations Coordinating Board (OCB) Central File Series, The Eisenhower Presidential Library, Abilene, KS.

17 Documents on Alison and Shigemitsu Meeting in December 27, 1954, Japanese Foreign Ministry. This document was declassified by request of the author on

220 *Hiroko Takahashi*

October 4, 2018（１９５４年１２月２７日、アリソン・重光会談文書、秘密指定解除・外交記録・情報公開室（２０１８年１０月4日）See Figure 10.1.
18 Shigemitsu was Foreign Minister of the wartime administration of Hideki Tojo, also a Class-A criminal.
19 From U.S. Embassy of Tokyo to Secretary of States, December 27, 1954. File: Japan General 1951-54, Division of Biology and Medicine, Entry 326-73 Box 12, Records of Atomic Energy Commission, Record Group 326, National Archives at College Park, College Park, MD. By FOIA request, this document was declassified in July 2014.
20 From Tokyo to Department of State January 3, 1955 in Atomic Energy Commission Compensation to the Japanese Government, Note by the Secretary, US DOE Archives.
21 Letter from William C. Noville, Manager of Tuna Research Foundation, Tokyo Branch, to Dr. Willis R. Boss, Division of Biology and Medicine, Atomic Energy Commission, on January 5, 1955. File: Organization & Management Japanese-American Conference 1954, Series Title: Division of Biology and Medicine, Radiation Exposure ("Special Case") Inclusive Date: 1945-1962, Entry 316-78-0003 Box 2, Records of Atomic Energy Commission, Record Group 326, National Archives at College Park, College Park, MD.
22 Statement by Lewis L. Strauss, Chairman, United States Atomic Energy Commission, February 15, 1955; Press Releases Issued by AEC Headquarters, 1947-1975, File No.598, Records of Atomic Energy Commission, Record Group 326, National Archives at College Park, College Park, MD.

References

Boudia, S. (2007). Global Regulation: Controlling and Accepting Radioactivity Risks. *History and Technology*, 23(4), pp. 389–406.

Boyer, P. (1994). *By the Bomb's Early Light: American Thought and Culture at the Dawn of the Atomic Age.* Chapel Hill, NC: University of North Carolina Press.

Hacker, B. (1994). *Elements of Controversy: The Atomic Energy Commission and Radiation Safety in Nuclear Weapons Testing, 1947–1974.* Berkeley, CA: University of California Press.

Higuchi, T. (2020). *Political Fallout: Nuclear Weapons Testing and the Making of a Global Environmental Crisis.* Stanford, CA: Stanford University Press.

Nakagawa, Y. (2011). *Zoho Hoshasen Hibaku no Rekishi: Amerika Genbaku Kaihatsu kara Fukshima Genpatsu Jiko made [A History of Radiation Exposure: From the Development of the Atomic Bombs by the US to the Fukushima Nuclear Power Plant Disaster].* Tokyo: Akashi-Shorten.

Nakao, M., Yamazaki, M., Higuchi, T., and Kurihara, T. (2015). *Special Exhibition of Tokyo Tech Museum and Archives: Scientist Yasushi Nishiwaki in the Nuclear Age.* Tokyo: Tokyo Tech Museum and Archives.

Sakamoto, K. (1994). Kakuheiki to Nichibeikankei: Bikini Jiken no Gaikosyori. *Nenpo Kindai Nihonkenkyu, .* [Nuclear Weapons and US-Japan Relation: Diplomatic Settlement of Bikini-incident, *Annual Report of Modern Japanese Studies*]. Tokyo: Yamakawashuppansha.

Takahashi, H. (2009). One Minute after the Detonation of the Atomic Bomb: The Erased Effects of Residual Radiation. *Historia Scientiarum*, 19(2), pp. 146–159.

Takahashi, H. (2012). *Shintei Zohoban: Fuin sareta Hiroshima Nagasaki [Classified Hiroshima and Nagasaki].* Tokyo: Gaifusha.

Takahashi, H. (2021). Daisansho Intokusareta Bikini Suibakuiikken Hibakusha [Concealed Hibakusha who were Exposed to the Hydrogen Bomb Test at Bikini Atoll]. In: Y. Wakao and E. Kido, eds., *Kaku to Hoshasen no Gendaishi* [Contemporary History of Nuclear and Radiation Exposure]. Kyoto: Showa-do.

Winkler, A. (1993). *Life Under a Cloud: American Anxiety about the Atom.* Oxford: Oxford University Press.

Yamashita, M. (2012). *Kakunoumino Shogen* [Testimony of the Nuclear Ocean]. Tokyo: Shin-nihon-shuppansha.

11 The dystopic Pieta: Chernobyl survivors and neoliberalism's lasting judgments

Kate Brown

The scene plays over and over in a timeless loop. The camera alights around a hospital, taking in the crowded ward, shabby curtains, broken pipes and tired nurses in starched white, working in what the narrator calls "primitive conditions." The photographers' pitiless stare follows the contours of disorder from architecture to human biology. The lens focuses on the twisted limbs of a toddler, pans to the flopping head of a hydrocephalic baby and centers on a beautiful boy flat on a sheet, listless and leukemic. A girl turns from the videographer to the wall to imagine herself somewhere else. Mothers next to the little cots knead their hands helplessly and hold back tears.[1] This is filmmaking at its most brutal.

It must have taken courage to allow the photographers to turn the camera on your child. The mothers refer to their children's infirmity as a third party in the room. Some children, the narrator says, are dying. The mothers hold them and rock them. The camera frames the figure of mother and child in a dystopic Pietà, a display that presents their bodies to the cameras in hopes of salvation, if not for them, then for humanity. In hopes that this nightmare might end.

The image of the Chernobyl child is one of the most lasting cultural artifacts of the disaster. After Soviet medicine failed them, after foreign experts turned their backs, survivors staged their children's bodies as sites of pollution and disease in a desperate, last-ditch effort to be seen as worthy of care. Trying to win the attention of audiences abroad, they presented a *tableau vivant* of bodies in pain.[2]

Documentaries such as *Chernobyl Heart* and *Children of Chernobyl* appealed to global, particularly Western audiences, to donate to Chernobyl children's funds. The more needy and helpless post-Soviet medicine appeared, the more money the charities believed they might generate. The strategy had unfortunate consequences. Emphasising helplessness compounded the assumption of Western superiority and former Soviet citizens' humiliation and degradation. In a vicious circle, the more Ukrainians and Belarusians made a case for aid, the more they appeared to be grasping, inferior and devious.

DOI: 10.4324/9781003227472-11

The dystopic Pieta   223

By presenting the nation in need, the filmmakers walked right into the buzz saw of Westerners' arguments about failed Soviet medicine and the alleged graft and incompetency of the socialist system. Critics charged that Ukrainians and Belarusians pushed their children in front of cameras to rattle the cup for international aid. They claimed they used any sick child as a lure to snag handouts. As Chernobyl children's programs multiplied, survivors' alleged addiction to welfare became the headline-grabbing problem, not radiation and the public health disaster. I find that to be an amazing misrepresentation.

As long as anyone could remember, farmers of the Chernobyl territories had met almost every need with their own labor—plowing, pumping, sawing, hauling, sowing, weeding, canning, milking and healing. The accident took away villagers' economic independence and turned them into supplicants. Yet, when they requested shipments of clean food, they were depicted as beggars. When they complained of health problems, they were "radio-phobic." If they kept farming to feed themselves, critics called them "nuclear fatalists" who refused to protect their families from danger.[3]

Cost-benefit analysis

For many foreign consultants, the antidote was clear. "Shock therapy" would fix both the economy and the psychological problems that allegedly plagued the lost and passive Soviet people. That's right: they dished up medical metaphors in place of medical aid. Following this train of thought, International Atomic Energy Agency (IAEA) officials insisted that relocating people from Chernobyl's contaminated lands was not a question of health but of economics.[4] They hired a British decision-making expert, Simon French, to consult with high-placed leaders, brainstorming over how to once and for all conclude the Chernobyl event. In Minsk, French pulled out an easel and gave a lesson on capitalist-style cost-benefit analysis. To the Belarusians' astonishment, everything could be assigned an absolute value in actuarial science—disease, risk, safety, even human lives (Boudia, 2014). French explained that, at each level of exposure, models could predict a numerical outcome. At a lifetime threshold radiation dose of 70 mSv (the level Ukrainian and Belarusian leaders recommended, breaking with the Moscow-designated 350 mSv lifetime dose), he computed using charts from the Japanese Life Span Study that they would save 240 people from getting cancer. If they elected the higher threshold of 350 mSv, the nation would be spared 600 cancers.

But, French hastened to remind his audience, if leaders lowered the permissible dose, more people would have to move—hundreds of thousands more.[5] In a flurry of calculations, French ran the numbers weighing protection against risk. With each lowered Sievert and every beneficial step toward safety, the price tag rose. Resettling people to comply with the maximum dose set by Ukrainian and Belarusian

224 Kate Brown

officials, French calculated, would amount to a total cost of over forty billion rubles. Where would they get that money? The state coffers were empty. Raising taxes was unpopular, to say the least. It was a grim trade-off.

French's lesson for Soviet leaders was that risk—in this case, in the form of man-made radioactivity—is inevitable and natural and needs to be brokered like anything else through the medium of capital (Langston, 2017: 181). The idea that life could be reduced to line items, to revenue coming in and expenses going out, was so incendiary that Belarusian leaders asked that the meeting be kept secret.[6]

In the neoliberal climate of the end of the Cold War, amid Chernobyl survivors' credible claims that they and their children were ill as a result of fallout, charities became the chief vehicle to deliver an extremely curtailed disaster relief. As I have written elsewhere, a grim picture of a public health emergency can be distilled from the Soviet-era Ministry of Health archives of Belarus and Ukraine. As the Soviet Union fell apart, international experts in radiation medicine, largely from UN agencies, took over managing scientific assessments of the Chernobyl disaster, deploying a carefully managed and blinkered science ill-attuned to human suffering (Brown, 2017; 2019).

Nuclear liabilities

Why were credentialed consultants, employees of UN agencies and representatives of Western nuclear agencies eager to help Soviet leaders minimise the health and environmental impacts of the Chernobyl disaster? For decades, propagandists in the West had been quick to trumpet Soviet accidents, including technological and scientific mishaps, as the inevitable result of a failed communist system. The first half of the 1980s was especially tense. US President Ronald Reagan won votes by exaggerating the Soviet military and ideological threat. The Chernobyl accident on April 26, 1986 came at just the right moment to become a case study of conflict between socialist and capitalist countries.

At first, the Cold War script played out predictably. With Soviet leaders reluctant to share information about the accident, American scientists used their own monitoring system to give an initial assessment that Chernobyl had emitted more radioactivity than *hundreds* of atmospheric tests. The blown fuel rods in the reactor were, in the dramatic words of Dr. Herbert Kouts of Brookhaven Lab, "like 1,600 howitzers pointed at the sky."[7] A pair of UN consultants predicted that 24,000 people would die of cancers resulting from Chernobyl exposures.[8] Over the summer of 1986, these scandalous figures were widely disbursed by western media to European and North American audiences growing increasingly wary of nuclear projects, military or civilian. A few weeks after the accident, IAEA director Hans Blix told his board of directors

The dystopic Pieta   225

that if another accident were to occur, "I fear the general public will no longer believe any contention that the risk of a severe accident was so small as to be almost negligible."[9] Recognising the political stakes of these dire warnings, Western officials radically dialed down their predictions. There would be about 5,100 cancers, UNSCEAR director Dan Beninson corrected himself—too few, really, to be detectable.[10]

Within three months of the accident, Western specialists had fallen into a rare and seamless accord with Soviet scientists on Chernobyl projections. The disaster could even be useful. Morris Rosen, deputy director of the IAEA, asserted cheerfully in August 1986 that "Chernobyl shows us that even in a catastrophic accident, we are not talking about unreasonable deaths."[11] Again, we must ask, why would Western experts reverse themselves and rush to defend the Soviet position that Chernobyl damage would be marginal?

Certain reasons spring to mind. The IAEA's mission included promoting peaceful uses of nuclear energy. Political leaders in Europe and the United States had committed to expensive nuclear reactor projects and feared an anxious public shutting them down. There were other problems, too, in the late 1980s and early 1990s that drove the unusual comity between the Soviet and Western military nuclear establishments.

No nuclear disaster is well-timed, but Chernobyl came at an especially poor moment for the political and technocratic elite promoting nuclear power and nuclear security in the United States and Europe. A series of lawsuits were underway, challenging the long-standing US government position that the testing and production of nuclear weapons on American soil had done no harm to either servicemen or the American public. In the 1980s, plaintiffs were lining up to sue contractors of the federal government for their exposures to manmade radioactivity in unauthorised, secret medical tests, emissions from weapons factories and the detonation of bombs at proving grounds. US government officials had a particular problem for two reasons. Only the Soviets rivaled the Americans in the volume of weapons produced and tested during the Cold War. Soviets blew up a few bombs in the Urals and Siberia but detonated most nuclear weapons on their polar and Kazakh peripheries. British and French military leaders chose remote sites in colonial holdings—Australia, Algeria and the South Pacific—for their tests. But the Americans, in addition to using their Pacific proving ground, had taken the unusual step of creating a nuclear test site in the American heartland of Nevada. They also blew up underground bombs that belched radioactivity from crevices in Mississippi and Alaska (Kohlhoff, 2002).

It was a risky move to turn to the continental United States to explode nuclear weapons. The decision was contentious at the time, opposed originally by David Lilienthal, head of the Atomic Energy Commission. Lewis Strauss, the second AEC commissioner also rejected the Nevada Test Site, at first.[7] High-level AEC officials had access to classified

226 *Kate Brown*

reports that showed that after the Trinity test in July 1945, large areas of New Mexico had been blanketed with fallout posing "a very serious hazard." By 1947, local health care officials provided radiation safety experts working for the nuclear testing program with charts confirming a sharp rise in infant deaths downwind of the test site in the months that followed Trinity (Tucker and Alvarez, 2019).

Nonetheless, commissioners finally justified turning Nevada's Yucca Flats into a test site because of the pressures of the Korean War and the race to test features of the hydrogen bomb. At the Los Alamos meeting dedicated to the selection of a new site, Enrico Fermi himself summed up the necessary precautions: the public should be warned about the testing and told to stay indoors, take showers and engage in other precautions to minimise fallout risk (Fradkin, 1989). That advice was not followed. People living near the Nevada Test Site (NTS) were not notified fallout coming their way until the sickly pinkish-gray clouds were upon them (Ball, 1986). Howard Ball, Peter Fradkin and Carole Gallagher have documented the experiences of ranchers, farmers, and townspeople living in Utah and Nevada, near the NTS (Fradkin, 1989; Ball, 1986; Gallagher, 1993). They show that while AEC personnel dismissed the claims of Utah ranchers, for instance, they had in hand classified data from tests in the Marshall Islands showing how blasts had stripped animals, fish and vegetation from Bikini Island. After recording extremely high levels of radioactivity, they moved Marshall Islanders from under clouds emanating 500 rads (a lethal dose for 50% exposed) for over 5,000 square miles.[12] The bombs, they knew, were impressive killing machines. When a handful of scientists backed up NTS-proximal publics on the dangers of fallout, Nevada senator George Malone called the scientists unqualified and claimed that they were spreading "scare" stories as part of a communist plot to get ahead in the Cold War (Fradkin, 1989).

Histories of fallout from the NTS rarely include the fact that the desert territories surrounding the NTS were, though close to the bomb blasts, not necessarily exposed to the bulk of the radiation emitted. As high-flying clouds winged away from Tonopah and Yucca Flats, precipitation brought fallout raining down along the belt between humid and dry climates of the continental US. That is, proximity to ground zero mattered little in the dissemination of radiation risk. In 1951, after a relatively low-yield test called Shot Simon in Nevada, an AEC reporter noted, "daily large amounts of radioactive dust fell out over about half the United States." Thirty-six hours later, radiation counters sounded alarms at Rensselaer Polytech in upstate New York. A UCLA monitor tracked Shot Smoky fallout to Rock Springs, Wyoming, where he found a hot spot that emerged after rainfall. He returned a year later and found strontium-90 in the bone marrow of rabbits at levels that equaled that found in rabbits at the Nevada proving ground. The discovery, "shook them up," Kermit Larsen remembered (Fradkin, 1989).

The dystopic Pieta   227

Despite these early warnings, bomb designers blasted away. Estimated doses in Tennessee were nearly as high as those in Utah and Arizona, near ground zero.[13] US Weather Bureau maps showed that 40% of Nevada fallout in the late 1950s passed over western Minnesota. Fallout from Plumbob skated across Minnesota 14 times as plumes from the blast split, then split again. The AEC recorded levels of Plumbob radioactivity in South Dakotan soils three times higher than in St. George, Utah, a town normally referred to as the epicenter of NTS fallout.[14] A thousand miles from the test site, in 1957, Minnesota farmer Joe Sauter noticed a strange, burned-out patch of clover as he watched his sheep mysteriously die, all together (Honicker, 1987). Milk from central North Dakota in the 1950s had the country's highest concentrations of bone-seeking strontium-90, while samples of wheat in Minnesota revealed the highest levels of strontium-90 in the US staple grain in 1959.[15] When rain fell in hard downpours, hot spots splashed across the Great Plains like a Jackson Pollock painting. Unnervingly, the most agriculturally productive territories in the United States were in the direct line of fire.

Scientists broke ranks, attempting to alert the nation to this problem. At the University of Minnesota, William Caster, trained in radiation biology, studied the effects of ionising radiation on the human heart and other organs. With AEC scientist Harold Knapp, Caster pointed out that the AEC had poorly calculated the absorption of strontium-90 in humans. The AEC, the sole funder of radiation-related research in the States, responded by calling Caster's department chair in Minnesota and telling them he need no longer apply for AEC grants (Honicker, 1987: 70–79). Knapp was asked to leave his job at the AEC after he questioned numbers generated by Gordon Dunning, in charge of the AEC's Division of Biology and Medicine. Scientists who monitored fallout within the AEC and the US Public Health Service learned to "confine their protests to memos for the files" (Fradkin, 1989: 182).

Despite the many complaints, AEC officials were in deep and there was no going back. By 1953, the federal government had invested $20 million in the NTS. With the large investment, even AEC and Army officials once dubious about continental testing were committed to pursuing the program. They engaged in cost-benefit calculations to rationalise this decision and many more. Taking measures to reduce radioactive emissions, for instance, would be "prohibitive" especially when weighed against the "benefits" of national defense. In the new equations, the balance of decisions was no longer whether to test in the continental United States or the colonised Pacific. Rather, Americans were asked to endure a bit of radioactive fallout (usually equated in press releases to x-rays and background radioactivity) in exchange for liberty and freedom. Willard Libby in 1957 spoke of weighing the "very small and rigidly controlled risk of radiation fallout" against "the risk of annihilation" (Ball, 1986: 41). Who could argue with that?

228   *Kate Brown*

Having to justify hazardous practices, US government officials used distance and containment, probabilities and estimates to assure Americans they were safe. A 1955 AEC pamphlet announced with almost blithe confidence: "fallout does not constitute a serious hazard to any living thing outside the test site." Strauss elaborated, "the hazard has been successfully confined to the controlled area of the test site" (Fradkin, 1989: 119). When miners with Geiger counters proved those statements to be false, the AEC's Dunning admitted that perhaps *some* fallout exceeded the boundaries of the test site. He did not report levels of radioactivity as counters detected them. Instead, AEC scientists first made calculations of doses to citizens that included a lot of estimates and probabilities. High-dose estimates for specific "hot spots" were hidden by averaging smaller populations receiving high doses with larger populations receiving lower doses. In Dunning's estimate of doses for seven years of testing, he improbably provided a number that was lower than that of a single shot (Fradkin, 1989). Low dose estimates were immeasurably helpful for public relations, because they could be favorably compared to an annual x-ray or background radioactivity to assure the public they were not endangered by nuclear tests.

Determining the spread and impact of fallout was assigned to a bewilderingly broad spectrum of US governmental agencies. Initially, the US Air Force was given the job of monitoring fallout from tests using planes equipped with air filters, while the AEC Nevada office recorded levels at and near the test site. These efforts, the AEC admitted in 1954, were meager.[16] As the press picked up on stories of exposure from US tests, the AEC was forced to do more. The US Department of Agriculture (USDA) and the AEC's Health and Safety Lab (HASL) began testing milk and soil in a handful of places in 1953, but worried about the fox guarding the hen house, the US Public Health Service assumed responsibility for offsite monitoring the next year.[17]

At first, they sampled widely, following the winds gusting with radioactive fallout. Investigators in 1957 recorded 42 mCi of strontium-90 per square mile in Mandan, North Dakota. Monitors detected radioactivity in milk in 1959 in Georgia, Texas, Illinois, Ohio, North Dakota, New York, California, Utah, Washington and Missouri. Public Health monitors found radioactive iodine in milk not just after weapons tests in Nevada, but from the Pacific and Soviet tests in Kazakhstan in 1956. Cows and sheep in Oregon, Ohio and Pennsylvania all had measurable levels of radioactivity. The animals' bodies, the researchers noted, worked like biological dosimeters (Wolff, 1957).

Public Health Service monitoring enflamed fears, especially when, in 1957, monthly tests from five US cities revealed milk lined with strontium-90 (Smith-Howard, 2017). In 1957, Edward Lewis, a Caltech biology professor, published an article in *Science* connecting fallout with a heightened potential for leukemia cases. He postulated a very low

The dystopic Pieta 229

threshold—or no threshold at all—for which radiation exposure could trigger the disease (Creager, 2015). In the same year, former Brookhaven employee Lyle Borst complained that the continental test site, the NTS, did not follow even basic safety measures to protect employees at nuclear sites. "In my experience, we have always removed pregnant women from contact with radiation." Writing from Long Island, he begged AEC officials to consider long-term impacts: "When I find contamination on my children the equivalent of any contamination I have ever received in 18 years of nuclear work, I cannot consider it inconsequential nor trivial" (Fradkin, 1989: 105). Despite these concerns, public agencies monitored food and water sources feebly and at a dwindling rate into the 1960s (Tarkalson, 1986: 16).[18]

While public monitoring operations kept up a calm facade, military agencies followed radioactive fallout in classified records. Project Gabriel, started in 1949 and updated in 1952, attempted to assess the long-range effects of fallout. Project Sunshine, run out of the Rand Institute from 1953, sought to trace the pathways and behavior of strontium-90 through the environment, up the food chain, and into human bodies (Tarkalson, 1986). The AEC set up Project Aureole to study the short-term, closed-in effects of nuclear testing; its data appears to still be classified (Bruno, 2003).

At the time the NTS was developed, the scientific community already knew that radiation exposure caused superficial injuries, leukemia, cancers, genetic defects, impaired fertility, cataracts, obesity and a shortened lifespan. What they did not yet know was how radioactivity caused these health problems, nor whether doses were cumulative. The most spectacular and clear cases (which were still at the time disputed) were the radium dial workers and Japanese bomb survivors who had received high radiation doses over relatively short periods. The big living experiment during the decades of global fallout was to observe how humans fare when exposed to chronic low doses of radioactivity.

Unfortunately, as the bombs fell and radioactive fallout spread across the heartland, federal agencies did little to study the effects of the manmade radioactive isotopes—it seemed they were not particularly interested in answering the longitudinal question. The Minnesota Department of Health asked the AEC for $49,000 to fund a lab to engage in systematic monitoring of farm produce from Minnesota fields (Honicker, 1987: 88). They were turned down. The National Cancer Institute undertook no studies connecting radioactivity with cancer during the Cold War. A few researchers who noticed disturbing patterns of leukemia and thyroid cancer clusters in Utah were dismissed, defunded and harassed by AEC officials.

The one major project publicly funded by US agencies (as opposed to secret studies with classified results) was the Atomic Bomb Casualty Commission's (ABCC) studies of atomic bomb survivors, organised in

230   *Kate Brown*

1947 and started in 1950. Leslie Groves, Director of the Manhattan Project, insisted that the bombs dropped on Hiroshima and Nagasaki contained no "residual radiation," later known as fallout. Groves was terrified that the expensive bombs he had helped bring into being would be banned, like chemical and biological weapons, if they were shown to have long-lasting health effects (Brodie, 2015). As a consequence, researchers on the ongoing ABCC study did not and *still* do not take radioactive fallout into account. Instead, ABCC emphasised study of the large, single gamma doses endured by Japanese survivors, while overlooking radioactive fallout that settled in soils, plants, and animals and worked its way into food streams (Neel and Schull, 1991; Lindee, 2016). The ABCC studies had another major drawback: because they began a full five years after the accident, these studies only included healthy survivors, omitting anyone who fell sick and died before 1950. US occupying forces confiscated Japanese physicists' data on radiation measurements gathered in 1945. In 1950, ABCC researchers reconstructed those measurements and started the long and checkered process of estimating bomb survivors' doses (Bruno, 2003; Lindee, 2016). The ABCC study, what later came to be known as the "gold standard" of radiation medicine, wholly ignored the most relevant issue born of global nuclear testing: fallout in ecologies and food sources. The knowledge gap would prove critical in the aftermath of Chernobyl.

Somewhat accidentally, the easy ability to trace radioactive isotopes through environments led to the emergence of ecological and environmental movements. Eugene Odum, who worked as an AEC contractor in the Marshall Islands, Puerto Rico and Panama, was inspired by following radioactive tracers in the environment to write his *Fundamentals of Ecology* (Bruno, 2003). Rachel Carson, in turn, used strontium-90 pathway studies to understand the spread of much harder to detect chemicals in the environment (Lutts, 1985). Aided by nuclear fallout, newly minted environmentalists started lawsuits pointing to health effects and chemical toxins (Sellers, 1997). That development threatened corporations that produced industrial toxins—corporations which, like the AEC, had insisted on the safety of their products and processes.

As Americans woke to the carcinogenic and hazardous toxins of the postwar era, something strange was happening in the realm of cancer research. In 1964, the National Cancer Institute abolished its Environmental Cancer Section, founded by Wilhelm Hueper, who had long been a thorn in the side of corporate chemical producers (Sellers, 1997). Robynne Mellor illuminates how the nature of US cancer research shifted in the 1950s; researchers began to emphasise lifestyle choices, such as diet, smoking, alcohol or weight, taking a neoliberal, personal responsibility turn toward individualising the causes of disease (Mellor, 2018). Researchers looked for genetic and viral causes rather than environmental sources of cancer. They spent millions seeking, but not finding, a "cancer virus" (Scheffler, 2014). In subsequent decades, they instead sought a "cancer gene." The neo-liberal turn in medicine meant redirecting funding and attention away from studies considering the environmental causes of cancer; if they could find individual or viral factors, business and government could be released from liability for the uptick in cancer clusters across the country.

The Chernobyl threat

All this history relates directly to the Chernobyl public health emergency. The paper trail of environmental contamination, the AEC's classification of information, dismissals, mistruths and harassment of scientists who broke ranks—it all existed in archival records which, at the end of the Cold War, were suddenly being declassified. That was a nightmare for the DoE, the heir to the AEC. Plaintiffs living near nuclear production sites and the Nevada and Pacific proving grounds were suing US-government indemnified contractors for millions of dollars (Ball, 1986; Johnston and Barker, 2008; Leopold, 2009; Fox, 2014; Smith-Norris, 2016; Pritikin, 2020). To head off a free-for-all of open-ended questions on the impact of the Chernobyl accident, American officials focused on damage control.

A year after the accident, in 1987, a speaker from the Department of Energy (DOE) addressed a meeting of American health physicists in suburban Maryland. During his talk, called "Radiation: The Offense and the Defense," the DOE lawyer argued that the biggest threat to the nuclear industry was not another nuclear accident, but lawsuits. Health physicists, he said, needed to be prepared to serve as expert witnesses defending US government interests in court. After the speech, attendees broke into groups for on-the-spot witness training from a Department of Justice lawyer.[19] People who would appear in court as "objective scientists" were schooled to be anything but.

Seeking to stifle a multitude of Chernobyl studies, the DOE also sent out a circular mandating that government-funded Chernobyl relief aid and research be channeled through the DOE.[20] The US Nuclear Regulatory Commission (NRC) published a study saying Chernobyl could never happen in the United States. Internally, however, one of the five NRC commissioners, James Asselstine, argued that it certainly could—and that the NRC was not prepared for it. His concerns dismissed, Asselstine left the NRC within the month.[21] At the United Nations, American delegates voted consistently to limit international investigations into Chernobyl's health effects, while, in 1988, DOE officials quietly created "Working Group 7.0" via back-channel negotiations with Soviet scientists to conduct joint studies of the Chernobyl-exposed.[22] As administrators at the National Cancer Institute put the brakes on thyroid cancer research on Utah downwinders, its researchers set to work on a Chernobyl thyroid

232 *Kate Brown*

study that took two decades to complete. Bruce Wachholz, transferred from the DOE to the NCI, was put in charge of both the Utah and Chernobyl thyroid studies.

In the early 1990s, as reports of a Chernobyl-caused pediatric thyroid epidemic were heavily disputed, US officials kept mum about their findings in the Marshall Islands. That study was still classified, most likely because the Brookhaven investigators had violated basic laws protecting human subjects in medical studies. The data, however, had shown that thyroid cancers and thyroid disease were present in 79% of exposed Marshall Islands children under age ten, many of whom also had anemia. Rongelap women exposed in the Bravo test had twice the number of stillbirths and miscarriages as unexposed women (Smith-Norris, 2016: 89–93). At the time, Marshall Islanders and downwinders of nuclear tests in Nevada were pursuing their case in US courts (Johnston and Barker, 2008), though, over decades, US officials held fast that medical examinations of the Marshall Islanders had shown "no aftermaths of fallout" and that the Islanders' "general health is satisfactory" (Smith-Norris, 2016). Closer to home, scientific administrators at the NCI and the US Public Health Service were sitting on studies indicating that, directly downwind from the NTS, children had three to seven times more cases of leukemia and thyroid cancers than other American children.[23] These were the liabilities—the known facts—that Chernobyl threatened to lay bare. The volume of spilled curies of radioactivity might only be topped by the number of dollars that would need to be spent on reparations should the fallout harms be publicly proven. Chernobyl was the disaster that, if examined too closely, could expose all other nuclear incidents to a heap of lawsuits.[24]

You can see where this is going. "A nuclear accident anywhere in the world," cancer expert Dr. Robert Gale noted, "is everywhere in the world."[25] UN officials claimed that Chernobyl was of "unprecedented dimensions," but it wasn't.[26] The US government was just one of several parties that had exposed earth-dwellers to a chronic blanketing of exposure to nuclear fallout. The total emissions from nuclear tests were a thousand times greater than emissions from Chernobyl. The Soviets, British, French, Chinese, Indians and Pakistanis also made nuclear bombs—a messy process—and blew them up, exposing people to radioactive emissions from 520 atmospheric and 1,500 underground detonations (underground tests also vented radioactivity into the atmosphere). From 1945 to 1998, military leaders exploded bombs in deserts, in polar regions, on tropical islands, underground, underwater and at high altitudes. They detonated nuclear bombs on towers and barges and suspended from balloons. Nuclear weapons tests are the primary man-made contributor of radioactive exposures to the world's population. Globally, atmospheric tests have released at least 20 billion curies of radioactive iodine alone.[27] Chernobyl accounted for just 48 million curries of I-131.[28]

The fact that three-quarters of fallout from nuclear testing landed in the Northern Hemisphere[29] was one problem with Chernobyl health studies; as Soviet researchers had shown, a generation of residents had already been exposed from nuclear testing.[30] Background levels of radioactivity and cancer rates had been on the rise in these territories for a decade before the Chernobyl acceleration.[31] By 1986, there was no longer a "natural" level of radioactivity or cancer rate to use as a benchmark.

With the Cold War in remission, officials had a hard time continuing to use "national security" as a reason to keep secrets about nuclear test emissions. Citizens learned the extent of their exposures and their governments' denials. Lawsuits mounted. So did resistance to nuclear reactors and nuclear weapons (Tompkins, 2016; Conze et al., 2017). Chernobyl was nothing short of a catastrophe for the global nuclear defense establishment.

"Mankind's greatest nuclear disaster"

But, if someone could show that Chernobyl, billed as "mankind's greatest nuclear disaster," caused only the deaths of a few score firemen and plant operators—with no other, wider health effects—all those lawsuits, uncomfortable investigations and recriminations could waft away.

And they did. In 1991, the UN General Assembly waited for the IAEA's assessment of Chernobyl damage before holding a pledge drive to raise $646 million for a large-scale epidemiological study of Chernobyl health effects and the relocation of over 200,000 people living in areas of high contamination. When the report stated the IAEA had found "no detectable Chernobyl health effects," the pledge drive netted less than 1% of its goal (under $6 million).[32] The big potential donors—the United States, Japan, Germany and the European Community—begged off, citing the IAEA report as a "factor in their reluctance to pledge."[33] The American delegation, especially, emphasised the IAEA assessment had shown conclusively that population resettlement was unnecessary.[34]

After the failed pledge drive, the UN Secretary-General created a Secretariat for Chernobyl Relief. The position would be passed around from agency to agency within the UN, with five directors appointed in five years. Chernobyl was a hot potato no one at the UN was willing to take.[35] Repeated appeals for international aid rarely raised more than a million dollars.[36] UN officials shrugged and mumbled about "donor fatigue,"[37] but it was clear that the IAEA and UNSCEAR's erroneous insistence that Chernobyl produced no health problems had strangled fund-raising. "No conclusive scientific proof of disease from Chernobyl exposure," a diplomat wrote in 1995, by which time few doubted the pediatric thyroid cancer epidemic, "led to a reluctance among the international community to offer decisive and meaningful assistance."[38] As the international community concluded that Chernobyl exposures had

234 *Kate Brown*

caused few health problems, lawsuits in the nuclear powers failed, one after the other—in the US, Great Britain, Australia, New Zealand, Russia and France, the legal cases were dismissed.

In subsequent years, post-Soviet leaders had no choice but to succumb to the rationale of cost-benefit analysis. New capitalist leaders (who were mostly former communist leaders) learned that dealing with Chernobyl was expensive and litigiously risky (Daston, 2017).[39] In the 1990s, in independent Russia, Ukraine and Belarus, subsidies for clean food and medical care dried up.[40] People slated for relocation in accordance with the 70 mSv lifetime guidelines adopted by Ukraine and Belarus received few subsidies and could not afford to move on their own. Nuclear power reactors earmarked for decommission, including the Chernobyl plant, continued to operate. Hospitals demanded hard currency for treatments that required foreign equipment or supplies, but few people had hard currency. In shops, where clean, packaged food finally appeared, customers had no money with which to buy it.

Hunger followed. This was not famine like that of the 1930s, but a gnawing, low-level malnourishment. Blow by blow, new capitalist leaders hacked away at the socialist welfare state. International consultants from the World Bank and the International Monetary Fund recommended the newly independent countries implement more austerity measures in order to qualify for loans. The leaders readily complied; foreign loans also generated personal fortunes. Dividing the wealth among themselves, these elected leaders voided the social contract (Kuzio, 2015).[41]

It follows that the 1990s were grim years for Chernobyl research. Inflation wiped out salaries and left labs in desperate need for just about everything. Most Russian scientists turned to other topics.[42] Chernobyl fell from the headlines (Kuchinskaya, 2014). Ukrainians and Belarusians kept research agendas alive but struggled alone (Petryna, 2013). Demodernisation and economic crisis were bad for health. Life expectancy spiraled downward and, with it, fertility rates.[43] People fed themselves from garden plots.[44] Young people went abroad. Rural areas depopulated. In this landscape, it became hard to distinguish the impacts of economic disaster from the impacts of nuclear catastrophe (Kasperski, 2015).

The UN helped its client states by repackaging the nuclear catastrophe. UN officials arranged for glossy brochures and articles in "up-market" publications on science and medicine.[45] They designed programs aimed at transforming Chernobyl "victims" into responsible citizens (Topçu, 2013; Boudia and Jas, 2013; Fairlie, 2016). Cut off from subsidies for clean food and medicine, residents were told they needed to learn how to "restore sustainable development" on Chernobyl farmland.[46] Colorful manuals instructed farmers how to sort hay and filter milk of radioactivity using equipment they had no money to purchase. Overworked mothers were taught painstaking new recipes to prepare radiation-free

The dystopic Pieta 235

food from contaminated produce, a sort of arduous alchemy devoid of magic (Lepicard and Hériard Dubreuil, 2001). Doctors underwent training in the latest medical technologies, which few hospitals could afford. Villagers who had no means to evaluate levels of radioactivity were told to choose whether to stay on contaminated land or go as relocation became voluntary and largely self-financed.[47] As the safety network retreated, state and international agencies shifted the burden of managing the post-accident risk society onto the shoulders of exposed residents—those with the fewest resources to do so.[48]

The defeat of the mothers with children in their arms, of doctors and scientists who tried to sound the alert about the public health disaster going on in the Chernobyl contaminated territories was the most lasting loss at the end of the Cold War. Western health physics, a science cut through with uncertainties due to its reliance on retrospective dose reconstructions and extrapolations between very different nuclear events, was adopted as the "gold standard." Belarusian and Ukrainian researchers' carefully documented records of damage in their patients' bodies from low-dose Chernobyl exposures were handily dismissed as the product of a failed and corrupt Soviet society.[49] That verdict radiated outward. Pointing to minimal deaths reported by the UN after Chernobyl, lawyers defending the US, UK, French and Russian nuclear industries won almost every lawsuit brought by atomic downwinders and veterans. *Chernobyl was the world's worst nuclear accident*, they repeated, *and only 33 people died*. The verdict was not the result of science, but the pitiable result of international relations and politics.[50]

Notes

1 *Children of Chernobyl*, directed by Clive Gordon. Aired on April 21, 1991, on Channel 4 [UK]).
2 See, for example, *Chernobyl Heart*, directed by Maryann De Leo, aired on September 9, 2004, on HBO; *Children of Chernobyl*, directed by James K. McNally in 1990 for Lethbridge (Alberta) TV. Available at: https://www.youtube.com/watch?v=Br2tDCqaVWw[Accessed June 30, 2021].
3 Sweet, B. (1999). Chernobyl's Stressful After-Effects. *IEEE Spectrum*, November 1; Rosenthal, E. (2005). Experts Find Reduced Effects of Chernobyl. *New York Times*, Section A, p. 10, September 6.
4 Lochard, J., Schneider, T., and French, S. (1992). *International Chernobyl Project—Input from the Commission of the European Communities to the Evaluation of the Relocation Policy Adopted by the Former Soviet Union.* Luxembourg: Office for Official Publications of the European Communities; Author telephone interview with an international expert in nuclear risk management, April 13, 2018.
5 Memo (1992). National Archive of the Republic of Belarus (hereafter NARB), 507/1/20, pp. 66–70.
6 IAEA Project for a Repeat Assessment of the Situation, Moscow (October 15, 1990). NARB 507/1/1, p. 33; Chernobyl—Nothing to Celebrate (1991). Green Peace Archive (GPA) 1804.

236 Kate Brown

7 Diamond, S. (1986). Reactor Fallout is Said to Match Past World Total. *New York Times*, Section A, p. 1, September 23.

8 Public Information, Nuclear Controversy, 270-N7.22.1, Box 15700, IAEA Archive, Chernobyl post review meeting.

9 Director General's Statement to the Board of Governors, May 12, 1986. IAEA Archive, Box 15717.

10 Stuart Diamond, Chernobyl's Toll in Future at Issue. (1986). *New York Times*, Section A, p. 1., August 29.

11 As quoted in Alexander Sich (1996). Truth was an early casualty. *Bulletin of the Atomic Scientists*, 52(3), p. 39.

12 Fortieth Meeting of the General Advisory Committee to the US Atomic Energy Commission (May 27–29, 1954), Washington, DC. DOE Opennet.

13 Author email correspondence with senior expert's risk assessment, specialised in radioactive dose evaluation. See also: Hoffman, O., Kocher, D., and Apostoaei, A. (2011). Beyond Dose Assessment: Using Risk with Full Disclosure of Uncertainty in Public and Scientific Communication, *Health Physics*, 101(5), pp. 591–601; and Hoffman, O., Apostoaei, A., and Thomas, B. (2002). A Perspective on Public Concerns about Exposure to Fallout from the Production and Testing of Nuclear Weapons. *Health Physics*, 82(5), pp. 736–48.

14 Springer, P. (1988). Forgotten Fallout: What is the Legacy of Radioactive Rains? *Fargo Forum*, May 1.

15 Springer, Forgotten Fallout.

16 Report on Project Gabriel, July 1954. Division of Biology and Medicine, AEC, DOE Opennet.

17 *Consideration of Three Proposals to Conduct Research on Possible Health Effects of Radiation from Nuclear Weapon Testing in Arizona, Nevada, and Utah, and Nuclear Weapon Testing and Studies Related to Health Effects: An Historical Summary: Responding to Recommendations by the Panel of Experts on the Archive of PHS Documents* (1980). DHHS, PHS, NIH, Bethesda, MD.

18 Starting in 1960, Public Health Service officials trimmed the cities down to New York, San Francisco and Chicago, but then dropped Chicago.

19 Author interview with senior expert in policy analysis involved in nuclear worker compensation legislation. See also: Takoma Park, MD (May 24, 2019). Tucker, K., and Alvarez, R. (2019). Trinity: The most significant hazard of the entire Manhattan Project. *Bulletin of the Atomic Scientists* (July 15). The attorney was Donald E. Jose, Assistant Director of the Torts Branch of the US DOJ civil division.

20 Department of Energy, Richland Operations Office, Requests for Assistance Resulting from Chernobyl, June 1, 1986, WH 423500, TFC UWSC Tom Foulds Collection, University of Washington Special Collections, Seattle, WA.

21 Chernobyl Implications Report, June 12, 1987. RG 431-01/1358, box 2, National Archives and Records Administration (NARA).

22 Progress Report, October 1993–January 1994. Chernobyl Studies Project, Working Group 7.0, DOE Opennet, UCRL-ID-110062-94-4.

23 Minutes, NCI Thyroid 131 Assessments Committee, August 24–25, 1987. National Cancer Institute (NCI), RG 43 FY 03 Box 5, part 3; *Cancer in Utah: Report No. 3, 1967–77: Utah Cancer Registry*, September 1979. Acc. no. 0331726, Nuclear Testing Archive (NTA); Joseph L. Lyon et al. (1979). Childhood Leukemias Associated with Fallout from Nuclear Testing. *New England Journal of Medicine*, 300, pp. 397–402. DOI: https://doi.org/10.105 6/NEJM197902223000804.

The dystopic Pieta   237

24 See, for example, Testimony of Dr. Rosalie Bertell, US Senate Committee on Veterans' Affairs (April 21, 1998).

25 Reuters, More Chernobyls Unavoidable, Dr. Gale Warns. *Los Angeles Times*, June 27, 1987. This came from the LA Times archive, no page number indicated. Available at: https://www.latimes.com/archives/la-xpm-1 987-06-27-mn-10881-story.html [Accessed July 2, 2021].

26 Quote from Report of the Economic and Social Council, October 29, 1990. United Nations Archive, New York (UN NY) S-1046/14/4, acc. 2001/0001.

27 Hancock, G., Tims, S., Fifield, L., and Webster, I. (2014). The Release and Persistence of Radioactive Anthropogenic Nuclides. In: C. Waters, J. Zalasiewicz, M. Williams, M. Ellis, and A. Snelling, eds., *A Stratigraphical Basis for the Anthropocene*. London: Geological Society, pp. 265–281; Cooper et al. (2003: 17); Hoffman et al., A Perspective on Public Concerns; R. H. Wyndham to Dr. S. Sella, November 15, 1973. UN NY S-0446-0106-09; Study of the Radiological Situation at the Atolls of Mururoa and Fangataufa, IAEA Board of Governors, Technical Cooperation Report for 1997, April 30, 1998. IAEA Archive, BOG, Box 33054. Report of the United Nations Scientific Committee on the Effect of Atomic Radiation to the General Assembly (2000). Available at: http://www.unscear.org/docs/reports/gareport.pdf [Accessed April 29, 2018]. On equivalency with Hiroshima bombs, see General Overview of the Effects of Nuclear Testing, CTBTO, available at: https://www.ctbto.org/nuclear-testing/the-effects-of-nuclear-testing/general-overview-of-theeffects-of-nuclear-testing/ [Accessed May 29, 2018].

28 Testimony of Owen Hoffman, September 16, 1998, National Cancer Institute's Management of Radiation Studies. Hearing before the Permanent Subcommittee on Investigations, US Senate. Washington, DC: GPO, p. 48.

29 Waters, C., et al. (2015). Can Nuclear Weapons Fallout Mark the Beginning of the Anthropocene Epoch? *Bulletin of the Atomic Scientists*, 71(3), pp. 46–57.

30 Marei, A., Barkhudaro, R., and Ia Novikova, N. (1974). *Global'nye vypadeniia Cs 137 i chelovek*. Moscow: Atomizdat.

31 "On the Work of Belarussian [BSSR] Health Ministry, 1986–1989," no earlier than March 1989, Natsionalnyi arkhiv respubliki Belarus (NARB), Minsk, Belarus 46/14/1260, pp. 1–15.

32 Anstee to Roland M. Timerbaev, November 1, 1991. World Health Organization Archive (WHO), Geneva, Switzerland, E16-180-4: 6; Brief for Secretary-General's Meeting, October 15, 1991. United Nations Archive, New York, (UN NY) S-1046/16/3.

33 International Co-operation in the Elimination of the Consequences of the Chernobyl Nuclear Power Plant Accident, May 24, 1990. UN NY S-1046/14/4; Third Meeting of the Inter-Agency Task Force on Chernobyl, September 19–23, 1991. WHO E16-445-11, p. 5; Briefing Note on the Activities Relating to Chernobyl, June 3, 1993. Department of Humanitarian Affairs (DHA), UN NY s-1082/35/6/, acc 2002/0207. Japan had previously pledged $20 million in February 1991, which became the basis for funding the IPHECA project (WHO E16-445-11, p. 3).

34 Anstee to Napalkov, January 17, 1992. WHO E16-445-11, p. 7.

35 Notes of the Secretary-General's Meeting with the Minister of Foreign Affairs of Ukraine, September 22, 1992. UN NY S-1046/14/4, acc. 2001/0001; From President Lukashenka to the Secretary-General, October 28, 1996. UN NY S-1082/46/5/ acc. 2007/0015.

36 Chernobyl: Mission to Russian Federation, Belarus, Ukraine, September 10–16, 1994. UN NY S-1082/46/5/ acc. 2007/0015; For Information on United Nations, Press Conference Chernobyl, November 30, 1995. UN NY

238   *Kate Brown*

S-1082/46/5/ acc. 2007/0015; A. M. Zlenko, A. N. Sychev, S. V. Lavrov to Mr. Boutros Boutros-Ghali, January 9, 1995. UN NY S-1082/46/5, acc. 2007/0015; Strengthening of the Coordination of Humanitarian and Disaster Relief Assistance, September 8, 1995. UN NY S-1082/46/5/ acc. 2007/0015; Strengthening of International Cooperation and Coordination of Efforts to Study, Mitigate and Minimize the Consequences of the Chernobyl Disaster, October 27, 1997 UN NY S-1092/96/5, acc. 2006/0160 Press Conference on Funding to Address Effects of Chernobyl Disaster, May 1, 1998 UN NY S-1092/96/5, acc. 2006/0160 Sergio Vieira de Mello, May 18, 1999 UN NY S-1092/96/5, acc. 2006/0160.; Note to the Secretary-General, April 23, 2001. UN NY S-1092/96/5, acc. 2006/0160.

37 Notes of the Secretary-General's meeting with the Minister of Foreign Affairs of Ukraine; Meeting of Jan Eliasson and Victor H. Batik, February 25, 1993; Meeting with Gennadi Buravkin, Belarus, March 4, 1993. WHO E16-445-11, p. 16.

38 Strengthening of the Coordination of Humanitarian and Disaster Relief Assistance, September 8, 1995. UN NY S-1082/46/5/ acc. 2007/0015.

39 Dr. I. Filyushikin, Institute of Biophysics, Moscow to Kreisel, April 27, 1993. WHO E16-3445-11: 16.

40 Protocol No. 3, Meeting of the Collegium State Committee, Belarusian Soviet Socialist Republic (BSSR), April 22, 1994. NARB 507/1/41, pp. 28–38; Yaroshinskaya, *Bol'shaia lozh'*, p. 334.

41 Maslyukov, V. (1998). A Report from Minsk. *Monthly Review*, 50(4), pp. 15–30.

42 Author interview with Russian scientist, a major protagonist of the counter-expertise on the consequences of Chernobyl, June 5, 2015, St. Petersburg.

43 Memo, no earlier than November 1993, Gosudarstvennyi arkhiv Mogilevskoi oblasti (GAMO), Mogilev, Belarus, 7/5/4156, pp. 81–94.

44 On the State of Children's Food, 1992, Tsentralnyi derzhavnyi arkhiv vyshchykh orhaniv vlady Ukrainy (TsDAVO), Kyiv, Ukraine 324/19/33, pp. 25–28.

45 Report of the Seventh Meeting of the Inter-Agency Committee for Response to Nuclear Accidents (Vienna, January 25–26, 1990), UNESCO Archive, Paris, 361.9(470) SC ENV/596/534.1, Part I.

46 Quote from Didier Louvat, Head, Waste Safety Section, IAEA, in *Commemoration of the Chernobyl Disaster: The Human Experience Twenty Years Later* (2007) [conference proceedings] (IAEA, Washington, DC, April 26, 2006), pp. 25–30.

47 Decision, December 29, 1993. GAMO 7/5/4156, pp. 78–94; Memo, no earlier than November 1993, GAMO 7/5/4156, pp. 81–94.

48 Memo, 1992. NARB 507/1/20, pp. 66–70; Sweet, Chernobyl's Stressful After-Effects.

49 Document R. 554, 1994, Conference Room Papers, United Nations Scientific Committee for Effects of Atomic Radiation Archives (UNSCEAR), Vienna.

50 For more recent, international studies that agree with the 1980s findings of Soviet researchers, see Stepanova, E., et al. (2008). Exposure from the Chernobyl Accident Had Adverse Effects on Erythrocytes, Leukocytes, and Platelets in Children in the Narodichesky Region, Ukraine: A 6-Year Follow-Up Study. *Environmental Health*, 7(1), p. 21; Sheikh Sajjadieh, M., Kuznetsova, L., Bojenko, V. (2011). Effect of Cesium Radioisotope on Humoral Immune Status in Ukrainian Children with Clinical Symptoms of Irritable Bowel Syndrome Related to Chernobyl Disaster. *Toxicology and Industrial Health*, 27(1), pp. 51–56; Svendsen, E., et al. (2010). Cesium 137

Exposure and Spirometry Measures in Ukrainian Children Affected by the Chernobyl Nuclear Accident. *Environmental Health Perspectives*, 118(5), pp. 720–725; Svendsen, E., et al. (2015). Reduced Lung Function in Children Associated with Cesium 137 Body Burden. *Annals of the American Thoracic Society*, 12(7), pp. 1050–1057; Pukkala, E. (2006). Breast Cancer in Belarus and Ukraine after the Chernobyl Accident. *International Journal of Cancer*, 119, pp. 651–658; Davis, S., et al. (2006). Childhood Leukaemia in Belarus, Russia, and Ukraine Following the Chernobyl Power Station Accident. *International Journal of Epidemiology*, 35(2), pp. 386–96. See also Noshchenko, A. Bondar, O., Drozdova, V. (2010). Radiation-Induced Leukaemia among Children Aged 0–5 Years at the Time of the Chernobyl Accident. *International Journal of Cancer*, 127(2), p. 214; Nyagu, A. et al. (2004). Effects of Prenatal Brain Irradiation as a Result of the Chernobyl Accident. *International Journal of Radiation Medicine*, 6(1–4), pp. 91–107.

References

Ball, H. (1986). *Justice Downwind: America's Atomic Testing Program in the 1950s*. New York: Oxford University Press.

Boudia, S. (2014). Managing Scientific and Political Uncertainty. In: S. Boudia and N. Jas, eds., *Powerless Science: Science and Politics in a Toxic World*. New York: Berghahn, pp. 95–112.

Boudia, S., and Jas, N., eds., (2013). *Toxicants, Health and Regulation Since 1945*. London: Pickering & Chatto.

Brodie, J. (2015). Radiation Secrecy and Censorship after Hiroshima and Nagasaki. *Journal of Social History*, 48(4), pp. 842–964.

Brown, K. (2017). Chernobyl's Hidden Legacy. *Physics World*. Available at: https://physicsworld.com/a/chernobyls-hidden-legacy/ [Accessed June 19, 2021].

Brown, K. (2019). *Manual for Survival: A Chernobyl Guide to the Future*. New York: Norton.

Bruno, L. (2003). The Bequest of the Nuclear Battlefield: Science, Nature, and the Atom during the First Decade of the Cold War. *Historical Studies in the Physical and Biological Sciences*, 33(2), pp. 237–260.

Conze, E., Klimke, M., and Varon, J. (2017). *Nuclear Threats, Nuclear Fear and the Cold War of the 1980s*. Cambridge, UK: Cambridge University Press.

Cooper, J., Randle, K., and Sokhi, S. (2003). *Radioactive Releases in the Environment: Impact and Assessment*. New York: Wiley.

Creager, A. (2015). Radiation, Cancer, and Mutation in the Atomic Age. *Historical Studies in the Natural Sciences*, 45(1), pp. 14–48.

Daston, L. (2017). What Is an Insurable Risk? Swiss Re and Atomic Reactor Insurance. In: N. Haueter and G. Jones, eds., *Managing Risk in Reinsurance*. Oxford: Oxford University Press, pp. 230–247.

Fairlie, I. (2016). *Torch-2016*. Vienna: Wiener Umwelt Anwaltshaft.

Fox, S. (2014). *Downwind: A People's History of the Nuclear West*. Lincoln, NE: Bison Books.

Fradkin, P. (1989). *Fallout: An American Nuclear Tragedy*. Tucson, AZ: University of Arizona Press.

Gallagher, C. (1993). *American Ground Zero: The Secret Nuclear War*. Cambridge, MA: MIT Press.

240 Kate Brown

Honicker, C. (1987). Premeditated Deceit: The Atomic Energy Commission Against Joseph August Sauter. MA thesis. University of Tennessee, Knoxville.

Johnston, B., and Barker, M. (2008). Consequential Damages of Nuclear War: The Rongelap Report. Walnut Creek, CA: Left Coast Press.

Kasperski, T. (2015). Nuclear Dreams and Realities in Contemporary Russia and Ukraine. *History and Technology*, 31(1) pp. 55–80.

Kohlhoff, D. (2002). *Amchitka and the Bomb: Nuclear Testing in Alaska*. Seattle, WA: University of Washington Press.

Kuchinskaya, O. (2014). *The Politics of Invisibility: Public Knowledge about Radiation Health Effects after Chernobyl*. Cambridge, MA: MIT Press.

Kuzio, T. (2015). *Ukraine: Democratization, Corruption, and the New Russian Imperialism*. Santa Barbara, CA: Praeger Security International.

Langston, N. (2017). *Sustaining Lake Superior: An Extraordinary Lake in a Changing World*. New Haven, CT: Yale University Press.

Leopold, E. (2009). *Under the Radar: Cancer and the Cold War*. New Brunswick, NJ: Rutgers University Press.

Lepicard, S., and Hériard Dubreuil, G. (2001). Practical Improvement of the Radiological Quality of Milk Produced by Peasant Farmers in the Territories of Belarus Contaminated by the Chernobyl Accident: The ETHOS Project. *Journal of Environmental Radioactivity, Remediation Strategies*, 56(1), pp. 241–253.

Lindee, S. (2016). Survivors and Scientists: Hiroshima, Fukushima, and the Radiation Effects Research Foundation, 1975–2014. *Social Studies of Science*, 46(2), pp. 184–209. DOI: http://doi.org/10.1177/0306312716632933.

Lutts, R. (1985). Chemical Fallout: Rachel Carson's Silent Spring, Radioactive Fallout, and the Environmental Movement. *Environmental Review*, 9(3), pp. 211–225.

Mellor, R. (2018). *The Cold War Underground: An Environmental History of Uranium Mining in the United States, Canada, and the Soviet Union, 1945-1991*. PhD dissertation. Georgetown University.

Neel, J., and Schull, W. (1991). *The Criteria of Radiation Employed in the Study*. Washington, DC: National Academies Press.

Petryna, A. (2013). *Life Exposed: Biological Citizens after Chernobyl*. Princeton, NJ: Princeton University Press.

Pritikin, T. (2020). *The Hanford Plaintiffs: Downwinders and the Fight for Atomic Justice*. Lawrence, KS: University of Kansas Press.

Scheffler, R. (2014). Following Cancer Viruses Through the Laboratory, Clinic, and Society. *Studies in History and Philosophy of Science*, 48(Part B), pp. 185–188.

Sellers, C. (1997). Discovering Environmental Cancer: Wilhelm Hueper, Post-World War II Epidemiology, and the Vanishing Clinician's Eye. *American Journal of Public Health*, 87(11), pp. 1824–1835.

Smith-Howard, K. (2017). *Pure and Modern Milk: An Environmental History Since 1900*. New York: Oxford University Press.

Smith-Norris, M. (2016). *Domination and Resistance: The United States and the Marshall Islands During the Cold War*. Honolulu, HI: University of Hawaii Press.

Tarkalson, R. (1986). *Radioactive Fallout Monitoring Before and After the 1963 Nuclear Weapons Test Ban Treaty*. MS thesis. University of Montana.

Tompkins, A. (2016). *Better Active than Radioactive!: Anti-Nuclear Protest in 1970s France and West Germany*. New York: Oxford University Press.

Topçu, S. (2013). Chernobyl Empowerment?: Exporting "Participatory Governance" to Contaminated Territories. In: S. Boudia and N. Jas, eds., *Toxic World: Toxicants, Health and Regulation in the 20th Century*. London: Pickering and Chatto, pp. 135–158.

Tucker, K., and Alvarez, R. (2019). Trinity: The most significant hazard of the entire Manhattan Project. *Bulletin of the Atomic Scientists*, July 15. Available at: https://thebulletin.org/2019/07/trinity-the-most-significant-hazard-of-the-entire-manhattan-project/ [Accessed June16, 2021].

Wolff, D. (1957). Radioactivity in Animal Thyroid Glands. *Public Health Reports*, 72(12), pp. 1121–1126.

12 Unfolding time at Fukushima

Harry Bernas[1]

The Fukushima Daiichi Nuclear Power Plant accident was first labeled by Japanese and foreign nuclear authorities as unforeseeable, the unanticipated result of a "natural catastrophe." The main purpose of this chapter is to show that the accident was not an isolated event but the result of a long-term social, economic, and political process. A review of the Japanese nuclear program's history shows that it was basically a predictable "normal accident," to use Charles Perrow's term (Perrow, 1984). The accumulation of complexities and unsolved technical problems was not random, but structured. The inevitability of an upcoming mega-earthquake and tsunami along the Fukushima coastline had been established in 2002, and all parties concerned were informed. Power and authority, as well as profits, naturally appear as prime motives. Decades of official documents show how nuclear power utilities, ministries and safety agency overseers largely ignored or denied the very possibility of major accidents, tolerated uncertainties and malpractices. As a result of this deliberate blindness, the destiny of Tokyo, Japan and beyond was left to depend only on the wind's direction and the post-tsunami aftershocks' intensity—i.e., on luck alone.

This historical perspective on the Fukushima Daiichi nuclear disaster emphasises a specific feature of the "Anthropocene." Technological risks have become primarily produced historically and socially; and when their impact reaches planet scale, they challenge the social structure that produced them . Nuclear energy implementation, termed a "Faustian bargain" in 1972 (Weinberg, 1972), was the first such mega-risk deliberately constructed and deployed by our species, Fukushima Daiichi history provides an incentive to include these long-term factors in a critical vision of possible futures.

Legend has it that Japan straddles a restless sea dragon. At 2:46 pm on March 11, 2011, the dragon shook its shoulders, causing the off-shore Great Tohoku Earthquake. The entire 1,000 km-long island of Honshu, Japan's main island—an area of 230,000 km^2 and 100 million people, moved 2.4 m toward North America. The Earth's rotation axis shifted. Some 25 km² of water were set into motion; one of the largest tsunamis in

DOI: 10.4324/9781003227472-12

recorded history, it killed an estimated 19,000 people. When explosions and three reactor core meltdowns started the next day at a nuclear facility called Fukushima Daiichi, the wind had just shifted toward the Pacific. Had the wind continued to blow southward, 50 million people would have attempted to rush from Tokyo to avoid the radioactive fallout. The havoc would have paralyzed, possibly destroyed, much of Japan.

The second fortuitous aspect of the unfolding disaster was the miraculous resistance of a single vacillating building. The quake turned the Fukushima Daiichi Unit 4 building into a shaky, fractured and leaning, weak-footed colossus. Its spent fuel pool, 30-odd meters above ground, was filled to the brim with 1,300 hot, highly radioactive fuel rods recently removed from three reactors requiring continuous water-cooling and protection to avoid melting. Hundreds of seismic aftershocks, including some up to magnitude 7, shook the building in the following weeks. For months, the plant's owner, Tokyo Electric Power Company (TEPCO), and nuclear experts around the world held their breath as the water splashed in the pool. Should it crack or dry out, a planet-sized radioactive catastrophe—several times Chernobyl—would occur. It didn't happen: Japan and a good part of our planet were saved by the wind's vagaries and the miraculous resistance of a broken building. A day or so after the explosions, we were saved again by the heroic team of Fukushima Daiichi operators led by Masao Yoshida, whose choice to ignore TEPCO headquarters' orders and drown the reactors in seawater[2] (Bernas, 2019) avoided a world-sized catastrophe. On the other side of the fence were most of the policy players—TEPCO and other nuclear power utilities, the regulating agencies and many of their academic members—whose decades-long inbreeding built up what became known as the Japanese "nuclear village" and created conditions more prone to lead to disaster.

As early as 2002, geologist Koji Minoura had been publicising evidence for an oncoming megaquake and tsunami on the Tohoku coast (see below). Nine years later, after the Fukushima Daiichi disaster, the Japanese government's Nuclear and Industrial Safety Agency (NISA) spokesman confirmed that both NISA and TEPCO had been aware of the risk and of Minoura's warning: "We were in the process of considering that," he said, "but this accident occurred during that process. It is now too late to say that we wish we checked earlier." Slow thinking, in the nuclear village.

Japanese and international investigation committees analyzed the causes of the Fukushima Daiichi demise. They reconstructed the time span from just before to after the explosions, detailing the organisational, technical and cultural conditions prevailing at and around the Fukushima Daiichi plant. Reports emphasised technical features, safety loopholes and plant operations. Perrow's criteria (1984) for what he terms a "normal accident" are all there: interactive complexity, a strong

244 Harry Bernas

interrelation and tight coupling among many operating subsystems, the probability that a local failure of even one small subsystem can create feedbacks disrupting the entire array. It was not the safety that was redundant, but the risk.

In this chapter, I argue that the Fukushima Daiichi disaster should also be seen as a time collapse. The economic and political conditions, the timing of Japanese nuclear power's birth and development affected both technical conditions and safety culture at all the nuclear power sites—including Fukushima Daiichi. The response of TEPCO and government agencies during the accident was the result of acquired methods and regulatory habits, and the future of the Fukushima Daiichi site and its surrounding province was largely written into them despite rare attempts to counteract the danger. The Fukushima Daiichi disaster is thus an integral part of nuclear and societal history. It reveals essential traits of nuclear technology as well as the societal conditions that promoted it, and on which it acts in turn.

A Poem Forebodes Disaster

Our sleeves were wet with tears
As pledges that our love
Will last until
Over Sue's Mount of Pines
Ocean waves are breaking[3]

Koji Minoura is a professor at the Institute of Geology and Paleontology at Tohoku University in Sendai, north of Fukushima. He roams Tohoku's landscapes and coastlines and finds time to read poetry. In the late 1980s, he read this love poem by Kiyohara no Motosuke, dating back to the tenth century. Poetry and geology mingled in Minoura's mind. The ancient Mount of Pines temple of Sue was 4 km into the sloped Sendai plain: the poem apparently referred to a tsunami. A perusal of Sandai-jitsuroku, the official history of the Jogan dynasty (859–878) written in the year 901 confirmed his guess (Minoura et al., 2001). A massive earthquake had occurred on July 11, 869, recorded as the "Jogan event," but the accompanying tsunami had been forgotten. The wave had been huge, reaching high ground up to some four kilometers inland.

Scientists' minds do not always walk straight lines. New ideas are like swifts or nightingales—they appear unbidden, or they sing in the dark. They come to those, like Minoura, with open and sharp minds. But once they appear, back to the workhorse drill: Minoura, students and colleagues explored the Sendai plain for months. Buried under recent deposits, they found a layer of ocean sand far inside the coastline and dated it to the ninth century—this was the physical evidence of the Jogan event. By digging further, they found two more sand layers, again separated in time by about a thousand years. They had discovered the existence and periodicity of a huge tsunami. The time intervals meant that another major earthquake and mega-tsunami were now overdue.

For a decade, Minoura and his students accumulated data, drawing the attention of seismologist colleagues and government officials to their finding and to the imminent danger. Colleagues were interested, but officials did not want to hear about it. Minoura finally published a paper in the aptly named *Journal of Natural Disaster Science*, officially published in 2001 but not actually appearing until March 11, 2002. It concluded that

> gigantic tsunamis occurred three times during the last 3,000 years.... The recurrence interval for a large-scale tsunami is 800-1,100 years. More than 1,100 years have passed since the Jogan tsunami ... the possibility of a large tsunami striking the Sendai plain is high ... A tsunami similar to the Jogan one would inundate the present coastal plain for about 2.5 to 3 km inland.
>
> (Minoura et al., 2001: 87)

Minoura reiterated this warning (Minoura et al., 2015) in scientific publications and in the press. It was endorsed and repeated for years by senior seismologists at ministry-level meetings with TEPCO, operator of Fukushima Daiichi. But neither TEPCO nor the supervising ministry's safety agency NISA would mention Minoura's studies before 2011.

The initial reports after the Fukushima disaster spoke of an unexpected disaster. Yet Minoura's warnings and information on TEPCO's decisions during plant building and operation showed that Japan's fate was in fact shaped by insufficient protection of a coast and the nuclear plants that lined it: prior warnings, also ignored, concerned other portions of Japan's coast. How was it that an entire industrial, scientific and governmental establishment, in one of the world's most sophisticated countries, blinded itself to the announced possibility of huge disasters? The earthquake was not only outside, but actually inside our civilisation.

"History happens to us"

Tony Judt's remark captures a fact. All the elements of this story did not happen by design: fortuity and contradictions blur the picture. History played two cruel tricks on Japan in the mid-twentieth century when the authorities, needing energy to rebuild a country devoid of fossil fuels, "chose" nuclear power. When the first nuclear power plants were being designed in the early 1960s, plate tectonics was still an emerging, barely recognised theory. Seismology was in its infancy, ignored by decision-makers and most engineers; geological fault lines had hardly been searched for. Seismic risk evaluations were based on equivocal historical

246 *Harry Bernas*

archives mentioning previous earthquakes of uncertain amplitudes. Nuclear plant sites were chosen by proximity to large industrial sites and availability of cooling water. The second play of fate worsened the first: there happened to be a 50-odd year lull in tectonic activity between the 1940s and the 1990s—scarcely a breather in Earth's history but an eternity for politicians and industrial managers. As their science progressed in the "Japanese Miracle" years of industrial development, seismologists did succeed in promoting architectural safeguards for buildings and transport projects.

The safety regulation of nuclear energy sites was much weaker: government and regulator saw the plants as too big and expensive to fail, and industry's need for electrical power preempted attempts to regulate a nuclear sector that had not yet revealed its weak points. When by 1995, the Kobe earthquake signaled that tectonic activity had resumed, it was too late. Fifty-four insufficiently protected nuclear reactors, providing 30% of Japan's electricity, dotted the most fault-ridden coastlines in the world. Over three decades, a tight bond had formed between government technocrats and power industry players. Expert committees assembled by regulating agencies heard increasingly detailed warnings by seismologist members, but such committees were primarily peopled by the power company and agency representatives. They contrasted the uncertain calendar of possible disasters presented by geologists with the huge, certain cost of implementing safety updates.

A highway to disaster

Japan's Ministry of International Trade and Industry (MITI, now called METI, Ministry of Economy, Trade and Industry) had been set up in 1949. When US occupation ceased in 1952, MITI revived a number of prewar corporations (zaibatsu) that had been dismantled under General Douglas MacArthur's authority as punishment for their massive contributions to Japanese militarism. Nuclear Japan was born in 1954, after President Dwight D. "Ike" Eisenhower's "Atoms for Peace" speech (Eisenhower, 1953) at the UN General Assembly (December 1953). Eisenhower offered to lift "atomic secrecy" and help countries develop peaceful uses of nuclear energy, including research and power reactors—the United States would even provide an initial load of enriched uranium (a move that led to proliferation). Japan, still under strong US influence, was first on the customer list.

At the time, there was not a single operating nuclear power plant in the world. After the very first demonstration in December 1942, several experimental reactors had tested conditions for nuclear fission. Starting in 1943, nine specially designed reactors were built in order to produce plutonium (Pu) for nuclear bombs, but such reactors are inadequate for nuclear power production. Designs of power reactors for submarines were initiated in late 1945 and the first US nuclear power-producing reactor only went into operation on a US Navy submarine in early 1955 and a civilian, upscaled version was connected to the power grid at Shippingport in 1957. So in 1953, the US Administration encouraged its own reluctant industries (working on military, hence entirely subsidised, reactors) to undertake civilian reactor design and production, in order to control any future market in nuclear energy. General Electric and Westinghouse finally complied. The UK Atomic Energy Authority designed and offered a competing reactor at the same time.

In the late 1950s, MITI undertook the construction of a Japanese nuclear energy program. The policy was to support a Japanese nuclear industry[4] and co-manage nuclear plants with it. Over the years, nationalist leaders made no secret of their complementary aim: to develop technical and infrastructure capacities for a military program when required.[5] A decade later, MITI and the revived Japanese industry conglomerates had founded ten non-competitive regional nuclear power utilities, TEPCO being the largest. Japanese reactors—notably Units 1 and 2 at Fukushima Daiichi—being among the world's first, were also first on the learning curve for possible flaws.[6] Thus, they were among the least safe. Moreover, no two reactors were alike. Each had its own possible flaws and unique safety challenges. In the United States, it took 26 years, mounting citizen protest, the Three Mile Island accident, and a sitting President's awareness of reactor meltdown dangers for safety to become a major concern of the nuclear industry.[7] In 1948, Edward Teller had been first to propose a "Reactor Safeguard Committee" to the US Atomic Energy Commission, responsible for all military and civil reactors. Over time it was reduced to a counseling role as budget considerations overwhelmed industrial power plant construction decisions. In Japan, it also took 28 years to create a Nuclear Safety Commission (NSC). In 1973 METI consolidated nuclear production and regulation inside its own Agency, which begat the Nuclear and Industrial Safety Agency (NISA) in 2001. For four decades, these agencies and nearly a hundred specialised subcommittees all promoted pro-nuclear industry policy from inside the dismal, grey government buildings of Tokyo's Kasumigaseki—the center of the "nuclear village."

In this "nuclear village" system, top officials navigated in a small world of revolving doors between government, nuclear monopolies and a few academic positions, honing the composition of their expert committees and the content of final regulations in order to minimise or avoid the hugely expensive safety precautions or retrofits that might be required to protect the nuclear reactors. Occasional whistleblowers, scandals and seismic damage opened possible moments in which a breach could have disrupted and corrected the village's hands-off procedures. But it took the Fukushima disaster to spawn an independent Nuclear Regulation Authority (NRA) in 2012. Its present leaders

248 *Harry Bernas*

attempt to ascertain independent safety assessments, often butting heads with a government keen to resume the former nuclear regime despite blatant structural and seismic risks.[8]

A brief timeline from its inception to 2011 reveals how the Japanese nuclear establishment literally built up the "normal accident" syndrome that led to Fukushima Daiichi. In 1966, as mentioned above, seismology was in its infancy. Few took it seriously enough as a predictive tool. The official assessment that allowed TEPCO to site a nuclear power plant at Fukushima was simply wrong: "The area around Fukushima Prefecture … is one of the regions with low seismicity in Japan…. [T]he area near the reactor construction site has never been hit by any earthquake."[9] By 1971, when Fukushima Daiichi's Unit 1 was powered up and Unit 2 had been authorised, pioneer seismologist Professor Kiyoo Mogi of Tokyo University had already published his objections against building nuclear reactors in a country that accounted for 10% of the planet's earthquakes. He repeatedly warned of an impending, dangerously shallow, magnitude-8 quake ("Tokai Earthquake") that would trigger a megatsunami affecting the most densely populated and highly industrialised area of Japan (between Tokyo and Nagoya). Six large reactors were being planned at Hamaoka, between those two cities, but Mogi's warnings were overruled inside expert committees for years, whether by operator-friendly majorities or ministerial decision. The same disconnect between knowledge of the danger—which had become public—and pursuit of Hamaoka reactor building occurred again in 1978, 1980, 1987 and 1998. Energy was required, economics ruled, and autocratic decisions, even when met by scientific and public opposition, were implemented.[10] Hamaoka moved ahead without any evaluation of whether its closely spaced reactor units, each containing 100–200 tons of radioactive fuel, could resist a megaquake and/or tsunami. Like the pendulum swinging toward its victim in Edgar Allen Poe's famous tale, so at Hamaoka the subducting tectonic plate inched and ground along for years. Japan's destiny and ours teetered on the edge. The nuclear plant was only shut after the Fukushima disaster.

Mogi's alarm was but the first in a long series. In 1994, worried by the discrepancy between existing regulations and the knowledge on seismic hazards accumulated since the 1970s, seismologist Katsuhiko Ishibashi of Kobe University published a book with an explicit title: *An Era of Underground Convulsions: A Seismologist Warns*. Whistleblowing proved no career booster: Ishibashi was formally reprimanded and forced to apologise to authorities at the Construction Ministry. Five months later, the Kobe earthquake killed 6,000 people. A panel of experts, including Ishibashi, was appointed, and very little change followed. Increasingly alarmed, Ishibashi became an advocate for radical changes to the decision-making processes around nuclear reactor implementations. In 1997, he published a peer-reviewed science paper (Ishibashi, 1997) describing what

Unfolding time at Fukushima   249

he termed "Genpatsu-Shinsai," drawing on the terms Genpatsu, meaning nuclear power plant, and Shinsai, meaning earthquake disaster: "a totally new type of natural-manmade disaster that human beings have never encountered ... especially dangerous because it could cause multiple failures at the same time, unlike a normal accident." In retrospect, the paper reads like an uncanny prediction of what would occur in Fukushima 14 years later. But when the Governor of Shizuoka Prefecture, where a new plant was to be set up, requested comment from the NISA safety agency, its key nuclear engineering expert member Haruki Madarame dismissed the prescient seismologist: "In the field of nuclear engineering, Ishibashi is a nobody."[11]

On August 29, 2002, a major tremor ran through the nuclear village when a former employee of General Electric (which had built the first Japanese nuclear plants and was responsible for their upkeep) anonymously informed METI that TEPCO had been falsifying plant safety inspection data for 30 years. An investigation revealed that six other nuclear power companies had done the same. TEPCO admitted to 29 falsified safety repair records, including the cover-up of 16 cracks in 13 nuclear reactor containment vessels at three plants—among them, Fukushima Daiichi Units 1 through 4. All 17 TEPCO nuclear plants were shut down for two years' inspection. The CEO resigned, glibly noting: "The company had to conceal the data because nuclear regulation in Japan was too strict."[12] NISA introduced an "allowable reactor defects" standard in order to avoid forcing the costly refurbishment of existing plants, prompting a *Japan Times* headline: "Japan's deadly game of nuclear roulette." Two years later, a burst pipe killed 5 workers at a Kansai Electric Power Company nuclear plant; NISA discovered that the pipe had not been inspected for 28 years.

In 2004, the respected chairman of METI's Coordinating Committee for Earthquake Prediction referred to Minoura's work as he warned of "the risk due to tsunamis on the Fukushima coast more than twice as tall as the forecasts of up to five meters put forth by regulators and Tokyo Electric."[13] A majority of committee members acknowledged the possibility of an earthquake but refused to mention a tsunami risk in their meeting reports; again, they declined to even signal that a nuclear plant might be in need of major refurbishment in order to withstand predictable catastrophe.

In 2006, another panel assembled by METI to strengthen earthquake safety guidelines was stacked with experts working for, or allied to, the utilities. Recognising mounting protests at sites hosting the plants, they again agreed on the possibility of an earthquake and again refuted the possibility of serious tsunami risk. The panel even suggested that plant safety be judged case-by-case, opening the door to local pressure politics rather than sensible, nationwide regulation. Ishibashi pleaded and fought. Then he resigned in protest. The nuclear utility spokesman was

250 *Harry Bernas*

unruffled: "Regulations have to be made by the people who use them. Nobody else has the expertise"[14] (One wonders how this policy would apply to guns or drugs).

The most revealing comment on the impact of the nuclear village's policy was made by NISA Director Kenkichi Hirose, responding to an NSC suggestion that officials establish evacuation zones in case of an accident: "Japan's nuclear disaster management has no particular problems, and changes are unnecessary.... The nation has finally put away its fear of nuclear accidents.... Why do we need to wake a sleeping child?"[15]

On July 16, 2007, the magnitude-7 Niigata-Chuetsu Earthquake damaged the world's largest nuclear power plant, the Kashiwazaki-Kariwa facility, run by TEPCO. The plant had been shaken three times harder than its initial design provided for. TEPCO had known since at least 2003 that an undersea fault, very close to the plant, could unleash a magnitude-7 quake. Today, we know that there are actually four major faults running under or very close to Kashiwazaki-Kariwa reactors. Falsifications, accidents and failures continued to be hidden or explained away by utilities and regulators.[16]

An evaluation of the nuclear plants' capacity to resist a major disaster was made by NISA in 2009. Notably, it focused on the older units at Fukushima Daiichi. The head of the Active Fault and Earthquake Research Center noted that the committee's discussion, in 22 meetings, made no mention of the tsunami danger revealed by Minoura. Neither TEPCO nor NISA mentioned it in the evaluation's conclusions. NISA approved the Fukushima Daiichi plant's safety report shortly after. After the disaster, a NISA spokesman lamely said: "We were about to start moving on to the next check and this disaster occurred ... It is now too late to say that we wish we checked earlier."[17]

Truth and consequences

After the Fukushima catastrophe, a few top-level decision-makers had an epiphany. Reading their testimonies to investigation committees in 2012 suddenly tinges the black-white-gray semblance of business and politics with the real world's colors. They admitted that the nuclear plant's demise was no "natural catastrophe," but a disaster largely of their own making. METI's former Director of Industrial Policy, Shigeaki Koga, recognised (Fackler, 2012) that "March 11 exposed the true nature of Japan's post-war system, that it is led by bureaucrats who stand on the side of the industry, not the people." Haruki Madarame, who was a major player in the nuclear village for decades, chief of the Nuclear Safety Agency and the Prime Minister's nuclear counselor during the Fukushima Daiichi crisis, broke down during his testimony to the Diet's Nuclear Accident Independent Investigation Commission.[18] He spoke of hubris and nationalistic pride, of "a long-term culture of complacency....

Unfolding time at Fukushima 251

[We] succumbed to a blind belief in the country's technical prowess and failed to thoroughly assess the risks of building nuclear reactors in an earthquake-prone country."

These confessions and regrets rang true in 2012. But as time goes on, the human, technical and political management of Fukushima Daiichi's aftermath reveals pressures to reopen insecure plants and suppress funds for displaced families in order to "encourage return" of populations to fallout-polluted areas. It seems government and utility leaders are not above a quiet return to old practices.

The remarkable indifference to populational risk (as opposed to technical operation problems) was a common feature of the otherwise very different Japanese and Soviet (Russian) histories of nuclear failure (Brown, 2019). At both Fukushima Daiichi and Chernobyl, planet-size catastrophes were averted only by luck—a lull in Japan's seismic activity, the chance avoidance of previous reactor core melts in other defective Soviet RBMK reactors, the wind's direction at Fukushima Daiichi, seismic aftershocks remaining just below the destruction threshold of shaky Fukushima Daiichi Unit 4's spent fuel pool—these are only a few examples. The history of US and European nuclear power plants reveals similar, if far less tragic, episodes. As in the case of the many military nuclear close calls of the Cold War (Schlosser, 2009), humanity has been very fortunate indeed.

Introducing one of the main reports to the Japanese Diet Committee on the Fukushima Daiichi accident, Chairman Kiyoshi Kurokawa wrote that the Fukushima Daiichi failure "cannot be regarded as a natural disaster. It was a profoundly manmade disaster—that could and should have been foreseen and prevented. And its effects could have been mitigated by a more effective human response." He went on to emphasise specifically "Japanese causes," including "reflexive obedience; reluctance to question authority; devotion to 'sticking with the program;' groupism; insularity," conceit and bureaucracy, "[which] led bureaucrats to put organisational interests ahead of their paramount duty to protect public safety."[19] The NAIIC Report provides much to reflect on regarding the catastrophe's circumstances and the impact of cultural features on reactions during and immediately after the Fukushima Daiichi incident. But though a reference to local factors is meaningful, it cannot be the whole story for at least two reasons. One was stated crisply by a political scientist: "to pin blame on culture is the ultimate cop-out. If culture explains the behavior, then nobody takes the responsibility" (Curtis, 2012). The second is that, over the last 60 years, "nuclear village" traits prioritising economic considerations over safety have repeatedly surfaced worldwide, even within international organisations, whenever serious incidents have affected nuclear reactor safety.

Contradicting Kurokawa's "Japanisation" of the Fukushima Daiichi failure, the accident obviously had all the characteristic technical features of a generic "normal accident" as defined by Charles Perrow (1984): the closely connected reactors involved such a degree of interactive complexity and so many feedback possibilities that the initial failure of the emergency generators propagated to disruptions in all parts of the system, causing the meltdowns and their consequences.

Also, major industrial "accidents" aren't isolated events: long-term development is crucial. The succession of events, their causes and how they were treated can be analyzed along two different, complementary lines. One is the buildup of a technically complex monster, in which successive decisions—from plant siting to implantation of spent fuel pools, hidden construction faults, inspection denials and so on—riddle most[20] of Japan's nuclear plants. All the features prepared for a "normal accident." Fukushima Daiichi, one of the oldest and most flawed plants, dangerously sited and under-protected, was a perfect target for disaster. The other vast pattern unfolds when we consider not just the series of official decisions and actions but how these were prepared, taken and implemented. Japan's nuclear history illustrates Barry Turner's (1978) pioneering emphasis on the importance of sociological and cultural features in creating the conditions for risks and accidents.

First, consider history on the decade-scale. A nuclear plant is far more than a technical maze. Years of construction and operation by thousands of on-site workers and external subcontractors produce a unique social structure and plant operation culture (Topçu, 2013a). When major accidents occur, social interactions affect the implementation of rescue strategies more than any automatised system. For example, as demonstrated at Chernobyl (Plokhii, 2018; Brown, 2019) and Fukushima, various group solidarities (or their absence) were crucial features of the crisis response, even before technological features.[21]

On the longer-term historical scale, the "nuclear village" is just one major piece of evidence that there is a more complex economic-industrial-political logic enveloping the Japanese nuclear establishment. US interests were heavily involved at the inception of nuclear energy in Japan. But the sector was soon taken over by the former zaibatsu influenced by imperialist traditions. Nuclear energy, comprising a quarter of Japanese industrial production, became a mainstay of the specific capitalistic environment of postwar Japan.[22] The nuclear village was its fitting complement, developing alongside the energy infrastructure. Both were instruments of nation rebuilding after the war's devastation.

The series of joint decisions by the utilities, regulators and Liberal Democratic Party politicians that led Japan over most of the post-war period draws a pattern of how risks to the population's health, livelihood and organisation are socially and historically produced. It did not go unopposed. Nuclear power, tainted by memories of Hiroshima, would remain a major battleground of Japanese society for at least 20 years. Issues such as the legitimacy of authority versus democratic protest, the

Unfolding time at Fukushima 253

weight of local versus national government decisions and the inclusion of scientific knowledge in decision processes often revolved around it. But in recent years, Japan's ruling instances have been developing strategies to live with the Fukushima Daiichi radioactive ruins, the 75,000 workers toiling amid the disaster's century-scale aftermath, the mega-ton accumulation of radioactive water and the 16 square km area piled with plastic bags replete with contaminated soil. The government aims to reestablish a pre-Fukushima Daiichi order, including a restart of nuclear plants. Attempts to limit contradiction and democratic decision processes are combined with incentives to repopulate contaminated zones. Nuclear energy thus remains the arena in which new modes of social pressure are tested, within and beyond Japan. This gives Fukushima Daiichi a special place in human history.

An Anthropocene syndrome?

In the early days of US nuclear power development, its most perceptive initiator Weinberg (1972) warned that the technology involved a "Faustian bargain": the price of "practically unlimited, cheap energy" would be stringent control of society to ensure safety, via a sort of "nuclear priesthood." Weinberg's comment was largely ignored except, ironically, by the most radical left-wing opponents of nuclear energy. They were no ideological soulmates, but they agreed that the problem was serious.

Now, the amplitude and the sequence of events at Chernobyl and Fukushima Daiichi demonstrated indisputably, in different but complementary ways, what a nuclear plant mega-risk actually meant. Events such as the near-fall of Fukushima Daiichi Unit 4's spent fuel pool and the continuous flow of radioactive water from the reactor cores were sufficiently "close calls" to give the world a clear vision of the danger inherent in anything but "complete control" over every aspect of the design, construction, and management of a nuclear plant—even if such perfection turned out to be illusory (Perrow, 1984). There had been many less dramatic forewarnings, but this time, the consequences could not be ignored.

Weinberg had sought technical fixes for problems posed by humans: new, safer types of nuclear power reactors, new designs for producing and distributing energy, and so on. Taken together, Chernobyl and Fukushima Daiichi had shown that even solving problems related to upstream triggers of the catastrophe—design faults or incompetence—was necessary but not sufficient to avoid possible destruction or irreparable harm. The nuclear "priesthood" could not be a straightforward compendium of technologies. Nuclear mega-risks are literally constructed, just like the power plants they endanger, by long-term human factors—economic, social, political—and their control implies a special use of technology. Nuclear energy promised

254 Harry Bernas

to involve a positive instrument of social control and guided change, via technical features (such as centralised power structuring industry and urbanism) and social constructs (such as blurred relations between the civil and military spheres). But it still grew to be the first example of a scientific innovation creating a planet-scale risk.

As power plants age, previously unknown limitations appear. Risks multiply. Plant operation means ever-more surveillance, ever-more protective measures for workers and the environment. Fukushima Daiichi's past and the nuclear village syndrome show that, irrespective of its final impact on safety, the authoritarianism officially bred for technological safety may become an effective instrument to control the economic and political power that stems from nuclear energy. And it may spread (Hecht, 2009): when the danger is world-scale, safety implies an absolute need for utmost social control, surveillance, and foresight. The Faustian bargain becomes a losing bet for democracy when the "priesthood" is our sole regulator (Smil, 2005; Mitchell, 2013).

Authoritarianism is only one way to exercise social pressure. A more subtle method involves techniques destined to induce changes in the people's vision of a protective society.[23] In recent years, several authors (Calhoun, 2006; Topçu, 2013a) have drawn attention to a far-reaching "privatisation of risks" strategy, as promoted by chemical companies, the nuclear power industry and international organisations. It is presently being tested in the Chernobyl (Topçu, 2013b) and Fukushima areas. In the latter case, let down by TEPCO and failing official health agencies in the aftermath of the tsunami and Fukushima Daiichi's demise, local populations with no technical knowledge of radioprotection bought their own Geiger counters and set up patrols, attempting to organise their own radioactivity warning systems (see Herran, chapter in this volume). Having "failed its mission," even unwittingly, the normal, top-down protection system of qualified state agencies was being replaced—and apparently being undermined—by an improvised, semi-anarchistic grassroots system.

In an astute maneuver, Shinzo Abe's government, supported by a cynical, soft-spoken international campaign based on previous experience at Chernobyl (Kimura, 2018), made every effort—including financial coercion—to transfer responsibility for decisions regarding travel, work, or resettlement in Fukushima Daiichi fallout areas from local governments and public agencies to private individuals. Such attempts to turn a spontaneous movement into a libertarian revolution are relatively new in Japan but are all too familiar in American history and lead to far-reaching consequences worldwide.

It also involves a degraded form of "citizen science." Citizens have every right and responsibility to scrutinise how scientists operate. But risks such as radiation fallout require means and preventive measures on the scale of national budgets, of organisational expertise in research or health. As time goes on, conditions at Fukushima Daiichi leave individual citizens without sufficient information to locate radioactive danger. Increasingly left to themselves, they are unable to organise their protection and distinguish truth from error when "information" is provided by conflicting sources (such as the Internet). The government eludes responsibility as well as potential health and insurance liability. For example, a trend of "organised ignorance" is set up in order to encourage inhabitants' return to the Daiichi area (Asanuma-Brice, 2018).

Also documented at Fukushima (Asanuma-Brice, 2018; Kimura, 2018; Ribault, 2019), present policy is a powerful means of increasing inequality. The rich, connected and knowledgeable are more insulated from the negative consequences of industry and government policy than are poor farmers or fishermen. The pattern fits in with the wave of individualism stimulated by so-called social networks. These, in fact, most often operate in anti-social modes, encouraging isolation and vulnerability, particularly in groups most sensitive to health and survival issues. Risk privatisation thus becomes a particularly effective tool of economic and political oppression, fragmenting protest and collective intelligence. It may also help disrupt the social fabric of mutual care and shared fate.

We face repeated attempts to transmute Chernobyl and Fukushima into isolated "events," free from history and context, unbound by rationality. Nuclear disasters first demonstrated the urgency of understanding and deconstructing this syndrome in order to solve, rather than ignore, our problems. Otherwise, our Anthropocene will be very short indeed.

Note added in proof: Citing a significant prewar example, M. Matsumoto has emphasized several longstanding traits (secrecy, hobnobbing, nationalist self-confidence) of the Japanese military-industrial complex which resurface in the Fukushima disaster. Whether both events may be grouped under a single "structural disaster" label is perhaps debatable. See M. Matsumoto (2014), The "Structural Disaster" of the Science-Technology-Society Interface From a Comparative Perspective with a Prewar Accident, in J. Ahn et al. (eds.), Chapter 10 in Reflections on the Fukushima Daiichi Nuclear Accident, Springer Open (doi 10.1007/978-3-319-12090-4_10). I thank B. Bensaude-Vincent for drawing my attention to this paper.

Notes

1 I thank the editors for the invitation to participate in this volume, and for days of lively discussions. I benefited greatly from comments by Angela N. H. Creager, John Krige, Hiroko Takahashi, and Ran Zwigenberg. I am deeply indebted to Kate Brown for our ongoing conversation on these topics.
2 ICANPS (2012). Final Report, Investigation Committee on the Accident at Fukushima Nuclear Power Stations of Tokyo Electric Power Company. Available at: https://www.cas.go.jp/jp/seisaku/icanps/eng/final-report.html [Accessed June 2, 2021].

256 *Harry Bernas*

3 Kiyohara no Motosuke, Poem 42. Available at: http://jti.lib.virginia.edu/japanese/hyakunin/hyakua.html [Accessed June 2, 2021].
4 With, among others, a Nuclear Facilities Development Division, Nuclear Fuel Cycle Industry Division, Nuclear Energy Policy Planning Division.
5 "I don't think Japan needs to possess nuclear weapons, but it's important to maintain our commercial reactors because it would allow us to produce a nuclear warhead in a short amount of time," said Shigeru Ishiba, ex-Defense Minister in the first Abe Government (Dawson, C., (2011). Japan, Provocative Case for Staying Nuclear. *Wall Street Journal*. October 28. Available at: https://www.wsj.com/articles/SB10001424052970203658804576638392537430156 [Accessed June 25, 2021].
6 Fukushima Daiichi Unit 1 opened in 1970.
7 President Jimmy Carter had participated as a Navy submarine engineer officer in the clean-up of a nuclear reactor after a power surge accident at Chalk River.
8 *Japan Times* (2017). Japan's nuclear safety chief raps TEPCO's attitude on Fukushima No. 1 crisis, restarting other reactors (July 10). Unfortunately, three years and a chairman change later, the NRA was ready to authorise the discharge of stored radioactive Fukushima Daiichi water into the ocean.
9 Partial conclusions from *Results of the Examination Performed by the Committee on Examination of Reactor Safety* by the Japanese Atomic Energy Commission (1966) (document in the personal archives of a colleague of the author).
10 K. Mogi summarised the problem in a 2004 review, noting that the possibility of an M8 class earthquake in the Tokai region had already been pointed out in October 1969. The Chairman of the [MITI] Coordinating Committee for Earthquake Prediction (CCEP) had announced it and it had been reported in the media. Only seven months later, Chubu Electric Company applied for the construction of a nuclear power plant at Hamaoka, in the center of the danger zone. The application was approved by the Prime Minister on December 10, 1970. Hamaoka Unit 1 went into operation in March 1976 and Unit 2 started up in November 1978. Mogi, K., (2004). Two Grave Issues Concerning the Expected Tokai Earthquake. *Earth Planets Space*, 56, pp. li–lxvi. Available at: http://www.terrapub.co.jp/journals/EPS/pdf/2004/5608/5608li.pdf [Accessed June 25, 2021].
11 Haruki Madarame, nuclear engineering expert and member of NISA, in a 1997 letter to the Shizuoka Legislature (disclosed by the press; see, for example, https://www.bloomberg.com/news/articles/2011-11-21/nuclear-regulator-dismissed-seismologist-on-japan-quake-threat [Accessed June 28, 2021]). Madarame spent 30 years in major government advisor capacities. A long-term member of NISA, which was supposed to regulate the nuclear industry through a maze of 99 subcommittees, he defended the industry's positions for decades, and he and his university received major funding from TEPCO. While other members of the "nuclear village" shuttle between government regulatory agencies and company boards, he remained an academic consultant to both sides, and in 2010 he became chair of the powerful Nuclear Safety Commission counseling the Prime Minister and Cabinet. He resigned after the Fukushima disaster.
12 Nobuya Minami, president of TEPCO, at his resignation press conference, mid-October 2002 (from TEPCO website, page now removed).
13 Professor Kunihiko Shimazaki, at Meeting of Coordinating Committee for Earthquake Prediction (METI), Feb. 19. 2004.
14 Quoted in Bloomberg, December 15, 2007.

Unfolding time at Fukushima 257

15 NISA Director Kenkichi Hirose (2006), letter to NSC, quoted in Hirata and Warschauer (2014).
16 According to a document revealed by Wikileaks, an IAEA official warned the G8 meeting of the Safety and Security Group in 2008 that "guides for seismic safety [in Japan] have only been revised three times in the last 35 years and the IAEA is now re-examining them." Quoted in *Economic Times* (2001). Japan warned over nuclear plants: WikiLeaks cables. March 16.
17 Masaru Kobayashi, NISA seismic safety office, quoted in Nakamura, D., and Harlan, C. (2011). Japanese Nuclear Plant's Evaluators Cast Aside Threat of Tsunami. *Washington Post*, March 23.
18 Testimony of Haruki Madarame, Chair of Nuclear Safety Agency, before the National Diet of Japan Nuclear Accident Independent Investigation Commission (NAIIC) on Fukushima Accident (2012). (Available at: https://warp.da.ndl.go.jp/info:ndljp/pid/3856371/naiic.go.jp/en/report/ [Accessed June 25, 2021].
19 Curiously, in the report's Japanese version, he does not highlight cultural factors as much. The National Diet of Japan Fukushima Nuclear Accident Independent Investigation Commission. Available at: https://warp.da.ndl.go.jp/info:ndljp/pid/3856371/naiic.go.jp/en/report/ [Accessed June 25, 2021].
20 This is not automatic. A significant reduction in risks is obtainable under severely controlled conditions, as was shown by the limited effect of the March 11, 2011 mega-tsunami on the Onagawa nuclear plant. Although 50 km closer than Fukushima Daiichi to the quake's epicenter, the impact was far weaker. Available at: https://en.wikipedia.org/wiki/Onagawa_Nuclear_Power_Plant [Accessed June 2, 2021].
21 Investigation Committee on the Accident at the Fukushima Nuclear Power Stations of Tokyo Electric Power Company (2012). Available at: https://www.cas.go.jp/jp/seisaku/icanps/eng/ [Accessed June 2, 2021].
22 The vulnerability of civil nuclear power reactors developed by the US industry after the Manhattan Project can be explored in a similar perspective. Prioritising access to profits in an immature technology has unsurprisingly been proven incompatible with plant safety and rational decisions.
23 Often initiated by RAND and Pentagon researchers in the Cold War "psychological warfare" context, once marginal and now flourishing think tanks such as the Cato Institute or the Heritage Foundation adapted them to expound on conservative and libertarian themes.

References

Asanuma-Brice, C. (2018). Fukushima, l'impossible retour dans les villages de l'ancienne zone d'évacuation: l'exemple d'Itate. *Géoconfluences*, October. Available at: http://geoconfluences.ens-lyon.fr/actualites/eclairage/fukushuma-iitate-impossible-retour [Accessed June 25, 2021].

Bernas, H. (2019). The Trail from Fukushima. *The American Historical Review*, 124(4), pp. 1364–1372. DOI: http://doi.org/10.1093/ahr/rhz313.

Brown, K. (2019). *Manual for Survival: A Chernobyl Guide to the Future*. New York: Norton.

Calhoun, C. (2006). *Public Culture*, 18(2), pp. 257–263. DOI: http://doi.org/10.1215/08992363-2006-001.

Curtis, G. (2012). Stop Blaming Fukushima on Japan's Culture. *Financial Times*, July 10. Available at: https://www.ft.com/content/6cecbfb2-c9b4-11e1-a5e2-00144feabdc0 [Accessed June 2, 2021].

258   *Harry Bernas*

Eisenhower, D. (1953). Address Before the General Assembly of the United Nations on Peaceful Uses of Atomic Energy. *New York City*, December 8. Available at: https://www.eisenhowerlibrary.gov/sites/default/files/file/atoms_for_peace.pdf [Accessed June 25, 2021].

Fackler, M. (2012). Nuclear Disaster in Japan Was Avoidable, Critics Contend, *New York Times*. March 9, Section A, p. 4. Available at: https://www.nytimes.com/2012/03/10/world/asia/critics-say-japan-ignored-warnings-of-nuclear-disaster.html [Accessed June 2, 2021].

Hecht, G. (2009). *The Radiance of France*. Cambridge, MA: MIT Press.

Hirata, K., and Warschauer, M. (2014). *Japan: The Paradox of Harmony*. New Haven, CT: Yale University Press.

Ishibashi, K. (1997). Nuclear Power Disaster with Large Earthquake. *Kagaku (Science)*, 67(10), pp. 720–724.

Kimura, A. (2018). Fukushima ETHOS: Post-Disaster Risk Communication, Affect, and Shifting Risks. *Science as Culture*, 27, pp. 98–117. DOI: http://doi.org/10.1080/09505431.2017.1325458.

Minoura, K., Imamura, F., Sugawara, D., Kono, Y., and Iwashita, T. (2001). The 869 Jogan Tsunami Deposit and Recurrence Interval of Large-scale Tsunami on the Pacific Coast of Northeast Japan. *Journal of Natural Disaster Science*, 23(2), pp. 83–88.

Minoura, K., Sugawara, D., Yamanoi, T., and Yamada, T. (2015). Aftereffects of Subduction-Zone Earthquakes: Potential Tsunami Hazards along the Japan Sea Coast. *Tohoku Journal of Experimental Medicine*, 237(2), pp. 91–102. DOI: http://doi.org/10.1620/tjem.237.91.

Mitchell, T. (2013). *Carbon Democracy: Political Power in the Age of Oil*. London: Verso.

Perrow, C. (1984). *Normal Accidents: Living with High-Risk Technologies*. New York: Basic Books.

Plokhii, S. (2018). *Chernobyl: The History of a Nuclear Catastrophe*. New York: Basic Books.

Ribault, T. (2019). Resilience in Fukushima: Contribution to a Political Economy of Consent. *Alternatives: Global, Local, Political*, 44(2-4), pp. 94–118. DOI: http://doi.org/10.1177/0304375419853350.

Schlosser, E. (2009). *Command and Control: Nuclear Weapons, the Damascus Accident, and the Illusion of Safety*. New York: Penguin Random House.

Smil, V. (2005). *Energy at the Crossroads: Global Perspectives and Uncertainties*. Cambridge, MA: MIT Press.

Topçu, S. (2013a). *La France nucléaire. L'art de gouverner une technologie contestée*. Paris: Seuil.

Topçu, S. (2013b). Chernobyl Empowerment? Exporting "Participatory Governance" to Contaminated Territories. In S. Boudia and N. Jas, eds., *Toxicants, Health and Regulation since 1945*. London: Pickering & Chatto.

Turner, B. (1978). *Manmade Disasters*. London: Wykeham Publications.

Weinberg, A. (1972). Social Institutions and Nuclear Energy, *Science*, 177(4043), pp. 27–34. DOI: http://doi.org/10.1126/science.177.4043.27.

Section IV
Timescaping through memory and future visions

13 Framing a nuclear order of time

Bernadette Bensaude-Vincent

For contemporary historians of the visions of the future, it is clear that nuclear technology is a paradigmatic example of innovations that pre-empt the future. That is, it has affected the entire planet and restricted the field of possibilities open to the generations to come. The vision of a future already there, embedded in past or present decisions, could have emerged from Hiroshima, when the visible impacts of nuclear weapons raised the fear of an imminent end to humanity. The vision of a future foreclosed could also be later generated by disasters at nuclear reactors, the accumulation of nuclear waste and the impact of radiation on living beings, which point at a dire non-future for *all* life on Earth. The purpose of this chapter is to more closely examine the impacts of nuclear technology on Western visions of the future. How, and to what extent, did the atomic bombs undermine the modern order of time, with its anthropocentric vision of the future? Did they really generate a new ontology of the future?

According to Barbara Adam, a futurist sociologist and historian, Western modernity is characterised by a shared notion of the future as an open realm to be filled by humans' plans and projects. But it was not always so. The ancient view of the future was a deity-directed fate. The Enlightenment period of western thought shifted toward widespread understandings of the future as an abstract, empty space calculated on the basis of present and past data (Adam and Grove, 2007). Allowing risk management and mastery of the future, this cultural model played a key role in western dominance over the world. "Imagined as an abstract, empty territory it [the future] is amenable to colonisation and control, plunder and pillage" (Adam, 2010: 366). Today, Adam stresses, the arrival of the atomic bomb has so disrupted the continuity of time that the once-open, modernist future has become a pure and obvious fiction.

The contrast between ancient and modern cultural views of the future is, surely, more nuanced. Cultural models of time are anything but neat, rigid and sequential structures—yet they document the evolution of ideas and attitudes toward time. Adam's historical analysis of the future echoes François Hartog's description of the modern regime of historicity,

DOI: 10.4324/9781003227472-13

262   Bernadette Bensaude-Vincent

or the idea of conceiving the present and the past *in relation to* the future (Hartog, 2015). However, Hartog argues, in the twentieth century this future-oriented approach to the past has been rivaled by a presentist attitude, favoring memorial practices instead of grand historical narratives projected into the future.

Examining the public discourses of scientists, intellectuals, journalists and political actors in three nuclearised countries (the United States, Japan, and France) in three key moments between 1945 and 1985, this paper tries to assess the impact of nuclear technology on the Western future-oriented experience of time. Hiroshima and Nagasaki did not mark the end of the arrow of progress. They did not immediately, or radically, undermine the established view of an open future. Indeed, in the immediate aftermath of these bombings, opposing visions (of a catastrophic end of humanity and of a bright future of endless energy) emerged from the same soil: the modern order of time in which the future makes sense of the present and of the past.

In the 1950s the Atoms for Peace program re-opened a future of modern comfort generated by nuclear energy, as illustrated in the slogan "electricity too cheap to meter" launched by Chairman of the US Atomic Energy Commission (AEC) Lewis Strauss in 1954 (Trischler and Bud, 2019). Thus, we see how memorialisation of Hiroshima established a nuclear order based on an intellectual divide between nuclear *weapons* and nuclear *energy*, morally tinged with the sense of bad and good nuclear technologies. Later on, the emergence of the environmental movement would reconfigure the nuclear order of time by shifting public attention to the global, long-term impacts of nuclear radiation for humans, the biosphere and the only planet on which we are known to survive. Nuclear technology provided a matrix for new representations of time, but it did not—could not—undermine the modern, future-oriented arrow of time.

This historical analysis of public discourses on nuclear technology instantiates the performativity of public discourses and metaphors (Austin, 1962; Lakoff and Johnson, 1980). It suggests that metaphors such as "nuclear apocalypse" or "nuclear winter" are constitutive of our experience of the world. They provide cultural patterns by which we make sense of what happens with regard to nuclear technology while occluding our full, detailed understanding of nuclear events and the human possibilities they create and destroy.

Hiroshima: end of humanity or new era?

Did Hiroshima mark the end of the modern faith in progress? Philosophers such as Günther Anders and Michel Serres have retroactively marked August 6, 1945, as a turning point. Anders, who corresponded with Hiroshima pilot Claude Eatherly, could not dissociate the mass destruction of Hiroshima from the mass destruction of Auschwitz: "There can be no question: The 'future' belongs to modern mass murder (to the extent that an appliance that produces 'futureless-ness' can be considered to have a future)" (Anders, 1979: 206; Liessmann, 2011). For Serres, too, the atomic bomb and the death camps were "tearing apart not just historic time but the time frame of human evolution" (Serres and Latour, 1995: 4, 15). Decades later, he declared that "Hiroshima remains the sole object of my philosophy."

Catastrophic visions of mass-destruction as a spur to collective suicide also sprang up immediately after the bombing. In France, for instance, Albert Camus wrote a famous editorial published on August 8, 1945 in the daily newspaper *Combat*: "The mechanical civilization has just reached the ultimate degree of savagery. Within the foreseeable future, we will have to choose between collective suicide or a clever use of scientific con-quests."[1] Two days later, Catholic novelist François Mauriac commented in his diary that the bombings of Hiroshima and Nagasaki represented a "planetary suicide" with a single benefit: to discredit the idea of the pro-gress of humanity (Mauriac, 2008). Striking a similar tone, influential American historian Lewis Mumford announced the end of the world in 1946, in a dramatic call to politicians entitled "Gentlemen: You Are Mad."

> The madmen are planning the end of the world. What they call continued progress in atomic warfare means universal extermina-tion, and what they call national security is organized suicide. There is only one duty for the moment: every other task is a dream and a mockery. Stop the atomic bomb. Stop making the bomb. Abandon the bomb completely. Dismantle every existing bomb.[2]

Remarkably the fear of extermination was a revival of an old trope from the early days of radioactivity research. By the tail end of the nineteenth century, when the discovery of radioactivity challenged the archaic no-tion of stable atoms undergirding the conservation of matter, fiction writers were drawing on the biblical tradition to tie the power of nuclear atoms to apocalyptic visions. Robert Cromie wrote the science fiction classic *The Crack of Doom,* imagining an atomic explosion, in 1895, and Herbert George Wells released *The World Set Free: A History of Humanity,* predicting a destructive and uncontrollable weapon, in 1914.

In the Bible, the Apocalypse is, to be sure, a moment of revelation: it unveils either the end of the world or the beginning of a sort of paradise, a peaceful world in which the wolf shall dwell with the lamb. The nuclear apocalypse, in turn, announced either the end of times or the start of a new era of plenty. Certainly, many parties subscribed to the latter vision. When US President Harry S. Truman announced on the radio that an atomic bomb had been dropped on Hiroshima by the US Air Force on August 6, 1945, this was his message:

264   *Bernadette Bensaude-Vincent*

The fact that we can release atomic energy ushers in a *new era* in man's understanding of nature's forces. Atomic energy may in the future supplement the power that now comes from coal, oil, and falling water, but at present it cannot be produced on a basis to compete with them commercially. Before that comes there must be a long period of intensive research. It has never been the habit of the scientists of this country or the policy of this government to withhold from the world scientific knowledge.[3]

In September and November 1945 two French physicists, Paul Langevin and Frédéric Joliot-Curie, adopted the same phrase—a new era—as they contextualised the atomic bomb for the French public.

One could not exaggerate the importance of the advent of the atomic bomb for the future of humanity. For it is something quite different from the invention of a new weapon of tremendous efficiency, hastening the end of a conflict that plagued the planet for six years. Actually, we are witnessing the dawn of a new era, the era of provoked transmutations, in a particularly dramatic way.

(Langevin, 1945: 3)

Based on the official report on the Manhattan Project by Henry Smyth (1945), Hiroshima was pictured as a normal episode in the history of radioactivity. A few weeks later, Langevin convened a conference at the Sorbonne where Joliot developed the promises of the new era. Three major features distinguished their view of the atomic bomb.

First, both insisted on the continuity between the new era and the history of physics, thus claiming credit for the contributions of French scientists like Pierre and Marie Curie as well as for Joliot's contributions to the new age. Second, they systematically downplayed the importance of its military uses to develop the promises of atomic energy. Langevin, a peace activist in the interwar period, did not mention the destructive power of the bomb but described it as the dawn of a new era of plenty. Third, they insisted that the "transmutation technology" was not, in itself, threatening. Langevin carefully concluded:

There is no real danger of a catastrophe.... [T]he only catastrophe to be afraid of would be the intentional and generalized use of this new potential for the sake of destruction. It depends on us to prevent it and to orient the technique of transmutations toward the improvement of human destiny.

(Langevin, 1945: 15)

For the advocates of a new era, the future was in our hands. It could be bright future, one starkly different from the vision of a collective suicide.

Disaster or new era? The striking ambivalence of earlier comments on the Hiroshima and Nagasaki bombings would shape nuclear power's Janus face for the public. It was both a weapon and a source of energy. Yet in the aftermath of the bomb, the only evidence most could see was the violence of an instant mass-destruction. Free electricity was just a promise, a way to reframe unimaginable horrors as just one side of a dual-use technology by way of a socially constructed mirror-image. Peaceful atomic power could provide welfare instead of warfare.

These visions of a better future prevailed, but not without cautions. The atomic apocalypse connoted a sense of urgency, captured by another biblical metaphor: the Doomsday Clock. In 1947, a number of atomic physicists founded the *Bulletin of Atomic Scientists*, a newsletter meant to inform the public of the risk of imminent annihilation of the human species. They powerfully connected medieval Doomsday descriptions with the ticking of the bomb in a famous image: a clock set to seven minutes before midnight.[4] The Doomsday Clock has been reset every other year since 1947. In 1949, after the first Soviet atomic bomb, the hand was set two minutes before midnight; it was moved back by ten minutes following the 1972 multi-national adoption of the Treaty on the Non-proliferation of Nuclear Weapons.

As Hannah Arendt notes, science and technology realise and affirm what people anticipate (Arendt, 1958: 1). Hiroshima did not significantly undermine the modern order of time. People easily made sense of the bombings by repurposing ready-made narratives from pre-existing cultural models. The biblical apocalypse dovetailed polar views of the atom as a promise for a better world or a harbinger of the end of humanity. Either way, the experience of time remained *future-oriented*. Even on the losers' side, in the city of Hiroshima City's mayor drew on the myth of the phoenix rising from the ashes as he launched a new slogan on the first anniversary of the bombing: "Hiroshima born anew on August 6" (Zwigenberg, 2015). This master narrative urged forward-thinking and rebuilding over mourning as the city reckoned with its devastation and victims' sufferings.

In the United States, France, Japan and beyond, bombing victims' pasts and presents would be invisible for a decade. When censorship began to lift in Japan in the early 1950s, a number of *hibakusha* started to talk. Each privately circulated testimony challenged the master narrative, however quietly.

An additional consequence of metaphorically adopting both new era and apocalyptic scripts was the comforting of human exceptionalism. The atomic bombs reinforced a western, *anthropocentric* view of history with two additional screen-effects. The prevailing image of a global threat to the entire human species transcended national borders and helped to depoliticise nuclear technology. Just as critics of the concept of Anthropocene claim that the very name conceals the responsibility of

266 Bernadette Bensaude-Vincent

capitalism in creating this new era, the perspective of nuclear technology as the potential end of all humanity concealed the responsibility of the United States in its introduction. Further, by inducing a single focus on the fate of the human species, radiation's effects on non-human life was overlooked.[5] The mushroom clouds generated a sense of human solidarity as well as a collective blindness to other forms of life.

History, memory and utopia

The two bombs dropped in 1945 did not immediately or seriously affect the western arrow of time, so how and why did Hiroshima transform into an icon of humanity's destructive enterprises, a twentieth-century cultural landmark? Depicting Hiroshima as a tragic expression of hardwired human violence and hubris catapulted the bombing out of the normal course of historical events. In the 1950s, through the program Atoms for Peace, Hiroshima reached a symbolic order by creating a "site of memory."

The Atomic Bomb Museum and the Peace Park at Hiroshima opened in August 1955. To memorialise the shock of the bomb and its victims, its local designers aimed to stimulate emotions rather than critical spirit in its visitors. The original museum made victims visible, their sufferings dramatically displayed to inspire empathy, identification, and a shared, universal model of human suffering. "Creating a sense of awe about the bomb by elevating it above the causes and effects," notes Daniel Seltz, is an important part of the culture of remembrance (1999). Thus, after walking through a dark, flame-lit entrance, visitors perused the clothing, watches, hair, and other personal effects of bomb victims, then traversed a section detailing the damages caused by the heat, by the blast, and by radiation.

The cultural view presented in Hiroshima's memorial museum stands in stark contrast with the historical approach chosen for the Nagasaki Atomic Bomb museum, opened in 1966. The Nagasaki Genbaku Shiryokan was, from the start, criticised as too political and not dedicated enough to promoting peace, and it was entirely redesigned in 1996. Hiroshima's choice to present a more consensual approach to history in the form of "site of memory" won out. Pierre Nora, who coined the phrase *lieux de mémoire*, argues that sites of memory, generally built by government officials, tend to erase local traditions, playing, for instance, a key role in the invention of a national memory in France (Nora, 1996). In the case of Hiroshima, this tendency to homogenise was pushed to the degree that it invented a universal memory, decoupled from *historical events*. The bomb dropped on August 6, 1945, was presented as a natural disaster, the destruction of Hiroshima a universal story of universal evil (Zwigenberg, 2014). There was no mention of who dropped the bomb or why; Japan's imperialist past and the United States' agency in its devastation were blotted out.[6] Displayed as the archetype of a mysterious violence with a metaphysical status, the bombing was detached from a chain of historical events. In this respect, Hiroshima museum conveyed a sense of nuclear fatalism in an effort to convince the victims that such sufferings were inevitable (Yoneyama, 2000). The symbolic weight conferred to Hiroshima is indebted to the sacred aura of its memorial.

This process of universalisation and sacralisation is close to the culture of memory that reconfigured the mass destruction of Jewish people as "the Holocaust" in the 1960s and 1970s, in the sense that it focused on the suffering of the victims (Alexander, 2002; Wieviorka, 2006). The two events converged in the Hiroshima-Auschwitz Peace March organised in 1962: symbolically turning the victims of these war-related mass killings into sacrificial lambs on the altar of Peace, survivors toured the world as witnesses whose sacrifice called for others to uphold higher moral standards (Zwigenberg, 2015). In other words, atoms need not be perceived as the end of civilisation—any technology's moral deployment hinged on the good or bad intentions of those using the power of atoms. The universalisation favored by the culture of memory in Hiroshima efficiently normalised and domesticated nuclear technology, and Hiroshima Peace Memorial Hall became a popular destination for school field trips from all over the world. Some 1.5 million people have visited the museum each year for 50 years straight.

Paradoxically, then, the culture of remembrance went hand in hand with a culture of oblivion. Once the bombing of Hiroshima was treated as an out-of-time event of transcendental status, with a strong normative power toward the quest for Peace, it became possible to divorce the tragic past from the present, the memorial from the new city. The frozen past, embodied in the clock stopped when the bomb detonated at 8:15 am on August 6, 1945, is contained on the island, within the perimeter of the Peace Memorial Park. Fifty meters away, a crowd of young people swarms around attractive shops with vibrant, pulsing neon lights. The temple of consumerism wraps its tentacles around the memorial.

Eager to improve everyday life and to take part in the modernisation of their country, Japanese society enthusiastically embraced nuclear power after World War II (see Zwigenberg, 2014). Japanese citizens were invited to enjoy the comfort of modern life. Yet beneath the *hedonistic present* of the emerging consumer society, in which every day Japanese favored the adoption of the American way of life, the 1950s also saw *increasing anxieties* around continued US nuclear tests in the Pacific Ocean—and the fallout they were creating.

On the US side, the progressive narrative gave way to a moral dramaturgy based on history rather than memory. On December 8, 1953, his country having conducted 42 atomic test explosions since Hiroshima and Nagasaki, President Dwight D. Eisenhower delivered a speech to the general assembly of the United Nations. In it, he launched a program called Atoms for Peace. Nuclear energy, Eisenhower announced, was a

268   *Bernadette Bensaude-Vincent*

global issue whose promise and danger were shared by all: "knowledge now possessed by several nations will eventually be shared by others—possibly all others." The present situation of global danger was, he explained, intolerable, as he switched to grand moral rhetoric about the ascent of mankind "toward decency, right and justice" imperiled by the two "atomic colossi" (the United States and USSR).

> Surely no sane member of the human race could discover victory in such desolation. Could anyone wish his name to be coupled by history with such human degradation and destruction? Occasional pages of history do record the faces of the "great destroyers," but the whole book of history reveals mankind's never-ending quest for peace and mankind's God-given capacity to build. It is with the book of history, and not with isolated pages, that the United States will ever wish to be identified.[7]

Eisenhower turned the biblical image of Doomsday into the "book of history" as Final Judge. Still, it remained a transcendental entity with no engagement in the political divides of the contemporary world. Eisenhower thus depoliticised Atoms for Peace, omitting the United States' military's move toward H-Bombs as well as its neo-colonial policies which were, even then, working to export US nuclear technology toward "third world" countries (Hecht, 2006; Krige, 2010).

The grand "history as judge" view was instrumentalised repeatedly throughout the twentieth century in order to justify political choices and projects.[8] With its Hegelian touch, it conveys the image of political leaders as geniuses capable of grasping the deep sense of History and guiding human societies in the right direction. Leaders of the Great Powers were the authors and owners of the global future. Eisenhower assumed that it was his responsibility to

> allow all peoples of all nations to see that, in this enlightened age, the great Powers of the earth, both of the East and of the West, are interested in human aspirations first rather than in building up the armaments of war.

Some western leaders, even as they extolled the virtues of spreading nuclear energy capacity, wanted to carry forward the understanding that it could always be used in destructive, murderous ways, and consequently iterated the "never forget" spirit. The future-oriented characteristic of History significantly shifted; the future that drove Eisenhower's mid-century decisions was no longer the vision of brighter tomorrows, but an unsettled legacy created for future generations, "the irreplaceable heritage of mankind handed down to us generation from generation." Promise had become a threat, elevating the priority of the conservation of human heritage.

In contrast, the same period in France saw a redoubling of the idea that nuclear technology signaled the dawn of a bright new era. It became a symbol of modernisation through a kind of nuclear tourism that was not driven by the culture of remembrance. In the 1950s, as an electrification campaign swept the country, the nuclear power station being built at Marcoule drew media attention and tourists. In 1955, Jean Cocteau, the famous French poet and filmmaker, scripted a commissioned film directed by René Lucot to celebrate nuclear technology.[9] Despite its conventional title, *À l'aube d'un monde (The Dawn of a World)*, the movie focused on the present and material aspects of nuclear technology: workers in uranium mines were portrayed as mythic heroes, "the atomic pile" as a domesticated atomic bomb, the burgeoning cobalt treatments of cancer as traditional cures, and the nuclear site at Marcoule as "a Parthenon waiting for its idol," plutonium. Notably, for the first time, nature was mentioned in a public discourse on nuclear technology, yet it was not as a victim of nuclear tests but as an allegory: "the coal field gets empty, the oil field gets empty.... Nature mysteriously points man's hand to an inexhaustible field" of atomic promise. French philosopher Gilbert Simondon has characterised *The Dawn of a World* as a "technophany," or a form of art issued from the expansion of technology, using a variety of classical archetypes without being too selective (Simondon, 2014). The film, the excitement and tours at Marcoule, it all helped integrate nuclear technology in France's popular culture in ways that were more tangible than even the ominous images of atomic mushroom clouds.

This intensive national propaganda campaign did not prevent protests against the French nuclear program. In 1955, a team of 665 atomic scientists and employees working in the Commissariat à l'énergie atomique (CEA), the French Atomic Energy Agency, were joined by 700 students to fight the construction of a third nuclear reactor in Marcoule (Topçu, 2013). It was much the same in Japan and the United States, where scientists also took the lead in protests and cautions. Instead of politicians' grand narratives, scientists took action on the public stage through international demonstrations, strikes, and manifestos. On July 9, 1955, Bertrand Russell stood in London to read a document known as the Russell-Einstein Manifesto. Co-signed by ten other scientists presenting themselves as members of the "human race," this momentous warning captured the world's attention. The document expressed concerns for our common fate. Given the destructive potential of H-Bombs (first demonstrated in 1952) and the long-term impact of lethal radioactive particles (as instantiated in the Lucky Dragon Incident), the authors underscored that the technological dangers to humans extended to their children and grandchildren. The worst was not certain, but it was *possible*. "Shall we put an end to the human race or shall mankind give up war?" became a focal dilemma for these thinkers, and it was

270   *Bernadette Bensaude-Vincent*

answered by an urgent call to find peaceful settlements to disputes between powerful nations in these formative years of the Cold War. The Russell-Einstein Manifesto provided the doctrine that would guide the Pugwash movement founded by Russell and Josef Rotblat in 1947 (resulting in a 1995 Nobel Peace Prize). During the Cold War, the Pugwash conferences and dozens of independent national Pugwash organisations around the world actively developed diplomatic skills as they laid the groundwork for agreements including the Partial Ban Treaty in 1963 and the Non-Proliferation Treaty in 1972. In 1988, the group extended its action to include environmental issues.

Despite all protests and the tensions of the Cold War the atom was celabrated as the icon of civilisation. A giant model, Atomium, was built for the 1958 World Fair in Brussels. It was meant as an icon for the fair's theme, "A World View: A New Humanism," and was located between the pavilions of the United States and the USSR,[10] attempting to release the tension between the eastern and western blocs' nuclear images and propaganda. Atomium clearly materialised the Atoms for Peace message, inaugurated with a call for world peace and social and economic progress and inviting 41 million visitors from April to October 1958 to learn about the inner structure of atoms. However, as a concrete metaphor, the Atomium had nothing to do with the atoms involved in nuclear bombs and nuclear reactors. It was a molecular model of a unit cell of iron crystal in which each sphere represented an atom. In shifting from the fissionable atoms of nuclear physics to the atoms of solid-state physics, Atomium substituted the images of destruction with construction. Atoms, in this presentation, were the building blocks of the molecular architectures designed by material chemistry. This silent shift in atomic inflection did not, to my knowledge, raise any comments at the time, but it presumably worked as a key device to acclimatise atoms as normal parts of everyday life. It disconnected the military uses of atoms from the domestication of atoms, reopening the future by conveying a positive image of atoms as the bricks with which humanity would build its limitless future.[11]

In sum, the nuclear escalation and nuclear tests of the 1950s more radically transformed visions of the future than did the 100,000 civilian deaths attributed to the bombings of Hiroshima and Nagasaki in late 1945. The nuclear race prompted a new geopolitical order in which the future depended on improbable agreements, miracle decisions. The modern vision of a future as an object of human will and creativity gradually gave way to concern for the future as legacy and heritage. At the same time, however, the propaganda campaigns around Atoms for Peace, supported by nuclear scientists, managed to keep a window open to the brighter future narrative by dissociating the destructive power of nuclear fission from the promises of constructive design using atoms. In the United States, France, and Japan, atoms were promoted with promises of consumer affluence and national security. Potential risks and health issues for nuclear workers were recast as a relatively small cost—just a part of the bargain.[12]

Nuclear winter: between apocalypse and collapse

The danger of a nuclear apocalypse is still around. The Doomsday Clock was moved again, set to two minutes before midnight, in 2018, amid North Korean claims about nuclear tests and tensions surrounding Iran. But the great fear once raised by the destructive power of nuclear technology seems to have faded in just 70 years. It took less than a century for the Doomsday Clock to become a routine barometer of the fluctuating tensions between nuclearised countries over time. Setting it forward or backward no longer attracts public attention. No one seems to care.

In public discourses and international policies, the perspective of an imminent apocalypse—the end of *mankind*—gave way to the anxiety of collapse—the end of the *world*. The time arrow is still oriented toward a tragic end, but this vision of time is less anthropocentric. This shift is correlated with the emergence of the environmental movement and concerns about how climate change, shaped by nuclear technology, has deeply reconfigured the order of time. How did the issues of nuclear bombs and climate change become intermingled?

In fact, they have always been connected. As early as the 1950s, RAND experts and US military research were developing calculations forecasting Soviet intentions and capabilities as well as computer models about the impact of weather on the spread of dust resulting from atomic explosions (Andersson, 2012; Andersson and Rindzeviciute, 2012). Irving Langmuir and Edward Teller seriously envisaged to use atomic bombs to conduct war through climate modification (Fleming, 2010). Most of these studies were classified, and they were exclusively concerned with local rather than global nuclear effects (Badash, 2009; Dörries, 2011). Nevertheless, they raised the environmental awareness of scientific writer Rachel Carson at the US Fish and Wildlife Service. Reading the reports of biological surveys in the Bikini Atoll before and after US nuclear tests (assembled by oceanographer Roger Revelle), Carson was convinced that human actions could pollute and endanger life everywhere. In her groundbreaking book *Silent Spring,* Carson transformed concerns about nuclear war into just one fear, alongside damage from chemical pesticides and other technologies, among many regarding the relationship between technology and nature. Does it mean that, due to the increasing concern for the conservation of nature, nuclear technology "changed ideas about humanity's role as an agent of catastrophic change," as Spencer Weart (1992) argues? To be sure, the impact of nuclear fallouts on the flora and fauna signaled that we needed to worry not only about the common fate of humanity, but the interdependence of humans and nature, writ large.

272   Bernadette Bensaude-Vincent

However, a global perspective on the impact of human technology on Earth emerged in atmospheric science, out of the closed circle of military and classified research on nuclear fallouts. It was prompted by the debate on ozone depletion in 1975, widely discussed in the public sphere. A few years later, Paul J. Crutzen, atmospheric chemist, and his colleague John W. Birks published a paper entitled "The Atmosphere after a Nuclear War: Twilight at Noon." Their computer simulation calculated that the explosion of an H-bomb would be followed by huge forest fires producing a thick smoke layer that would drastically reduce the amount of sunlight reaching Earth's surface. Darkness would persist for many weeks, attended by a significant drop in temperatures all over the globe (Crutzen and Birks, 1982). The perspective sparked a fierce controversy over the hypothesis of a "nuclear winter," as amply covered in the media from 1982 to 1985.

In the United States, a group of five scientists, Carl Sagan, James B. Pollack, Richard P. Turco, Owen B. Toon and Thomas Ackerman— under the acronym TTAPS—developed and publicised this nuclear winter hypothesis, arguing that cities burning would cause global temperatures to drop to −15°C. Sagan, an expert on planetary research with a famous TV series, *Cosmos,* used this scenario to advocate for nuclear disarmament. The debate among scientists became inextricably political; both in the United States and the Soviet Union, the nuclear winter hypothesis was taken up by advocates of the ban on nuclear weapons (Dörries, 2011; Rubinson, 2014). In America, the controversy would focus narrowly on the scientific validity of the hypothesis. Edward Teller, for instance, disparaged Crutzen and Birks's calculations as "dangerous myths about nuclear arms" (1982), and the journal *Nature* spread skepticism (Maddox, 1984). Nevertheless, the nuclear winter scenario gained acceptance on the political stage, especially with the support of politician Albert Gore, then a US congressman. In the Soviet Union, the hypothesis was more broadly supported, as the government leveraged it for anti-US-imperialist propaganda and Soviet peace activists and dissidents, including Vladimir Brodski, exiled to Siberia, adopted the framework to push for disarmament.

The entanglement of science and politics in the debates around nuclear winter, accurately described by Matthias Dörries (2011) and Paul Rubinson (2014), sheds light on the process that reconfigured the nuclear order of time. Both the metaphor of a nuclear winter and the ensuing public debate were key in overcoming the modern (and artificial) divide between *society* and *nature.* Just as Carson's metaphor of a silent spring (made silent by mass destruction) posed a decade earlier, nuclear winter connoted the impact of human technological choices on the natural cycle of seasons. Human history ceased to be detached from the history of Earth.

Computer simulations enhanced this vision of a tragic future in two dimensions: spatially, they established that even a local nuclear war would threaten all human cultures and all forms of life on Earth, and

Framing a nuclear order of time 273

chronologically, the nuclear winter controversy extended the time frame of nuclear debates into the unforeseeable future. Visualisations allowed a sense of the infinite timescales of nuclear aftereffects. The nuclear winter scenario drew public attention to the invisible and unexpected impacts of nuclear technology, due to the interdependency of all the world's inhabitants. It pointed out that, beyond the spectacular impacts of the atomic mushroom, a form of "slow violence" due to the pollution by radionuclides, silently and inexorably affects the whole planet (Nixon, 2011). It insisted the future is already determined, colonised by nuclear dust and its interaction with sunlight, plants and animals—the entire environment in which human history plays out.

Still, given the context of renewed tensions between the East and the West in the early 1980s, the debate over nuclear winter remained centered on the issue of nuclear war, without addressing the potential impact of an accident in nuclear reactors. Even after the Chernobyl accident in 1986, the extension of the nuclear winter debate to civil nuclear plants was hindered because some environmentalists reframed nuclear power as a low-carbon technology capable of saving rather than destroying the planet.

Climate change generated a distinctive form of catastrophism. The end of time is no longer envisioned as a punctual event, a bang. Big fires, floods, tsunamis, the mass-extinction of living species—the nuclear world breaks apart in a gradual process of climate collapse marked by a sequence of violent episodes.

Like the nuclear apocalypse, this more recent notion generates a sense of urgency. However, it marks the end of nuclear exceptionalism by positing a "great acceleration" of all sorts of technology such that a disastrous convergence of, for instance, overpopulation, mass species extinction, greenhouse gas effects, peak energy and economic inequality,[13] is amplified by rather than attributable to nuclear technology. Just as many nuclear catastrophists, today's collapsologists are more concerned with the times-before-the end (*katechon* in Greek) than with the end of times (*eschaton*). Both share the hope that humans are still the masters of their future. For instance, Pablo Servigne, Raphael Stevens and Gauthier Chapelle captured public attention with a sort of manual of collapsology and avoidance (Servigne et al., 2015) and a follow-up, *Another End of the World Is Possible* (Servigne et al., 2018). Others, such as Yves Cochet (2019), envision the "end of the world" as a decade of destruction followed by the advent of a better and softer world. This vision of disaster as a kind of purification is reminiscent of the ambivalence in the competing memorial narratives presented in Hiroshima and Nagasaki.

Conclusion

A brief survey of 40 years of public discourse about nuclear technology shows the remarkable resilience of modern visions of the future. Indeed, the atomic bombs reversed the arrow of progress toward an apocalyptic end of history. In the context of the Cold War, aspirations to new heights of progress gave way to concerns about legacy and heritage, and a culture of memory. However, advocates of and opponents to nuclear power converged in their attempts to open the future. Whether they struggled for control or for survival, they integrated nuclear technology into capital-H History, the grand narrative of modernity as humans' emancipation from nature. The perspective of sorcerers' apprentices threatening the future of mankind with their atomic tinkering was systematically balanced by the promise that atoms could shape the world to create a better human future.

Remarkably, neither military nor civilian nuclear technology could eradicate the deeply rooted prevalence of the future as a guide for present action. The imminent danger of mass destruction even reinforced the normative power of the future: the development of futurology as a new science meant using forecasts as a form of mobilisation for social and political actions at a global level. The future became "a field of world making" (Andersson, 2012: 1429).

In the decades following World War II, the experience of time was not exclusively shaped by nuclear technology. Despite the high visibility and spectacular impacts of atomic bombs, the quotidian use of oil and plastics by millions of people contributed more actively to framing the order of time in popular culture. As the future continues to drive the present, atoms nevertheless diversified visions of the future. They generated the threat of a nuclear apocalypse as the mirror image of the promise of a brilliant future, and by the end of the twentieth century, a combination of environmental and nuclear concerns generated a future envisioned as an amalgamation retaining traces of the past—predetermined by the choices of present and past generations. This vision of a preempted, colonised future gained traction with the increasing concern about nuclear waste management and the long-lasting effects of nuclear accidents.

Nuclear technology is no longer uniquely associated with the end of time, although atoms retain a specificity that should not go unnoticed. Atoms, implanted with nucleic clocks, directly confront our human and social notion of time. Radionuclides have a half-life time of their own, independent of anything else and, in some cases, incommensurable with our familiar timescales. Their inner clocks allow radioisotopes to be used for estimating the age of Earth. Even in the implausible scenario of total nuclear disarmament and decommissioning of all nuclear reactors on the planet, the future of Earth would be colonised by the various radionuclides left over from nuclear bombs and reactors. Whatever political decisions are taken about nuclear weapons, nuclear energy, and for the management of nuclear waste, future generations of humans and of all living beings will have to coexist with dangerous radionuclides. They are here, and they are meant to last.

Framing a nuclear order of time 275

The clocks in Hiroshima, stopped at 8:15 am on August 6, 1945, and the clocks of Fukushima, stopped at 2:44 pm on March 11, 2011, cannot create a temporal record of a bright, nontoxic future. They are stopped. Because the future depends on what has already happened in the past, we in the present have no choice but to learn how to share the world with these atomic traces and scars, the alien and dangerous creatures borne of human innovation whose temporality far exceeds ours.

These multiple coexisting times are not compatible with the linear chronological time (*chronos*). They favor, instead, the notion of *kairos*, the opportunity, the right time for action. Living in a devastated world should encourage us to give up the old cliché of the end of times and planetary suicide, just mirror images of the endless progress of humanity. It is time (so to speak!) to consider the multiple temporal regimes that make up our inescapably nuclear world. This is an opportunity to make technological and political choices aimed at reducing the asynchrony of the ongoing processes that end up in iterative crises. In other terms, living in a nuclear world requires a radical revision of time.

Notes

1 Camus, A. (1945). Combat. *Combat*, August 8, 1945, p. 1. Available at: https://www.humanite.fr/albert-camus-sur-hiroshima-leditorial-de-combat-du-8-aout-1945-580990 [Accessed June 17, 2021].
2 Mumford, L. (1946). Gentlemen: You are Mad. *The Saturday Review of Literature*. Available at: https://librarianshipwreck.wordpress.com/2017/08/09/atomic-warfare-means-universal-extermination/comment-page-1/ [Accessed June 8, 2021].
3 Truman, H. (1945). Speech delivered on August 6, 1945. Available at: https://www.youtube.com/watch?v=e3Ib4wTq0jY [Accessed June 8, 2021].
4 Interestingly this association provided a new cultural pattern for all kinds of scenarios of the end of the world as instantiated by Paul Ehrlich bestseller *The Population Bomb*, published in 1968.
5 Even when the damage caused on marine life by the US nuclear tests in the atolls of the Pacific Ocean became public in 1954, tuna was merely considered to be an economic resource for Japanese fishermen. It was just a matter of financial compensation for the loss rather than the warning sign of the large-scale impact of human technology on the environment.
6 The renovated museum, opened in 2019, still carefully avoids raising issues of responsibility, even in the section entitled "What led the US to drop an atomic bomb on Hiroshima?" Shiga Kenji, the director of the Museum, deliberately chose to downplay contextualisation and information in order to focus on the fate of individuals (Shiga et al., 2018). The main thrust of the historical exhibit of the east building, clearly separated from the section Reality of the Atomic Bomb focused on memory, is to describe the danger of atomic weapons. It describes the Cold war, the non-proliferation treatise, the protests against atomic weapons but ignores the construction of nuclear reactors. Only one caption mentions that Hiroshima doctors helped for radiation medicine after Chernobyl, but Fukushima is never mentioned. Clearly the memorial museum dedicated to the abolition of nuclear weapons and

276 Bernadette Bensaude-Vincent

peace activism in the name of human spiritual values reduces the "nuclear age" to its military face.

7 Eisenhower, D. (1953). Atoms for Peace draft. Address to the General Assembly of the United Nations, December 8. Available at: https://www. eisenhowerlibrary.gov/sites/default/files/research/online-documents/atoms-for-peace/atoms-for-peace-draft.pdf [Accessed June 17, 2021].

8 A few decades earlier the authority of the "tribunal of history" was called by Adolf Hitler in conclusion of his declaration at the trial following his failed attempt at a push in Munich in 1923:

"For it is not you, gentlemen, who pass judgment on us. That judgment is spoken by the eternal court of history…. Pronounce us guilty a thousand times over: the goddess of the eternal court of history will smile and tear to pieces the State Prosecutor's submissions and the court's verdict; for she acquits us"

(German History Documents, vol. 6 Weimar Documents (1919-1933) Hitler's Speech at the Putsch trial (February 1924). Available at: https://ghdi.ghi-dc.org/sub_document.cfm?document_id=3913 [Accessed June 17, 2021].

9 Lucot and Cocteau were by no means exceptional in celebrating new technology. Other French *avant-garde* artists celebrated plastics. See for instance *Le chant du styrène* (1958) a movie made by Alain Resnay, on the script written by the novelist Raymond Queneau.

10 The Soviet pavilion displayed a facsimile of Sputnik and of the first Lenin nuclear icebreaker, while the US pavilion offered fashion shows, color TV and an electronic computer.

11 A more conceptual version of the message was delivered by Nobel laureate physicist Richard Feynman at the 1959 meeting of the American Physical Society. He envisioned a program of bottom-up design of materials starting from atoms (Feynman, 1959). With its catchy title "There is plenty of room at the bottom," this talk became famous 30 years later as a prophetic anticipation of nanotechnology (Drexler, 1986). It inspired the motto of the 2000 United States National Nanotechnology Initiative, "shaping the world atom by atom."

12 On the condition of US and Soviet nuclear workers during the Cold War and how they were silenced, see Brown (2013), and Hecht (2012) for African workers in uranium mines.

13 The concept of collapse has been introduced by historian Jared Diamond (2005), who identified five mechanisms responsible for the collapse of societies based on several historical examples of civilisations collapsed.

References

Adam, B. (2010). History of the Future, Paradoxes and Challenges. *Rethinking History*, 14(3), pp. 361–378.

Adam, B., and Grove, C. (2007). *Future Matters*. London: Brill.

Alexander, J. (2002). On the Social Construction of Moral Universals: The "Holocaust" from War Crime to Trauma Drama. *European Journal of Social Theory*, 5(1), pp. 5–85.

Anders, G. (1979). *Besuch im Hades*. Munich: Beck.

Andersson, J. (2012). The Great Future Debate and the Struggle for the World. *American Historical Review*, 117(5), pp. 1411–1430. Available at: http://ahr.oxfordjournals.org/content/117/5.toc [Accessed June 1, 2021].

Andersson, J., and Rindzeviciute, E. (2012). The Political Life of Prediction. The Future as a Space of Scientific World Governance in the Cold War Era. *Les Cahiers européens de Sciences Po*, pp. 1–25. Available at: https://hal.archives-ouvertes.fr/hal-01361235/file/andersson-rindzeviciute-2012-the-political-life-of-prediction-the-future-as-a-space-of-scientific-world-governance-in-the-cold-war-era.pdf [Accessed June 1, 2021].

Arendt, H. (1958). *The Human Condition*. Chicago: University of Chicago Press.

Austin, J. (1962). *How to Do Things with Words*. Oxford: Clarendon Press.

Badash, L. (2009). *A Nuclear Winter Tale: Science and Politics in the 1980s*. Cambridge, MA: MIT Press.

Brown, K. (2013). *Plutopia: Nuclear Families, Atomic Cities, and the Great Soviet and American Plutonium Disasters*. Oxford: Oxford University Press.

Cochet, Y. (2019). *Devant l'effondrement. Essai de collapsologie*. Paris: Les liens qui libèrent.

Crutzen, P., and Birks, J. (1982). The Atmosphere after a Nuclear War: Twilight at Noon. *Ambio*. 11, pp. 114–125.

Diamond, J. (2005). *Collapse: How Societies Chose to Fail or Survive*. New York: Penguin Books.

Dörries, M. (2011). The Politics of Atmospheric Sciences: Nuclear Winter and the Global Climate Change. *Osiris*, 26, pp. 198–223.

Drexler, K. (1986). *Engines of Creation*. New York: Anchor Books.

Feynman, R. (1959). Plenty of Room at the Bottom, Lecture given at the American Physical Society in Pasadena, December 1959. Available at: https://web.pa.msu.edu/people/yang/RFeynman_plentySpace.pdf [Accessed June 21, 2021].

Fleming, J. (2010). *Fixing the Sky: The Checkered History of Weather and Climate Control*. New York: Columbia University Press.

Hartog, F. (2015). *Regimes of Historicity, Presentism and the Experience of Time*. New York: Columbia University Press.

Hecht, G. (2006). Negotiating Global Nuclearities: Apartheid, Decolonization and the Cold War in the Making of the IAEA. In J. Krige and K. Barth, eds., *Global Power Knowledge: Science and Technology in International Affairs*. Chicago: Chicago University Press, pp. 320–331.

Hecht, G. (2012). *Being Nuclear: Africans and the Global Uranium Trade*. Cambridge MA: MIT Press.

Krige, J. (2010). Techno-Utopian Dreams, Techno-political Realities: The Education of Desire in the Peaceful Atom. In M. Gordin, H. Tilley, and G. Praksh, eds., *Utopia/Dystopia: Conditions of Historical Possibility*. Princeton, NJ: Princeton University Press, pp. 151–175.

Lakoff, G., and Johnson, M. (1980). *Metaphors We Live By*. Chicago: Chicago University Press.

Langevin, P. (1945). L'ère des transmutations. *La Pensée*, 5, pp. 3–16.

Liessmann, K. (2011). Thought After Auschwitz and Hiroshima: Günter Anders and Hannah Arendt. *Eranohar*, 46, pp. 123–135.

Maddox, J. (1984). Nuclear Winter not Yet Established. *Nature*, 308(5954), p. 11.

278 *Bernadette Bensaude-Vincent*

Mauriac, F. (2008). *Journal et mémoires politiques*. Paris: Robert Laffont.

Nixon, R. (2011). *Slow Violence and the Environmentalism of the Poor*. Cambridge: Harvard University Press.

Nora, P., ed. (1996). *Realms of Memory: Rethinking the French Past. Volume 3, Symbols*. Chicago: Chicago University Press.

Rubinson, P. (2014). The Global Effects of Nuclear Winter: Science and Antinuclear Protests in the United States and the Soviet Union during the 1980s. *Cold War History*, 14(1), pp. 47–69.

Seltz, D. (1999). Remembering the War and the Atomic Bombs: New Museums, New Approaches. *Radical History Review*, 75, pp. 92–108.

Serres, M., and Latour, B. (1995). *Conversations on Science, Culture and Time*. Ann Arbor, MI: University of Michigan Press.

Servigne, P., Stevens, R., and Chapelle, G. (2015). *Comment tout peut s'effondrer: petit manuel de collapsologie à l'usage des générations présentes*. Paris: Seuil.

Servigne, P., Stevens, R., and Chapelle, G. (2018). *Une autre fin du monde est possible*. Paris: Seuil.

Shiga, K., Daimaru, K., Becker, A., Nagiscarde, S., and Mesnard, P. (2018). Hiroshima, une muséographie en recherche. *Memories at Stake*, 7, pp. 126–130.

Simondon, G. (2014). *Sur la technique*. Paris: Presses Universitaires de France.

Smyth, H. D. (1945). *Atomic Energy for Military Purposes. A general Account on the Development Methods of Using Atomic Energy for Military Purposes*. Official Report. Available at: https://ocw.mit.edu/courses/science-technology-and-society/sts-003-the-rise-of-modern-science-fall-2010/readings/MITSTS_003F10_read05_smyth.pdf [Accessed June 21, 2021].

Teller, E. (1982). Dangerous Myths about Nuclear Arms. *Readers Digest*, November, pp. 139–144.

Topçu, S. (2013). *La France nucléaire. L'art de gouverner une technologie contestée*. Paris: Seuil.

Trischler, H., and Bud, R. (2019). Public Technology: Nuclear Energy in Europe. *History & Technology*. DOI: http://doi.org/10/1080/07341512.2018.15700674.

Weart, S. (1992). From the Nuclear Frying Pan into the Global Fire. *Bulletin of the Atomic Scientists*, 48(5), pp. 18–27.

Wieviorka, A. (2006). *The Era of the Witness*. Ithaca, NY: Cornell University Press.

Yoneyama, L. (2000). *Hiroshima Traces: Time, Space and Dialectics of Memory*. Berkeley, CA: University of California Press.

Zwigenberg, R. (2014). *The Origin of the Global Memory Culture*. Cambridge: Cambridge University Press.

Zwigenberg, R. (2015). Never Again: Hiroshima, Auschwitz and the Politics of Commemoration. *The Asia-Pacific Journal*, 13(3), pp. 1–22.

14 Nuclear dreams and capitalist visions: the peaceful atom in Hiroshima

Ran Zwigenberg

In late April 1956, a mere 11 years after a US nuclear weapon destroyed Hiroshima, an American fighter plane flew a different kind of sortie over the city. The bomber's payload was rather peculiar: over 100,000 Japanese language leaflets urging residents in the Hiroshima area to visit the Atoms for Peace exhibit at the Hiroshima Peace Memorial Museum. The United States Information Agency (USIA), which sponsored the event and the aerial leafleting, did not, apparently, see the historical irony of atomic PR materials dropping from US bombers over Hiroshima (Jones, 2012). Indeed, the whole idea of having a "nuclear power for peaceful purposes" exhibit in Hiroshima, seems to us now, as it did to some far-sighted contemporaries, almost surreal in its impudence. Yet, for many involved at the time, it all made perfect sense: the fact that Japan, twice a victim to the atomic bomb, could whole-heartedly adopt atomic energy was not out of the bounds of common sense. Most Japanese, including A-bomb survivors and members of the anti-nuclear movement, were forward-looking, and nuclear energy was, at that particular moment, the future. It would be the late 1960s and into the 1970s before a serious movement to oppose nuclear energy developed in Japan. Even then, except for the *Gensuikin* faction of the movement (*Gensuibaku kinshi nihon kokumin gikai* 原水爆禁止日本国民会議) which came out against nuclear power in 1970, the larger *hibakusha* movement would not actively oppose nuclear power until after Chernobyl.[1] Briefly, this chapter considers how and why so many in Hiroshima—even within its anti-nuclear movement—supported nuclear power for so long.

Much of the historical research on the introduction of atomic power into Japan frames it as an American import. As this chapter demonstrates, however, that is an incomplete story. The Atoms for Peace importation into Japan was a shared American and Japanese story. The Americans employed much of their machinery of soft and hard power in their campaign to promote the Atoms for Peace campaign and looking at Japan through a post-colonial framework (in relation to India, as done below) supports the idea that Japan and the United States were far from political equals in the post-war period. Still, the atom was not simply forced upon the Japanese—it was *welcomed* by them. The Atoms for Peace campaign was successful, I

DOI: 10.4324/9781003227472-14

280 Ran Zwigenberg

argue, because it was promoted in terms intimately familiar to the Japanese people. It was billed as the very apex of modernisation, the model for which was America's consumer glamour and technological advancements. That is, the adoption of the Atoms for Peace program in Japan was about the twin forces of desire and reason, each symbolised (however ironically) by America and connecting the atom to the improvement of everyday life and the ongoing consumerisation and modernisation of Japanese society.

As Shunya Yoshimi[*] argued, as the image of wartime and occupation-era America receded, "'America' became a model of lifestyle consumption" (Yoshimi and Buist, 2003: 439). The Japanese desired to be modern and affluent so they could, in the words of one promoter of the Hiroshima atom exhibit, "live the dream of tomorrow."[2] Modernity was American. America projected affluence and promoted science-driven progress and rationality. Atoms for Peace stood for both of these forces. Significantly, only when the underlying assumptions fueling Japanese dreams of consumerism and American-inspired prosperity were challenged by the environmental movement and the counterculture of the late 1960s did the anti-nuclear power side start to oppose nuclear power in earnest.

Given the dual American and Japanese focus of this paper, I will tell this story through the actions of two figures, one American and one Japanese. Concentrating on these two figures and the 1956 exhibit gives us a lens into the history of the Atoms for Peace idea. The American promoter of the exhibit was the head of the American Cultural Center (ACC) in Hiroshima, Abol Fazl Fotouhi, and the Japanese figure was Ichiro Moritaki, a noted activist who was among the founders of the anti-nuclear movement. Both were far from typical.

Fotouhi was no shady operator. As his name indicates, he was not even a typical American diplomat; he was an Iranian immigrant to the United States, meaning he, too, was from a developing country—an apt figure to be part of this story. Like many of the principal actors in the Hiroshima drama, Fotouhi embodied many contradictions and ambivalences, which make casting the story of nuclear energy in Hiroshima as a black-and-white morality play impossible. Although he actively promoted the exhibit, Fotouhi was simultaneously and clearly uncomfortable with some aspects of the State Department's approach. Together with his wife and daughter, who attended a Japanese public school, Fotouhi immersed himself in Japanese culture and became immensely popular in Hiroshima.[3] In his writings, he contrasted his attitude and local knowledge with those of what he called the "stockade dwellers," other American and Western diplomats who resided mostly in Western enclaves and wasted little time on trying to understand local Japanese culture.[4]

---

[*] The names and surnames of Japanese persons have been reversed and macrons are removed to be consistent with the volume's other chapters.

Nuclear dreams and capitalist visions   281

Moritaki, a professor of ethics and a *hibakusha*, was, at the time, already a symbol of Japanese and Hiroshima's resistance to the A-bomb. Kenzaburo Oe called him simply "the philosopher" (Oe, 1997: 101). With his selfless activism, including lengthy sit-ins in front of the A-bomb cenotaph, he could have been a perfect "resister." Yet he, too, supported nuclear energy at first.[5] If Fotouhi was not a typical diplomat, Moritaki was not a typical activist. He was introspective and rejected self-righteousness—a quality that was manifested in his readiness to admit his own mistakes in relation to nuclear energy.

Moritaki and Fotouhi might have been exceptional in many regards, but they shared with many of their generation, both Japanese and American, a common-sense understanding of the benefits of reason and progress and a loathing for "extremism." Promoters of the Atoms for Peace campaign could astutely build on both broad inclinations.

Fotouhi and Moritaki first met in the context of Moritaki's work against American nuclear tests in the Pacific following the Lucky Dragon Incident, in which Japanese civilian fishermen were irradiated in March 1954 by the Castle-Bravo nuclear test in the Bikini Atoll. US actions were immensely unpopular in those days. Fotouhi recalled,

> The continuation of the Hydrogen Bomb experiments … had lowered the United States prestige considerably. Groups of citizens visit me almost daily to express concern over the 'apparent indifference' of the United States to the dangers from fall outs [sic]. To each group I would patiently explain the United States position and the role it was playing through the United Nations to harness the atom and control its powers.[6]

Indeed, one important "line of defense" Fotouhi and the Americans employed in defending the power's immense nuclear buildup and frequent tests was to argue it was promoting the atom not only as a force for war, but also as a force for peace. It was the same logic behind the original Atoms for Peace campaign launched by US President Dwight D. Eisenhower at the UN.

In this initiative and others, Atoms for Peace was tied to disarmament and lowering the tensions among global superpowers. When Moritaki, in December 1955, protested the continuation of nuclear testing in a letter to President Eisenhower and other world leaders, Fotouhi was tasked with drafting the American reply. In his February 1956 answer, sent to Moritaki and published in Hiroshima's newspapers, Fotouhi argued that the United States was consistently working to get the atom under international control as a step toward disarmament. He insisted that, in this goal, the United States was being thwarted by Soviet obstruction, but that "the government of the United States has been seeking an international system to promote the peaceful use of atomic energy, and to this end has signed agreements with many countries for cooperation."[7]

282 *Ran Zwigenberg*

Fotouhi's answer did little to persuade Moritaki or influence Japanese public opinion. In an editorial published on February 5, 1956, the *Yomiuri Shimbun* attacked Fotouhi's position curtly: "The question of banning H-bombs tests was flatly dodged."[8] *Yomiuri's* editorial stance might seem odd as, by this time, the newspaper was involved in a deep partnership with the United States to promote the Atoms for Peace across Japan. It was, in fact, the primary sponsor of a huge campaign, starting in Tokyo's Hibiya Park in December 1955, to convince Japanese of the civilian benefits of the atom. Such duality—the fierce opposition to nuclear tests and the equally strong support of nuclear energy adoption—was not, however, wholly unusual in this period. Significantly, while Moritaki and other *hibakusha* argued against both the Atoms for Peace exhibit and the introduction of atomic power into Hiroshima, they did not do so out of a principled resistance to all nuclear technology. Quite the contrary. Some *hibakusha*, including noted ones like Hiroshima mayor Shinzo Hamai, were avid supporters of the Atoms for Peace and saw it as a force for "life" balanced against the military atom, which was so obviously a force for "death" (Tanaka, 2011: 257). Thus, many, like Seiji Imahori in his later work *The Age of the H-Bomb*, construed atomic power as progress—a transformative path from a dark atomic past under the nuclear mushroom cloud into a bright atomic future lit by cheap, clean, modern nuclear energy (Imahori, 1960: 15).

This dynamic was clear in 1955, even before the Atoms for Peace show, when a proposal by US congressman Sydney Yates split the anti-bomb movement in Hiroshima. Yates's plan was to provide Hiroshima with a nuclear reactor as "a symbol of peace and cooperation" (Zwigenberg, 2012). The legislator explicitly connected the bomb and nuclear energy, using the above-mentioned logic, as he described "using atomic energy for life rather than death" (Tanaka, 2011: 251). Yates suggested that sending such technology to Japan first was a sort of concession: "giving preference for Hiroshima, which was the first victim of the atomic bomb in access to the resources of the peaceful atom" (Hiroshima shi, 1984: 208). The plan also called for the construction of a special hospital for the thousands of citizens of Hiroshima who had been exposed to the bomb and suffered ongoing medical issues as a result.[9] Others had made similar arguments; in October 1954, for example, the US Atomic Energy Commission's (AEC) Thomas E. Murray, using almost identical terms, called on his government to give a reactor to the city of Hiroshima as, "a dramatic and Christian gesture ... a lasting monument to our technology and our good will" (Zwigenberg, 2012). That the Yates proposal came, like the movement to decrease the US military footprint across the archipelago, following the Lucky Dragon Incident alarmed his fellow US policymakers. Removing bases from urban areas was "intended to 'scotch the idea so prevalent in Japan that that country was still occupied,' as Eisenhower's Secretary of Defense, Charles Wilson, put it," and "If we could not succeed in

Nuclear dreams and capitalist visions 283

destroying this idea, we stood to lose our entire position in the Japanese islands" (Kovner, 2016: 91). In the meantime, Shunya Yoshimi argues, the late 1950s saw America's image bifurcate in Japan: in urban areas, it was seen less and less as a violent and militarised influence, while, in Okinawa and other former Japanese territories, militarised America remained the norm (Yoshimi and Buist, 2003: 439). Constructing an enormous reactor in Hiroshima, of all places, went against this trend.

Consequently, Fotouhi and the embassy came out against the Atoms for Peace scheme. In a June 1955 letter, the director of the Atomic Bomb Casualty Commission (ABCC, an American medical research center in Hiroshima), Robert Holmes, proposed to the embassy "that Hiroshima should be the atomic center of Japan with ABCC as a natural center of activities of this nature." Holmes planned a campaign in Hiroshima, which included promoting treatment in the ABCC for sick *hibakusha*, promoting cooperation with the Hiroshima Medical University, and donating materials to the Hiroshima Peace Museum that would counter the current ideological line of the museum. As his interlocutor in the embassy commented,

> Dr. Holmes believes that there will be anti-US material [at the museum] possibly including skeletons etc., but thinks it better to join the exhibition and refute anti-US propaganda with material pointing up the beneficial uses of atomic energy and the function of the ABCC rather than leave the anti-US propaganda unrefuted.

Holmes apparently saw the reactor proposition as a welcome addition to his plan and was surprised when the embassy did not follow through. He felt "that the embassy erred in not recommending Hiroshima as the site for the first atomic reactor." Holmes also "took strong exception to the views of the PAO (Public affairs officer) in Hiroshima [Fotouhi] who has apparently not been overly enthusiastic."[10]

Moritaki and the local *gensuikyo* had been opposed to the Yates offer from the get-go. It was not on principle, but because an atomic power plant could become a target for Russian attack. That is, constructing a nuclear plant in Hiroshima could put it at risk for another nuclear attack. Hiroshima's *gensuikyo*, including Moritaki, supported nuclear energy, just with reservations. In their statement against the Yates proposal they cautioned,

> [we] hope that this immense energy source of the future will supply us with boundless sources of power. This is especially important for our resource poor country. But [we must remember] this great source of energy was also used in Hiroshima as a tool of slaughter, so we must ensure that it will be used (now) for the welfare of mankind. (Hiroshima City, 1984: 208–209)

284 *Ran Zwigenberg*

Gensuikyo's opposition angered Mayor Hamai, who told the press,

> I have been calling on the United States to spearhead the peaceful use of nuclear energy for the past two years [now]... starting the peaceful use of nuclear energy in the first city victimized by atomic energy would serve as our tribute to the deceased victims. Our citizens, I am sure, will welcome it.... I want to believe that this [nuclear plant] is intended as a life-affirming gift of goodwill. (Hiroshima City, 1984: 208)

The mayor was not far off the mark when he assured his readers of public support for the reactor. Such optimistic attitudes were widely shared across Japan. Tying atomic power with science and progress was a natural extension of the Japanese discourse of modernisation that held sway across the ideological spectrum in Japan. As Miriam Kingsberg demonstrated, the late 1940s saw a monumental shift in Japanese social sciences, with spillover effects on society at large. The shift started with a concentrated American effort to mold "Japanese research practices according to American cultural values and to restructure the transnational intellectual network of the prewar years into a US-dominated entity that served national political ambitions in the Cold War era" (Kingsberg, 2019: 151). As Americans claimed they were promoting scientific and universal "'truth' free from proclivity or bias, as the defining value of legitimate scholarship," in practice, these arguments about objective science masked a clear ideological agenda (Kingsberg, 2019, p. 152). After the shock of defeat, however, many Japanese social scientists believed that they had a role in promoting rationality, modernisation and democracy alongside American social scientists transitioning away from wartime racism. Ruth Benedict's *The Chrysanthemum and the Sword,* perhaps the most influential text of its time (in this context), rejected racism and insisted that the Japanese could embrace democracy (Kingsberg, 2019: 152).

Furthermore, going along with the American model, especially the atom, had its own inciting benefits. Both progressives and conservatives shared optimism about the nuclear project. Itty Abraham, in his work on the Indian atomic power program, observed that in the non-western, post-colonial world, the atom was entangled with the discourse of development and state power (Abraham, 1999: 10). This is certainly how power-broker figures like the LDP's Yasuhiro Nakasone and Matsutaro Shoriki, owner of the *Yomiuri Shimbun,* saw it. Nakasone famously commented that if Japan did not participate in "the largest discovery of the twentieth century," it would "forever be a fourth-rate nation" (Zwigenberg, 2012). Such anxiety pushed these men into cooperation with the United States and the Atoms for Peace program. As Abraham noted, "post-colonial"

Nuclear dreams and capitalist visions   285

elites, arguably including post-occupation Japanese elites, demonstrated deep concern vis-à-vis both the first world and their own population (Abraham, 1999: 11). "Post-colonial time is always time in waiting," Abraham writes, "in being able to see the future in the present through conditions prevalent in advanced states yet always being behind them" (Abraham, 1999: 11). The ensuing sense of urgency translated into a strong desire to modernise and rationalise; a desire to transform not only the economy, but also the psychological makeup of Japanese citizens. In other words, this was an enlightenment-derived project, with which the Japanese were closely familiar.

Japanese elites from Meiji on had tried to modernise and educate imperial subjects. The very emergence of Japanese nationalism and the idea of the national subject was tied to the modernisation project. Atomic power exhibits, like the many other industrial exhibits popular throughout post-Meiji Japan, were meant to inform, educate, and awe the populace with the power of science. Faced with enormous models of reactors, spaceships, and complex scientific jargon, organisers believed, the everyday citizen could not resist the pull of the future. In many ways this was, Abraham argues, "science as modern fetish." Atomic energy was treated as a triumph of science and rationalism; to stand against it was, thus, to stand against science and rationality, to be caught in the past and "against progress" (Abraham, 1999: 11).

The Atoms for Peace exhibit went forward in Hiroshima, but it seemed some were not overwhelmed by science, at least not completely. It all had a very rocky start. Strapped for funds and without an adequate space, the city removed over 2,000 articles from the Hiroshima Peace Memorial Museum to make room for the Atoms for Peace's exhibit. Local residents and the *Gensuikyo* sprang to action. Moritaki led the opposition to this move. Again, he found himself standing against activists and politicians who welcomed the exhibit. Just as it had with the Yates proposal, the *Gensuikyo* resisted the Atoms for Peace exhibit not on principle, but primarily because of the removal of the articles. They explained, conscripting the dead to support their argument (in a way not dissimilar to Hamai's rhetorical tendency): "We are not against the exhibit as such [but against the use of the museum for that purpose]. Behind these a-bomb artifacts there are the 200,000 victims ... these are more important than the exhibit and should not be moved."[11] Others were more indignant. Fotouhi quoted the main grievances in newspaper reports: "The energy which destroyed the city," claimed one survivor, "is now used as a tool to remove our most sacred relics from their permanent home with the possibility of never putting them back again."[12] Another resident voiced a widespread concern that the exhibit would contain active radioactive material and "contaminate our city again." The most prevalent complaint, however, voiced by Moritaki and others,

286 Ran Zwigenberg

was, "if the city and prefecture have funds for this, they should pay for *hibakusha* welfare."[13]

Responding to critics, the exhibit's sponsors organised a public symposium and debate in March. The editor of the *Chugoku Shimbun* spoke first, saying, "hundreds of thousands of people have seen the exhibition which depicts the miraculous use of the destructive atom in many peaceful ways," and urged Hiroshima residents not to lag behind. Fotouhi then told the meeting that,

> as a friend of the Hiroshima people and as a member of the community I felt that the Hiroshima people should not be deprived of the opportunity to see the many benefits that the atomic energy is now providing the mankind [sic]. My government therefore agreed to include Hiroshima in the scheduled showings.[14]

Fotouhi, pressed by the editor about the complete absence of the bomb from the exhibit, conceded that the exhibit was, "indeed, only about nuclear power. The dark side [of atomic power] the bomb is spoken of incessantly, thus, I would like the exhibit to inform people more about the side of peaceful use" (Moritaki, 2015). The *hibakusha* representatives offered mild retorts. Yuko Yamaguchi from the Hiroshima Society for the Protection of Children, for instance, countered that the Atoms for Peace might dilute the message of the anti-bomb movement. Heiichi Fujii of the local *Gensuikyo* repeated the organisation's position on the issue, but also said that one could *not* ignore "the dark side" of nuclear power and it must be incorporated for the exhibit to be acceptable. Both voiced concerns over radiation.[15]

Takeo Fujiwara, from Hiroshima University, argued, unaware of the historical irony weighing his words, "It is absurd to think that an advanced nation like America would knowingly bring unprotected fissionable material to any country."[16] When another resident spoke of the items in the museum as "relics," Fujiwara drew on the kind of elite anxiety discussed above:

> What is the museum? Is it a shrine? Is it a place like our Miyajima? If that is so, why then don't you have the marking of a shrine? Why should our ancestors object to anything if it means the future welfare of mankind?.... We need to understand the basic principles of peaceful living. We must see what the future promises.

It was as though his strongest argument was that irrational attachment to the relics of the dead (*ihin*) must not stand in the way of science.[17]

In April, following his second letter to the United States protesting nuclear tests, Moritaki directly confronted Fotouhi on the matter. According to Moritaki's diary entry on April 25:

Nuclear dreams and capitalist visions 287

> I tried to persuade the director [Fotouhi] that he should definitely not remove the atom bombing exhibits from the museum for this exposition, and that he should listen closely to the feelings of the hibakusha in the city. In closing, I said in a pretty forceful tone, 'If I were you, I would most definitely not have made this decision.' At this, Fotouhi responded, 'I'll paint Hiroshima over with "peaceful use." Mind you, with "peaceful use!" Just you wait and see!.'
> (Moritaki, 2015)

This outburst seems a bit out of character for Fotouhi, a rather mild-mannered man, but Moritaki's recollection of it suggests palpable impatience with those he saw as standing in the way of progress.

Fotouhi, who grew up in a reform-minded, land-owning family in Iran, had displayed similar feelings toward those he saw as standing in his father's way by sabotaging his electricity and irrigation projects. Fotouhi's upbringing seems also to have made him quite hostile toward communists, who once tried to assassinate members of his family. In this, Fotouhi was very much in line with the general trend in the United State Information Agency (USIA) and the US State Department, both of which were vehemently anti-communist. The USIA produced countless films and other propaganda pieces, especially aimed at audiences in the developing world. In one example, a USIA-produced cartoon titled "The New Adventures of Hanuman" (1958) used Thai and Hindu mythology to teach children about the dangers of communism. The movie was a joint Japanese-Thai production and spawned similar films in both countries and beyond (Holmstrom, 2019). Fotouhi, constantly worried about communism, became convinced in the fight over the Atoms for Peace exhibition that "*gensuikyo* was infiltrated by communist [sic] who wanted to use the organisation to further their goals."[18]

The specter of communism, as it happened, proved more phantom than reality. Fotouhi did not have to work too hard to overcome opposition to the Atoms for Peace program, as Hiroshima was quite enthusiastic for it.[19] The *hibakusha* were opposed not only by the ACC but also most of the city's leadership. As Fotouhi commented, "was not Hiroshima boasting for being the 'peace city,' so why not Atoms for Peace?" (Zwigenberg, 2012: 12). Indeed, in presenting Atoms for Peace as the wave of the future, the organisers of the exhibit utilised the very logic that underlined Hiroshima's own message of moving from the darkness of war into the light of peace.

Hiroshima had rebuilt itself along these same lines. The 1949 Hiroshima Peace City law equated building a "city of peace" with building a rational metropolis. Much of Hiroshima's official aim in the post-war period was about change and transformation. Kenzo Tange, who designed the memorial museum, saw his work as one of spiritual renewal, part and parcel of "the making of Hiroshima into a factory for

288   Ran Zwigenberg

peace" (Zwigenberg, 2012). Accepting nuclear energy, which was presented as a "key to the future," was a natural extension of this trajectory that equated peace with industrial modernity (Zwigenberg, 2014). Furthermore, Hiroshima City's stance was decisively apolitical. The city constantly averted conflict and sought to keep itself outside the ugly politics of Japan in the late 1950s. As Masaya Nemoto demonstrated, this stance was a side effect of the combination of "nuclear universalism" (i.e., the idea that Hiroshima was a universal tragedy that transcended national borders) and a peculiar brand of local patriotism or "regionalism" (Nemoto, 2018: 15). The City, Mayor Hamai in particular, gained much political power from the rise of the anti-nuclear movement, and sought to disassociate itself from national politics connecting the supposed local and peculiar connection of Hiroshima and peace with the global and universal message of nuclear disarmament (Nemoto, 2018: 20). This move was supposed to sidestep the contentious realm of national politics and was perceived as the rational and progressive response.

In this context, rationality, progress, and progressivism were all conflated. This was expressed symbolically by hosting the exhibition in the Peace Museum: it literally brought together the ideas of science and peace. In the exhibition's official brochure, Joseph Evans, head of the USIA Tokyo branch, told visitors,

> [I] would like to show Japanese and make them understand the true role of the atom in tomorrow's world.... How [the atom] can contribute to economic development, increased leisure, the welfare and lengthening of human life ... [and] contribute to the achievement of peace. (Zwigenberg, 2014: 118)

The brochure went on to explain the uses of the atom in agriculture, medicine, industry, and transportation with splendid illustrations of futuristic looking machines. The phrase "atomic bomb" was never mentioned.

On opening day, local media fully cooperated, praising the exhibit, speaking of "a new human civilisation" and of man gaining control over "a second sun" (Zwigenberg, 2014: 118). Local dignitaries were equally ecstatic. The head of the prefectural chamber of commerce told the papers, "we are entering a splendid era (*subarashii jidai*) ... it is good that I achieved old age [to see it]. [This era] is full of wonder and [we are laying] the infrastructure to make it happen" (Zwigenberg, 2015: 165). Others, especially scientists, stressed the importance of understanding the atom, furthered by the Atoms for Peace exhibition. A Japanese scientist from the ABCC commented, "The region of Hiroshima has an inseparable relationship with nuclear power and thus should have a correct understanding [of it]." Mayor Hamai said, similarly, "I heard

Nuclear dreams and capitalist visions 289

much about this. It is good to see it firsthand ... it is the first step that people should talk of deepening our understanding of nuclear power" (Zwigenberg, 2015: 165). The equation of American science and ideas of progress with neutral or positive values was ever-present.

Among the doubters, radiation and its effect on human life and the environment was the chief concern. Koichiro Tanabe from the Japan Pen Club insisted, "I am fundamentally in agreement with atomic power ... it will bring human civilization to a new stage. It is highly advantageous." But, Tanabe added,

> there is also one problem: radiation. After being used for electricity, there is allot [sic] of residual radiation. I heard that in the US they bury radioactive material deep in the earth. There is also the idea of dumping it at the bottom of the sea.... [Where] it is a danger to water and ocean life.... [The exhibit] does not dispel my unease over the problem of the ashes of death.

Moritaki was even more adamant:

> the people of Hiroshima are especially sensitive to effects of radiation.... [Thus] before we have atomic power, we should better understand radiation. [Furthermore] how will they treat the waste? Why is there no explanation of it.... They do not show what they will do in case of a malfunction in the reactor, or what they will do with the waste ... [and] the ashes of death. I would very much like them to address these issues. (Zwigenberg, 2012: 9)

Essentially, though critics were in the minority, critical reviews of the exhibit evidence that not everyone was convinced that the exhibit told the true scientific story of atomic energy nor that such projects could safely move forward without revictimising the people of Hiroshima. As the exhibit progressed, these voices were highlighted less and less.

It was not easy spoiling the party for Hiroshima. The Atoms for Peace exhibit was quite an event. This was, after all, the 1950s, and most Japanese still lived in poverty (Fotouhi recalled driving through mounds of rubble almost a decade after the bomb). The exhibit brought color, excitement, and a view of another world to the city. Visitors saw what they were told was the latest technology, and they were showered with information and brochures, all with futuristic imagery and bright colors. The exhibition's enormous banners, flanked by the flags of countries participating in Atoms for Peace, lent the usually solemn museum "a festive atmosphere." Newspapers magnified the celebration with daily features (including cartoons) about the exhibit, its contents, and visitors' reactions with a gusto usually accompanying events like the World's Fair. The items on display included a full-scale model of an experimental

290 *Ran Zwigenberg*

nuclear reactor and a model illustrating a nuclear fission reaction that used electric lights and panel displays to introduce nuclear physics. Attractions showed atomic power revolutionising daily life and leisure for the Japanese, as well as the atom's medical benefits and its uses in the space race. A particular hit was the "magic hands" display, a type of mechanical arm operated by visitors. The device was originally designed for handling radioactive materials, but attendees at the exhibit used it to pick up a brush and write *bunka shakai* (cultured society); the very design of the exhibit coerced visitors to equate nuclear technology with the ethos of progress and enlightenment (*bunmei kaika*) promoted in Japan since the Meiji era (Zwigenberg, 2012).

Like the Meiji reformers, Atoms for Peace promoters were successful in reforming Japanese opinions. A group of atomic bomb "maidens" (young women who suffered visible scars from the bombing), another symbol of Hiroshima and the peace movement, visited the museum and wrote,

> At first, as we were victims of the bomb, we were anxious about [the exhibit] … but after going through the exhibit we understand that Atomic Power can be used not only for war but also can be useful for the advancement of mankind. (Zwigenberg, 2012: 119)

Perhaps the most dramatic evidence of transformation came when the millionth visitor, who happened to be a schoolboy on an organised visit (as were the bulk of the exhibition's visitors), was rewarded with a precious prize: a television set. The TV was offered up by a local merchant, a *hibakusha* who contacted Fotouhi to say,

> My parents and children were all killed by the bomb. I have seen the exhibition and am thrilled with what atomic energy can do for the future welfare of mankind. I wish therefore to offer a large television set to be awarded the millionth visitor. (Zwigenberg, 2012: 121)

It was more than the Americans or their local supporters could have dreamed.

The gift of a TV was a near-perfect symbol, encapsulating the modernisation Atoms for Peace stood for. When it came to everyday people in Japan, modernisation was not just about science labs and reactors but also washing machines and electric fans. Fotouhi frequently referred to his background as an Iranian immigrant and spoke of how, like the Japanese, he was a firm believer in modernisation. He saw himself as the successful embodiment of what Christina Klein has called America's "politics of integration," in which Asian "others" were refashioned into honorary Whites in the Cold War West. For Fotouhi, though, this was not just a Cold War strategy—it was his life story (Klein, 2003: 12). With little

Nuclear dreams and capitalist visions   291

patience for the arrogance of visiting Americans, Fotouhi saw the Japanese as equally able of making the same journey he had. And he did all he could to build on this feeling of solidarity with the Japanese. The dream of bringing modernity to Japan via Atoms for Peace became a recurring theme in his speeches and diary entries. The same was true for Homi J. Bhabha, India's leading atomic scientist, who captured what Atoms for Peace meant to non-Westerners in a 1955 address at the Geneva Convention, "Atomic power... [will enable] the full industrialisation of the under-developed areas, for the continuation of our civilisation and its further development, atomic energy ... is an absolute necessity." Bhabha continued, "Everyone, even in country as vast as India, would eventually be able to *reach a standard of living equivalent to the preset US levels*" (emphasis added). Atoms for Peace he concluded, would "authorize an enormous leap into modernity" of just the sort the Japanese desired (Krige, 2010: 153). Along with other American imports, including jazz, William Faulkner, and modern kitchen implements, Atoms for Peace represented a "leap into modernity" and into "US living standards." The ACC did all it could to blend political progress, material comforts, and scientific advancements into one. This was part of a USIA-sanctioned policy that talked of "rapid economic, cultural and social improvement through application of power reactors" (Osgood, 2008: 26).

The ACC was formerly the local CIE (Civil Information and Educational Section) library, itself an arm of SCAP (Supreme Commander for the Allied Powers), which undertook a campaign of reeducating and democratising the Japanese people. As Hiromi Ochi noted, this center for democracy was often conflated with American affluence on account of the many American films, magazines and books it offered to borrowers (Ochi, 2012: 101). In April 1949, for instance, *Asahi Shimbun* featured a huge picture captioned "Fashion Season," explaining that "Tokyo's CIE library is very crowded with young women because of its American fashion magazines" (Ochi, 2012: 104). Ochi wrote, "At a time when few Japanese people could understand English, the visual images of the United States in the magazine pages served as a vehicle to present the brand-new idea of democracy as affluence." In the pages of those magazines were "many advertisements featuring happy housewives dressed beautifully in kitchens full of electric appliances" (Ochi, 2012: 104). Kitchens and atomic reactors might seem unrelated, but in Atoms for Peace exhibits, both were objects of consumerist lust, tied together by the reactors' production of the electric energy needed to power appliances and the new, modern lifestyle. This was true beyond Japan. General Electric's "Kitchen of the Future," for instance, became an integral part of the Atoms for Peace exhibit in the Netherlands, drawing as much, if not more attention as the nuclear reactors on display (Cieraad, 2009: 114).

292   *Ran Zwigenberg*

The Fotouhi family adopted this American strategy whole-heartedly. At the same time that her husband was promoting American science throughout Japan, Agnes Fotouhi toured Hiroshima and neighboring prefectures with a mobile display kitchen "showing how average Americans live at home."[20] According to a USIA pamphlet, "she introduced American cooking, improved Japanese housekeeping, [and] taught preparation of inexpensive, nutritious meals."[21] Japanese women, according to the *Asahi Shimbun,* enthusiastically accepted "this [lesson] in scientific home economics" (Ochi, 2012: 101). Agnes Fotouhi's participation in her American husband's more "muscular" diplomatic and military pursuits in Japan was not exceptional. The American government, in cooperation with American universities, had established home economics programs in Japan and Okinawa. American military families were used again and again by Fotouhi and other diplomats in "people to people" diplomacy with the Japanese; "transcending barriers," as Fotouhi put it, through "simple human interaction." This division of gendered labor might be seen as corresponding to "soft" (feminine) and "hard" (masculine) power. Yet, as Mire Koikari has pointed out, such binaries are overly simple ways to frame the coordinated efforts: as women learned and taught "a 'modern,' 'scientific,' and 'American' food preparation and home management," they too claimed a space in the modern world—and the modernisation of their world in a Western mold (2017: 82). Japanese people, whether male or female, wanted to be more "scientific" and "modern," from atomic reactors to "nutritious" meals, and Westerners, whether male or female, could show them the way (Koikari, 2017; Hopson, 2020).

John Krige has aptly called Atoms for Peace "an exercise in... the education of desire" (Krige, 2010: 152). Krige, who wrote on India and other postcolonial states' embrace of AFP, interpreted Atoms for Peace as a channeling of the desire of non-Westerners to modernise. This formulation is especially apt in the Japanese case, in which the post-war period made the necessity of modernisation seemingly plain. Although Japanese intellectuals had a strong tradition of doubting and problematising modernity, their objections were largely absent in the 1940s and 1950s. Ideas about "overcoming modernity," explored at length by thinkers including Hideo Kobayashi and Kyoto-school philosopher Kitaro Nishida, were tarred with the brush of fascism and imperialism, then cast aside after 1945 (Sakai and Isomae, 2010). In this climate, resisting Atoms for Peace and Americanisation, especially in its peculiar casting by the ACC as a blend of progress and affluence, was quite difficult. To go back to Kingsberg, following the war and occupation, many Japanese and Americans had a "shared conviction that the values of democracy, capitalism, and peace were bases of knowledge" (Kingsberg, 2019: 166). In Hiroshima, the order of operations was just slightly different: here, democracy, capitalism, and knowledge would lead to peace. And *peace* was Hiroshima's totem.

Even Ichiro Moritaki came around. In Nagasaki in August 1956, he proclaimed as part of Hidankyo's founding statement, "Atomic power ... must absolutely be converted to a servant for the happiness and prosperity of humankind. This is the only desire we hold as long as we live" (Zwigenberg, 2012). Even the more unorthodox and politically active among Japan's scientists and thinkers would not challenge nuclear energy. The career of Nobel Prize-winning physicist Hideki Yukawa provides a case in point. The Lucky Dragon Incident had shocked Yukawa, "making him aware of his social responsibility as a scientist, as well as of nuclear weapons' imminent danger to humanity" (Kurosaki, 2018: 115). One of his first actions was to publish an extremely influential essay in the *Mainichi Shimbun* titled "Atomic Energy and the Turning Point of Humanity." This was a start of a very active career that sent him to Pugwash and other political forums. But neither in this essay nor elsewhere did Yukawa and his colleagues challenge the Atoms for Peace's separation of *nuclear weapons* from *nuclear energy*.

Moritaki would not backtrack to reject the Atoms for Peace's foundational ideas until the 1970s, when he became, like leading international activists, deeply concerned about radiation. Many of these thinkers, with whom he was interacting on the global stage, had started to come out against nuclear power, building on the first stirrings, in the 1960s, against the project of fast-paced Japanese modernisation and economic growth. Moritaki and others had come, together, to see the many connections between unbridled consumerism, developmental capitalism, environmental degradation and radiation hazards. They started to protest nuclear power. As Akira Kurosaki has demonstrated, many Japanese scientists led a critique of nuclear orthodoxy, now from within the peace movement (Kurosaki, 2018: 102).

The roots of this change can be found deep in the struggles over the nuclear test ban and related Cold War issues, when a number of pro-Soviet and pro-Chinese factions split from *Gensuikyo*. *Gensuikin* (Moritaki's branch of the movement) was against all tests and weapons, "socialist" or "imperialist" bombs alike. The mid-1960s were also an era of rising environmental salience. The Minamata disease and other incidents had disturbed the Japanese "dream of tomorrow." Moritaki recalled that the change "resulted largely from our deepening understanding of nuclear issues, [and] its backdrop lay in escalating environmental destruction and pollution occurring in Japan due to high-speed economic growth as well as the impact of the United Nations Conference on the Human Environment held in Stockholm in June of the same year [1972]" (Moritaki diary).

Moritaki starts the story of his "conversion" with a 1969 meeting at Yaizu, where the Lucky Dragon No. 5 was based. Anti-Vietnam and

294   Ran Zwigenberg

other activist groups gathered, and, in a sub-committee meeting on nuclear power (incidentally, headed by a representative from Fukushima) Moritaki noted that *Gensuikin* decided to "earnestly take up the issue of nuclear power." He added that he, personally, was by this time vehemently against the construction of any new nuclear power stations (Moritaki, 2015: 34). The meeting mostly moved on to discuss Vietnam, Okinawa, and other issues, but the location of these first declarations show the context of counter-culture politics where this change was taking place. Moritaki recalled his realisation that, even without the active "military use of nuclear weapons" the danger of radiation was real and ever-present; it started, he said, in 1967, with the struggle against the introduction of nuclear aircraft carriers and submarines to Sasebo in Nagasaki, the accidental dropping of nuclear weapons in Spain, and the evidence of the lingering impact of radiation in the Marshall Islands (Moritaki, 2015: 20). Still, he would cling to science and enlightenment, affirming at the time that

> we have to re-learn the problem [of nuclear power] seriously again. But we have to do so from the point of view of natural science. In order to enlighten the people (on the matter) we have to have the knowledge and ability [to do so]. (Moritaki, 2015)

It was dissident scientists' turn against nuclear power that eventually swayed Moritaki and the movement he led. Anti-Vietnam and other anti-establishment activism were as important globally as it was locally, in 1971, when Moritaki traveled to Washington. There he met anti-nuclear chemist Linus Pauling, with whom he had a long correspondence, and Patricia Lindop, a physicist from St. Bartholomew's Medical College who was active in PSR (Physicians for Social Responsibility, another peace group). Through these meetings, Moritaki came to know another anti-nuclear scientist, John Gofman. As Soraya Boudia demonstrates in this volume, Gofman's work on low-dose exposure and the campaign he led against the AEC were transformational for public discussion about radiation in the United States. Gofman and Lindop made a profound impression on Moritaki (Moritaki, 2015: 22). He was particularly impressed by Lindop, who argued at the meeting, "What is radiation? You cannot see it, you cannot smell it or taste it but radiation is affecting our children ... and spreading cancer, we cannot forgive the scientists who conceal this [truth] and [keep it] quiet" (Moritaki, 2015: 23). All three scientists pointed out the connections and similarities between environmental pollution and radiation from tests and nuclear accidents. All three suspected a similar cover-up around both.

That same year, Moritaki traveled to Paris, where he met with French and German "green activists," including scientists calling for a fight against "radiation pollution" (Moritaki, 2015: 23). "In this trip," wrote

Moritaki, "I realized ... that European and American scholars began to seriously think and act on pollution problems associated with the peaceful use of nuclear energy" (Moritaki, 2015: 24). When he returned to Japan, Moritaki actively worked to include in the next *gensuikin* conference a statement connecting nuclear power and environmental pollution. At the world conference marking the 27th anniversary of the atomic bombing (1972), the movement adopted the slogan, "Let us oppose the introduction of nuclear power plants and spent fuel reprocessing facilities, which cause major environmental disruption and radioactive pollution" (Moritaki, 2015: 23).

But, again, the global developments had built upon local grassroots activism. The national Japanese movement against nuclear power started locally, focused on the sites of the early nuclear plants built in the mid-1960s and into the early 1970s (Craig, 2011). Protests reflected a range of concerns, from nuclear safety to possible economic disruptions, but also connected to a much wider dissatisfaction and anger over the costs of development. Moritaki saw in these protests similarities to anti-nuclear and anti-pollution protests he had encountered in Brittany on another trip to France in 1974 (Moritaki, 2015: 28).

Gensuikin thus actively sought to connect with local movements like the one in Ikata, where local residents had started a legal fight against the construction of a nuclear power plant in 1973. Ikata activists had not initially been concerned with the larger anti-nuclear struggle, but wanted to avoid the large-scale declines in fish populations that had been seen in other cities that played host to nuclear plants. The economy was largely based on fishing, and a vast die-off would decimate Ikata's local economy. In the same year that Ikata went to trial, the *Genshiryoku Shiryo Johoshitsu* (known in English as the Citizen's Center for Nuclear Information, or CNIC), was founded by grassroots activists (Craig, 2011). The coming together of movements like the CNIC and the older peace movement was the beginning of a wider shift in attitudes. Yet, for the general public, the anti-nuclear movement would not gain prominence until the Chernobyl accident. Doubts over nuclear power were, indeed, noticeable in the 1970s, and they steadily gained ground as nuclear accidents multiplied.

The dream of boundless energy fizzled, but only through a multitude of developments and the coming together of local protest, global political mobilisation and the broader radicalisation and rethinking of values that came with the anti-Vietnam War movement. The resulting counterculture brought Moritaki and other *hibakusha* activists to resist nuclear power by reintroducing doubts over modernity and its costs. Even then, it must be remembered, theirs was a minority position. *Gesnuikyo* was hesitant to come out against nuclear power; according to Moritaki, it did not want to be seen acting "against science." Such was the power of the *idea* of the AFP and its powerful, symbolic confluence of progress, science and affluence. AFP built on the desire of the Japanese for a "bright future" and a "bright peace." It required the equation of both with consumer desire and capitalist visions of the "dream of tomorrow." This project was construed as a natural continuation of the Meiji slogans of culture and enlightenment and as paths to modernisation. Disastrously, its grip on the Japanese imagination lasted well into the twenty-first century.

Notes

1 Both Gensuikyo (原水爆禁止日本協議会) and Hidankyo (日本原水爆被害者団体協議会) officially supported "nuclear power for peaceful purposes."
2 *Chuugoku Shimbun*, May 29, 1956.
3 Interview with Farida Fotouhi, October 1, 2011.
4 *Louisville Courier Journal*, December 26, 1954.
5 Moritaki, who was certainly not comfortable with Oe's and others' compliments, acknowledged his own imperfections and, in the case of nuclear energy, wrote at length explaining his past mistake in supporting it
6 I thank Farida Fotouhi for giving me access to her father's personal archive. The references to "Fotouhi" refer to Abol Fazl Fotouhi, unpublished memoir, (Fotouhi Papers). This quotation: Fotouhi, p. 206.
7 Fotouhi, p. 207.
8 *Yomiuri Shimbun*, February 5, 1956.
9 *Chugoku Shimbun*, February 5, 1955.
10 C. Segwick to Mr. Morgan and Mr. Hackle, Dr. Holmes (20 June 1955), RG 34, Box 187, Folder 3, United States National Archives, College Park, MD.
11 Fotouhi, p. 200. See also the *Chugoku Shimbun*, March 22, 1956 for an edited text of the meeting.
12 Fotouhi, p. 200.
13 Fotouhi, p. 198.
14 *Chugoku Shimbun*, March 22, 1956.
15 *Chugoku Shimbun*, March 22, 1956.
16 The *Chugoku Shimbun* account of the symposium did not mention this exchange. This quote is from Fotouhi's papers.
17 *Chugoku Shimbun*, March 22,1956.
18 Fotouhi, p. 181.
19 The ACC was only one of five sponsors of the exhibit, and it received the enthusiastic support of Hiroshima City leadership, Hiroshima prefecture, Hiroshima University, and the *Chugoku Shimbun*.
20 Undated *Chugoku Shimbun* clipping, Fotouhi papers.
21 United States Information Agency, 8th review of Operations, Fotouhi papers, p. 2.

References

Abraham, I. (1999). *The Making of the Indian Atomic Bomb: Science, Secrecy and the Postcolonial State*. New Delhi: Orient Longman.
Cieraad, I. (2009). The Radiant American Kitchen: Domesticating Dutch Nuclear Energy. In: R. Oldenziel and K. Zachmann, eds., *Cold War Kitchen: Americanization, Technology, and European Users*. Cambridge, MA: MIT Press, pp. 113–159.

Craig, N. (2011). "The Energy of a Bright Tomorrow": The Rise of Nuclear Power in Japan. *Origins*, 4(9). Available at: https://origins.osu.edu/article/energy-bright-tomorrow-rise-nuclear-power-japan [Accessed June 26, 2021].

Hiroshima City. (1984). *Hiroshima shinshi: rekishi hen*. Hiroshima: Hiroshima City.

Holmstrom, H. (2019). Animatics and Anti-Communism: Payut Ngaokrachang Animates Hanuman for the USIA. The Unwritten Record [blog], National Archives, May 15, 2019. Available at: https://unwritten-record.blogs.archives.gov/2019/05/15/animatics-and-anti-communism/ [Accessed June 26, 2021].

Hopson, N. (2020). Ingrained Habits: The 'Kitchen Cars' and the Transformation of Postwar Japanese Diet and Identity. *Food, Culture and Society*, 23, pp. 589–607.

Imahori, S. (1960). *Gensuibaku jidai: gendaishi no shogen*. Kyoto: San'ichishobō.

Jones, M. (2012). *After Hiroshima: The United States, Race and Nuclear Weapons in Asia, 1945*. Cambridge, UK: Cambridge University Press.

Kingsberg, M. (2019). Transnational Knowledge, American Hegemony: Social Scientists in US-Occupied Japan. In: J. Krige, ed., *How Knowledge Moves: Writing the Transnational History of Science and Technology*. Chicago: University of Chicago Press, pp. 149–174.

Klein, C. (2003). *Cold War Orientalism: Asia in the Middlebrow Imagination, 1945–1961*. Berkeley, CA: University of California Press.

Koikari, M. (2017). *Cold War Encounters in US-Occupied Okinawa: Women, Militarized Domesticity and Transnationalism in East Asia*. Cambridge, UK: Cambridge University Press.

Kovner, S. (2016). The Soundproofed Superpower: American Bases and Japanese Communities, 1945–1972, *Journal of Asian Studies*, 75(1), pp. 87–109.

Krige, J. (2010). Techno-Utopian Dreams, Techno-Political Realities: The Education of Desire for the Peaceful Atom. In: M. Gorodin, G. Prakash and H. Tilley, eds., *Utopia/Dystopia: Conditions of Historical Possibility*. Princeton, NJ: Princeton University Press, pp. 151–175.

Kurosaki, A. (2018). Japanese Scientists' Critique of Nuclear Deterrence Theory and Its Influence on Pugwash, 1954–1964. *Journal of Cold War Studies*, 20 (1), pp. 101–139.

Moritaki, I. (n.d.). Diary. Available at: http://www.gensuikin.org/data/mori1.html [Accessed May 28, 2019].

Moritaki, I. (2015). *Kaku to jinrui wa kyooson dekinai: kaku zettai hitei e no ayumi*. Tokyo: Kabushiki Kaisha Nanatsumori Shokan.

Nemoto, M. (2018). *Hiroshima paradokusu: sengo Nihon no hankaku to jindoo ishiki*. Tokyo: Bensei Shuppan.

Ochi, H. (2012). Democratic Bookshelf: American Libraries in Occupied Japan. In: G. Barnhisel and C. Turner, eds., *Pressing the Fight: Print, Propaganda, and the Cold War*. Amherst, MA: University of Massachusetts Press, pp. 89–111.

Oe, K. (1997). *Hiroshima Notes*. London: Marion Boyars.

Osgood, K. (2008). *Total Cold War: Eisenhower's Secret Propaganda Battle at Home and Abroad*. Lawrence, KS: University of Kansas.

Sakai, N., and Isomae, J. (2010). *Kindai no chookoku to Kyoo to gakuha: kindaisei, teikoku, fuhensei*. Kyoto-shi: Ningen Bunka Kenkyu Kiko Kokusai Nihon Bunka Kenkyu Senta.

298   Ran Zwigenberg

Tanaka, T. (2011). Genshiryoku heiwa ryo to Hiroshima: senden kosaku no tageto ni sareta hibakushatachi. *Sekai*, 25, pp. 248–261.

Yoshimi, S., and Buist, D. (2003). "America" as Desire and Violence: Americanization in Postwar Japan and Asia during the Cold War. *Inter-Asia Cultural Studies*, 4(3), pp. 433–450.

Zwigenberg, R. (2012). "The Coming of a Second Sun": The 1956 Atoms for Peace Exhibit in Hiroshima and Japan's Embrace of Nuclear Power. *The Asia-Pacific Journal*, 10(6,1), 1–15. Available at: https://apjjf.org/2012/10/6/Ran-Zwigenberg/3685/article.html.

Zwigenberg, R. (2014). *Hiroshima: The Origins of Global Memory Culture*. Cambridge: Cambridge University Press.

Zwigenberg, R. (2015). Aboru Futsui to Moritaki Ichiro: genshuryoku no yume to Hiroshima. In: T. Morris Suzuki, S. Yoshimi and M. Chikanobu, eds., *Choosen no Sensoo: 1950-nendai*. Tokyo: Iwanami Shoten, pp. 158–177.

15 Slow disaster and the challenge of nuclear memory[1]

Scott Gabriel Knowles

Memorial practices are some of the strongest tools we have for making sense of disasters over time. What gets remembered and the traditions surrounding those memories—these offer deep insight into the ways that societies craft meaning and structure out of disaster, what gets learned and also unlearned. Wars are the disasters most commonly memorialised in stone and structures. But other types of disasters provoke memory and artifacts, too, even without the construction of monuments. In songs and stories, art and architecture, and the recording of events through manifold channels of documentation, disasters mark their time in both the individual and collective consciousness (Figure 15.1).

The nuclear defies ordinary timelines and measures of impact, rendering and rupturing memorial practices and public memory in ways that shift and change like the landscape around atomic incidents. The Japanese 3.11 "triple disaster" was not the first time nations, communities, corporations and public history-makers have struggled to memorialise and make sense of nuclear disaster—Hiroshima, Nagasaki, Chernobyl and Three Mile Island present cases for comparison, as do sometimes lesser-known nuclear witnesses like the workers of Weldon Spring, Missouri.

This chapter sketches out the political and cultural impediments to nuclear memory, while also charting creative modes of memorialisation. How do events speak across distances of time, and what burdens do the maintainers of these dialogues bear—how does the maintenance of nuclear memory create new victims? How can memorials effectively convey loss when the timescale of that loss is incalculable?

Throughout, this essay argues for the use of a slow disaster methodology, proposing the history of disaster memory as a way to think about the nuclear not only as a set of material realities, but also as an assemblage of ideas and cultural practices, warnings and hopes and nightmares. Nuclear memory can be an aid to an impoverished historical record, so full of erasures, and also open the way for new critical approaches to disaster governance, climate change activism, and explorations of the Anthropocene.

DOI: 10.4324/9781003227472-15

Figure 15.1 Weldon Spring Site Remedial Action Project Disposal Cell, Weldon Spring, Missouri. Photo by Scott Gabriel Knowles, 2019.

Scales of disaster

Disasters come in the violence of moments, but also lifetimes—beyond lifetimes. That is, all disasters have multiple temporal dimensions. Attentiveness to disasters of the present, of the past, of the deep past, into the deep future or ongoing across time—each is a choice of focus for individuals and for societies. Studying the myriad ways people choose to illuminate or ignore these many disaster temporalities can reveal long-inherited values and commitments, as well as contemporary social and political contexts and agendas. We come to know about these choices through the historical record of disaster activities: death and dollar counts, relief payments, agency functions and dysfunctions, technological interventions.

Challenge of nuclear memory   301

The temporal scale of the "disaster event" dominates most discussion, most research and certainly drives media coverage, bureaucratic function and policy debate. At the scale of an event-in-time, a disaster kills and breaks and overwhelms. This definition of disaster came to dominate social science disaster research in the 1950s, articulated in a classic form by sociologist Charles Fritz in 1961 as "an event ... concentrated in time and space, in which a society ... undergoes severe danger and incurs such losses ... that the social structure is disrupted and the fulfillment of all or some of the essential functions of the society is prevented" (Knowles, 2013).

Stretching out in time, beyond the event, is a temporal scale I refer to as "risk management." Beginning with the invention of risk in the nineteenth century, the expert cultures of technoscience, public health, insurance and accounting, and the military have converged on a managerial approach to disasters. These disaster experts threw away their grandfathers' "Acts of God" and focused on disasters as acts of man and of nature. Hazards and risks are to be investigated and mapped over time, space, deaths and illnesses analyzed and recorded toward actuarial comfort. As Ulrich Beck suggests in *Risk Society: Towards a New Modernity* (1992), the time scale of risk management is part and parcel of industrialisation, embodying a worldview that sees disaster only as an irritating externality of wealth creation and land transformation (Beck, 1987; 1992; 1995; 1999; 2009; Giddens and Pierson, 1998; Giddens, 1999; Lupton, 1999). Risk management refers to a time bounded by research questions that can be asked and also answered, environmental change processes that can be documented and studied, profits and losses that can be tallied, and policy decisions that can be charted through a few election cycles.

Slow disaster is an intentional refutation of the notion that disaster can be articulated as an event-in-time. Whereas risk management focuses on decades, slow disasters move over centuries, a temporal frame beyond the range of most of risk management's practitioners. Slow disaster thinking invites researchers to remain open to the possibility of intermittent visitations of violence, distributed in time and place but still connected to a common ancestor. The idea itself seems to undermine the explanatory power of the disaster concept as it is commonly used—slow disaster simultaneously describes long-term phenomena and exposes the intense present-mindedness of conventional disaster analysis.

In conceptualising slow disaster, I draw inspiration from Rob Nixon's 2013 volume *Slow Violence and the Environmentalism of the Poor*. Nixon calls for the formation of an environmental politics capable of linking causes and effects across long stretches of time. "Climate change, the thawing cryosphere, toxic drift, biomagnification, deforestation, the radioactive aftermaths of wars, acidifying oceans, and a host of other slowly unfolding environmental catastrophes present formidable

302 *Scott Gabriel Knowles*

representational obstacles that can hinder our efforts to mobilize and act decisively," Nixon argues (Nixon, 2013; Knowles, 2014).[2]

My ambition in translating "slow violence" into the language of disaster studies is twofold. First, I want to explore the historical forces at work in centering the awareness of disaster so overwhelmingly on an *event*. Why have experts and political leaders, even average people, been so eager to suffer and then "recover" from disaster when long-term, ever-unfolding impacts on the natural and built environment, human bodies and human minds are often so abundantly clear? Moreover, what are the politics of such an impoverished disaster memory? Second, I want to locate the formation of temporal scales themselves in the work of disaster researchers and practitioners over the past decades, which have been so crucial in the formation of laws and practices of disaster preparedness and recovery. How have they aligned their notions of temporal scale with the disasters they study? How have these scalar choices shaped the possibilities of imagination and memory? My point is to assess how and what we come to know about these conflicting disaster temporalities through the study of disaster memory.

In the case of the nuclear, one temporal frame is *NEVER* adequate—we must think at the scale of the event, risk management and the slow disaster. Indeed, it is the nuclear that led most forcefully to the formation of these different scales. Charles E. Fritz, before taking up his training in sociology, worked as a photographer for the US Strategic Bombing Survey in World War II. Fritz's first research into human reactions to disaster were funded by US civil defense officials worried over what would happen to American society in the event of a nuclear attack. Fritz's work, and that of social science disaster research into the 1990s, remained focused on the event as a space within which to peer into the underlying psychological realities of communities under stress—that is to say, the stress of the atomic bomb (Dynes and Drabek, 1994; Quarantelli, 1994).[3]

Likewise, the risk management scale has been strongly shaped by the global expert communities of nuclear weapons production, nuclear power production and the prediction, avoidance and monitoring of disasters in both. Comprehending and managing the life spans of nuclear missiles, command and control systems, nuclear power plants and nuclear workers all emerged after 1945 as signal responsibilities of the nuclear state. And it's in the realm of the nuclear that the state has struggled to bound time and violence with bureaucratic tools. A Nuclear Regulatory Commission or Department of Defense seems adequate for the production and maintenance of a nuclear weapon or energy complex, but what about the aftermath of a nuclear war, or the aftermath of a nuclear power disaster, or the location and monitoring of nuclear waste, or the long-term health of soldiers or workers exposed to radioactivity, or their children, or their children's children? Risk management slips into slow disaster at the edges of expert control.

Challenge of nuclear memory   303

As Lee Clarke points out, there are plenty of "fantasy documents" the nuclear state uses to provide cover for the experts, but the underlying realities of unpredictability and unmanageability remain (Oakes, 1994; Clarke, 1999; Davis, 2007). The slow disaster is this time zone, ending only at the end of human life. This is a persistent concern of the nuclear age. Yet there is no Department of Armageddon. And why not? Again, the choices of disaster temporality reflect the realities of a society in its time and place. The "Doomsday Clock" of the *Bulletin of the Atomic Scientists* is always counting down to midnight—it has been since 1947. Still, it has required re-setting and re-adjustment as munitions and policies and polities and climates and technologies change. In the nuclear age, the focus among industrialised nations is the present, perhaps the decades to each side of the event. Arms control and nuclear power oversight have been presented as the natural remedies to the dangers of nuclear risk. But slow disaster is a crucial temporality for the charting of the nuclear, as well as its apocalyptic kin, climate change.

Over the past two decades, the emergence of the Anthropocene debate has vividly demonstrated the conceptual power of deep history and long projection. Though confined largely to geology and ecology in the sciences, the social sciences, the arts, and activist communities have embraced discussions over the extreme long-term implications of industrialisation as an ongoing process. The debating club of Anthropocenic origins goes around and around: does the age begin with agriculture (10,000 BCE), with settler colonialism in the Americas, industrial carbon (1750), or with radioactivity (1945) (Ruddiman, 2003; McNeill and Engelke, 2014; Davis, 2017; Lovelock and Appleyard, 2019)? Wherever you land on this question, you are operating at a slow-disaster scale, looking for changes in the land and the inhabitants of the land that might not be visible in a single storm or cancer death but will become legible over centuries and millennia. And what if those records aren't written most powerfully in government archives or scientific studies, but in the memories of those who live and die under nuclear fear?

Remembering the event: Hiroshima

When he visited the Hiroshima Peace Park and museum with his wife in 1962, the American psychologist Robert Lifton was so moved that he decided to stay, to undertake a long series of interviews with survivors. In collecting and analyzing their stories, Lifton broke new ground in understanding how human beings deal with trauma. He also carefully documented a generation of survivors, a contextualised record unique to its time and place. Lifton discovered that the experience of the bombing did not end for survivors—and he described the phenomenon of survivors' guilt. It was a disaster often pictured in terms like John Hersey's "noiseless flash," with utter and immediate devastation, yet for survivors the suffering carried onward indeterminately, grinding in what Lifton termed "death in life."[4]

Lifton's interviews shined light on the uniqueness of nuclear war as a heretofore unseen type of disaster. Nuclear disaster had a psychological, memory dimension different from the conventional warfare and bombing that most of Europe and all of Japan had endured during World War II. Lifton paid particular attention to the lack of a pre-existing model for the type of destruction the atomic bomb would bring.

> People were unprepared for the atomic bomb on many psychological dimensions: the immediate relaxation induced by the all-clear signal, the feeling of being in some way protected, the general sense of invulnerability which all people in some measure possess even (or especially) in the face of danger, and the total inability to conceive of the unprecedented dimensions of the weapon about to strike them. As one man put it: "We thought something would happen, but we never imagined anything like the atomic bomb."
>
> (Lifton, 1967/1991: 18)

Lifton observed the broadly shared memory that the disaster event of the atomic bombing seemed like the end of the world to many survivors. And, a related phenomenon, Lifton terms the "ultimate horror," a "memory which epitomizes the relationship of death to guilt … a specific image of the dead or dying with which the survivor strongly identifies himself, and which evokes in him particularly intense feelings of pity and self-condemnation" (Lifton, 1991). This ultimate horror, with the lack of a pre-existing frame of reference for the scale of nuclear destruction, combined with the unfolding disaster of radiation sickness in Hiroshima and Nagasaki to mark the disaster event of atomic attack as something as yet unseen. The results, too, were unforeseen, profoundly shaping the memories of victims, the worldviews of those who would connect with and study victims, and the scope of possibility for those who would deny and later regret their denial of victims and their narratives. The event could neither be contained nor forgotten (Zwigenberg, 2018).

Disaster memorials and museums work to "contain" specific narratives of loss and pain and translate them into more general experiences that transcend time and space. Open to the public, usually outdoors and chiseled out of stone, steel or other durable materials, memorials have historically served as centerpieces of national cultures of war memory. Context, history, and morals are inscribed in this memorial architecture: choices of materials and aesthetics; the symbolism of animals, plants and people in different configurations; and the presence (or absence) of contextualising names and dates can often render mute stones into very noisy sites of meaning. The public participates in the ongoing formation of meaning at memorials, performing ceremonies on critical days of

Challenge of nuclear memory 305

remembrance, leaving tributes at other times or removing and even destroying memorials in times of strife and revolution.

Only in more recent decades have formal museums been created to work alongside memorials, providing even more in-depth exhibits, teaching and performance spaces. In the memorial museum, a more deliberative practice of archiving, historical research and pedagogy has the opportunity to flourish—it is here that the disaster event can be transformed into a much longer process of analysis and historical provocation. Edward T. Linenthal has written about this shift, one that seems to have begun in the United States with the Oklahoma City Bombing Memorial and Museum in the 1990s and carried over into the post-9/11 culture of memorial museums so prevalent today (Linenthal, 2001; Doss, 2012). The trend, however, could be said to have started in Hiroshima.

The formation of a nuclear moment into an ongoing site of memorial and learning in Japan is a process that began after the end of World War II and continues today. In its workings, this process takes an event the world had never before witnessed, captures it as a moment in time, and delivers it, over and over again, to visitors. Conveying the violence and terror of the moment, the process of memorial learning makes this unthinkable moment and its unfolding aftermath relevant to each visitor, on each visit. This process is also political. Creating the memorial in Hiroshima and Nagasaki produced controversies—how violent should they be, how much should they serve as theaters of blame—and ongoing concerns, including how they provide "lessons" to take away from the experience as those lessons and learners evolve?

The Hiroshima Peace Memorial remains a haunting, instructing, focusing memorial, geared around the annual recognition of the exact time that an atomic bomb was dropped on the city—and made apparent a nuclear future—on August 6, 1945. It is often cautioned that young children should not visit the museum without the close consideration of parents, a cruel irony given the amount of effort focused on telling the stories of children who suffered in Hiroshima. A humble and solemn grass mound a short distance from the museum marks the resting place of thousands of unknown dead, cremated and interred in the dazed days after the disaster. The entire area is decorated with paper origami cranes of all sizes, a symbol of peace and reference to the 1,000 cranes folded by bombing and eventual leukemia victim Sadako Sasaki (DiCicco et al., 2018). Every year, on the evening of August 6, people arrive at the river to set lantern boats loose to the current.

The content of the museum centers on the event and the sufferers—many of its exhibits tell the tale of the physical violence of the act. One of the most profound spaces in the museum is the wall of letters, a living record including each letter that a mayor of Hiroshima has written to register concern over nuclear testing and nuclear stockpiling somewhere in the world. Time extends past August 6. We can contemplate a sort of

306 *Scott Gabriel Knowles*

global Hiroshima of nuclear sufferers. The event gives way to decades of activism.

July of 2015. We sat together in a modest underground classroom on the grounds of the Hiroshima Peace Memorial Park. This summer day was not long before the 70th memorial of the disaster. We were a small group of American students and disaster researchers, joined by three Japanese women, each in her 70s, each with a unique story of the shared disaster: the atomic bombing of their city on a summer morning.

Mrs. K., a Japanese woman, remembers that day clearly—she heard a big metallic sound, as if the world was breaking. Her two older sisters worked in the city, and she took the train in to look for them. To her it seemed that the city was simply gone, replaced with a blackened field. As Mrs. K. walked into the ruins, others walked the other way—people who looked like ghosts, with skin hanging from their fingertips. She was wearing sandals, and she remembers the "soft" sensation of walking over dead bodies. Even today, walking across a particular bridge in Hiroshima, she can hear the voice of a woman begging for help—a woman for whom she could do nothing. Mrs. K. tells us she can hear the voices of the young people who died, they want to be with their friends, to play, to read books.

Mrs. H. went into the destroyed city to look for her grandparents. She was six years old. She accidentally walked over the neck of a dead body and apologised. She was asked by a burned person for some water. She brought her hands close to the lips of the victim, shaking a few drops of water into their mouth. The person thanked her, then died. A nurse ran over, pushing the child, admonishing her not to give water to burn victims, telling her the person had died because of this small sip of water, this small act of kindness from a child. She experienced insomnia and nightmares about the search for her grandmother. Mrs. H. married at age 21, but did not tell her husband of her radiation exposure. After 14 years her husband found out—she thought he would divorce her, but her husband said he had suspected it and they stayed together.

Mrs. K. and Mrs. H. represent a group of disaster victims known as *hibakusha* or radiation-affected people (Sato, Zwigenberg, this volume). These atomic bombing survivors lived in obscurity and silence until 1952 when official censorship was lifted and their story could begin to be told.[5] As the years went by, the *hibakusha* suffered, often in silence. Their disaster sometimes manifested in leukemia and other cancers, but more often in a slow and grinding fear—what we now would call Post Traumatic Stress Disorder. Cultural stigmatisation could be as devastating as the direct effects of survival. Because of the fear of radiation and genetic mutation, *hibakusha* found it difficult to marry and start families after the war. Because of the scars on their bodies, they often found it difficult to re-integrate into society. Because of the special attention paid to these two cities, they even faced the backlash of fellow countrymen—a nation full of war victims who sometimes wondered if the people of

Hiroshima and Nagasaki received too much special attention among the overwhelming trauma.

A Memorial Peace Park and Museum opened in Hiroshima and also in Nagasaki in the 1950s. The nation re-entered normal relations with the world, rebuilt its economy and the war slipped into memory. Through it all, the *hibakusha* suffered. Despite the memorial buildings, despite the passage of time, the *hibakusha* still often found it difficult to tell their stories. Mrs. H. began to tell her story only after her dying mother asked of her to "make sure the story of the atomic bomb is not lost." (Figure 15.2)

Remembering nuclear risk management

The US Department of Energy manages almost 100 active nuclear clean-up locations across the United States under the auspices of its Legacy Management program. Preserving public health is the number one goal of the program. Its second goal is that it: "Preserves, protects, and makes accessible legacy records and information."[6] In other words, Legacy Management is charged with maintaining a historical archive of nuclear America. Much of this work involves providing documents mandated through various legislative and legal actions that began in the 1960s. In

Figure 15.2 Hiroshima Lantern Festival and the "A-Bomb Dome" on August 6, 2015. Photo by Scott Gabriel Knowles.

308 Scott Gabriel Knowles

some instances, though, the Legacy Management task veers into active curatorial acts: of sites, artifacts, and interpretive history.

At the site of the former Mallinckrodt factory, where uranium was processed for nuclear weapons from 1957 to 1966, the visitor can today tour a museum explaining the heroic history of the place and the people who worked there.[7] Thanks to the activism of local environmental justice crusaders like Denise Brock, this museum now includes a memorial to the dozens of workers who developed cancer due to unmonitored radioactive exposures at the plant.[8] For decades the site sat abandoned, until the Legacy Management program took control and created the Weldon Spring Site Remedial Action Project Disposal Cell. Here, the debris of the old factory and acres of radioactive soil were piled up into a mound and covered with stones to stabilise the radioactivity for long-term monitoring and storage.[9]

The museum of legacy management is an artifact of a political struggle over risk management. For decades, Mallinckrodt, the company, and the government evaded responsibility and avoided making clear decisions over the site. Legend tells that an attempt to make Agent Orange at the site during the Vietnam War was thwarted because it was far too polluted already. Eventually, community action forced the government's hand. The content of the museum was carefully scripted to tell a story of a victorious nation in WWII, of the heroic sacrifices made by workers. Local Civil War history is even included. However, eventually worker families insisted that the names of those made sick and killed by this work were included—Denise Brock was instrumental in erecting a memorial St. Louis Arch in the space.

Climb to the top of the containment cell and survey the landscape—you could be forgiven for assuming that it is a great modernist work of art. In fact, though, you are sitting on top of the remains of the Cold War in St. Louis, an entire factory complex raised and piled and scraped and covered by the Department of Energy as a way to bring an "end" to the story of the nuclear in this place. We (a group of visiting researchers) looked around, uncertain. As the wind whipped and we stood dumbstruck, the track team from the high school next door ran up to the top, their stern-faced coach panting behind them. The teenagers looked us over, gave us a sort of "why are you here but really who cares?" glance, then ran back down. At Weldon, *we* stood atop a memorial to the nuclear, but to the runners it was just a place to exercise.

In Pennsylvania, at Three Mile Island (TMI), nuclear memory is also stuck in risk management rhetoric. You drive along the "three-mile island," realising that, not so very long ago, the Department of Energy wished for Americans to marvel at the architecture of the nuclear. The nuclear fear of 1979 remains mostly unmarked, except for the structures, those unmistakable cooling towers—two of which sit silent. And if you stand in front of the now permanently closed Exelon visitor center, the only sounds you hear are birds and the ceaseless rattling of the dosimeter measuring the air around you for radiation releases.

The visitors' center is directly opposite the plant, built with a second-level veranda looking out across the river at the plant. At some point, the intention was obviously to allow visitors to get a great view and take pictures. On the grounds of the visitors' center, I note one interesting, poignant artifact: a beautiful grove of cherry trees growing behind the building. They were a gift from a Japanese nuclear power organisation that visited to learn from what happened at TMI in the 1990s. They left the trees as a marker of friendship. (Figure 15.3)

On the side of the road, at the edge of the property, we find the only acknowledgement that anything untoward ever occurred here. It is one of those ubiquitous blue Pennsylvania roadside history plaques, yet its final text was once a source of major controversy. Exelon (the current owner of TMI) conflicted with Eric Epstein, the chairman of the Three Mile Island Alert. The sign's original draft language stressed that no lives were lost as a result of the March 28, 1979 partial melt-down—a debatable point then and now. Though acknowledging the accident forced a massive regional evacuation, the sign on the site today ends on a hopeful "lessons learned" note: "Events here would cause basic changes

Figure 15.3 Three Mile Island. Cherry tree grove behind former visitor center—a gift of friendship from Japanese nuclear power operators. Photo by Scott Gabriel Knowles.

throughout the world's nuclear power industry." In the battle over this sign, we discover the difficulty in remembering an event that, for all intents and purposes, ended the growth of the American nuclear power industry. TMI today stands in for most people as a symbol of technology gone awry, with fearful consequences. (Figure 15.4)

Figure 15.4 Historical plaque across from Three Mile Island. Photo by Scott Gabriel Knowles.

Challenge of nuclear memory 311

The Three Mile Island disaster came in the midst of a national turn against nuclear power. Forty-one reactors were commissioned in 1973 but only two in 1978. Accidents had been in the news. A Michigan plant nearly melted down in 1966, causing authorities to prepare an evacuation of Detroit. A major fire broke out at Brown's Ferry (Alabama) Nuclear Power Station in 1975.[10] The Clamshell Movement started in 1976 at the New Hampshire Seabrook reactor site.[11] Radioactivity was being documented in animals, soil, water and milk near power plants across the nation.

The health impacts of the disaster are still disputed today, but TMI has come to stand in for an entire generation of down-winder deaths, worker exposures, animal deaths and fear. It is a memorial to an accident in which the government denies any deaths, which nonetheless acknowledges that thousands might have been killed with only slightly different outcomes in March of 1979. A memorial to diffuse technological effects is difficult to conceptualise—what would it look like, would there be names? At TMI, there is the closed viewing building and the blue sign. These are the best we have for now.

Slow disaster and nuclear memory

As Robert Lifton has explained, all of the certainties of the flow of time were upended by the consciousness that human life on earth could be extinguished by nuclear weapons. The awareness was/is too much to reckon with and forces us into what Lifton refers to as a state of "psychic numbing." Numb and disoriented might be a much better description of Cold War culture, more appropriate to human psychology than the civil defense mantra of "command and control." Nuclear war, nuclear power, nuclear waste—none of these operates in the tidy modernist boxes that had defined war, industrialisation and environmental impacts before 1945. We may live our lives in one direction, but memory—just like the nuclear—is not linear, effects are not neatly tied to causes, breaks and gaps in the record are all too real.

Reflecting on disaster memory generally requires that we attend, seriously, to the discovery of deliberate acts of historical erasure. We can mark as well the normal function of societal forgetfulness, the slow lack-of-tending to graves, genealogies and artifacts that might accrue as generations unfold and people move. Formal disaster memorials are a relatively new medium of memory, synchronised with our enriched understanding of disasters not as natural acts or inevitable moments but as reflections of broader inequities, unmanageable risks and injustices. This task is difficult enough for a fire or a flood—disaster events that seem to have bounded temporalities. The same conceptual "luxuries" are not available in the slow disaster of the nuclear.[12]

312   *Scott Gabriel Knowles*

Aside from funereal markers themselves, war memorials are perhaps the oldest and clearest expressions of communal grief and loss that exist. The vocabulary of war memorials, in other words, is very well defined. Disaster memorials have a less established set of traditions, though they do exist across different types, especially in disasters that are war-adjacent, such as the September 11 memorials or terrorism memorials like that Oklahoma City Bombing memorial. The nuclear sends memorial challenges mushrooming. The event is unbounded in time. The violence can be invisible. The disaster reaches populations that may or not be known. As such, nuclear memorialisation demands a "slow disaster" thinking that runs counter to the "disaster event" thinking so dominant in the discourse around disaster government, sense-making and memory.

How do you memorialise an event that is ongoing, global in scale, with victims who may not be dead, visibly damaged or even known? We have here entered the same puzzle that climate change activists are forcing us to think about—intergenerational, slow disaster, claiming lives and health across vast distances and time-scapes. As a focusing act, memorialisation makes loss material and establishes a moral economy—that may itself be a source of dispute—but serves the purposes of grounding a disaster in the political. There are strong incentives to memorialise slow disasters like climate change, toxicity and nuclear exposure.

A further point might be relevant here: slow disaster memorialisation also forces a reconceptualisation of more traditional memorial practices. For example, PTSD is now recognised as a slow disaster affecting vast numbers of military and civilian combatants after conflicts. There are no PTSD memorials—why not? How does the discussion of climate change and the nuclear open the possibility for a rethinking of the process of making memory material? Is it appropriate to mourn the victims of the manmade atrocities of opioid addiction, auto crashes, and slavery?

What exactly are we trying to remember when we remember the nuclear? There is war and violence—the suffering of civilian victims, children and old people especially. The "noiseless flash" was different from the allnight bombing raids. It came without warning. The scale of violence was utterly unprecedented, let alone as the result of a single weapon. Certainly, this is one of the aspects of nuclear war memory. The force of the blast was extreme, though the blast and the fires that followed fit well with so-called "conventional" bombing memory. The black rain hinted that there was something different in this experience of blast and fire. But only when the radiation sickness began did the special character of the atomic bomb reveal itself, and in this, memory took a turn—here we see the transition from the memory of an *event in time* to an *event through time*.

Another dimension of nuclear memory that must be reckoned with, frustrating the inert "sacrifice" narratives of war memorials: the memory of the human capacity for cruelty. Not all memorials are memorials to victims or reserved for the victim experience. There is the collective memory of national suffering and sacrifice. And there is the memory of the human ability to set aside morality in the name of "winning a war"—a situational ethics that gnaws at the conscience. Here, for example, the Hiroshima memorial leaves the visitor guessing; in the inert, passive phrases of its informational panels, the "bomb was dropped" (Zwigenberg, 2014). This distancing is perhaps puzzling except when one considers the strong influence of the United States in the post-war memorial cultures of Japan and the large numbers of American tourists who visit Hiroshima every year—the passivity is itself a continuation of the post-war reconciliation, forced by an occupying army and continued by Japanese leaders eager to place the past firmly in the past. Even in this memorial, we sense the deep desire of officials to name the war a mistake, move forward to normalcy, and return to their seats among leading nations (Dower, 2000).

But the passivity blocks a fuller exploration of the memory of cruelty—and it's here that the nuclear sets itself apart, both in war and in peace. One way to come to this discussion is to look at the ways that the pre-war history of the atomic bomb is studied—treated as the signal scientific achievement of the twentieth century in western histories (Rhodes, 2012). The race to defeat the Nazis gives way to a confused policy apparatus in the United States, a war-weary nation late to involvement and a fabled invasion of Japan that necessitated the use of the bomb. Though wave after wave of revision concentrates on the "decision," it is seemingly impossible to divorce the atomic project from the techno-enthusiasm, bordering on supernatural ascriptions of power to the Manhattan Project. Lock scientists on a mountaintop, give them a moral cause and enough money, and they produce a result so impossibly effective that it defies all known categories of production.

In this sense, the "Manhattan Project for everything" phenomenon was born. This emphasis on expertise-toward-purpose has a momentum that is hard to slow, even today—but what if the purpose goes awry? Oppenheimer's self-critical "I have become death" mythology softens it slightly, as does the Franck Report—but the disjunction of the Manhattan Project narrative and the cruelty narrative produce a highly difficult memorial culture. How can we at one and the same time remember with great reverence and excitement a technical achievement of human ingenuity, then switch our brains into a memory of unparalleled, meticulously planned human cruelty? Contemporary and ongoing debates in the United States about "the apology for the bomb" (still not forthcoming) show that even 75 years later we have made little progress on this question.

Another conundrum: Approaching a memorial site requires a certain psychological condition of meditation and an effect of reverence—a "memorial mindset." The degree to which memorials resemble churches or cemeteries shows the ways in which architects and memorial planners

314   *Scott Gabriel Knowles*

have historically wished to hush the crowd into contemplation upon entry into the memorial space. This reverence takes on a secondary set of reverential characteristics with the gnawing element of danger. Because of the special, quiet, invisible nature of radioactivity, visitors to spaces where nuclear violence and nuclear disaster have occurred frequently find the experience unsettling. Writing about Chernobyl, Philip R. Stone invokes the Foucauldian notion of the "heterotopia"—a place that resides outside of the everyday space-time frameworks that give our lives consistency and comfort (White and Frew, 2013). The nuclear sites of Three Mile Island, Chernobyl, and Fukushima are certainly heterotopic. But they go further, veering into the realm of immediate, bodily concern. *Is it safe to visit this memorial?* The confusion is doubled when the visitor, as at Chernobyl or Fukushima, is required to sign indemnification papers releasing the governments of Ukraine or Japan from liability for any injuries they may sustain as a result of their memorial site visit.

In nuclear spaces that have not yet turned into formal memorials, the informal takes over—small tokens, broken pieces, reminders of tragedy signal to visitors, hinting at the violence that has taken place, at varying possible storylines about what happened in this space. But without a formally sanctioned experience, one is left to wonder: is it safe to be here; and more, is it disrespectful to victims to visit? Even when guided by experts or survivors with every right to be on site, the experience is bewildering. Abandoned buildings, sometime intact, sometimes in disrepair after evacuation, leave visitors guessing about their own safety and their new role as witnesses. These specific experiences are captured hauntingly in the post-Fukushima films *A Journey to Namie* and *Healing Fukushima*, directed by sociologist of risk Sulfikar Amir.[13] Understandable concerns over safety and respect for victims potentially work against the communitarian possibilities of mourning made possible in memory sites that are still in the danger zone. Touring Daiichii, Pripyat, or a depopulated city like Namie brings the visitor directly into a space of nuclear injury. Such an experience may be fine for the more devoted disaster memorial visitor; for most people, though, such memorial pilgrimages just aren't worth the risk.

Conclusion: memories awaken

In March of 2011, with the triple disasters of Fukushima, the only nation to experience nuclear warfare now entered the small group to have experienced a nuclear power disaster.

Among the many pathways from Fukushima, one led back to 1945, traversing across 66 years of history. After Fukushima, many aging *hibakusha* from Hiroshima and Nagasaki began to speak out forcefully. Many traveled to Fukushima to offer aid and comfort to a new generation of *hibakusha*—those who had suffered radiation exposure from the nuclear power disaster. Their history became a ground for recovery.

Challenge of nuclear memory 315

The *hibakusha* of today—those of 1945 and of 2011—can find some solace in sharing their stories, in reinterpreting the memorials of Hiroshima and Nagasaki, and in agitating through teaching and activism for a safer Japanese future. Their work has been crucial to the political aftermath of Fukushima, to the ensuing decade of democratic discourse over the future of the Japanese energy sector. Most nuclear power plants in Japan have been shuttered since 2011. A program to gather oral history interviews has brought a new generation—the grandchildren of Hiroshima and Nagasaki—into the work of nuclear memory. This forms a therapeutic community for *hibakusha* of past and present. Meanwhile, across Fukushima, Miyagi, and Iwate Prefectures, disaster archives, museums and memorials are taking shape at every conceivable scale.

Forgetting is convenient for policymakers and industry interests, who would draw a hard line between the end of a disaster and the beginning of a new era. For them, closure is essential. With the tenth anniversary of Fukushima passing and the area still littered with toxic waste—officials scrambled to "close" the disaster in time for the 2020 Olympics (delayed not by the threat of nuclear consequence but a novel contagion). And yet thousands have not yet returned to their homes—many homes in towns like Tomioka or Namie remain inside "forbidden zones," too dangerous to re-inhabit. Miles-long depots of radioactive soil are kept in "temporary" holding until "permanent" disposal solutions can be discovered. It is not an easy disaster to bring to a conclusion.

Although these disasters may seem different—one in war and the other in peace, separated by time—the example of Japan's *hibakusha* is a crucial one as we think about disaster memory. In both 1945 and 2011, the type of disaster event was only of passing interest compared to the underlying issues of governmental responsibility, the trust of citizens in the political system and in scientific experts, the strength (or weakness) of culture and community, and the power of memory over long stretches of time.

For the *hibakusha*, disaster is slow. Remembering is often inconvenient, but historical memory is the ground upon which any future disaster resilience in Japan—or anywhere in the world, for that matter—will be forged. As Mrs. K. tells us so succinctly: "To look back to the past is to take responsibility for the future."

Notes

1 The author wishes to acknowledge research funding from the Japan Society for the Promotion of Science (2015), the Haus der Kulturen der Welt (2019), and Drexel University.
2 Dawson, A. (2011). Slow Violence and the Environmentalism of the Poor: An Interview with Rob Nixon. *Social Text* Online, August 31. Available at: https://socialtextjournal.org/slow_violence_and_the_environmentalism_of_the_poor_an_interview_with_rob_nixon/ [Accessed July 1, 2021].

316 *Scott Gabriel Knowles*

3 For a narrative history of Charles E. Fritz and early disaster researchers in the United States, see Knowles (2013: 218–229); for an internalist history from a founder of the Disaster Research Center see Quarantelli, E. (n.d.). The Early History of the Disaster Research Center. Disaster Research Center. Available at: https://www.drc.udel.edu/content-sub-site/Documents/DRC%20Early%20History.pdf [Accessed July 1, 2021].
4 Hersey, J. (1946). Hiroshima. *New Yorker*, August 31.
5 United Nations Office for Disarmament Affairs (n.d.). Hibakusha-Atomic Bomb Survivors. Available at: https://www.un.org/disarmament/education/slideshow/hibakusha/ [Accessed February 7, 2020].
6 US Office of Legacy Management (n.d.). Mission. Available at: https://www.energy.gov/lm/mission [Accessed July 1, 2021); Office of Environmental Management (n.d.). Cleanup Sites. Available at: https://www.energy.gov/em/mission/cleanup-sites [Accessed February 7, 2020].
7 Fentem, S. (2019). Cleanup Of Manhattan Project Site In Downtown St. Louis Nears Completion. St. Louis Public Radio. Available at: https://news.stlpublicradio.org/post/cleanup-manhattan-project-site-downtown-st-louis-nears-completion [Accessed July 1, 2021].
8 Dreiling, G. (2007). A Conversation with Denise Brock. *St. Louis Magazine*, March 6. Available at: https://www.stlmag.com/St-Louis-Magazine/March-2006/Q-A-A-Conversation-With-Denise-Brock/ [Accessed June 30, 2021]; see *The Safe Side of the Fence*, directed by Tony West, released July 19, 2015.
9 Missouri Department of Natural Resources (2017). Weldon Spring Site Remedial Action Project. Available at: https://dnr.mo.gov/env/hwp/fedfac/ffs-doe.htm [Accessed June 30, 2021].
10 Hiltzik, Michael. "Column: 50 Years after 'we Almost Lost Detroit,' America's Nuclear Power Industry Faces Even Graver Doubts." *Los Angeles Times*, October 3, 2016. Available at: https://www.latimes.com/business/hiltzik/la-fi-hiltzik-detroit-nuclear-20161003-snap-story.html [Accessed June 30, 2021].
  Lochbaum, D. (2016). Nuclear Plant Accidents: Browns Ferry Fire. *All Things Nuclear* (blog). Union of Concerned Scientists, July 19. Available at: https://allthingsnuclear.org/dlochbaum/nuclear-plant-accidents-browns-ferry-fire [Accessed June 30, 2021].
11 Clamshell Alliance (n.d.). About Clamshell. Available at: https://www.clamshellalliance.net/about/ [Accessed June 30, 2021].
12 For a review of contemporary disaster research approaches to temporality and memory, see Felt et al. (2017: 1003–1028); for a review about tendencies in memory practices relevant to this paragraph, see: Ricœur Blamey and Pellauer (2010: 146–176, 412–452).
13 Amir, S. (2015). *A Journey to Namie*. Documentary film; Amir, S. (2016). *Healing Fukushima*. Documentary film.

References

Beck, U. (1987). The Anthropological Shock: Chernobyl and the Contours of the Risk Society. *Berkeley Journal of Sociology*, 32, pp. 153–165.
Beck, U. (1992). *Risk Society: Towards a New Modernity*. London: SAGE Publications.
Beck, U. (1995). *Ecological Enlightenment: Essays on the Politics of the Risk Society*. Atlantic Highlands, NJ: Humanities Press.
Beck, U. (1999). *World Risk Society*. Malden, MA: Polity Press.

Challenge of nuclear memory 317

Beck, U. (2009). *World at Risk*. Cambridge, UK: Polity Press.

Clarke, L. (1999). *Mission Improbable: Using Fantasy Documents to Tame Disaster*. Chicago, IL: University of Chicago Press.

Davis, H. (2017). On the Importance of a Date, or Decolonizing the Anthropocene. *ACME*, 16(4), pp. 761–780.

Davis, T. (2007). *Stages of Emergency: Cold War Nuclear Civil Defense*. Durham, NC: Duke University Press. DOI: http://doi.org/10.1215/9780822389637.

DiCicco, S., Adams, K., Nakagoshi, N., and Masakiro, M. (2018). *The Complete Story of Sadako Sasaki*. Santa Barbara, CA: Armed with the Arts, Inc.

Doss, E. (2012). *Memorial Mania: Public Feeling in America*. Chicago, IL: University of Chicago Press.

Dower, J. (2000). *Embracing Defeat: Japan in the Wake of World War II*. New York: Norton.

Dynes, R., and Drabek, T. (1994). The Structure of Disaster Research: Its Policy and Disciplinary Implications. *International Journal of Mass Emergencies and Disasters*, 12(1), pp. 5–23.

Felt, U., Fouché, R., Miller, C., and Smith-Doerr, L., eds. (2017). *The Handbook of Science and Technology Studies*. 4th edition. Cambridge, MA: MIT Press.

Giddens, A. (1999). Risk and Responsibility. *The Modern Law Review*, 62(1), pp. 1–10.

Giddens, A., and Pierson, C. (1998). *Conversations with Anthony Giddens: Making Sense of Modernity*. Stanford, CA: Stanford University Press.

Knowles, S. (2013). *The Disaster Experts: Mastering Risk in Modern America*. Philadelphia, PA: University of Pennsylvania Press.

Knowles, S. (2014). Learning from Disaster? The History of Technology and the Future of Disaster Research. *Technology and Culture*, 55(4), pp. 773–784. DOI: http://doi.org/10.1353/tech.2014.0110.

Knowles, S., and Loeb, Z. (2021). The Voyage of the Paragon: Disaster as Method. In: J. Remes and A. Horowitz, eds., *Critical Disaster Studies: New Perspectives on Disaster, Risk, Vulnerability, and Resilience*. Philadelphia, PA: University of Pennsylvania Press.

Lifton, R. (1991). *Death in Life: Survivors of Hiroshima*. Chapel Hill, NC: University of North Carolina Press.

Linenthal, E. (2001). *The Unfinished Bombing: Oklahoma City in American Memory*. Oxford: Oxford University Press.

Lovelock, J., and Appleyard, B. (2019). *Novacene: The Coming Age of Hyperintelligence*. London: Allen Lane.

Lupton, D. (1999). *Risk: Key Ideas*. London: Routledge.

McNeill, J., and Engelke, P. (2014). *The Great Acceleration: An Environmental History of the Anthropocene since 1945*. Cambridge, MA: The Belknap Press.

Nixon, R. (2013). *Slow Violence and the Environmentalism of the Poor*. Cambridge, MA: Harvard University Press.

Oakes, G. (1994). *The Imaginary War: Civil Defense and American Cold War Culture*. New York: Oxford University Press.

Quarantelli, E. (1994). Disaster Studies: The Consequences of the Historical Use of a Sociological Approach in the Development of Research. *International Journal of Mass Emergencies and Disasters*, 12(1), pp. 25–49.

318 *Scott Gabriel Knowles*

Rhodes, R. (2012). *The Making of the Atomic Bomb*. New York: Simon and Schuster.

Ricœur, P., Blamey, K., and Pellauer, D. (2010). *Memory, History, Forgetting*. Chicago, IL: University of Chicago Press.

Ruddiman, W. (2003). The Anthropogenic Greenhouse Era Began Thousands of Years Ago. *Climatic Change*, 61(3), pp. 261–293. DOI: http://doi.org/10.1 023/B:CLIM.0000004577.17928.fa.

White, L., and Frew, E. (2013). *Dark Tourism and Place Identity: Managing and Interpreting Dark Places*. New York: Routledge.

Zwigenberg, R. (2014). *Hiroshima: The Origins of Global Memory Culture*. New York: Cambridge University Press.

Zwigenberg, R. (2018). Healing a Sick World: Psychiatric Medicine and the Atomic Age. *Medical History*, 62(1), pp. 27–49. DOI: http://doi.org/10.1017/ mdh.2017.75.

Contributors

Bernadette Bensaude-Vincent is a historian and philosopher of science and technology, professor (emeritus) at Université Paris 1 Panthéon-Sorbonne. Her current research addresses the regimes of temporality in the Anthropocene. Among her recent publications, she authored *Temps-paysage. Pour une écologie des crises* (2021), *Carbone, ses vies, ses oeuvres.* (S. Loeve co-author 2018). She co-edited *Research Objects in their Technological* Settings (2017), and *French Philosophy of Technology. Classical Readings and Contemporary Approaches* (2018). In 2021, she was awarded the George Sarton Medal by the History of Science Society.

Harry Bernas is Research Director (emeritus) at CNRS (French National Center for Scientific Research) and University of Paris-Saclay, France. He has authored some 250 papers on condensed matter physics and materials science topics, and held management positions in the French and European research systems. A long-term interest in societal interactions of science has led him, over a decade ago, to study the impact of politics on the aims and practice of science and technology. Nuclear energy, being emblematic in this regard, is the main focus of his current work.

Soraya Boudia is a science and technology studies scholar, Professor of sociology at University of Paris. Her work explores the role of scientific knowledge in environmental issues. She has extensively worked on the history of nuclear governance. She has published with N. Jas, *Gouverner un monde toxique* (Quae, 2019), *Powerless Science? Science and Politics in a Toxic World* (Berghann, 2014), *Toxicants, Health and Regulations Since 1945* (Pickering & Chatto, 2013), and with E. Henry, *La Mondialisation des risques. Une histoire politique et transnationale des risques sanitaires environnementaux* (Presses Universitaires de Rennes, 2015).

Kate Brown is Professor of Science, Technology and Society at the Massachusetts Institute of Technology. She is the author of several prize-winning histories, including *Plutopia: Nuclear Families, Atomic Cities and the Great Soviet and American Plutonium Disasters*

320 Contributors

(Oxford 2013). Her latest book, *Manual for Survival: A Chernobyl Guide to the Future* (Norton 2019), translated into nine languages, is a finalist for the 2020 National Book Critics Circle Award, the Pushkin House Award and the Ryszard Kapuściński Award for Literary Reportage.

Angela N. H. Creager is the Thomas M. Siebel Professor in the History of Science at Princeton University, where she teaches in the Department of History and advises graduate students through the Program in History of Science. She earned her PhD in biochemistry at University of California, Berkeley, where she developed an interest in the history of biology. She is author of two books, most recently *Life Atomic: A History of Radioisotopes in Biology and Medicine* (2013). Her current work addresses science and regulation in the 1960s through the 1980s, focusing attention on how researchers conceptualized and developed techniques for detecting environmental carcinogens.

Maël Goumri is a PhD Candidate in Science and Technology Studies at the University of Paris. His thesis analyses on a long-term perspective the prevention of nuclear severe accidents. He highlights how the nuclear industry and regulation institutions developed knowledge and practices to master the risk of accident in a context of radical uncertainty. His thesis work was supported by the French Institut de Radioprotection et de Sûreté Nucléaire (IRSN) and Electricité de France (EDF) Foundation committee for the History of Electricity and Energy.

Néstor Herran is Associate Professor at the Sorbonne University, Paris. His first book, *Aguas, semillas y radiaciones: el laboratorio de radioactividad de la Universidad de Madrid, 1904–1929*, is an original history of the applications of radioactivity in Spain in the early twentieth century. Author of several collective volumes on the history of physics in Spain and on the historiography of sciences, he has recently co-edited with David Aubin the book *Chronologie de l'histoire des sciences* (2019). His current academic interests focus on the history of nuclear science and technology, computer science, geophysics and environmental sciences in the Cold War.

Scott Gabriel Knowles, Professor at Graduate School of Science and Technology Policy in Seoul, is a historian of disaster worldwide. He is the author of *The Disaster Experts: Mastering Risk in Modern America* (2011), editor of *Imagining Philadelphia: Edmund Bacon and the Future of the City* (2009), and co-editor (with Richardson Dilworth) of *Building Drexel: The University and Its City, 1891–2016* (2016) and (with Art Molella) *World's Fairs in the Cold War: Science, Technology, and the Culture of Progress*. He is series co-editor (with Kim Fortun) of "Critical Studies in Risk and Disaster" (UPenn Press).

Contributors 321

John Krige is a Professor Emeritus at the Georgia Institute of Technology. He researches on the intersection between science, technology and foreign policy, and has published widely on nuclear policy. In 2019 he was awarded the biennial Francis Bacon Prize in the History and Philosophy of Science and Technology. His latest monograph, co-authored with Mario Daniels, is entitled *Knowledge Regulation and National Security in Cold War America* (University of Chicago Press, 2022). He has also just produced a new edited collection entitled *Writing the Transnational History of Knowledge Flows in a Global Age* (University of Chicago Press, 2022).

Joseph Masco is Professor of Anthropology and Social Sciences at the University of Chicago. He is the author of three books on US nuclear nationalism and the world shaping force of nuclear technologies. These include: *The Nuclear Borderlands: The Manhattan Project in Post-Cold War New Mexico* (2006, Princeton University Press); *The Theater of Operations: National Security Affect from the Cold War to the War on Terror* (2014, Duke University Press); and *The Future of Fallout, and Other Episodes in Radioactive World-Making* (2020, Duke University Press).

Mary X. Mitchell is Assistant Professor in the Centre for Criminology & Sociolegal Studies and the Institute for the History and Philosophy of Science and Technology at the University of Toronto, St. George Campus. Trained as an attorney and scholar in Science and Technology Studies, Mitchell's work focuses on the interplay between the unequally distributed burdens of nuclear technologies and emerging forms of sovereignty and governance. Her recent publications include "The Cosmology of Evidence: Suffering, Science, and Biological Witness after Three Mile Island" (2021, *Journal of the History of Biology*). She is currently completing a manuscript that explores the sociolegal history of US nuclear weapons Nuclear weapons ban blasting in Oceania.

Maria Rentetzi is Professor and chair of Science, Technology and Gender Studies at Friedrich-Alexander Universität Erlangen-Nürnberg. She works at the intersection of science and technology studies, nuclear diplomacy, and gender. Her research focuses on two intertwined areas of inquiry: the investigation of the politically and historically situated character of technoscience and the critical examination of gender as a major analytic category in technoscientific endeavors. She is an ERC Con grantee and an affiliate of the Max Planck Institute for History of Science, previously a guest professor at the TU Berlin, Silverman Professor at Tel Aviv University, and professor at the National Technical University of Athens.

Tania Navarro Rodríguez is a sociologist and political scientist, and research affiliate at the University of Paris. Her work explores the

322 *Contributors*

relationship between science, policy and society and offers a socio-historical perspective in the areas of risk management, expertise production and public policies. She currently explores the development of radioactive waste management policies in France and at the international level, as well as the governance of crisis in nuclear industry. Her previous work examined electoral and alter-globalization movements as well as child feeding practices in France in the mid-twentieth century. She has published in French and Mexican journals (in English, French and Spanish).

Kyoko Sato is Associate Director of the Program in Science, Technology, and Society at Stanford University. Her work addresses the entanglement of technical expertise, cultural politics, and technoscientific governance in democracy. She currently studies the history of nuclear technology in Japan and the United States, as well as the politics of expertise in Japan's Covid-19 governance. Her previous work examined interdisciplinary knowledge production in the United States and the politics of genetically modified food in France, Japan, and the United States. She has published in journals such as *Science, Technology and Human Values*; *Theory and Society*; and *Journal of Science and Technology Studies* (in Japanese).

Hiroko Takahashi is Professor at Nara University, Department of History. She examines the history of Japan-US relations, nuclear technology, and global nuclear damage and survival. She is the author of numerous publications, including *Fuinsareta Hiroshima-Nagasaki: Bei Kakujikken to Minkan Boei Keikaku* [Classified Hiroshima and Nagasaki: US Nuclear Test and Civil Defense Program] (2008) and "One Minute after the Detonation of the Atomic Bomb: The Erased Effects of Residual Radiation" (2009, *Historia Scientiarum*). She serves as a member of the Research Committee for Historical Materials at the Hiroshima Peace Memorial Museum, the Expert Panel for the Peace Foundation of Daigo Fukuryu Maru Exhibition Hall, and the Steering Committee of Pugwash Japan.

Ran Zwigenberg is an Associate Professor at Pennsylvania State University. His research focuses on modern Japanese and European history, with a specialization in memory and cultural history. He has taught and lectured in the United States, Europe, Israel, and Japan, and published on issues of war memory, heritage, psychiatry, and survivor politics. Zwigenberg's first book, *Hiroshima: The Origins of Global Memory Culture* (Cambridge University Press, 2014), won the 2016 Association for Asian Studies' John W. Hall book award.

Index

A

Acceptable 72, 96, 119, 149, 153, 155, 158, 161, 162, 191–92, 194, 204, 286

Accident 1, 2, 5, 9–11, 27, 120, 122, 132–33, 136, 138–42, 148–62, 169, 173, 177, 185–87, 189, 191–96, 198, 204, 223–25, 230–32, 235, 242–44, 247–52, 255, 273–74, 294–95, 309, 311; design-basis 154, 156–57; hypothetical 9, 150, 153, 155, 159, 161–62; normal 11, 159, 161, 242–43, 248–49, 252; nuclear 1, 27, 122, 140–141, 150–51, 154–55, 158–59, 162, 185, 189, 191, 193–94, 196, 198, 204, 231–32, 235, 250, 255, 273–74, 294–95

Accountability 1, 6, 24, 63, 152

Ackerman, Thomas 272

Advisory Committee for Reactor Safeguards (ACRS) 149, 151–53, 159

Air Force 52, 54, 56–57, 95, 132–33, 135–36, 228, 263

Albright, Madeleine 67

American Physical Society (APS) 191

Ancestral 88, 90, 102, 167

Annexation 95–98, 101

Anthropocene 3, 16, 60–61, 63, 242, 253, 255, 265, 299, 303

Anti-Vietnam War movement 293–95

Apollo Mission 6, 51

As Low as Reasonably Achievable (ALARA) 192

Association pour le contrôle de la radioactivité dans l'Ouest (ACRO) 195

Atomic Bomb Casualty Commission 28, 229, 283

Atlantic Charter 87, 95–96, 98, 102

Atomic Energy Act 71, 151

Atomic Energy Agency (UK AEA) 155–156

Atomic Energy Commission (US AEC) 50, 54, 56, 70, 73,101, 117, 134, 149, 151–55, 158, 166, 170, 172, 174, 190–91, 204–10, 214–15, 225–31, 247, 262, 282, 294

Atomic mushroom – mushroom cloud 6, 36, 51, 266, 269, 273, 282

Atomium 114, 270

Atoms for Peace 5, 8, 14, 70, 111, 113–14, 137, 148, 151, 155, 178, 246, 262, 266–68, 270, 279–93

Aubinière (General Robert) 74

Auschwitz 263, 267

B

B29 bombers 96–97

Ban (see Test Ban Treaty)

Barriers 24, 34, 38, 155, 160, 167–69, 175–76, 179, 189, 292

Beck, Clifford 153–55

Beninson, Dan 225

Bhabha, Homi 76, 291

Bhutto, Zulfiqar Ali 68

Bikini Atoll 10, 30–31, 52, 99, 100–01, 203, 214–15, 271, 281

Bikini Incident (see Lucky Dragon)

Biological Effects of Atomic Radiation (BEAR) 116

Biological Effect of Ionizing Radiation (BEIR) 191

Biosphere 16, 48, 51, 59–60, 169–70, 174, 262

324   *Index*

Birks, John 272
Black rain 4, 26, 32, 37–39, 215, 312
Blix, Hans 224
Body-bodies (human) 3, 5–6, 24–25, 28, 30, 34, 45, 48, 56, 58, 63, 85, 88, 90, 124, 142, 153, 186, 189, 205, 209, 215, 222, 228–29, 235, 302, 306
Bomb 4–5, 7–10, 14, 23–40, 45–46, 48, 50–51, 53, 55–56, 58, 61, 66, 68, 70, 72, 74–81, 86–87, 99, 101, 116, 134, 136, 149, 161, 185–87, 194, 205, 207, 214–15, 225–27, 229–30, 232, 246, 261, 263–72, 274, 279, 281–83, 285–86, 288–90, 293, 302, 304–05, 307, 312–13; A-bomb 4, 7, 14, 16, 23–36, 38–40, 45–46, 48, 55, 61, 70, 101, 116, 134, 136, 186, 194, 205, 214–15, 229, 261, 263–66, 269, 271, 274, 279, 281–83, 285, 288–90, 302, 304–05, 307, 312–13; H-bomb 30, 134, 205, 207, 226, 268–69, 272, 281–82
Boris Kidric Institute 120
Bourgeois, Jean 148
Bravo-shot – (Castle) Bravo Test 7, 134–35, 203, 205–07, 214–15, 232, 281
Brookhaven National Laboratory 154, 224, 229, 232
Büchler, Carlos 117–119
Bundy, McGeorge 75
Bura Bura disease 25
Bush, Georges H.W. 79

C
Cancer 11, 24, 29, 33–34, 36, 116, 190–91, 223–25, 229–33, 269, 294, 303, 306, 308
Capitalism – capitalist – capitalistic 71, 156, 223–24, 234, 252, 266, 279, 292–93, 296
Carter, Jimmy 159
Central Intelligence Agency (CIA) 133, 204, 206–08, 211, 214
Centre d'Étude sur l'Évaluation de la Protection dans le domaine Nucléaire (CEPN) 194–95
Cesium-137 (Cs-137) 38, 51, 60, 139, 141
Chamorro people 91

Charter – charting 85, 87, 95–96, 98–99, 102, 299, 303
Chernobyl – accident – disaster – catastrophe 2, 5, 9, 11–12, 133, 139–41, 185–86, 192–94, 198, 224–25, 230–33, 243, 251–53, 255, 273, 275, 279, 295, 299; Chernobyl survivors 29, 222–24
Citizen 5, 9, 11, 15, 40, 46, 59, 80–81, 97, 132–33, 135, 141–42, 150, 195–97, 206, 214, 222, 228, 233–34, 247, 254–55, 267, 281–82, 284–85, 315
Citizen's Center for Nuclear Information (CNIC) 295
Citizen science 142, 196, 254
Climate change 1, 8, 15, 271, 273, 299, 301, 303, 312
Cockcroft, John 122
Cold War 4, 6–8, 11, 28, 46, 54, 56, 58–60, 62, 66–67, 71, 73–74, 79, 112–13, 116, 118, 120, 123, 125, 132, 197, 206, 208, 211, 224–26, 229, 231, 233, 235, 251, 270, 274, 284, 290, 293, 308, 311
Cole, Sterling 118–20, 207
Colonial – colonialism – colonialist – colonised – colonies 7, 15, 46, 68–69, 73–74, 85–89, 91–92, 95–99, 112, 124, 187, 225, 227, 261, 273–74, 303
Commissariat à l'énergie atomique (CEA) 151, 156–57, 160–61, 173, 178, 194, 269
Commission de Recherche et d'Information Indépendantes sur la Radioactivité (CRIIRAD) 141–42
Committee on Radiation Protection and Public Health (CRPPH) 194
Concertation (social) 167
Containment 4, 7, 9–12, 152–56, 161, 167–69, 171, 174–80, 186, 189, 190, 228, 249
Control 4, 7–10, 28–29, 36, 59–60, 67–68, 71–72, 74, 78–81, 88–89, 91–92, 95–96, 101, 111, 116–19, 152, 156, 159, 161, 187–88, 191, 193–94, 198, 208, 231, 247, 253–54, 261, 274, 281, 288, 302–03, 308, 311
Controversy – controversies – controversial 9, 15, 37, 99, 118,

120, 132, 134–37, 139, 141–42, 158, 160, 166–68, 170–71, 175, 177, 187, 189–90, 205–06, 208, 272–73, 305, 309
Core meltdown 151, 154–56, 158–59, 243
Cost-benefit analysis 192, 223, 227, 234
Counter-expertise (*see* expertise)
COVID-19 1
Crisis – crises 2, 8, 12, 16, 68–69, 74, 79, 111, 141, 159–61, 189–92, 194, 196–98, 234, 250, 252, 275
Crutzen, Paul J. 272
Cuban missile crisis 2, 189
Curie, Marie & Pierre 264

D
Daiichi (*see* Fukushima)
Decolonialisation – decolonialising 75, 87, 111
de Laguna, Wallace 172
Deny – denial – denied – denying 4, 6, 9–11, 23, 25, 32–33, 35, 37–38, 59, 68, 74, 78, 140, 190, 193, 196, 205, 207–08, 215, 217, 233, 242, 252, 304
Département de Sûreté Nucléaire (DSN) 156–57
Department of Defense (DOD) 50, 54, 56, 211, 302, 308
Department of Energy (DOE) 56, 191, 231–32, 307–08
Disaster 1–5, 11, 15–16, 27–29, 38, 40, 122, 133, 140–41, 150, 155, 161, 192–93, 197–98, 204, 216–17, 222–25, 232–35, 242–53, 255, 261, 265–66, 273, 299–306, 311–12, 314–15
Disposal (*see* waste)
Doomsday 2, 6, 16, 265, 268, 271, 303
Dosimeter 6, 56, 58–59, 63, 228, 309
Dual-use 3, 7, 9, 70, 77–78, 265
Dulles, John Foster 68, 76, 101

E
Earth system 60–61, 63
Edgerton, Germehausen and Greir (EG&G) 51
Eisenhower, Dwight David 68, 70–71, 74–76, 111, 118, 148, 208, 211, 246, 267–68, 281–82
Eklund, Sigvard 123, 125

Électricité de France (EDF) 157–59, 161, 194
Emelyanov, Vasilij 119
Emotion – emotional 69, 74, 76, 80, 87, 266
Enewetak Atoll 93, 101
Environmental Protection Agency (EPA) 136, 191–92
Environmental Radiation Monitoring System (ERAMS) 136
Environmental radioactivity 132–38; monitoring 132–42
Epidemiological study 233
ETHOS project 195–96
Euratom 72–74, 113, 118, 122, 125, 137, 139–40, 188, 194
EURDEP 132
European Commission (EC) 140, 193
European Defense Community (EDC) 72
European Nuclear Energy Agency (NEA) 113, 122, 137, 171, 178–79, 193–94
Exceptionality – Exceptionalism – exceptional 11–12, 55–56, 67–68, 73, 96, 161–62, 185, 187, 190, 265, 273, 281, 292
Exclusion 5, 56, 59, 152–53, 193
Exelon 308–09
Exhibition – exhibit 58, 88, 113–15, 279–80, 282–83, 285–91, 305
Expert – expertise 2–4, 8–12, 24, 28, 36, 38–41, 46, 50, 91, 113–16, 118–23, 137–38, 148–51, 153–55, 157–58, 160, 162, 167–79, 185–97, 222–26, 231–32, 243, 246–50, 254, 271–72, 301–3; counter-expertise 5, 9–10, 27, 41, 135, 141–42, 190; expert's judgment 153, 157, 176
Exposure 5–6, 23–25, 27–30, 34–40, 45–46, 48, 55–56, 58–61, 63, 112, 116, 122, 138, 153, 161, 187–91, 196, 203–5, 207, 215–17, 223–25, 228–29, 232–33, 235, 294, 306, 308, 311–12, 314

F
Fallout 2, 7–11, 15, 24, 26, 28–30, 36, 38, 45–46, 48, 50, 60–61, 70, 116, 133–42, 154, 161, 172, 186–87, 190, 193, 203, 205–10, 214–15, 224, 226–30, 232–33, 243, 251, 254, 267, 271–72

326 Index

Farmer, Frank Reginald 156
Farrell, Thomas F. 205
Faustian bargain 10, 242, 253–54
Federal Civil Defense Administration
  (FCDA) 134
Fischer, David 118
Food and Agriculture Organisation
  (FAO) 116, 171
Food and Drug Administration
  (FDA) 192
Forbidden zones 315
Foreign Operations Administration
  (FOA) 136, 208, 211
Forsmark 140
Fotouhi, Abol Fazl 280–83, 285–87,
  289–92
Framatome 156–57
Fukushima – accident – disaster –
  catastrophe 1–3, 5, 11–12, 15,
  27–29, 38, 40, 132, 141–42, 179,
  185–86, 192–93, 195–96, 198, 204,
  216–17, 242–45, 247–55, 275, 294,
  311, 314

G
Galapagos Island 100
Gamma radiation – rays 34, 120,
  207, 230
Geiger counter 50, 142, 197, 228, 254
General Electric 152, 176, 247,
  249, 291
Genshiryoku Shiryo Johoshitsu 295
Gensuikin 279, 293–95
Ghadafi, Muammar 70
Gilpatric, Roswell 75–76
Global Network of Isotopes in
  Precipitation (GNIP) 137, 139
Global North 2, 76
Global South 2, 9, 112–13, 116
Gofman, John 190–91, 294
Great Tohoku Earthquake 242
Green revolution 116
Groves, General Leslie 133, 230

H
Häfele, Wolf 150
Hague Conventions 92
Hamai, Shinzo 282, 284–85, 288
Hanford 58, 169, 172–73,
  176–77, 185
Hazard – hazardous 10–12, 116–18,
  137–38, 140–49, 151–52, 154,
  166–70, 173–75, 177, 185–90,

192–93, 196–98, 206, 215, 226,
  228, 230, 248, 293, 301
Health and Safety Committee (HSC)
  137–139
Hegemon – hegemony 67, 74, 112
Hibakusha 5, 23–33, 35–40, 215, 265,
  279, 281–83, 286–87, 290, 295,
  306–07, 313–315; identity 27–28;
  relief 25, 31–32; status 5, 23–26, 29,
  31–32, 35–39
Hibaku taikensha 23, 25, 35–36
High Altitude Sampling Program
  (HASP) 135
High modernism 25
Hiroshima 2–4, 10, 14–16, 23–24,
  27–31, 33, 35, 37–39, 46, 48, 66,
  133, 185, 187, 194, 198, 204–06,
  215, 218, 252, 261–67, 270, 273,
  275, 279–90, 292–93, 299, 303–07,
  313–15
Hixon, Walter 67–68
Human health 3, 28, 38, 137, 142,
  167, 171, 175, 204

I
Ibuse, Masuji 37
Ichiro, Moritaki 280, 293
Idaho Falls National Laboratory –
  National Engineering Laboratory
  (INEL) 155
Ignorance 8, 30, 255
Imaginary 6, 13, 26, 40, 46
Inclusion (social) – inclusive 167, 197
Indigenous – indigeneity 7, 55, 77,
  86–92, 97, 99, 100, 102
Institut de Radioprotection et de
  Sûreté Nucléaire (IRSN) 194–95
Insurance – insurers 122–23, 154,
  187, 255, 301
Intercontinental Ballistic Missiles 86
International Atomic Energy Agency
  (IAEA) 8–9, 12, 111–25, 135, 137,
  139–41, 156, 167, 176, 179, 188,
  193, 223–25, 233
International Commission on
  Radiological Protection (ICRP) 12,
  29, 40, 122–23, 138, 162, 188,
  192–95, 197, 216–17
International Committee for
  Radiological Units (ICRU) 123
International Monetary Fund 69, 234
International Radiation Protection
  Association (IRPA) 194

Index 327

Iodine-131 (I-131) 132, 141, 156, 228, 232

J
Johnson, U. Alexis 77
Johnson, Boris 80–81
Joint Dosimetry Experiment 120
Joliot-Curie, Frédéric 264
Jong-un, Kim 80–81

K
Kahn, Hermann 75
Kennedy, John F. 68, 75
Khrushchev, Nikita 75
Kihonkon report 32, 38–39
Kissinger, Henry 78–79
Kobe earthquake 246, 248
Kochi 203, 216
Kodak 6, 48, 50–51, 54, 56, 60, 63
Korean war 67, 226
Kouts, Herbert 224
Kuran, Peter 54
Kyshtym (disaster) 122, 140

L
Langevin, Paul 264
League of Nations 87–88
League of Nations' South Pacific 85
Leakage 155–56, 173, 175
Leukemia – Leukaemia – Leukemic 36, 222, 228–29, 232, 305–06
Liability 118–19, 122–23, 125, 133, 139, 154, 187, 213–14, 231, 255, 314
Libby, Willard F. 134, 227
Life Span Study (LSS) 29, 34, 223
Lifton, Robert 303–04, 311
Limited Test Ban Treaty (*see* Test ban treaty)
Linenthal, Edward T. 305
Lochard, Jacques 193–95
Long Island 154, 229
Lookout Mountain Laboratory 52–53, 56, 58
Low-dose – low-level radiation – radioactivity 40, 59, 116, 159, 166, 187, 190–91, 228–29, 235, 294
Lucky Dragon Incident (or Bikini incident) 30–31, 203–16, 269, 281–82, 293

M
MacArthur, Douglas 246

Majuro Atoll 85, 88, 92
Malone, George 226
Manhattan Project 8, 14, 152, 205, 230, 264, 313
Marcoule 176, 269
Marianas 85
Market 9, 50, 114, 121–23, 125, 203, 247
Marshall Islands – Islanders 7, 10, 30, 46, 54, 85–88, 90–94, 203, 206–78, 212–14, 226, 230, 232, 294
Mastery – mastering 8–9, 149, 155, 159, 162, 187–89, 193, 196, 198, 261
Mathé, Georges 120
Maximum Credible Accident (MCA) 153–54, 156, 158–59, 162
Mayak 132, 169, 185 (disaster, *see* Kyshtym)
McCarthy era 50
McCullough, C. Rogers 149
McMahon Act (*see* Atomic Energy Act)
McNamara, Robert 77
Medicine 7, 11, 15, 113, 116–17, 120, 171, 209, 214, 222–24, 227, 230–31, 234, 288
Memorials 267, 299, 304–06, 308, 311–15
Method of barriers 155
Metrology 124
Minoura, Koji 243–45, 249–50
Mitigation – Mitigating 197–98
Modernisation 15, 76, 267, 269, 280, 284–85, 290, 292–93, 296
Mollet, Guy 72
Morgan, Karl Ziegler 144
Moritaki, Iriko 280–83, 285–87, 289, 293–95
Murray, Thomas E. 282
Muskie, Edmund 190

N
Nace, Raymond 172–73
Nader, Ralph 190
Nagasaki 2, 4, 10, 14, 16, 23–24, 27–31, 34–37, 46–48, 66, 133, 185, 187, 194, 198, 204–6, 215, 230, 262–63, 265–67, 270, 273, 293–94, 299, 304–05, 307, 314–15
Nakasone, Yasuhiro 78, 284
National Academy of Sciences (NAS) 116, 170, 191–92

328 Index

National Aeronautics and Space Administration (NASA) 76–77
National Institute of Radiological Sciences (National Institute for Quantum and Radiological Science and Technology) 204
National Institutes of Health (NIH) 192
National Research Council (NRC) 54, 58, 116, 192
National Science Foundation (NSF) 192
Nazi 313
Nehru, Jawaharlal 135
Nevada Test Site 34, 56, 59, 225–26
New Mexico 5, 46, 48, 169, 179, 226
Nitze, Paul 67
Nixon, Richard 79, 81
Nonalignment 74, 76
North Atlantic Treaty Organization (NATO) 78, 138
Norwegian Defense Research Institute (FFI) 138
Nuclear age 7, 10, 13–16, 28, 39, 45–46, 48, 50, 53, 55, 62–63, 70, 185, 303
Nuclear and Industrial Safety Agency (Japanese NISA) 243, 245, 247, 249–50
Nuclear apartheid 6, 69, 80, 112
Nuclear fatalism 68, 267
Nuclearity 26
Nuclear Regulation Authority (Japanese NRA) 247
Nuclear Regulatory Commission (NRC) 157, 159–60, 179, 191, 231, 302
Nuclear security 68, 189, 225
Nuclear umbrella 40, 66
Nuclear village 243, 247, 249, 250–52, 254
Nuclear weapon 4–5, 7, 15–16, 23, 25, 27, 30–31, 40, 50, 54, 58, 62–63, 66–81, 86, 96, 99, 101–102, 112, 117–18, 120, 125, 134, 189–90, 206, 215, 225, 232–33, 261–62, 265, 272, 274, 279, 293–94, 302, 308, 311
Nuclear winter 262, 271–273

O
Oak Ridge 114, 120, 172, 175
Obama, Barack 81

Occupational Safety and Health Administration (OSHA) 192
Okinawa 283, 292, 294
Okrent, David 153
Operation Castle 203, 206
Operation Fitzwilliam 133
Oppenheimer, Robert 313
Organization for European Economic Co-operation (OEEC) 137–38

P
Pacifist movements 135, 186
Pakistan Atomic Energy Commission 111
Participation (public) 88, 97, 102, 133, 142, 167, 192, 195
Pauling, Linus 294
Pearl Harbor 90
Pellerin, Pierre 140
Permissible dose 166, 210, 223
Plutonium (Pu-239) 16, 46, 51, 58, 60–62, 169, 246, 269
Pollack, James B. 272
Post-accident – post-Chernobyl, post-Fukushima, post-disaster 39–40, 194, 196–97, 235, 314
Post-colonial 76, 111, 124, 279, 284–85, 292
Post-traumatic stress disorder (PTSD) 23, 36, 312
Pradel, Jacques 178
Preparedness 197, 302
Price Anderson Act 154
Pripyat 193, 314
Probabilistic safety assessment (PSA) 158
Productive fiction 59
Proliferation – non-proliferation 3, 7, 10, 15, 68–71, 75–76, 73–79, 112, 117, 120–21, 125, 135, 246
Pugwash 270, 293, 322
Putin, Vladimir 80

R
Race (human) – racial – racialised 4, 6–8, 45, 58, 66, 68, 73–75, 80–81, 86, 89, 92, 94–95, 97, 99, 268–69
Radiation Alert Network (RAN) 134–35
Radiation Effects Research Foundation (RERF) 29
Radioactivity Environmental

Monitoring data bank
(REMdb) 141
Radioisotopes 8–9, 60, 111, 113–14,
116, 119, 121–22, 124, 132, 134,
139, 141, 170, 172, 274
Radiophobia – radiophobic 40, 223
Radioprotection 162, 179,
194–95, 254
RadNet 132, 136
RAND 229, 271
Rasmussen, Norman Carl 158;
report 158
Reactors 2, 5, 7–8, 10–11, 15, 70, 75,
78, 112, 118, 120, 122–25, 133,
138, 140, 142, 148–61, 171–72,
176, 185, 188–89, 193, 224–25,
233–34, 243, 246–49, 251–53, 261,
269, 282–85, 289–92, 311; safety
reactor 148–49, 151, 251
Realpolitik 72
Regulation 4, 8, 10, 59, 89, 113, 121,
124, 135, 138, 149, 152–53,
155–56, 161–62, 176, 187–88, 191,
217, 246–50
Resilience 198, 273, 315
Risk 2, 4, 5, 7–12, 15, 27, 59, 70, 72,
97, 102, 116–17, 120, 122, 132,
148–52, 154–56, 158–62, 170,
173–76, 178–79, 185–87, 189–99,
204–05, 223–27, 234, 235, 242–45,
248–49, 251–55, 265, 270, 283,
301–03, 308, 311, 314;
management – managers 12,
186–87, 190, 192, 194, 197, 261,
301–02, 308
Rochester 48, 50, 54
Rosen, Morris 225
Rubinson, Paul 272
Rusk, Dean 76
Russell, Bertrand 205, 269–70
Ruthenium-106 132

S
Safeguards 71, 112, 116–21, 151–52,
156, 246
Safety standards 29, 112–13, 116–17,
121–24, 137
Sagan, Carl 272
Sarabhia, Vikram 76, 77
Scud missile 79
Service Central de Protection Contre
les Rayonnements Ionisants (SCPRI)
139–41

Servigne, Pablo 273
Shippingport 153, 247
Slow disaster 15–16, 299, 301–03,
311–12
Slow violence 6, 25, 40, 58, 273,
301–02
Smyth, Henry 264
Sousselier, Yves 178
Standard – standardisation –
standardising 2, 5, 8, 24–25, 27, 29,
34, 40, 100, 111–13, 116–25,
137–39, 149, 156, 160, 188–89,
209–10, 216–17, 230, 235, 249,
267, 291
Stimson, Henry L. 95
St. Louis Arch 308
Strauss, Lewis 117, 206–8, 225,
228, 262
Strontium 51, 60, 134, 139, 226–230
Survivors 3, 5, 15–16, 19, 23–40, 116,
205–06, 214–15, 222–24, 229–30,
267, 279, 285, 303–04, 306, 314
(*see* hibakusha)
Swedish Defense Research Agency
(FOI) 132

T
Tamplin, Arthur 190–91
Teller, Edward 78, 247, 271–72
Tepco (Tokyo Electric Power
Company) 1, 142, 216, 243–45,
247–50, 254
Test 3, 5–7, 9–10, 16, 27, 46, 48–50,
54, 58, 66, 70, 75–76, 78, 80, 99,
134–37, 139, 141, 155–56, 158,
172, 185,189, 191–92, 203–04,
206–09, 212–15, 224–29, 232–33,
267, 269–71, 281–82, 286,
293–94
Test Ban Treaty 51, 61, 69, 132, 137,
141; Partial Test Ban Treaty
(PTBT) 137
Three Mile Island 2, 5, 150–51, 157,
159–61, 192, 247, 299,
308–11, 314
Thyroid 153, 229, 231–33
Tinian Island 85
Tokai Earthquake 248
Trauma 25–26, 36, 39, 303, 307
Treaty on the Non-Proliferation of
Nuclear Weapons 69–70, 265
Treaty on the Prohibition of Nuclear
Weapons 16, 40

330   *Index*

Truman, Harry S. 99, 101, 151, 211, 263
Trump, Donald 79–81
Trusteeships 85, 87–88, 95, 97–98, 101–02; agreements 98–99, 101; system 97–99
Tsunami 1, 11, 142, 242–45, 248–50, 254, 273
Turco, Richard P. 272

U

Uncertainties – Uncertainty 1, 11–12, 15, 25, 27–28, 39, 151, 156–57, 235, 242
Union of Concerned Scientists (UCS) 157–58, 191
United Nations (UN) 11, 16, 61, 70, 74, 77, 80, 87, 88, 95–99, 101–02, 111, 113, 117, 120, 125, 135, 148, 224, 231–35, 246, 267, 281, 293
United Nations Educational, Scientific and Cultural Organization (UNESCO) 135
United Nations Scientific Committee on the Effects of Atomic Radiation (UNSCEAR) 12, 40, 135, 138–39, 188, 225, 233
United States Department of Agriculture (USDA) 228
United States Information Agency 279, 287
United States Public Health Service 227, 228, 232
Uranium 10, 58, 61, 115, 133, 141, 246, 269, 308

V

Victims 11, 14–15, 23, 25–28, 31–32, 35–37, 187, 154, 198, 204–05, 214–15, 234, 248, 265–67, 269, 279, 282, 284–85, 290, 299, 304–06, 312, 314

Vinča 120
Violence 3–7, 11–12, 25, 46, 48, 55, 62, 69, 91, 100, 187, 265–67, 300–02, 305, 312, 314; categories and demarcation 4–7; managing 4–7

W

Washington Naval Conference 89
Waste 10–11, 15–16, 116, 121, 166–80, 185, 261, 274, 289, 302, 311, 315, 322; disposal 9, 118, 167–69, 171–78, 180; environment 174–177; high-level 175, 178; sea disposal 168–171, 173, 175–76; storage 9, 121, 167–169, 171, 178, 180
Webb, James 77
Weinberg, Alvin R. 10, 148, 253
Weldon Spring 299–300, 308
Westinghouse 156, 247
Whistleblowing – whistleblowers 247–48
Wilson, Charles 282
Wisner, Frank 208
Workers 6, 11, 31, 40, 55–56, 58–59, 61, 116, 120, 122, 137–38, 170–71, 188, 198, 229, 249, 252–54, 269, 271, 299, 302, 308, 311
World Health Organisation (WHO) 120
Wotho atoll 92

X

Xenon-133 133
X-rays 50, 116, 227–28

Y

Yucca Mountain Nuclear Waste Repository 167

Printed in the United States
by Baker & Taylor Publisher Services